DPT
Your All-in-One Resource

On the CD that accompanies this book, you'll find additional resources to extend your learning.

The reference library includes the following fully searchable titles:

- Windows Vista Product Guide
- *Microsoft Computer Dictionary*, 5th ed.
- Sample chapter and poster from *Look Both Ways: Help Protect Your Family on the Internet* (Linda Criddle, 2007)

The CD interface has a new look. You can use the tabs for an assortment of tasks:

- Check for book updates (if you have Internet access)
- Install the book's practice files
- Go online for product support or CD support
- Send us feedback

The following screen shot gives you a glimpse of the new interface.

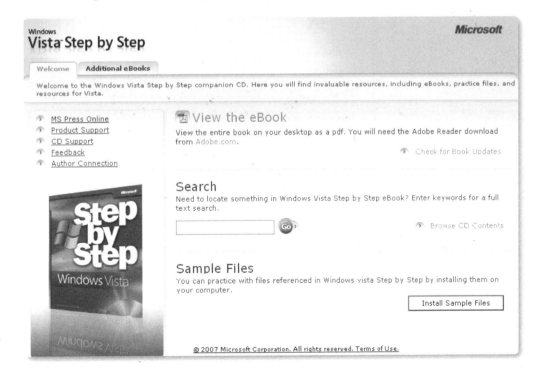

Microsoft®

Windows Vista®
Step by Step,
Deluxe Edition

Joan Preppernau and Joyce Cox
Online Training Solutions, Inc.

PUBLISHED BY
Microsoft Press
A Division of Microsoft Corporation
One Microsoft Way
Redmond, Washington 98052-6399

Library of Congress Control Number: 2007942091

Printed and bound in the United States of America.

1 2 3 4 5 6 7 8 9   QWT   3 2 1 0 9 8

Distributed in Canada by H.B. Fenn and Company Ltd.

A CIP catalogue record for this book is available from the British Library.

Microsoft Press books are available through booksellers and distributors worldwide. For further information about international editions, contact your local Microsoft Corporation office or contact Microsoft Press International directly at fax (425) 936-7329. Visit our Web site at www.microsoft.com/mspress. Send comments to mspinput@microsoft.com.

Microsoft, ActiveX, Aero, BitLocker, ClearType, DirectX, Excel, Hotmail, Internet Explorer, Microsoft, Microsoft Press, MSN,OneNote, Outlook, PowerPoint, ReadyBoost, SharePoint, SideShow, Verdana, Windows, Windows Live, Windows Media, Windows Mobile, Windows Server, and Windows Vista are either registered trademarks or trademarks of Microsoft Corporation in the United States and/or other countries. Other product and company names mentioned herein may be the trademarks of their respective owners.

The example companies, organizations, products, domain names, e-mail addresses, logos, people, places, and events depicted herein are fictitious. No association with any real company, organization, product, domain name, e-mail address, logo, person, place, or event is intended or should be inferred.

This book expresses the author's views and opinions. The information contained in this book is provided without any express, statutory, or implied warranties. Neither the authors, Microsoft Corporation, nor its resellers, or distributors will be held liable for any damages caused or alleged to be caused either directly or indirectly by this book.

Acquisitions Editor: Juliana Aldous Atkinson
Developmental Editor: Sandra Haynes
Project Editor: Sandra Haynes
Editorial Production: Online Training Solutions, Inc.

Body Part No. X14-40123

Contents

About the Authors xi

Introducing Windows Vista xiii

   Windows Vista Editions xiv

      Sidebar: Upgrading to Windows Vista xviii

   Let's Get Started! xviii

The Microsoft Business Certification Program xix

   Selecting a Certification Path xx

   Becoming a Microsoft Certified Application Specialist—Windows Vista xx

   Taking a Microsoft Business Certification Exam xxi

   For More Information xxii

Information for New Computer Users xxiii

   Using Your Mouse xxiv

   Working with Windows xxv

   Giving Instructions. xxvi

   Message Boxes. xxviii

Features and Conventions of This Book xxix

Using the Companion CD xxxi

   What's on the CD? xxxi

   Minimum System Requirements xxxiv

   Installing the Practice Files. xxxvi

   Using the Practice Files. xxxvii

   Removing and Uninstalling the Practice Files xxxviii

Getting Help xxxix

Quick Reference xli

What do you think of this book? We want to hear from you!

Microsoft is interested in hearing your feedback so we can continually improve our books and learning resources for you. To participate in a brief online survey, please visit:

www.microsoft.com/learning/booksurvey/

1   Getting Started with Windows Vista   1

Logging On to Windows Vista 2

    Sidebar: Networks, Domains, and Workgroups. 3

Activating Windows 7

    Sidebar: Identifying Genuine Windows Software .11

    Sidebar: The Perils of Piracy 12

Updating Windows System Files. 12

    Sidebar: Switching Quickly Among Users. 17

Ending a Computing Session. 18

Making Your Computer Easier to Use 22

Key Points 26

Keyboard Shortcuts. 27

2   Working Efficiently in Windows Vista   29

Finding Your Way Around the Windows Desktop 30

Using and Modifying the Start Menu 32

Finding Your Way Around Your Computer 42

Using and Modifying the Taskbar. 49

Controlling Your Computer by Using Voice Commands. 57

    Sidebar: Speech Recognition Command Reference 62

Creating Shortcuts to Files, Folders, and Programs. .68

Rearranging and Deleting Items on the Desktop 71

Key Points 73

Keyboard Shortcuts. 73

3   Working with Folders and Files   75

Navigating to Folders and Files. 76

    Sidebar: Accessing Your Entire Network 82

Viewing Folders and Files in Different Ways. 84

Viewing Information About a Folder or File 93

Creating, Renaming, and Deleting Folders and Files. 97

Moving and Copying Folders and Files 102

Finding Specific Information 105

Key Points 110

Keyboard Shortcuts. 111

4   Personalizing Windows Vista   **113**

Changing the Look of Windows Vista on Your Screen 114

Optimizing Visual Effects 118

Changing the Desktop Background 126

Selecting and Managing a Screen Saver 130

Managing Your System Date and Time 133

Changing Your Computer's Name 137

   Sidebar: Changing the Name of the Computer Folder 138

Key Points 139

Keyboard Shortcuts 139

5   Installing and Configuring Devices   **141**

   Need More Ports? 143

Displaying More on Your Monitor 144

Configuring Your System for Multiple Monitors 147

   Sidebar: Expanding Your Laptop with Peripheral Devices 150

Changing the Way Your Mouse Works 151

Changing the Keyboard Input Language 154

Configuring Tablet PC Options 160

Installing and Sharing a Local Printer 166

Connecting to a Remote Printer 173

   Sidebar: Updating Device Drivers 175

Setting Up Speakers 176

Setting Up a Microphone 180

Key Points 183

Keyboard Shortcuts 183

6   Safely and Efficiently Accessing the Internet   **185**

Connecting to the Internet 186

Displaying Web Sites in Internet Explorer 7 190

   Sidebar: Protecting Personal Information 196

Blocking Pop-Up Windows 196

Changing Your Home Page 198

Changing the Appearance of Web Content 199

Finding, Saving, and Returning to Web Sites 202

Printing Web Pages. 205

Sending Web Pages and Links to Other People. 208

Discovering and Subscribing to RSS Feeds 210

Restricting Objectionable Content. 212

 Sidebar: Protecting Children's Privacy. 213

Key Points 219

Keyboard Shortcuts. 219

7   Working with Programs   221

Installing and Removing Programs. 222

Managing Hard Disks 227

Starting Programs Automatically 229

Specifying the Default Program for a Type of File. 232

Recovering from Software Errors 234

 Sidebar: Changing Your Default Middleware Programs. 235

Playing Games 236

Key Points 238

Keyboard Shortcuts. 239

8   Making Connections   241

Connecting Your Computer to a Workgroup 242

Setting Up a VPN Connection. 245

 Sidebar: Creating an Ad Hoc Wireless Network 250

Connecting Your Computer to a Domain 251

Accessing Your Domain Computer Remotely. 254

 Sidebar: Storing and Managing Network Passwords 259

Sharing Drives and Folders 260

 Sidebar: Restricting Permission to a Shared Folder. 262

Key Points 263

Keyboard Shortcuts. 263

9   Communicating with Other People   265

Setting Up Windows Mail. 266

 Sidebar: Mail Server Addresses for Popular Providers 267

 Sidebar: E-Mail Concepts. 268

 Sidebar: Blocking Unwanted Messages. 273

Sending and Receiving E-Mail Messages 277
    Sidebar: Joining a Newsgroup 283
    Sidebar: Instant Messaging. 284
Faxing and Scanning Documents 284
Conducting Online Meetings 287
Key Points 292
Keyboard Shortcuts. 293

10   Staying Organized   295
Using and Modifying Sidebar Gadgets 295
Recording Notes 301
Keeping Track of Contacts 304
Keeping Track of Appointments and Meetings 314
    Sidebar: Tracking Tasks 315
    Sidebar: Changing Windows Calendar Defaults 316
Key Points 322
Keyboard Shortcuts. 323

11   Working with Graphics and Documents   325
Creating Simple Graphics. 326
Changing the Content, Size, and Orientation of Graphics 337
    Sidebar: Using Custom Colors 344
    Sidebar: Using a Graphic as Your Windows Desktop 345
Saving Graphic Files in Different Formats 345
    Sidebar: Understanding Graphic Formats. 348
Printing Graphics 348
Creating Simple Documents 352
Formatting Words and Paragraphs 354
Inserting Text and Graphics. 358
Printing Documents 362
Key Points 364
Keyboard Shortcuts. 365

12   Working with Digital Media   367
Viewing, Cataloging, and Fixing Pictures 368
Playing Music 375
Configuring Windows Media Center Options. 382

Burning Audio and Data Discs. 385
        Sidebar: Retrieving Images from a Digital Camera or Scanner. 388
Sharing Pictures and Other Digital Media Files 389
Key Points 391
Keyboard Shortcuts. 392

13   Managing Computer Security   **395**
Administering Windows User Accounts. 396
Managing Your Windows User Account 401
        Sidebar: Backing Up Your Windows Password. 404
Limiting Access to the Computer, to Programs, and to the Internet 405
Analyzing Your Computer's Security 409
Configuring Internet Security Zones 416
        Sidebar: Protecting Yourself from Phishing Sites. 422
Key Points 423
Keyboard Shortcuts. 423

14   Optimizing Your Computer System   **425**
Locating System Information. 426
Monitoring Your Computer's Performance. 432
Improving Your Computer's Performance. 437
Turning Windows Features On and Off. 444
Managing Cached Files. 445
Removing Unnecessary Files 447
Key Points 450
Keyboard Shortcuts. 451

15   Identifying and Solving Problems   **453**
Finding Solutions to Common Problems. 454
        Sidebar: Reporting Problems 458
Finding Information Through a Newsgroup. 459
        Sidebar: Getting Help from Microsoft Product Support 460
Getting Help from Other Windows Users. 460
        Sidebar: Starting Your Computer in Safe Mode. .464
        Sidebar: Enabling and Disabling Remote Assistance 465

Backing Up and Restoring Files. 466
Restoring Your Operating System. 472
Transferring Software, Settings, and Files to Another Computer 476
Key Points 478
Keyboard Shortcuts. 478

Glossary 479

Index. 491

What do you think of this book? We want to hear from you!

Microsoft is interested in hearing your feedback so we can continually improve our books and learning resources for you. To participate in a brief online survey, please visit:

www.microsoft.com/learning/booksurvey/

About the Authors

Joan Preppernau

Joan has worked in the training and certification industry for 10 years. As President of OTSI, Joan is responsible for guiding the translation of technical information and requirements into useful, relevant, and measurable training, learning, and certification deliverables. Joan is a Microsoft Certified Professional and Microsoft Certified Application Specialist, and the author or co-author of more than a dozen books about Windows and the Microsoft Office system.

Joan has lived and worked in New Zealand, Sweden, Denmark, and various locations in the U.S. during the past 16 years. Having finally discovered the delights of a daily dose of sunshine, Joan is now happily ensconced in America's Finest City—San Diego, California—with her husband Barry and their daughter Trinity.

Joyce Cox

Joyce has 25 years' experience in the development of training materials about technical subjects for non-technical audiences, and is the author of dozens of books about Microsoft Office and Windows technologies. She is the Vice President of Online Training Solutions, Inc. (OTSI). She was President of and principal author for Online Press, where she developed the *Quick Course* series of computer training books for beginning and intermediate adult learners. She was also the first managing editor of Microsoft Press, an editor for Sybex, and an editor for the University of California.

Joyce and her husband Ted live in downtown Bellevue, Washington, and escape as often as they can to their tiny, offline cabin in the Cascade foothills.

The Team

This book would not exist without the support of these hard-working members of the OTSI publishing team:

- Susie Bayers
- Jan Bednarczuk
- Jeanne Craver
- Marlene Lambert
- Jaime Odell
- Barry Preppernau
- Jean Trenary
- Lisa Van Every

We are especially thankful to the support staff at home who make it possible for our team members to devote their time and attention to these projects.

As always, Juliana Aldous (Acquisitions Editor) and Sandra Haynes (Series Editor) provided invaluable support on behalf of Microsoft Press.

Online Training Solutions, Inc. (OTSI)

OTSI specializes in the design, creation, and production of Office and Windows training products for information workers and home computer users. For more information about OTSI, visit

www.otsi.com

Introducing Windows Vista

Windows Vista is the latest and greatest in the illustrious line of Windows operating systems from Microsoft. The successor to Windows XP, this operating system is specifically designed to fill the needs of both business and personal users. As soon as you turn on a computer running Windows Vista, you'll notice the slick look of the new user interface. If your computer has the hardware necessary to display the Windows Aero color scheme, the high-quality visual effects will contribute significantly to your overall computing experience.

But this new version of Windows isn't just pretty to look at. It takes secure computing to a new level. In addition to providing accessory programs that help you monitor and protect your computer, it works behind the scenes to help keep malicious programs and malicious people at bay, and alerts you if a program or a person tries to make any changes that might affect the stability of the system.

After you get used to its sophisticated design and you come to rely on its new security features, you will probably start noticing the many Windows Vista features that increase your efficiency and productivity. Finding files has never been simpler or faster; simply type a word you know exists in the file you are looking for, and Windows Vista instantly shows you all the files stored on your system that contain the word. Getting the information you need to complete the task at hand is a snap; simply click the help links in windows and dialog boxes to learn about the available choices. Need to see whether a particular date falls on a weekend, keep track of the time in another country, or remove the red-eye from the photograph you want to use on your new business card? Take advantage of the many programs that come with Windows Vista to take care of these and other tasks, all from your computer desktop.

Because Windows Vista has so many new features, we don't identify them with a special margin icon as we did in previous versions of this book. We do, however, list the features here, categorized by Windows Vista edition.

Many of the features introduced in Windows Vista run behind the scenes and don't require you to do anything. We don't cover these features in this book because it is unlikely that you will have to work with them.

Windows Vista Editions

Windows Vista comes in five editions—three designed for varying levels of personal computing, and two specifically tailored for business computing needs.

Windows Vista Home Basic

This edition is designed for home users with the most basic computing needs, such as Internet and e-mail access. It delivers security and reliability without the extra features that many home users might not need. Windows Vista Home Basic includes the following features:

- Integrated desktop search makes it easy to find files, folders, messages, programs, and Windows Vista tools and controls from the Start Search box at the bottom of the Start menu or from the Search box in the upper-right corner of every Windows Explorer window.

- Windows Internet Explorer 7, with multi-page browsing and enhanced security, offers many convenient new features to simplify the process of locating, displaying, and returning to information on the Internet, including a built-in RSS reader for subscribing to Web feeds.

- Windows Explorer displays information about the properties and contents of folders and files.

- Sleep mode, a fast-acting hibernation function that shuts down or starts up your computer in seconds, and Windows ReadyBoost, which borrows from USB flash drive memory to expand the available system memory (RAM), help increase your efficiency.

- Windows Sidebar displays "gadgets" that make information such as news, photos, notes, weather, and more available full time from your desktop.

- Windows Mail, the new version of Microsoft Outlook Express, provides e-mail functionality without the need for other software.

- Windows Calendar provides personal and shared schedules and task tracking.
- Windows Photo Gallery and personal and public Pictures folders make it easy to view, label, organize, and share digital images.
- Microsoft Speech Recognition provides the means to control your computer by using your voice rather than the keyboard and mouse.
- Parental Controls enable you to limit the time children spend on the computer and the programs and sites they can access.
- Windows Backup And Restore Center safeguards against lost information by automatically backing up information on your computer at regular intervals and before any major system change. If you experience system trouble after installing a program, you can restore your system to the previous version without losing changes you have since made to documents or other content on your computer.
- The Network File And Sharing Center provides real-time monitoring of network connections from your computer and options for controlling what areas of your computer can be accessed from other computers.
- The Ease Of Access Center provides accessibility features and a questionnaire for determining which features can help you to better interact with your computer.
- Sync Center provides a central location for synchronizing content between your computer and portable devices such as Microsoft Windows Mobile devices and personal music systems, and for monitoring synchronization activities.
- Enhanced protection features help you ensure the security of your computer and the information on it. Windows Security Center provides real-time monitoring of the security controls in place on your computer and whether your operating system files are up to date. Windows Firewall protects against unauthorized connections to and from your computer. Windows Defender protects against malicious software (malware) attacks. User Account Control (UAC) prevents unauthorized changes to your computer by requiring administrator permission to carry out restricted tasks.

Windows Vista Home Premium

This edition is designed for home users who use their computers for more than the basics. It includes all the features of Windows Vista Home Basic, plus the following:

- The Windows Aero (authentic, energetic, reflective, and open) user interface provides an enhanced visual experience with features such as transparent window frames, additional color schemes, and live previews of open windows from the taskbar and when switching between windows.

- Windows Media Center provides the means to enjoy all forms of digital entertainment—photos, videos, television, and music—from one central location. If your system includes a television tuner and Windows Media Center–compatible remote control, you can use your computer as an all-in-one entertainment center. With the addition of Windows Media Extender hardware units, you can broadcast content from your computer to multiple locations in your home or office.

- Windows Tablet and Touch Technology enables you to interact with a Tablet PC–compatible computer by using a digital pen or your fingertip. Continuous feedback helps your computer do an increasingly accurate job of recognizing your handwriting.

- Windows SideShow provides auxiliary display support for next-generation hardware with external displays, making it possible, for example, to check your schedule without opening the lid of your laptop.

Windows Vista Ultimate

This edition is designed for home users who want to do it all. Ideal for home-based businesses, Windows Vista Ultimate includes business, mobility, and entertainment functions, with all the features of Windows Vista Home Premium, plus the following:

- Windows Movie Maker enables you to create, edit, enhance, narrate, and package video clips.

- Windows BitLocker Drive Encryption protects your system by encrypting the entire hard disk on which Windows Vista is installed. BitLocker automatically encrypts the files you move to or save on the system drive, and it decrypts them when you move them from the system drive to another drive. BitLocker also protects against intrusion by monitoring the startup and logon processes; if it detects anomalies, it requires the entry of a special BitLocker password to gain access to the computer.

- Advanced networking capabilities allow you to join a domain as well as provide Group Policy support and features such as Remote Desktop.

Windows Vista Business

Designed for small, mid-sized, and large businesses, this edition includes all the features of Windows Vista Home Premium, plus the following:

● Windows Mobility Center provides access to all the settings you might want to adjust when using a mobile PC, so you don't need to search for them individually.

● Windows Meeting Space provides a convenient online meeting interface for sharing information with and among a group of people. Participants can collaborate on documents, share control of a computer, distribute handouts, and chat with each other.

● Business and technology resources designed for small businesses are available, along with enhanced networking, backup, and fax and scan capabilities.

Windows Vista Enterprise

This edition is designed for mid-sized and large enterprises with complex IT infrastructures. It is available only to Microsoft Volume License customers, through the Microsoft Software Assurance and Microsoft Enterprise Agreement programs. It includes all the features of Windows Vista Business, plus the following:

● Windows BitLocker Drive Encryption (see the earlier description under Windows Vista Ultimate).

● Virtual PC Express allows users to run two operating systems on one computer by using Microsoft Virtual PC technology.

● Subsystem for Unix-based Applications (SUA) makes it possible to run UNIX-based programs and scripts on Windows Vista.

● Support for all 35 available interface languages makes global deployment easier.

> **Tip** Some features of Windows Vista work only if you have the hardware to support them. For information, see "Using the Companion CD" later in this book.

See Also For detailed descriptions of the Windows Vista editions and features, visit *www.microsoft.com/windowsvista/getready/editions/*.

The exercises in this book cover the features of Windows Vista that you are most likely to use at home and at work, and assume that you have *administrative privileges* on your computer. Screenshots depict the Windows Vista Ultimate user interface.

Upgrading to Windows Vista

Upgrading is the process of replacing your computer's operating system with a newer version, without disturbing the programs installed on your computer, your personal preferences and settings, or existing information, such as documents, spreadsheets, and data files. You can upgrade to Windows Vista from Windows XP. You might be able to upgrade from a computer running an earlier version of Windows, but many computers purchased more than two years ago won't meet the Windows Vista hardware requirements.

Although upgrading to Windows Vista should not affect your personal files and settings, it is always a good policy to back up important files before upgrading. The time and effort it takes to back up files and settings will likely be far less than the time and effort required to re-create the same information.

See Also For information about backing up files and settings in Windows XP, consult *Microsoft Windows XP Step by Step* (ISBN 0-7356-2114-4) by Online Training Solutions, Inc. (Microsoft Press, 2005) or consult Windows Help And Support.

If you have questions or concerns about whether you can upgrade your existing computer to Windows Vista, you can download the Windows Vista Upgrade Advisor from

www.microsoft.com/windowsvista/getready/upgradeadvisor/

After installing the program on your computer, you can run it to generate a list of any known compatibility issues with your computer and the peripheral devices connected to it. The Upgrade Advisor can recommend solutions for fixing some issues and also provides information about which edition of Windows Vista best fits the way you plan to use your computer.

Let's Get Started!

It might seem a bit strange to sing the praises of an operating system. In the past, a computer's operating system was supposed to do its job so unobtrusively that we only noticed it when something went wrong. Not so with Windows Vista. Its sophisticated design values and superior collection of tools and programs mean that after we've shown you around, you will be looking at this operating system in a whole new light.

The Microsoft Business Certification Program

Desktop computing proficiency is becoming increasingly important in today's business world. As a result, when screening, hiring, and training employees, more employers are relying on the objectivity and consistency of technology certification to ensure the competence of their workforce. As an employee or job seeker, you can use technology certification to prove that you already have the skills you need to succeed, saving current and future employers the trouble and expense of training you.

The Microsoft Business Certification (MSBC) program is designed to assist employees in validating their Windows Vista skills and 2007 Microsoft Office program skills. There are two paths to certification:

- A Microsoft Certified Application Specialist (MCAS) is an individual who has demonstrated worldwide skill standards for Windows Vista or for the 2007 Microsoft Office suite through a certification exam in Windows Vista or in one or more of the 2007 Microsoft Office programs, including Microsoft Office Word 2007, Microsoft Office Excel 2007, Microsoft Office PowerPoint 2007, Microsoft Office Outlook 2007, and Microsoft Office Access 2007.

- A Microsoft Certified Application Professional (MCAP) is an individual who has taken his or her knowledge of the 2007 Microsoft Office suite and of Microsoft SharePoint products and technologies to the next level and has demonstrated through a certification exam that he or she can use the collaborative power of the Office suite to accomplish job functions such as *Budget Analysis and Forecasting*, or *Content Management and Collaboration*.

After attaining certification, you can include the MCAS or MCAP logo with the appropriate certification designator on your business cards and other personal promotional materials. This logo attests to the fact that you are proficient in the applications or cross-application skills necessary to achieve the certification.

Selecting a Certification Path

When selecting the Microsoft Business Certification path that you would like to pursue, you should assess the following:

- The program and program version(s) with which you are familiar
- The length of time you have used the program
- Whether you have had formal or informal training in the use of that program

Candidates for MCAS-level certification are expected to successfully complete a wide range of standard business tasks, such as formatting a document or worksheet. Successful candidates generally have six or more months of experience with Windows Vista or the specific Office program, including either formal, instructor-led training or self-study using MCAS-approved books, guides, or interactive computer-based materials.

Candidates for MCAP-level certification are expected to successfully complete more complex, business-oriented tasks utilizing advanced functionality with the combined 2007 Microsoft Office suite of products. Successful candidates generally have between six months and one or more years of experience with the programs, including formal, instructor-led training or self-study using MCAP-approved materials.

Becoming a Microsoft Certified Application Specialist—Windows Vista

Every MCAS and MCAP certification exam is developed from a set of exam skill standards that are derived from studies of how Windows Vista and the 2007 Office system programs are used in the workplace. Because these skill standards dictate the scope of each exam, they provide you with critical information on how to prepare for certification.

To become certified as a Microsoft Certified Application Specialist in Windows Vista, you must demonstrate proficiency in these seven areas:

- **Protecting your computer.** You must demonstrate the ability to manage Windows Firewall, manage malicious software protection, configure Windows Update settings, lock a computer, manage Windows Internet Explorer security, and configure local user accounts.

- **Managing mobile and remote computing.** You must demonstrate the ability to manage the computer power state, network connections, and remote access to your computer; connect to another computer; and access files stored in shared network folders when your computer is offline.

- **Managing software, disks, and devices.** You must demonstrate the ability to manage software, storage disks, devices, and drivers; manage display settings; configure multiple monitors; and install and configure a printer.

- **Managing files and folders.** You must demonstrate the ability to manage Windows Explorer settings; manage, organize, and search for files and folders; secure and share folders; and back up and restore files and folders.

- **Collaborating with other people.** You must demonstrate the ability to collaborate in real time and present information to an audience through Windows Meeting Space, and to communicate in real time by using Windows Live Messenger.

- **Customizing your Windows Vista experience.** You must demonstrate the ability to modify the Start menu and the taskbar, personalize the desktop and system sounds, and manage Windows Sidebar.

- **Optimizing and troubleshooting your computer.** You must demonstrate the ability to increase processing speed, locate the information about your system needed to troubleshoot a problem, repair a network connection, recover from software errors, troubleshoot printing errors, recover the operating system from a problem, and request and manage Remote Assistance.

Taking a Microsoft Business Certification Exam

The MCAS and MCAP certification exams for Windows Vista and the 2007 Office system programs are performance-based and require you to complete business-related tasks by using an interactive simulation (a digital model) of the Windows Vista operating system or one or more programs in the Office suite.

Test-Taking Tips

- Follow all instructions provided in each question completely and accurately.

- Enter requested information as it appears in the instructions, but without duplicating the formatting unless you are specifically instructed to do otherwise. For example, the text and values you are asked to enter might appear in the instructions in bold and underlined (for example, **text**), but you should enter the information without applying these formats.

- Close all dialog boxes before proceeding to the next exam question unless you are specifically instructed otherwise.

- Don't close task panes before proceeding to the next exam question unless you are specifically instructed to do otherwise.

- If you are asked to print a document, worksheet, chart, report, or slide, perform the task, but be aware that nothing will actually be printed.

- Don't worry about extra keystrokes or mouse clicks. Your work is scored based on its result, not on the method you use to achieve that result (unless a specific method is indicated in the instructions), and not on the time you take to complete the question.

- If your computer becomes unstable during the exam (for example, if the exam does not respond or the mouse no longer functions) or if a power outage occurs, contact a testing center administrator immediately. The administrator will restart the computer and return the exam to the point where the interruption occurred with your score intact.

Certification

At the conclusion of the exam, you will receive a score report, which you can print with the assistance of the testing center administrator. If your score meets or exceeds the passing standard (the minimum required score), you will be mailed a printed certificate within approximately 14 days.

For More Information

To learn more about the Microsoft Business Certification exams and courseware, visit

www.microsoft.com/learning/mcp/msbc/

Information for New Computer Users

Windows Vista is the latest edition of the Microsoft Windows *operating system*. Your computer's operating system basically tells your computer what to do and how to do it. For your computer to work, Windows Vista must do the following:

- Coordinate interactions among its components, such as receiving input from the keyboard and mouse, displaying output on the monitor, and locating programs and files.

- Act as the interface between you and your computer, so that you can work in a visual way by clicking items on the screen instead of having to type precise sequences of commands.

- Enable your computer to communicate with other computers and with peripheral devices such as printers, scanners, and modems.

- Interact with programs installed on your computer.

The programs you purchase and install on your computer run on Windows Vista, meaning that they call on the operating system whenever they need to work with your computer's components or with peripheral devices. They also build on the interface provided by the operating system to communicate with you. This relationship allows the programs to concentrate on their specialized tasks, such as word processing or performing calculations in a worksheet, while the operating system handles the basic behind-the-scenes tasks.

The Windows operating system has been around long enough that it has spawned its own jargon. If you are a new computer user, some of the terms associated with Windows Vista and the programs that run on it might be new to you, so we will briefly cover them here to bring you up to speed.

Using Your Mouse

A mouse is a hardware device with which you control the location of the on-screen pointer; for example, to specify what user interface element to click, or the location of the insertion point. A standard mouse includes two buttons; your mouse might also include a scroll wheel, tilt wheel, or roller ball that provides additional methods of moving the pointer around the screen.

For new computer users who are not familiar with the standard Windows mouse actions, here's a quick summary:

- *Pointing to* an object involves moving the mouse so that the cursor (the visible representation of the mouse location on the screen) is over the object.
- *Clicking* an object involves pointing to the object and quickly pressing and releasing the primary mouse button once. (By default, the primary mouse button is the left one, but you can change this.)
- *Double-clicking* an object involves pointing to the object and pressing and releasing the primary mouse button twice in rapid succession. You can adjust the speed at which Windows recognizes two clicks as a double-click.
- *Right-clicking* an object involves pointing to the object and clicking the secondary mouse button once. This action displays a *context menu* (also called a *shortcut menu*) listing actions that can be performed with the object you right-clicked. You select the action you want by clicking it on the context menu.
- *Dragging* an object involves pointing to the object, holding down the primary mouse button, moving the mouse until the pointer is in the location where you want the object to appear, and releasing the mouse button. You can also drag through multiple objects in a list to select them, or drag to draw an object on a page.

If you prefer to click, double-click, and drag by using the right mouse button, you can switch the buttons by adjusting the Mouse settings in Control Panel.

See Also For information about switching the action of the left and right buttons and adjusting the speed of a double-click, see "Changing the Way Your Mouse Works" in Chapter 5, "Installing and Configuring Devices."

On a mobile computer (usually referred to as a *laptop*) or on a Tablet PC, you might use an alternative pointing device, such as a touch pad, TrackPoint device, or Tablet PC pen.

See Also For information about the Tablet PC pen equivalents of mouse actions, see "Configuring Tablet PC Options" in Chapter 5, "Installing and Configuring Devices."

Working with Windows

Windows Vista displays information in *windows*. A window can either fill the entire screen or occupy only part of the screen. Each window is encased in a *frame* displaying information about the window contents and containing controls for managing the window and its contents. When a window is not maximized to fill the screen, you can drag the edges of the frame to change the size of the window.

At the top of the window is space allocated to a *title bar*, which might tell you the window's purpose, the name of the program running in the window, or the name of the file open in the program. You can maximize or reduce the size of a window by double-clicking its title bar. When a window is not maximized, you can move it on the screen by dragging it by its title bar.

At the right end of the title bar are the Minimize, Maximize/Restore Down, and Close buttons. You click the Minimize button to collapse the window into a button on the Windows Vista taskbar (called *minimizing the window*); you click the Maximize/Restore Down button to switch the window from filling the screen (often *maximizing the window*) to occupying only part of it (*reducing* the window), and to switch it back again; and you click the Close button to close the window. If the window is displaying a program or file, closing the window might also exit the program or close the file.

Below the title bar, the window might have a *menu bar*, *toolbar*, or other visual representation of the instructions (commands) you can give Windows Vista regarding the contents of the window.

When a window is not big enough to show all its contents, vertical and/or horizontal *scroll bars* appear so that you can move the contents within the window. You use the vertical scroll bar to move the contents up and down, and the horizontal scroll bar to move the contents from side to side, as follows:

- Clicking the arrow at either end of a scroll bar moves the contents one line or column at a time.
- Clicking directly on the scroll bar on either side of the scroll box moves the contents one "windowful" at a time.
- Dragging the scroll box on the scroll bar moves the contents in larger increments.

The position of the scroll box in relation to the scroll bar tells you where you are in the contents. For example, when the scroll box is in the middle of the scroll bar, the window is displaying the portion of its contents located about halfway through.

Giving Instructions

To get any useful work done, you have to be able to give your computer instructions about what to do. These instructions are called *commands*. Some commands are simple, and you can give them by clicking an item on a menu, clicking a button on a toolbar, or pressing a key or combination of keys on the keyboard. If Windows Vista or the program you are working in needs information from you in order to know how to carry out a command, it might display a different window, a *task pane*, or a *dialog box*. These might present only one set of options, but they can also be quite complex, involving several layers of options you can use to refine your instructions. However, they all request information in consistent ways and use these common components:

- **Tabs.** If a dialog box contains too many options to fit in the dialog box window, the options are arranged in logical groups on separate pages, indicated by page tabs. You click a tab to display that set of options.

- **Command buttons.** Most dialog boxes have at least two command buttons: an OK button that carries out the command, and a Cancel button that cancels the command. Clicking either button also closes the dialog box. Other buttons might be available, such as the Apply button that applies changes without closing the dialog box. If a button label includes an ellipsis (...), clicking the button opens another dialog box. A dark border indicates the active button; you can press Enter to implement that command.

- **Option buttons.** In a group of mutually exclusive options where only one option can be selected at a time, each option is preceded by an option button (a small circle). When you click an option or its button, a dot appears in the circle to indicate that the option is *selected*. Because only one option in the group can be selected at a time, selecting an option removes the dot from the previously selected option.

- **Check boxes.** Options that can be either selected or not selected, but are not mutually exclusive, are preceded by a check box (a small square). Clicking an empty check box selects the associated option; a check mark appears inside the box to indicate that the option is *selected* or *turned on*. Clicking the box again removes the check mark to indicate that the option is *deselected*, *cleared*, or *turned off*. Check boxes operate independently, so if a dialog box presents a group of check boxes, you can select none, one, some, or all of the options, as required for the task at hand.

- **Text boxes.** You enter information, such as a file name, by typing it in a text box. To replace an existing entry, select the entry and delete it, or overtype the old text with the new.

- **List boxes.** A list of options from which you can select one or more is sometimes displayed in a list box. When more choices are available than can fit in the list box, the list box has a scroll bar. Regardless of the format of a list box, you select an option by clicking it. The option is then highlighted in the list. To select multiple options in a list box, select the first option, press the Ctrl key, and select the additional options.

- **Drop-down list boxes.** To conserve space, options are sometimes displayed in a drop-down list. A drop-down list appears initially as a text box containing an option. Clicking the arrow at the right end of the box displays a list of the other available options. To select an option, you simply click it in the list. That option then appears in the box. You can select only one option from a drop-down list.

- **Combo boxes.** Sometimes a text box and a drop-down list box are combined to form a combo box in which you can either type information or select from a list.

- **Spin boxes.** If a text box must contain only one of a specific set of options (usually numbers), it sometimes has a pair of up and down arrows at its right end. You change the entry either by selecting the existing number and typing a new one or by clicking one of the arrows to increase or decrease the number.

- **Sliders.** Settings can also be represented by the position of a slider on a horizontal or vertical bar. To change the setting, you drag the slider or click the bar to either side of it.

- **Links.** Clicking a link in a window might open another window or it might take you to information stored on your computer or on the Web. When you point to a link, it becomes underlined and the pointer changes to a hand.

You can move between options in a dialog box by pointing to them with the mouse, or by pressing the Tab key.

Message Boxes

Windows Vista displays message and warning boxes when a command you have chosen can't be carried out, or to request confirmation of a potentially risky action that you might later regret (for example, when you delete files).

You can click OK or Yes to acknowledge the message and continue the command. Click Cancel or No to close the message box and cancel the command.

Features and Conventions of This Book

This book has been designed to lead you step by step through all the tasks you are most likely to want to perform in Windows Vista, and the tasks you need to know how to perform if you are going to seek certification as a Microsoft Certified Application Specialist in Windows Vista. If you start at the beginning and work your way through all the exercises, you will gain enough proficiency to be able to work with all the common Windows elements and manage and maintain your own computer. However, each topic is self contained. If you have worked with a previous version of Windows, or if, after completing all the exercises, you later need help remembering how to perform a procedure, the following features of this book will help you locate specific information:

- **Detailed table of contents.** Scan a listing of the book's topics and sidebars.
- **Chapter thumb tabs.** Easily locate the beginning of the chapter you want.
- **Topic-specific running heads.** Within a chapter, quickly locate the topic you want by looking at the running head of odd-numbered pages.
- **Quick Reference.** Refresh your memory about a task while working with your own documents by following general instructions for each procedure covered in specific detail elsewhere in the book.
- **Detailed index.** Look up specific tasks and features and general concepts in the index, which has been carefully crafted with the reader in mind.
- **Companion CD.** Install the practice files you use while working through the step-by-step exercises, and browse a fully searchable electronic version of this book and other useful resources.

In addition, we provide a glossary of terms for those times when you need to look up the meaning of a word or the definition of a concept.

You can save time when you use this book by understanding how the *Step by Step* series shows special instructions, keys to press, buttons to click, and so on.

Convention	Meaning
	This icon at the end of a chapter introduction indicates information about the practice files provided on the companion CD for use in the chapter.
USE	This paragraph preceding a step-by-step exercise indicates the practice files that you will use when working through the exercise.
BE SURE TO	This paragraph preceding or following an exercise indicates any requirements you should attend to before beginning the exercise or actions you should take to restore your system after completing the exercise.
OPEN	This paragraph preceding a step-by-step exercise indicates files that you should open before beginning the exercise.
CLOSE	This paragraph following a step-by-step exercise provides instructions for closing open files or programs before moving on to another topic.
1 2	Blue numbered steps guide you through step-by-step exercises and Quick Reference versions of procedures.
1 2	Black numbered steps guide you through procedures in sidebars and expository text.
→	An arrow indicates a procedure that has only one step.
See Also	These paragraphs direct you to more information about a given topic in this book or elsewhere.
Troubleshooting	These paragraphs explain how to fix a common problem that might prevent you from continuing with an exercise.
Tip	These paragraphs provide a helpful hint or shortcut that makes working through a task easier, or information about other available options.
Important	These paragraphs point out information that you need to know to complete a procedure.
Save	The first time you are told to click a button in an exercise, a picture of the button appears in the left margin. If the name of the button does not appear on the button itself, the name appears under the picture.
Enter	In step-by-step exercises, keys you must press appear as they would on a keyboard.
Ctrl + Home	A plus sign (+) between two key names means that you must hold down the first key while you press the second key. For example, "press Ctrl + Home" means "hold down the Ctrl key while you press the Home key."
Program interface elements	In steps, the names of program elements, such as buttons, commands, and dialog boxes, are shown in black bold characters.
User input	Anything you are supposed to type appears in blue bold characters.
Glossary terms	Terms that are explained in the glossary at the end of the book are shown in blue italic characters.

Using the Companion CD

The companion CD included with this book contains practice files you can use as you work through the book's exercises, as well as other electronic resources that will help you learn how to use Windows Vista.

What's on the CD?

The following table lists the practice files supplied on the companion CD.

Chapter	Folder\Files
Chapter 1: Getting Started with Windows Vista	None
Chapter 2: Working Efficiently in Windows Vista	None
Chapter 3: Working with Folders and Files	*Files\AlbumSlides.pptx* *Files\Bamboo.docx* *Files\Bamboo1.jpg* through *Bamboo3.jpg* *Files\BookBeat.docx* *Files\BookSales.xlsx* *Files\CakePlate.jpg* *Files\Cat.jpg* *Files\ColorSlides.pptx* *Files\ComparisonShop.docx* *Files\Costs.xlsx* *Files\Crow.jpg* *Files\FabricSpecial.docx* *Files\FengShuiSlides.pptx* *Files\Figurine.jpg* *Files\Frog.jpg* *Files\Frog.jpg* *Files\Introduction.wav* *Files\Lady.jpg* *Files\LoanPayment.xlsx* *Files\MusicBox.jpg* *Files\OrgSlides.pptx*

Chapter	Folder\Files
Chapter 3: Working with Folders and Files (continued)	Files\PlanningSlides.pptx
	Files\Procedures.docx
	Files\RoomMakeover.docx
	Files\SalesMtgSlides.pptx
	Files\TagAnnounce.docx
	Files\TagIntroduce.docx
	Files\TeaPot.jpg
	Files\Welcome.docx
	Files\Narrations folder (empty)
	Files\Photographs folder (empty)
	Files\Presentations\Background.jpg
	Files\Presentations\TagTemplate.pptx
	Files\Videos\HouseHome.wmv
	Files\Videos\YinYang.png
Chapter 4: Personalizing Windows Vista	Backgrounds\Arizona01.jpg through Arizona10.jpg
Chapter 5: Installing and Configuring Devices	None
Chapter 6: Safely and Efficiently Accessing the Internet	None
Chapter 7: Working with Programs	Programs\MusicBox.bmp
Chapter 8: Making Connections	Connections\Changes.docx
	Connections\FindingWord.docx
	Connections\SavedText.docx
Chapter 9: Communicating with Other People	None
Chapter 10: Staying Organized	None
Chapter 11: Working with Graphics and Documents	Graphics\Brochure.rtf
	Graphics\ClassDesc1.rtf through ClassDesc3.rtf
	Graphics\FinalBrochure.rtf
	Graphics\GardenCompany.rtf
	Graphics\GCLogo.bmp
	Graphics\RedFlower.jpg
	Graphics\TeamPhoto.jpg
	Graphics\ToyTrain.bmp

Chapter	Folder\Files
Chapter 12: Working with Digital Media	*Media\Arizona01.jpg* through *Arizona10.jpg* *Media\Background.jpg* *Media\Bamboo01.jpg* through *Bamboo03.jpg* *Media\CakePlate.jpg* *Media\Cat.jpg* *Media\Crow.jpg* *Media\Figurine.jpg* *Media\Frog.jpg* *Media\Home01.wmv* through *Home03.wmv* *Media\MusicBox.jpg* *Media\TeaPot.jpg* *Media\YinYang.jpg*
Chapter 13: Managing Computer Security	*Security\Angelic.jpg*
Chapter 14: Optimizing Your Computer System	None
Chapter 15: Identifying and Solving Problems	*Solutions\BookBeat.docx*

In addition to the practice files, the CD contains some exciting resources that will really enhance your ability to get the most out of using this book and Windows Vista, including the following:

- *Windows Vista Step by Step, Deluxe Edition* in eBook format

- *Microsoft Computer Dictionary*, 5th ed. eBook

- Sample chapter and poster from *Look Both Ways: Help Protect Your Family on the Internet* (Linda Criddle, 2007)

> **Important** The companion CD for this book does not contain the Windows Vista operating system. You should purchase and install that operating system before using this book.

Minimum System Requirements

Windows Vista

To run Windows Vista, your computer needs to meet the following minimum hardware requirements:

- 800 megahertz (MHz) processor
- 512 megabytes (MB) RAM
- DirectX 9–capable graphics processor
- 20 gigabytes (GB) hard disk drive capacity with 15 GB available space

Computers that meet these requirements may be labeled by their manufacturers as *Windows Vista Capable.*

To get an even better Windows Vista experience, including the Windows Aero visual effects, your computer needs to meet these minimum requirements:

- 1 GHz processor
- 1 GB of system memory
- DirectX 9–capable graphics processor with a Windows Vista Display Driver Model (WDDM) driver, 128 GB of graphics memory (if the GPU uses dedicated memory; otherwise, no additional graphics memory is required), Pixel Shader 2.0 and 32 bits per pixel
- 40 GB hard disk drive capacity with 15 GB available space
- Internal or external DVD-ROM drive
- Audio output capability
- Internet access capability

Computers that meet these requirements may be labeled by their manufacturers as *Windows Vista Premium Ready.*

See Also For information about the Windows Aero visual effects, see "Optimizing Visual Effects" in Chapter 4, "Personalizing Windows Vista."

The TV Tuning, Microsoft BitLocker Drive Encryption, and Tablet PC features available with certain editions of Windows Vista require additional hardware, as indicated in the following table:

Feature	Available in	Additional hardware requirements
Windows Media Center television functionality	Windows Vista Ultimate, Windows Vista Home Premium	A TV tuner card and a remote control that complies with the Windows Vista Remote Control specification
BitLocker Drive Encryption	Windows Vista Enterprise, Windows Vista Ultimate	Integrated Trusted Platform Module (TPM) 1.2 chip or USB 2.0 key
Tablet PC features	Windows Vista Enterprise, Windows Vista Business, Windows Vista Ultimate, Windows,Vista Home Premium	A PC that meets the Tablet PC specification and includes an electromagnetic digitizer pen

Step-by-Step Exercises

In addition to the hardware required to run Windows Vista, you will need the following to successfully complete the exercises in this book:

- Windows Vista Home Basic, Windows Vista Home Premium, Windows Vista Ultimate, Windows Vista Business, or Windows Vista Enterprise

   See Also For information about the features available in different editions of Windows Vista, see "Introducing Windows Vista," earlier in this book.

- Monitor with minimum 800×600 screen resolution; 1024×768 or higher recommended

- Keyboard and mouse or compatible pointing device

- Internet connection, 128 kilobits (Kbps) or greater, for download and activation of products, accessing online Help topics, and any other Internet-dependent processes

- Access to the following peripheral devices:
  - Scanner
  - Printer
  - Speakers
  - Camera
  - External storage device
  - Microphone
- 30 MB of available hard disk space for the practice files

Installing the Practice Files

You need to install the practice files in the correct location on your hard disk before you can use them in the exercises. Follow these steps:

1. Remove the companion CD from the envelope at the back of the book, and insert it into the CD drive of your computer.

    The Step By Step Companion CD License Terms appear. Follow the on-screen directions. To use the practice files, you must accept the terms of the license agreement. After you accept the license agreement, a menu screen appears.

    > **Important** If the menu screen does not appear, click the Start button and then click Computer. Display the Folders list in the Navigation pane, click the icon for your CD drive, and then in the right pane, double-click the StartCD executable file.

2. Click **Install Practice Files**.

3. Click **Next** on the first screen, and then click **Next** to accept the terms of the license agreement on the next screen.

4. If you want to install the practice files to a location other than the default folder (*Documents\Microsoft Press\WindowsVistaSBS_Dlx*), click the **Change** button, select the new drive and path, and then click **OK**.

    > **Important** If you install the practice files to a location other than the default, you will need to substitute that path within the exercises.

5. Click **Next** on the **Choose Destination Location** screen, and then click **Install** on the **Ready to Install the Program** screen to install the selected practice files.

6. After the practice files have been installed, click **Finish**.

7. Close the **Step by Step Companion CD** window, remove the companion CD from the CD drive, and return it to the envelope at the back of the book.

Using the Practice Files

When you install the practice files from the companion CD that accompanies this book, the files are stored on your hard disk in chapter-specific subfolders under *Documents\ Microsoft Press\WindowsVistaSBS_Dlx*. Each exercise is preceded by a paragraph that lists the files needed for that exercise and explains any preparations needed before you start working through the exercise. Here are examples:

USE the *Angelic* image. This practice file is located in the *Documents\Microsoft Press\ WindowsVistaSBS_Dlx\Security* folder.

BE SURE TO log on to Windows and have an active Internet connection available before beginning this exercise.

OPEN Control Panel, and then display the User Accounts window.

You can browse to the practice files in Windows Explorer by following these steps:

Start

1. On the Windows taskbar, click the **Start** button, and then click **Documents**.

2. In your *Documents* folder, double-click *Microsoft Press*, double-click *WindowsVistaSBS_Dlx*, and then double-click the specific chapter folder.

You can browse to the practice files from a dialog box by following these steps:

1. In the **Favorite Links** pane in the dialog box, click **Documents**.

2. In your *Documents* folder, double-click *Microsoft Press*, double-click *WindowsVistaSBS_Dlx*, and then double-click the specific chapter folder.

Removing and Uninstalling the Practice Files

You can free up hard disk space by uninstalling the practice files that were installed from the companion CD. The uninstall process deletes the practice files that were installed in the *Documents\Microsoft Press\WindowsVistaSBS_Dlx* chapter-specific folders, but does not delete any additional files you created while working through the exercises.

Follow these steps to uninstall the standard practice files:

Start

1. On the Windows taskbar, click the **Start** button, and then click **Control Panel**.

2. In **Control Panel**, under **Programs**, click the **Uninstall a program** task.

3. In the **Programs and Features** window, click **Windows Vista Step by Step Deluxe**, and then on the toolbar at the top of the window, click the **Uninstall** button.

4. If the **Programs and Features** message box asking you to confirm the deletion appears, click **Yes**.

To remove files you created while working through the exercises, open Windows Explorer, browse to the files, and select and delete them.

> **Important** Microsoft Product Support Services does not provide support for this book or for its companion CD.

Getting Help

Every effort has been made to ensure the accuracy of this book and the contents of its companion CD. If you do run into problems, please contact the sources listed below for assistance.

Getting Help with This Book and Its Companion CD

If your question or issue concerns the content of this book or its companion CD, please first search the online Microsoft Press Knowledge Base, which provides support information for known errors in or corrections to this book, at the following Web site:

www.microsoft.com/mspress/support/search.asp

If you do not find your answer at the online Knowledge Base, send your comments or questions to Microsoft Press Technical Support at:

mspinput@microsoft.com

Getting Help with Windows Vista

If your question is about Windows Vista, and not about the content of this Microsoft Press book, first consult the resources listed in Chapter 15, "Identifying and Solving Problems." If you do not find your answer in Windows Help And Support, or through the other resources listed, please search the Windows Vista Solution Center or the Microsoft Knowledge Base at:

support.microsoft.com

In the United States, Microsoft software product support issues not covered by the Microsoft Knowledge Base are addressed by Microsoft Product Support Services. Location-specific software support options are available from:

support.microsoft.com/gp/selfoverview/

Quick Reference

1   Getting Started with Windows Vista

To activate Windows manually

1. In **Control Panel**, click **System and Maintenance**, and then click **System**.
2. In the **System** window, in the **Windows activation** area, click **Activate Windows now**.
3. In the **Windows Activation** dialog box, click **Activate Windows online now**. Then after Windows verifies that your copy of Windows is genuine, click **Close**.

To automatically download and install critical updates

1. In **Control Panel**, click **Security**, and then click **Windows Update**.
2. In the left pane, click the **Change settings** task. Then select the **Install updates automatically** option, if it is not already selected.
3. In the second **Install new updates** list, select a time at which your computer will usually be on and online. If you want more control over the update process but still want automatic updates, select the **Download updates but let me choose whether to install them** option.
4. With the **Include recommended updates** and **Use Microsoft Update** check boxes selected, click **OK**.

To install available Windows updates

1. In **Control Panel**, click **Security**, and then click **Windows Update**.
2. If updates are available, click the **View available updates** task in the update status box.
3. In the list of available updates, select the check box for any update you want to install. Then click **Install**.

To log on to a user account while another is active

1. On the **Start** menu, click the **Shut Down Options** button, and then click **Switch User**.
2. On the **Welcome** screen, click the user account you want to log on to, and enter the password if one is required.

To lock your computer

→ On the **Start** menu, click the **Lock** button.

To unlock your computer

→ If your account is password protected, on the **Welcome** screen, enter your password in the **Password** box, and then press Enter. Otherwise, click your user account picture.

To put your computer into Sleep mode

→ On the **Start** menu, click the **Sleep** button.

To wake your computer from Sleep mode

→ Depending on your specific hardware, press ⌨️Enter⌨️ or press your computer's power button to wake your computer.

To log off from Windows

1. On the **Start** menu, click the **Shut Down Options** button, and then click **Log Off**.
2. If you don't have any unsaved work, click **Log off now** to complete the process and display the Welcome screen. Otherwise, click **Cancel** to return to your computing session; then save and close open files, shut down running programs, and click **Log Off** in the **Shut Down Options** list to complete the process.

To shut down your computer

→ If you've already logged off from your computer, in the lower-right corner of the **Welcome** screen, click the **Shut Down** button.

→ If you haven't yet logged off, on the **Start** menu, click the **Shut Down Options** button, and then in the **Shut Down Options** list, click **Shut Down**.

To open the Ease Of Access Center

→ In **Control Panel**, click **Ease of Access**, and then click **Ease of Access Center**.

2   Working Efficiently in Windows Vista

To change the number of recently opened programs displayed on the Start menu

1. Right-click the **Start** button, and then click **Properties**.
2. On the **Start Menu** tab of the **Taskbar and Start Menu Properties** dialog box, with the **Start menu** option selected, click **Customize**.
3. In the **Start menu size** area of the **Customize Start Menu** dialog box, type or select the number of programs you want displayed, and then click **OK**.
4. In the **Taskbar and Start Menu Properties** dialog box, click **OK**.

To start a program from the Start menu

1. On the **Start** menu, click **All Programs**.
2. In the **All Programs** list, click a program name, or click a folder containing a program you want to open, and then click the program name.

To add a shortcut to the pinned programs area of the Start menu

→ Right-click a program icon in the **All Programs** list of the **Start** menu, or in Windows Explorer, and then click **Pin to Start Menu**.

→ Drag a program icon from the recently opened programs area or **All Programs** list of the **Start** menu to the pinned programs area.

→ Drag a program icon from Windows Explorer to the **Start** button, and then when the **Start** menu opens, to the pinned programs area.

To remove a shortcut from the pinned programs area of the Start menu

→ In the pinned programs area, right-click the program icon, and then click **Unpin from Start Menu**.

To browse the folder structure of your computer

1. In the **Navigation** pane, display the **Folders** list.
2. Click the arrow beside a folder name or double-click the folder name to show its list of subfolders; or in the Address bar, click the arrow to the right of the folder name to display its list of subfolders, and then click the folder name you want in the list.

To resize a window

→ In an open window, click the **Maximize** or **Restore Down** button in the upper-right corner of the window.

→ In a non-maximized window, point to the window's frame. When the pointer changes to a double-headed arrow, drag the frame to the size you want.

To hide a window

→ In an open window, click the **Minimize** button in the upper-right corner of the window.

To close a window

→ Click the **Close** button in an open window, or if the window is hidden, click the window's taskbar button, and then click **Close**.

To switch between multiple windows

→ On the **Quick Launch** toolbar, click the **Switch between windows** button, and then click the window you want to display.

To minimize all open windows

→ On the **Quick Launch** toolbar, click the **Show desktop** button.

To view a group of windows at the same time

→ Right-click the taskbar button for a group of programs, and then click **Show Windows Stacked**.

To lock or unlock the taskbar

→ Right-click an empty area of the taskbar, and then click **Lock the Taskbar**.

To modify what appears on the taskbar

1. Right-click an empty area of the taskbar, and then click **Properties**.
2. In the **Taskbar and Start Menu Properties** dialog box, select the options you want on each tab, and then click **OK**.

To resize the taskbar

→ Point to the top of the taskbar. When the pointer changes to a double-headed arrow, drag the border up or down until it's the size you want.

To create a desktop shortcut

1. Right-click an open area of the desktop, point to **New**, and then click **Shortcut**.
2. In the **Create Shortcut** wizard, type in the location of the item; or click **Browse**, navigate to and click the program you want, and then click **OK**.
3. In the **Create Shortcut** wizard, click **Next**.
4. In the **Type a name for this shortcut** box, type a name, and then click **Finish**.

To rearrange items on the desktop

→ Drag a shortcut on your desktop to the location you want it to appear.

→ Right-click an empty area of the desktop, point to **View**, and then click **Auto Arrange**.

To delete an item from the desktop

→ Right-click the shortcut, click **Delete**, and then in the confirmation message box, click **Yes**.

To configure your Windows Vista computer to recognize your voice

1. Click the **Start** button, type speech recognition in the **Start Search** box, and then press ⌷ Enter ⌷.
2. Read the information on the **Welcome to Speech Recognition** page of the **Set Up Speech Recognition** wizard, and then click **Next**.
3. Select the option for the type of microphone you are using, and then click **Next**.
4. On the **Set up your microphone** page, read the instructions, and then click **Next**.
5. On the **Adjust the microphone volume** page, read the microphone test paragraph aloud in your normal speaking voice. Click **Next**, and then on the page confirming that your microphone is set up, click **Next** again.
6. Read the information on the **Improve speech recognition accuracy** page, and then with **Enable document review** selected, click **Next**.
7. On the **Print the Speech Reference Card** page, click **Next**.
8. If you do not want speech recognition to start automatically, clear the **Run Speech Recognition at startup** check box. Then click **Next**.
9. If you are already comfortable with speech commands, click **Cancel**. Otherwise, click **Start Tutorial**; follow along with the tutorial instructions, and then click **Finish**.

To control your computer by using speech commands

→ Say Start listening into your microphone, and then give any speech commands to your computer that you want. When you finish, say Stop listening, or click the microphone on the **Speech Recognition** command bar. If you want to stop Speech Recognition, click the **Close** button on the command bar.

3   Working with Folders and Files

To display the contents of folders, drives, and storage devices accessible to your computer

→ On the **Start** menu, click **All Programs**, click **Accessories**, and then click **Windows Explorer** to display the contents of your *Documents* folder.

→ Right-click a folder, and then click **Explore**.

→ Click a folder link on the **Start** menu to open that folder. For example, click **Computer** or **Network** to display an overview of all the hard disk drives and storage devices accessible to your computer.

To navigate recent files in Windows Explorer

→ Click the **Back** button or **Forward** button to display the contents of folders you have already viewed in the Content pane.

→ Click the **Recent Pages** button to see a list of folders you have viewed so that you can select the one you want to display.

To add a folder to the Favorite Links list

→ In the **Contents** pane of Windows Explorer, drag the folder you want to add to the list.

To map a drive

1. On the **Start** menu, click **Computer**.
2. On the toolbar above the Content pane, click **Map network drive**. Then in the **Map Network Drive** window, specify the letter by which you want to identify this drive.
3. Click **Browse**, navigate to the drive or folder you want to map, and then click **OK** to return to the **Map Network Drive** window with the path entered in the **Folder** box.
4. If you want to connect to this location only until the end of the current Windows session, clear the **Reconnect at logon** check box. Then click **Finish**.

To disconnect from a mapped drive or folder

→ In Windows Explorer, right-click the drive or folder, and then click **Disconnect**.

To display or hide panes in Windows Explorer

→ On the **Organize** menu, point to **Layout**, and then in the list, click the pane you want to change.

To change the view of folders or files

→ On the Windows Explorer toolbar, click the **Views** button to cycle through the four most common views; or, click the **Views** arrow, and then select the view you want by dragging the slider.

To change the sort order in a Windows Explorer list view

→ Click the heading that you want to sort by. Click it again to reverse the sort order.

To delete a column in a Windows Explorer list view

→ Right-click a column heading, and then in the attributes list, click the attribute you want to add.

To change the properties of a file

→ Display the folder containing the file in Windows Explorer. Click the file, and then modify its properties in the **Details** pane.

To remove properties from a file

1. Select a file in Windows Explorer, and then on the **Organize** menu, click **Remove Properties**.

2. In the **Remove Properties** dialog box, select the properties you want to remove.

To create a folder from Windows Explorer

1. On the **Organize** menu, click **New Folder**.

2. With the *New Folder* file name highlighted, type the name you want for the folder, and then press `Enter`.

To compress a file

→ In Windows Explorer, right-click the file you want to compress, point to **Send To**, and then click **Compressed (zipped) Folder**.

To delete multiple files

1. In Windows Explorer, click the first file you want to delete, hold down the `Ctrl` key, and then click the other file(s) you want to delete; or to select a range of files, click the first file, hold down the `Shift` key, and then click the last file.

2. Press the `Del` key. Then in the **Delete Multiple Items** message box, click **Yes**.

To permanently delete items from the Recycle Bin

→ Open the Recycle Bin, verify that you do not want to retain any items, and then on the toolbar, click **Empty the Recycle Bin**. In the **Delete Multiple Items** message box, click **Yes** to permanently delete all items.

→ On the desktop or in the **Folders** list, right-click the **Recycle Bin**, and then click **Empty Recycle Bin** to delete all items without first reviewing them.

→ Open the Recycle Bin, select specific items you want to permanently delete, press `Del`, and then in the **Delete File** message box, click **Yes**.

To restore files from the Recycle Bin

→ Open the Recycle Bin. Then without selecting any items, on the toolbar, click **Restore all items** to return all deleted items to their previous locations.

→ Open the Recycle Bin, and select specific items you want to restore. Then on the toolbar, click **Restore this item** to return selected items to their previous locations.

To copy files to other folders

→ In Windows Explorer, click the file you want to copy, and on the **Organize** menu, click **Copy**. Then display the folder you want to copy the file to, and on the **Organize** menu, click **Paste**.

→ Using the secondary mouse button, drag the file to its new location. Then when you release the mouse button, click **Copy Here**.

→ Hold down the Ctrl key, and drag the copy to its new location, releasing first the mouse button and then the Ctrl key.

To search for items on your computer and on the Internet

→ Click the **Start** button, and then in the **Start Search** box, type what you want to search for. To use the Internet for your search, at the bottom of the **Start** menu, click the **Search the Internet** link.

→ On the **Start** menu, click **Search**. Then in the **Search** box, type what you want to search for. To use advanced criteria to help focus your search, click the **Advanced Search** arrow, and fill in any extra information you want.

4   Personalizing Windows Vista

To switch between themes

1. In **Control Panel**, click **Appearance and Personalization**.
2. Under **Personalization**, click the **Change the theme** task.
3. Click the **Theme** arrow, and then in the list, click the theme you want to use. Then click **OK**.

To change the desktop background to your own picture

1. Save the picture you want to use in your *Pictures* folder.
2. In **Control Panel**, under **Appearance and Personalization**, click the **Change desktop background** task.
3. In the **Picture Location** list, click **Pictures**.
4. Click the thumbnail of the picture you want. Then click **OK**.

To change the desktop background to a Windows Vista picture

1. In **Control Panel**, under **Appearance and Personalization**, click the **Change desktop background** task.

2. In the **Picture Location** list, click **Windows Wallpapers**.

3. In the **Windows Wallpapers** gallery, click the thumbnail of the picture you want. Then click **OK**.

To use your photos as a screen saver

1. In **Control Panel**, click **Appearance and Personalization**, and under **Personalization**, click the **Change screen saver** task.

2. In the **Screen Saver Settings** dialog box, click the **Screen saver** arrow, and then in the list, click **Photos**. Then click **Settings**.

3. In the **Photos Screen Saver Settings** dialog box, to the right of **Use pictures and videos from**, click **Browse**.

4. In the **Browse For Folder** dialog box, browse to the folder that has the photos you want to use, and then click **OK**. Adjust the slide show speed if you want, and then click **Save**.

To adjust the refresh rate and the color depth of your monitor

1. In **Control Panel**, under **Appearance and Personalization**, click the **Adjust screen resolution** task.

2. In the **Display Settings** dialog box, click **Advanced Settings**.

3. In the **Advanced Settings** dialog box, click the **Monitor** tab. In the **Monitor Settings** area, click the **Screen refresh rate** arrow to display a list of valid refresh rates for the selected monitor.

4. Select a screen refresh rate of at least 10 Hertz, preferably 70 or over. Then click **OK**. If your computer system includes multiple monitors on the same graphics adapter or multiple enabled graphics adapters, select the other monitors in turn, click **Advanced Settings**, confirm the available graphics memory, select an appropriate refresh rate, and click **OK**.

5. In the **Display Settings** dialog box, click the **Colors** arrow to display the available color qualities. Set the color quality to at least **32 bit**. Then click **OK**.

To enable window transparency

1. Apply the **Windows Aero** color scheme.

2. In **Control Panel**, under **Appearance and Personalization**, click the **Change the color scheme** task.

3. On the **Window Color and Appearance** page, select the **Enable transparency** check box. Then click **OK**.

To change the desktop background color

1. In **Control Panel**, under **Appearance and Personalization**, click the **Change desktop background** task.

2. In the **Picture Location** list, click **Solid Colors**.

3. In the **Solid Colors** gallery, click the color you want. Then click **OK**.

To change the system time

1. Right-click in the notification area at the right end of the status bar, and then click **Adjust Date/Time**.

2. In the **Date and Time** dialog box, click **Change date and time**.

3. Drag the mouse pointer over the hour, minutes, or AM/PM setting displayed in the digital clock to select it, and then type or select (by clicking the arrows) the time you want.

4. Click **OK** in each of the open dialog boxes.

To connect to an Internet time server for an automatic update

1. Right-click in the notification area at the right end of the status bar, and then click **Adjust Date/Time**.

2. In the **Date and Time** dialog box, click the **Internet Time** tab, and then click **Change settings**.

3. In the **Internet Time Settings** dialog box, with the **Synchronize with an Internet time server** check box selected, click the **Server** arrow. In the list, click the server you want to use, and then click **Update now**.

To view the computer name

→ On the **Start** menu, click **Computer**. The computer name appears in the lower-left corner of the **Computer** window.

To change the computer name

1. On the **Start** menu, right-click **Computer**, and then click **Properties**.

2. In the **Computer name, domain, and workgroup settings** area of the **System** window, click **Change settings**.

3. On the **Computer Name** tab of the **System Properties** dialog box, click **Change**, and replace the existing computer name with the name you want. Then click **OK**.

To change the name of the link to your *Computer* folder

→ On the **Start** menu, right-click **Computer**, click **Rename**, type the name you want to appear, and then press Enter.

5 Installing and Configuring Devices

To change your screen resolution

1. In **Control Panel**, under **Appearance and Personalization**, click the **Adjust screen resolution** task.

2. In the **Display Settings** dialog box, drag the **Resolution** slider to the setting you want, and then click **Apply**.

3. In the **Display Settings** message box that appears, click **Yes**.

To configure your computer to display your Windows desktop across two monitors

1. In **Control Panel**, under **Appearance and Personalization**, click the **Adjust screen resolution** task.

2. In the preview area, click monitor 2, select the **Extend my Windows desktop onto this monitor** check box, and then click **Apply**.

3. In the **Display Settings** message box that appears, click **Yes**.

To change the primary monitor

1. In **Control Panel**, under **Appearance and Personalization**, click the **Adjust screen resolution** task.

2. In the preview area, click the monitor you want as the primary.

3. Select the **This is my main monitor** check box, and then click **Apply**.

4. In the **Display Settings** message box that appears, click **Yes**.

To adjust the relationship of the displays to each other

1. In **Control Panel**, under **Appearance and Personalization**, click the **Adjust screen resolution** task.

2. In the preview area, drag monitor **2** to the location you want it to be in relationship to monitor **1**.

To change the way the mouse buttons work

1. In **Control Panel**, under **Hardware and Sound**, click **Mouse**.

2. On the **Buttons** tab of the **Mouse Properties** dialog box, in the **Button configuration** section, select the **Switch primary and secondary buttons** check box to change the default primary button from left to right.

3. In the **Double-click speed** area, drag the slider to the speed you want. Then click **OK**.

To change how the mouse pointer looks and works

1. In **Control Panel**, under **Hardware and Sound**, click **Mouse**.

2. On the **Pointers** tab of the **Mouse Properties** dialog box, in the **Scheme** list, click one of the 21 available system schemes to change the pointer set.

3. In the **Customize** list, click any pointer, and then click **Browse**. Then in the **Browse** dialog box displaying the contents of your *Cursors* folder, double-click any cursor to replace the selected pointer.

4. Click the **Pointer Options** tab, and set the pointer speed, movement, and visibility options. Then click **OK**.

To change how the mouse wheel works

1. In **Control Panel**, under **Hardware and Sound**, click **Mouse**.

2. On the **Wheel** tab of the **Mouse Properties** dialog box, in the **Vertical Scrolling** area, select either the **The following number of lines at a time** option (and then type or click the arrow keys to set the number of lines you want to scroll) or the **One screen at a time** option to control how much of the screen scrolls as you turn the mouse wheel.

3. If your mouse supports horizontal scrolling, in the **Tilt the wheel to scroll the following number of characters at a time** box, enter the number of characters you want to scroll horizontally when you tilt the mouse wheel left or right. Then click **OK**.

To configure your computer to enter keystrokes as though you are typing on a different-language keyboard

1. In **Control Panel**, click **Clock, Language, and Region**, and then under **Regional and Language Options**, click the **Change keyboards or other input methods** task.

2. In the **Regional and Language Options** dialog box, on the **Keyboards and Languages** tab, click **Change keyboards**.

3. In the **Text Services and Input Languages** dialog box, in the **Default input language** list, click the language you want. Or, to accept input from a language-specific keyboard not in the list, click **Add** in the **Installed services** area.

4. In the **Add Input Language** dialog box, in the list of languages, click the **Expand** button to the left of the language keyboard you want, and then click the **Expand** button to the left of **Keyboard**.

5. In the **Keyboard** list, select the language's check box, and then click **OK** in the **Add Input Language** dialog box.

6. In the **Text Services and Input Languages** dialog box, click **OK**.

7. On the **Language Bar**, click the input language button. Then in the input language list, click your chosen language.

To remove a different-language keyboard

1. In **Control Panel**, click **Clock, Language, and Region**, and then under **Regional and Language Options**, click the **Change keyboards or other input methods** task.

2. In the **Regional and Language Options** dialog box, on the **Keyboards and Languages** tab, click **Change keyboards**.

3. In the **Installed services** area, click the keyboard you want to remove, and then click **Remove**.

To change the screen orientation of your Tablet PC

1. In **Control Panel**, tap **Mobile PC**, and then tap **Tablet PC Settings**.

2. On the **Display** tab of the **Tablet PC Settings** dialog box, in the **Orientation** list, tap the orientation you want. Then click **Apply**.

To set the pen equivalents of various mouse actions

1. In **Control Panel**, tap **Mobile PC**, and then tap **Tablet PC Settings**.

2. Tap the **Other** tab, and then tap the **Go to Pen and Input Devices** link.

3. On the **Pen Options** tab of the **Pen and Input Devices** dialog box, select the options you want.

To change the position of the Input Panel

1. Tap the **Input Panel** tab.

2. On the **Input Panel**, tap **Tools**, and then in the list, tap the option you want.

To install a local printer and test the installation by printing a test page

1. Connect the printer to the appropriate port on your computer.

2. Connect the printer to a power outlet, and then if necessary, turn it on.

3. If Windows Vista does not recognize the printer, skip to step 5. Otherwise, click the alert to display the progress of the printer installation.

4. After Windows Vista declares the printer ready to use, close the **Driver Software Installation** window. If the installation does not complete successfully, continue with step 5.

5. Open **Control Panel**, and under **Hardware and Sound**, click **Printer**.

6. On the toolbar of the **Printers** window, click **Add a printer**.

7. On the **Add Printer** wizard's first page, click **Add a local printer**.

8. On the **Choose a printer port** page, select the port to which your printer is connected from the **Use an existing port** list, and then click **Next**.

9. If you have an installation CD for your printer, insert it in the appropriate drive, click **Have Disk**, and then follow the instructions on the screen to install your printer. Otherwise, in the **Manufacturer** list, click the brand name of your printer.

10. In the **Printers** list, click the model of your printer (which you can usually find printed on the top or front of the printer). Then click **Next**. (If the Printers list doesn't include your specific model, select a model with a similar name, or download the necessary

drivers from the printer manufacturer's Web site, return to the **Install the Printer Driver** page, and click **Have Disk** to install the printer manually.)

11. On the **Type a printer name** page, change the printer name if you want, or accept the default name. If you want Windows and any programs you install, such as Microsoft Office Word, to print to this printer when you click the **Print** button, select the **Set as the default printer** check box. Then click **Next**.

12. On the wizard's confirmation page, click **Print a test page**.

13. In the confirmation message box, click **Close**. Then in the **Add Printer** wizard, click **Finish**.

To change your default printer,

1. In **Control Panel**, click **Hardware and Sound**, and then click **Printers**.

2. In the **Printers** window, double-click the printer you want to set as the default. Then on the **Printer** menu of the printer's management window, click **Set as Default Printer**.

To share a printer

1. In **Control Panel**, click **Hardware and Sound**, and then click **Printers**.

2. In the **Printers** window, right-click the printer you want to share, and then click **Sharing**.

3. In the **Properties** dialog box, click **Change sharing options**.

4. On the **Sharing** tab, select the **Share this printer** check box. Then in the **Share name** box, type a simple name for the printer (or leave the default).

5. In the **Properties** dialog box, click **OK**.

To connect to a network printer

1. In **Control Panel**, under **Hardware and Sound**, click **Printer**.

2. On the toolbar of the **Printers** window, click **Add a printer**.

3. On the **Add Printer** wizard's first page, click **Add a network, wireless, or Bluetooth printer**.

4. On the **Select a printer** page, click the printer you want to connect to, and then click **Next**.

5. In the **Printers** message box, click **Install driver**.

6. On the **Type a printer name** page, change the printer name if you want, or accept the default name. If you want Windows and any programs you install, such as Word, to print to this printer when you click the **Print** button, select the **Set as the default printer** check box. Then click **Next**.

7. In the **Add Printer** wizard, click **Finish**.

To connect speakers to your Windows Vista computer, and adjust the audio output levels

1. Remove the speakers from their packaging, if you have not already done so. If you are using an alternate audio configuration, such as a headset microphone, connect the input and output cables appropriately, and then skip to step 6.

2. Link the two speakers by using the connector cable.

3. Position the speakers to the left and right of your monitor to provide stereo sound quality.

4. Connect the speakers to a power outlet by using the AC adapter cord.

5. Plug the speakers into the speaker jack on the computer by using the connector cable.

6. Open **Control Panel**, click **Hardware and Sound**, and then click **Sound.**

7. In the **Sound** dialog box, click each of the tabs, and explore the options available. Then on the **Playback** tab, click your speakers, and click **Configure**.

8. On the **Choose your configuration** page of the **Speaker Setup** wizard, select the appropriate audio channel, and then click **Test**. Try testing each of the configurations to hear the different options. Finally, select the channel you want, and then click **Next**.

9. If the **Select full-range speakers** page appears, click **Next** to complete the configuration, and then on the **Configuration complete** page, click **Finish**.

To connect a microphone to your Windows Vista computer, and adjust the audio input levels

1. Remove the microphone from its packaging, if you have not already done so. If you are using a USB microphone, ensure that you are logged in as an administrator before connecting the microphone to the USB port.

2. Plug the microphone connector cable into the audio input jack on your computer, or into a USB port, depending on the connection type.

3. Open **Control Panel**, and then click **Ease of Access**.

4. In the **Ease of Access** window, under **Speech Recognition Options**, click **Set up a microphone**.

5. In the **Microphone Setup** wizard, select the option for the type of microphone you are using, and then click **Next**.

6. On the **Set up your microphone page**, read the instructions, and then click **Next**.

7. On the **Adjust the microphone volume** page, read the microphone test paragraph aloud in your normal speaking voice.

8. When you finish reading the paragraph, click **Next**. Then click **Finish** to complete the wizard.

6   Safely and Efficiently Accessing the Internet

To connect to the Internet through a broadband or dial-up connection

1. In **Control Panel**, click **Network and Internet**.
2. Under **Network and Sharing Center**, click the **Connect to a network** task.
3. At the bottom of the page in the **Connect to a network** wizard, click the **Set up a connection or network** link.
4. On the **Choose a connection option** page, click **Connect to the Internet**, and then click **Next**.
5. On the **How do you want to connect** page, click either **Broadband** or **Dial-up**, and then click **Next**.
6. Enter the requested connection information, and then click **Connect** to close the window and create the connection.

To start Internet Explorer

→ On the **Start** menu, click **Internet**.

→ If Internet Explorer is not your default browser, point to **All Programs** on the **Start** menu, and then click **Internet Explorer**.

To open Web sites

→ In Internet Explorer, click once in the **Address** box, type the address of the Web site you want to visit, and then click the **Go** button or press `Enter`.

To open a recently visited Web site

1. Click the **Start** button, and in the **Start Search** box, type http://.
2. In the results shown on the **Start** menu, click the site you want to open.

To return to a previous Web page

→ In Internet Explorer, to the left of the **Address** box, click the **Back** or **Forward** button; or, to the right of the Back and Forward buttons, click the **Recent Pages** button, and then in the list, click the page you want to go to.

To change tabbed browsing settings

1. On the Internet Explorer **Tools** menu, click **Internet Options**.
2. In the **General** tab of the **Internet Options** dialog box, in the **Tabs** area, click **Settings**.
3. In the **Tabbed Browsing Settings** dialog box, review the types of changes you can make, and change any settings that you want. Then click **OK** in each open dialog box.

To modify Pop-up Blocker settings

→ On the Internet Explorer **Tools** menu, point to **Pop-up Blocker**, and then click **Pop-up Blocker Settings**.

To turn off Pop-up Blocker

➜ On the Internet Explorer **Tools** menu, point to **Pop-up Blocker**, and then click **Turn off Pop-up Blocker**. Then in the **Pop-up Blocker** message box requesting confirmation, click **Yes**.

To change your home page

1. In Internet Explorer, display the Web page you want to set as your home page.
2. On the **Command** bar, click the **Home** arrow, and then in the list, click **Add or Change Home Page**.
3. In the **Add or Change Home Page** dialog box, select the **Use this webpage as your only home page** option, and then click **Yes**.

To add a second home page

1. In Internet Explorer, display the Web page you want to set as your second home page.
2. In the **Home** list, click **Add or Change Home Page**. Then in the dialog box, select the **Add this webpage to your home page tabs** option, and click **Yes**.

To display your home page

➜ On the Internet Explorer **Command** bar, click the **Home** button.

To set a blank home page

➜ In Internet Explorer, in the **Home** list, point to **Remove**, and click **Remove All**. Then in the **Delete Home Page** dialog box, click **Yes**.

To change the size of the text on Web pages that don't specify text size

➜ On the Internet Explorer **Page** menu, point to **Text Size**, and then click the size you want: **Smallest**, **Smaller**, **Medium** (the default), **Larger**, or **Largest**.

To change the text and background colors used on Web pages without color specifications

1. On the Internet Explorer **Tools** menu, click **Internet Options**.
2. On the **General** tab of the **Internet Options** dialog box, in the **Appearance** area, click **Colors**.
3. In the **Colors** dialog box, clear the **Use Windows colors** check box.
4. Click the **Text**, **Background**, **Visited**, or **Unvisited** color button, select the color you want to use for that feature, and then click **OK** in each open dialog box.

To override the default color and font options on Web sites

1. On the Internet Explorer **Tools** menu, click **Internet Options**.
2. On the **General** tab of the **Internet Options** dialog box, in the **Appearance** area, click **Accessibility**.

3. In the **Formatting** area of the **Accessibility** dialog box, select the **Ignore colors specified on webpages** check box and the **Ignore font sizes specified on webpages** check box. Then click **OK**.

To search the Web

→ In the Internet Explorer **Live Search** box at the right end of the **Navigation** bar, type a plain-text query, and then click the **Search** button.

To add search providers to the Search Options list

→ At the right end of the Internet Explorer **Live Search** box, click the **Search Options** arrow. Then in the **Search Options** list, click **Find More Providers**.

To add a page to your Favorites list

1. In Internet Explorer, display the page you want to add. On the toolbar, click the **Add to Favorites** button, and then in the list, click **Add to Favorites**.

2. In the **Add a Favorite** dialog box, click **Add** to make the current page available from your Favorites list.

To view your Web browsing history

1. To the left of the page tabs, click the **Favorites Center** button.

2. In the **Favorites Center**, click the **History** arrow, and then click the sort order you want.

To display the Favorites Center as a pane

1. On the Internet Explorer toolbar, click the **Favorites Center** button.

2. In the upper-right corner of the **Favorites Center**, click the **Pin the Favorites Center** button.

To preview a Web page before printing

→ In Internet Explorer, display a Web page you want to print. Then on the **Command** bar, click the **Print** arrow, and click **Print Preview**.

To print a Web page

1. On the Internet Explorer **Command** bar, click the **Print** button.

2. Select the printer you want to use, and then click **Print**.

To send a Web page in an e-mail message

1. On the Internet Explorer **Page** menu, click **Send Page by E-mail**. Then in the **Internet Explorer Security** message box that appears, click **Allow**.

2. Address the e-mail message, and then send it.

To send a link to a Web page in an e-mail message

→ On the Internet Explorer **Page** menu, click **Send Link by E-mail**. Then address and send the e-mail message.

To configure the Content Advisor settings

1. On the Internet Explorer **Tools** menu, click **Internet Options**, and then in the **Internet Options** dialog box, click the **Content** tab.
2. In the **Content Advisor** area, click **Enable**.
3. In the **Select a category** list of the **Content Advisor** dialog box, click each category and then adjust the slider to the restriction level you want.
4. Click the **Approved Sites** tab, and add any sites you want to this list.
5. Click the **General** tab, and set the options you want.
6. In the **Supervisor password** area, click **Create password**.
7. In the **Create Supervisor Password** dialog box, type a password in the **Password** and **Confirm password** boxes, and click **OK**. Then click **OK** in the message box confirming that the password was successfully created.
8. In the **Content Advisor** dialog box, click **OK**. Then click **OK** in the message box confirming that Content Advisor has been enabled, and close the open dialog box.

To display a Web page that Content Advisor has blocked

→ In the **Content Advisor** window that opens when you attempt to view a blocked Web page, select the **Always allow this website to be viewed** option, type the password in the **Password** box if necessary, and then click **OK**.

To disable Content Advisor

1. On the Internet Explorer **Tools** menu, click **Internet Options**, display the **Content** tab, and then click **Disable**.
2. If necessary, in the **Supervisor Password Required** message box, type the password in the **Password** box, and then click **OK**. If a message box appears, notifying you that Content Advisor has been turned off, click **OK**. Then close the **Internet Options** dialog box.

7   Working with Programs

To uninstall a program

1. In **Control Panel**, under **Programs**, click the **Uninstall a program** task.
2. On the **Programs and Features** page, select the program you want to remove.
3. On the toolbar, click **Uninstall**. Then in the message box asking you to confirm that you want to proceed, click **Yes**.
4. If a message box informs you that you need to restart your computer to finish the uninstall process, click **Yes** to restart your computer, or click **No** to complete the uninstall process when you next start or restart your computer.

To start a program automatically

1. On the **Start** menu, point to **All Programs**, right-click **Startup**, and then click **Explore All Users**.

2. In the **Folders** list, display the contents of the folder containing the program you want.

3. If necessary, scroll the **Navigation** pane until the *Startup* folder is visible.

4. In the **Content** pane, hold down the right mouse button, and drag the program to the *Startup* folder in the **Navigation** pane, releasing the mouse button when you see the *Move to Startup* ScreenTip.

5. On the context menu, click **Copy Here**.

To change the default program for a file type

1. In Windows Explorer, right-click the file for which you want to change the associated program, point to **Open With**, and then click **Choose Default Program**.

2. In the **Open With** dialog box, under **Recommended Programs**, click the program you want to use, or click **Browse** and then navigate to the program you want to use.

3. Select the **Always use the selected program to open this kind of file** check box, and then click **OK**.

To change the default middleware settings

1. On the **Start** menu, click **Default Programs**.

2. Click the **Set program access and computer defaults** task.

3. In the **Set Program Access and Computer Defaults** dialog box, select the **Microsoft Windows**, **Non-Microsoft**, or **Custom** option, make any necessary changes, and then click **OK**.

To add a Games link to the Start menu

1. Right-click the **Start** button, and then click **Properties**.

2. On the **Start Menu** tab of the **Properties** dialog box, click **Customize**.

3. Scroll the list in the **Customize Start Menu** dialog box, and under **Games**, select the **Display as a link** option. Then click **OK** in each of the open dialog boxes.

To display information about the storage disks connected to your computer

1. On the **Start** menu, right-click **Computer**, and then click **Manage**.

2. In the left pane of the **Computer Management** console, expand **Storage**, and then click **Disk Management**.

To start Windows Task Manager

→ Press [Ctrl]+[Alt]+[Del] (once only). On the screen that appears, click **Start Task Manager**.

8   Making Connections

To join your computer to a new workgroup

1. In **Control Panel**, click **System and Maintenance**, and then click **System**.
2. In the **System** window, under **Computer name, domain, and workgroup settings**, click **Change settings**.
3. On the **Computer Name** tab of the **System Properties** dialog box, to the right of **To use a wizard to join a domain or workgroup**, click **Network ID**.
4. On the first page of the **Join a Domain or Workgroup** wizard, with the **This computer is part of a business network** option selected, click **Next**.
5. Select the **My company uses a network without a domain** option, and then click **Next**.
6. In the **Workgroup** box, type a name to describe your workgroup. Then click **Next**.
7. On the wizard's final page, click **Finish**. Then in the **System Properties** dialog box, click **OK**.
8. Close any open files and quit any running programs. Then in the message box, click **Restart Now**.

To create a VPN connection over the Internet

1. Display **Control Panel**, and then click **Network and Internet**.
2. In the **Network and Internet** window, under **Network and Sharing Center**, click the **Connect to a network** task, and then at the bottom of the **Connect to a network** window, click the **Set up a connection or network** task.
3. In the **Connect to a network** wizard, scroll to the end of the **Choose a connection option** list, click **Connect to a workplace**, and then click **Next**.
4. On the **How do you want to connect** page, click **Use my Internet connection (VPN)**.
5. On the **Type the Internet Address to connect to** page, in the **Internet address** box, type the remote access server's host name or IP address, and in the **Destination name** box, type a name for the connection.
6. Specify whether you want to make the connection available to other users of your computer or keep it to yourself, and then click **Next**.
7. On the **Type your user name and password** page, enter your network credentials, click **Connect**, and then in the **Connect to a workplace** wizard, click **Close**.
8. If the **Set Network Location** window appears, click **Work**.

To set up an ad hoc network

1. On the **Start** menu, click **Connect To**.
2. In the **Connect to a network** window, click the **Set up a connection or network** task.
3. On the **Choose a connection option** page, click **Set up a wireless ad hoc (computer-to-computer) network**, click **Next**, read the information on the page, and then click **Next** again.

4. Provide a network name, select whether the network is open or requires authentication, provide a security phrase if necessary, and then click **Next**.

To disconnect from an ad hoc network

1. On the **Start** menu, click **Connect To**.

2. In the **Connect to a Network** window, click the ad hoc network, and then click **Disconnect**.

To connect a computer to a domain

1. Connect your computer to your corporate network, either physically or through a VPN connection.

2. Display **Control Panel**, click **System and Maintenance**, and then click **System**.

3. In the **System** window, under **Computer name, domain, and workgroup settings**, click **Change settings**.

4. In the **System Properties** dialog box, click **Network ID**.

5. In the **Join a Domain or Workgroup** wizard, with the **This computer is part of a business network** option selected, click **Next**.

6. With the **My company uses a network with a domain** option selected, click **Next**.

7. Make sure you have all the necessary information, click **Next**, and then enter your user name, password, and domain name.

8. Click **Next**, and then in the message box, click **Yes**.

9. If you want to enable your user account, click **Next**. Otherwise, select the **Do not add a domain user account** option, and then click **Next**.

10. Unless you are the domain's network administrator, accept the default **Standard Account** option, click **Next**, and then click **Finish**.

11. In the **System Properties** dialog box, click **OK**. Then close any open files, quit any running programs, and in the message box, click **Restart Now**.

12. When your computer restarts, press [Ctrl]+[Alt]+[Del] to display the Welcome screen. Then type your password, and press [Enter] to log on to the domain.

To set up your computer so that it can be accessed via Remote Desktop

1. In **Control Panel**, click **System and Maintenance**, and then under **System**, click the **Allow remote access** task.

2. In the **System Properties** dialog box, under **Remote Desktop**, to allow Remote Desktop connections from any other Windows computer, select the **Allow connections from computers running any version of Remote Desktop** check box. To restrict connections to computers running Windows Vista, select the **Allow connections only from computers running Remote Desktop with Network Level Authentication** check box.

3. If a **Remote Desktop** message box appears, advising you that you won't be able to connect through Remote Desktop while the computer is in sleep mode, click **OK**.

4. In the **System Properties** dialog box, click **OK**.

To connect to your computer by using Remote Desktop

1. From another computer on the network, on the **Start** menu, click **All Programs**, click **Accessories**, and then click **Remote Desktop Connection**.

2. If the multi-tabbed dialog box area is not displayed, click **Options**.

3. On the **General** tab of the **Computer** box, type the name of the remote computer you want to access, and then click **Connect**.

4. In the **Windows Security** dialog box, enter your computer or domain credentials and, if you will be connecting to the remote computer from this computer on a regular basis, select the **Remember my credentials** check box. Then click **OK**.

To store a network password

1. In **Control Panel**, click **User Accounts and Family Safety**, and then click **User Accounts**.

2. In the **Tasks** list, click **Manage your network passwords**.

3. In the **Stored User Names and Passwords** dialog box, click **Add**.

4. In the **Stored Credential Properties** dialog box, enter the server, Web site, or program for which you want to store credentials in the **Log on to** box.

5. In the **User name** box and **Password** box, enter your credentials for the server or Web site.

6. Under **Credential type**, select the type of entity for which you are storing credentials. Then click **OK**.

To share a folder on your computer with everyone else on your network

1. In Windows Explorer, display the folder you want to share. Then on the toolbar, click **Share**.

2. On the first page of the **File Sharing** wizard, click the arrow to the right of the empty box, click the option you want, and then click **Add**.

3. Click **Share**.

4. After the folder is shared, click **Done**.

To customize permissions for a shared folder

1. Right-click the shared folder, and then click **Properties**.

2. On the **Sharing** tab of the **Properties** dialog box, click **Advanced Sharing**.

3. In the **Advanced Sharing** dialog box, select the **Share this folder** check box, and then click **Permissions**.

4. In the **Permissions** dialog box, with **Everyone** selected, click **Remove**. Then click **Add**.

5. In the **Select Users or Groups** dialog box, enter the Windows user account names or domain user account names of the people you want to have access to the shared folder, and then close the four open dialog boxes.

9   Communicating with Other People

To start Windows Mail

→ On the **Start** menu, click **All Programs**, and then click **Windows Mail**.

To begin configuring Windows Mail to connect to an e-mail account

1. On the **Tools** menu, click **Accounts**.
2. In the **Internet Accounts** dialog box, click the **Add** button, click **E-mail account**, and then **click Next**.

To connect to an e-mail account the first time you start Windows Mail

1. In the **Add E-mail Account** wizard, enter your name as you want it to appear to recipients of e-mail messages from you, and then click **Next**.
2. On the **Internet E-mail Address** page, enter the e-mail address, and then click **Next**.
3. In the **Incoming e-mail server type** list, click the type of server that handles your incoming mail, and then enter the names of your incoming and outgoing mail servers in the boxes.
4. If your outgoing e-mail server requires authentication, select the check box. Then click **Next**.
5. On the **Internet Mail Logon** page, enter your e-mail account name and password.
6. Click **Next**, and then click **Finish**.

To change the configuration of an existing account

1. Click **Accounts** on the **Tools** menu.
2. In the **Internet Accounts** dialog box, click the account you want to configure, and then click **Properties**.

To change the layout of the Windows Mail program window

→ On the **View** menu, click **Layout**.

To filter messages

→ In the **Search** box, type the characters, word, or words you want to locate.

To sort messages

→ Click any column header.

To add a message sender to Windows Contacts

1. In the message header, right-click the sender, and then click **Add to Contacts**.
2. In the contact record that opens, click **OK**.

To display the contents of a message

→ Click the message header in the message pane to display its contents in the preview pane.

→ Double-click the message header to open the message in its own window.

To access newsgroups from Windows Mail

→ On the **Tools** menu, click **Newsgroups**.

To send a fax from Windows Fax And Scan

1. Click **Fax** in the **Navigation** pane, and then click the **New Fax** button on the toolbar.
2. In the **New Fax** window, enter the receiving phone number (or the contact to whom you are sending the fax) and a subject.
3. Compose the fax or a cover sheet, optionally attach a file or insert a picture or scanned document, and then click **Send**.

To scan a printed document

1. Turn on the scanner, and insert the document you want to scan.
2. Start Windows Fax And Scan, click **Scan** at the bottom of the **Navigation** pane, and then click the **New Scan** button on the toolbar.
3. Adjust the settings in the **New Scan** window, and then click **Preview**. If you are satisfied with the preview, click **Scan**.

To fax, e-mail, or save a scanned document

→ Click the **Forward As Fax** or **Forward As E-Mail** button on the toolbar, or click the **Save As** button to save the scanned document as a file.

To open People Near Me

→ In **Control Panel**, click **Network and Internet**, and then click **People Near Me**.

To start Windows Meeting Space

→ On the **Start** menu, click **All Programs**, and then click **Windows Meeting Space**.

To join a meeting for which you have an invitation file and a password

1. On the **Windows Meeting Space** home page, click **Open an invitation file**.
2. In the **Open** dialog box, navigate to the invitation file. Click the file, and then click **Open**.
3. On the meeting entry page, enter the password, and then click the **Join a meeting** button.

To join a meeting for which you have only a password

1. On the **Windows Meeting Space** home page, click **Join a meeting near me** to display a list of active meetings.
2. Click the meeting you want to join.
3. On the meeting entry page, enter the password, and then click the **Join a meeting** button.

To initiate a meeting

1. On the **Windows Meeting Space** home page, click **Start a new meeting**.
2. Assign the meeting a name and password (which you'll distribute to meeting attendees).
3. Click the **Create a meeting** button.

To share a file with meeting participants

→ Click **Share a Program or Your Desktop**, and then browse to and double-click the file.

To distribute a file to meeting participants

→ Click **Add a Handout**, and then browse to and double-click the file.

To edit a handout

1. Double-click the handout in the meeting window to open a local copy.
2. Take turns with other participants making changes that are reflected in all the open copies of the handout file.

10 Staying Organized

To display Windows Sidebar

→ On the **Start** menu, click **All Programs**, click **Accessories**, and then click **Windows Sidebar**.

To remove Sidebar from the Windows desktop

→ Right-click an empty area of Sidebar, and then click **Close Sidebar**.

To change Sidebar gadget options

→ Point to the gadget to display the gadget controls, and then click the **Options** button, labeled with a wrench icon.

To add a gadget to Sidebar

1. On the **Sidebar control** at the top of Sidebar, click the **Add** button (labeled with a plus sign).
2. Drag the gadgets you want from the **Gadgets** window to Sidebar. Then close the **Gadgets** window.

To display a Sidebar gadget on the desktop

→ Right-click the gadget, and then click **Detach from Sidebar**.

To reattach a Sidebar gadget

→ Right-click the gadget, and click **Attach to Sidebar**.

To change the position of a gadget on Sidebar

→ Drag the gadget to the position you want.

To change Sidebar properties

1. Right-click an empty area of Sidebar, and then click **Properties**.
2. In the **Windows Sidebar Properties** dialog box, change the options you want, and then click **Apply** or **OK**.

To make Sidebar always available

1. Right-click an empty area of Sidebar, and then click **Properties**.
2. In the **Windows Sidebar Properties** dialog box, select the **Sidebar is always on top of other windows** check box, and then click **OK**.

To start Sticky Notes on a Tablet PC

→ On the **Start** menu, click **All Programs**, and then click **Sticky Notes**.

To start Sticky Notes on a non-Tablet PC

→ On the **Start** menu, click **All Programs**, click **Accessories**, click **Tablet PC**, and then click **Sticky Notes**.

To share sticky notes with other people

→ Drag written notes to other programs by using the **Drag and Drop** handle on the toolbar.

→ Copy and paste written or voice notes by clicking the **Copy** button on the toolbar, switching to the other program, and then clicking the **Paste** button in that program.

→ Click **Export** on the **Tools** menu, and then name and save the file. Send the exported file to another person or copy it to another computer.

To keep Sticky Notes open on top of other programs

→ On the **Tools** menu, point to **Options**, and then click **Always On Top**.

To record notes in Sticky Notes

→ Write notes by using the Tablet PC pen or dragging the mouse pointer.

→ If a microphone is installed on your computer, click the **Record** button at the bottom of the **Sticky Notes** window. Speaking into the microphone, dictate additional information about the note. When you finish, click the **Stop** button.

To display the *Contacts* folder

→ On the **Start** menu, click **All Programs**, and then click **Windows Contacts**.

To display the *Contacts* folder commands by setting the folder type

1. In your personal folder, right-click the *Contacts* folder, and then click **Properties**.
2. In the **Contacts Properties** dialog box, click the **Customize** tab.

3. In the **Use this folder type as a template** list, click **Contacts**. Then select the **Also apply this template to all subfolders** check box.

4. In the **Contacts Properties** dialog box, click **OK**.

To import contacts from a file

1. In the *Contacts* folder, on the toolbar, click **Import**.

2. In the **Import to Windows Contacts** dialog box, select the format of the file you are importing, and then click **Import**. If you are importing a CSV file, click **Browse** in the **CSV Import** dialog box.

3. In the **Open** dialog box, navigate to the source file, and then click **Open**.

4. Select the fields you want to import and, if necessary, map the source file fields to the Windows Contacts fields. Then click **Finish**.

To export all contacts to a file or files

1. In the *Contacts* folder, on the toolbar, click **Export**.

2. In the **Export Windows Contacts** dialog box, select the format you want to export contacts to, and then click **Export**.

3. If you are exporting to a CSV file:

    a. Click **Browse** in the **CSV Export** dialog box.

    b. In the **Save As** dialog box, navigate to the folder in which you want to save the exported file, enter the file name you want in the **File name** box, and then click **Save**.

    c. In the **CSV Export** dialog box, click **Next**. Select the fields you want to export, and then click **Finish**.

4. If you are exporting to vCard files, in the **Browse For Folder** dialog box, navigate to the folder in which you want to save the exported file(s), and then click **OK**.

5. In the **Windows Contacts** message box confirming the export, click **OK**. Then in the **Export Windows Contacts** dialog box, click **Close**.

To create a contact record

1. On the toolbar, click **New Contact**.

2. On the tabs of the **Properties** dialog box, enter the information you want to include in the contact record. Then click **OK**.

To create a contact group

1. On the toolbar, click **New Contact Group**.

2. In the **Properties** dialog box, on the **Contact Group** tab, type the group name in the **Group Name** box.

3. Click **Add to Contact Group**. In the **Add Members to Contact Group** dialog box, select the contacts you want to add to the group. Then click **Add**.

To add members who don't have contact records to a contact group

→ To add the person to the group and save a contact record at the same time, click **Create New Contact**, enter the person's contact information in the contact form, and then click **OK**.

→ To add the person to the group but not create a contact record, enter his or her name and e-mail address in the **Contact Name** and **E-Mail** boxes, and then click **Create for Group Only**.

To send an e-mail message to a contact or to all members of a contact group

→ In the *Contacts* folder, click the contact record or contact group, and then on the toolbar, click the **E-Mail** button.

To start Windows Calendar

→ On the **Start** menu, click **All Programs**, and then click **Windows Calendar**.

To create an appointment in Windows Calendar

1. Select the timeslot you want.
2. On the toolbar, click the **New Appointment** button.
3. Type a name for the appointment, and then press Enter.
4. In the **Details** pane, change any appointment details you want.

To change an appointment to an all-day event

→ In the **Appointment Information** section of the **Details** pane, select the **All-day appointment** check box.

To change an appointment to a meeting

1. In the **Details** pane, enter the meeting location in the **Location** box.
2. If necessary, scroll the **Details** pane to display the **Participants** section. In the **Participants** section, click the **Attendees** button.
3. In the **Windows Calendar** dialog box displaying your Windows Contacts, for each contact you want to invite to the meeting, click the contact name and click the **To** button. Then click **OK**.
4. In the **Participants** section of the **Details** pane, click the **Invite** button.
5. Make any changes you want to the meeting invitation message that opens, and then send the message.

To locate Internet calendars from Windows Calendar

1. On the **Share** menu, click **Subscribe**.
2. In the **Subscribe to a Calendar** dialog box, click the **Windows Calendar Website** link.

11   Working with Graphics and Documents

To resize the drawing canvas in Microsoft Paint

→ On the **Image** menu, click **Attributes**, click the **Default** button or set the width and height you want, and then click **OK**; or

→ Point to a move handle on the canvas. When the pointer changes to a double-headed arrow, drag the handle.

To display the Paint toolbox

→ Click **Tool Box** on the **View** menu.

To set the primary color in the Paint color palette

→ In the color palette, click the color you want.

To set the secondary color in the Paint color palette

→ In the color palette, right-click the color you want.

To save a graphic in Paint

1. On the **File** menu, click **Save As**.
2. In the **Save As** dialog box, browse to the folder where you want to save the file
3. In the **Save as type** list, click the file format you want.
4. Type a name for the graphic in the **File name** box, and then click **Save**.

To change the dimensions and orientation of a graphic

→ Change the size of the canvas by dragging its move handles or by specifying its exact dimensions in the **Attributes** dialog box.

→ Enlarge or shrink the image horizontally, vertically, or entirely, by a specific percentage.

→ Skew the image horizontally or vertically.

→ Flip the image horizontally or vertically.

→ Rotate the image in 90-degree increments.

To open an existing graphic in Paint

→ Start Paint. On the **File** menu, click **Open**. In the **Open** dialog box, browse to the file you want to open, click the file, and then click **Open**.

To change the zoom level in Paint

→ On the **View** menu, point to **Zoom**, point to **Custom**, and then click the percentage you want.

→ Press Ctrl+Page Up to zoom out and Ctrl+Page Down to zoom in.

→ In the toolbox, click the **Magnifier** button, and then click the area you want to zoom in to.

To view a picture that is larger than the work area

→ Click **View Bitmap** on the **View** menu; or press `Ctrl`+`F`. To return to Paint, click the primary mouse button.

To use the tools in the Paint toolbox

→ Click the **Free-Form Select** button, and then, in the options box at the bottom of the toolbar, click a background style (filled or transparent). Drag to outline the area you want to select.

→ Click the **Select** button, and then, in the options box at the bottom of the toolbar, click the background style you want. Drag at an angle to define the outside edges of the selection area. To restrict the selection area to a square shape, hold down the `Shift` key while dragging.

→ Click the **Eraser/Color Eraser** button, and then, in the options box at the bottom of the toolbar, click the eraser size you want. Drag the **Eraser** over the area of the picture that you want to erase to replace the erased area with the current secondary color.

→ Click the **Fill With Color** button, and then click inside a defined area to fill it with the primary color or right-click inside a defined area to fill it with the secondary color.

→ Click the **Pick Color** button, and then click anywhere in the graphic to set the selected color as the primary color, or right-click to set the selected color as the secondary color.

→ Click the **Magnifier** button, and then in the options box at the bottom of the toolbar, click or drag to select a zoom level; or click in the graphic to zoom and center that location.

→ Click the **Pencil** button, and then drag to draw a line in the primary color, or right-drag to draw a line in the secondary color.

→ Click the **Brush** button, and then, in the options box at the bottom of the toolbar, click the brush shape you want. Click or drag to paint with the primary color; right-click or right-drag to paint with the secondary color.

→ Click the **Airbrush** button, and then, in the options box at the bottom of the toolbar, click the spray pattern you want. Click or drag to paint with the primary color; right-click or right-drag to paint with the secondary color.

→ Click the **Text** button, and then, in the options box at the bottom of the toolbar, click the background style you want. Click to position the text insertion box and display the Fonts toolbar, and then type the text. While the text box is active, you can resize and move the text box, and change the font, font size, and text formatting.

→ Click the **Line** button, and then, in the options box at the bottom of the toolbar, click the line width you want. Drag to draw a straight line in the primary color, or right-drag to draw a straight line in the secondary color. To restrict the angle of the line to any multiple of 45 degrees, hold down the Shift key while dragging.

→ Click the **Curve** button, and then, in the options box at the bottom of the toolbar, click the line width you want. Drag to draw a straight line from the start point to the end point of the curve, click to place the center of the arc, and then drag the line handles to adjust the curve.

→ Click the **Rectangle, Rounded Rectangle, or Ellipse** button, and then, in the options box at the bottom of the toolbar, click the fill style you want. Drag diagonally to define the outer edges of the shape. To restrict the shape to a square or circle, hold down the Shift key while dragging.

→ Click the **Polygon** button, and then, in the options box at the bottom of the toolbar, click the fill style you want. Drag to draw one line of the shape, click to form the additional angles of the shape, and then double-click to complete the shape. To restrict angles to multiples of 45 degrees, hold down the Shift key while drawing the shape.

To change the size of a picture

1. With the **Select** tool, drag to draw a selection box around the image.
2. Point to any corner resize handle. When the pointer changes to a double-headed arrow, drag toward the center of the image or diagonally outward, releasing the mouse button when the image is the size you want.

To move a picture

1. With the **Select** tool, drag to draw a selection box around the image.
2. Point to the inside of the selected image. When the pointer changes to a four-headed arrow, drag the image to where you want it on the canvas.

To change the orientation of a picture

1. With the **Select** tool, drag to draw a selection box around the image.
2. On the **Image** menu, click **Flip/Rotate**.
3. In the **Flip and Rotate** dialog box, with **Flip horizontal** selected, click **OK**. To flip the entire canvas, choose this command without selecting a specific part of the image.

To duplicate an image

1. With the **Select** tool, drag to draw a selection box around the part of the image you want to copy. Press and hold the Ctrl key, and then drag the selection to where you want to place the copy.
2. Click away from the selection to release it, and then, if necessary, resize the canvas to fit the image.

To set a graphic as your Windows Vista desktop background

→ Open the graphic you want to use for the background in Paint. Then on the **File** menu, click one of the following options:

- **Set As Background (Tiled)**
- **Set As Background (Centered)**
- **Set As Background (Stretched)**

To fit an oversized image on one page

1. On the **File** menu, click **Page Setup**.
2. In the **Scaling** area of the **Page Setup** dialog box, click **Fit to**, and then enter 1 in each of the corresponding boxes to fit the picture onto one page.
3. In the **Page Setup** dialog box, click **OK**.

To start WordPad

→ On the **Start** menu, click **All Programs**, click **Accessories**, and then click **WordPad**.

To select the entire contents of a document

→ On the **Edit** menu, click **Select All**; or press Ctrl+A.

To format the fonts and paragraphs in a document

→ To change the font, on the Format bar, click the **Font** arrow to display the list of available fonts, and then in the list, click the font you want to use.

→ To change the text alignment, on the Format bar, click the button representing the alignment you want.

→ To change the color of the text, click the **Color** button to display the list of available text colors, and then in the list, click the color you want.

→ To apply character formatting, on the Format bar, click the button of the formatting you want (Bold, Italic, or Underline).

→ To change the font size, on the Format bar, in the **Font Size** list, click the size you want.

To select one paragraph

→ Triple-click anywhere in the paragraph.

To create a bulleted list and change the indent of the list

1. Select the text you want to format as a list, and then click the **Bullets** button.
2. On the **Ruler**, drag the left upward-pointing triangle to where you want the indent to be.

To change the measurement units in WordPad

→ On the **View** menu, click **Options**. In the **Options** dialog box, click the **Options** tab, click the units you want to display, and then click **OK**.

To display the Ruler

→ Click **Ruler** on the **View** menu.

To insert graphics from external files into an existing document

1. On the **Insert** menu, click **Object**.
2. In the **Insert Object** dialog box, click **Create from File**.
3. Click **Browse**. In the **Browse** dialog box, navigate to the folder with the graphic, click the graphic, and then click **Open**.
4. In the **Insert Object** dialog box, click **OK** to insert the graphic into the document.

To print a document from WordPad

1. On the **File** menu, click **Page Setup**.
2. In the **Page Setup** dialog box, change any settings you want, and then click **OK**.
3. On the **File** menu, click **Print Preview**.
4. On the **Print Preview** window toolbar, click **Print**.
5. In the **Print** dialog box, if you want to print the document to a printer other than the default, click that printer in the **Select Printer** area. Then click the **Print** button.

12   Working with Digital Media

To start Windows Photo Gallery

1. On the **Start** menu, click **All Programs**, and then click **Windows Photo Gallery**.

To add a folder to Windows Photo Gallery

→ Display a photo in Windows Photo Gallery, and then click **Add Folder to Gallery**; or

1. On the **File** menu, click **Add Folder to Gallery**.
2. In the **Add Folder to Gallery** dialog box, navigate to the folder you want to add, and then click **OK**.

To adjust the exposure or color of a picture, crop a picture, or fix red eyes

1. Display the photo in Windows Photo Gallery.
2. On the toolbar, click **Fix**.
3. In the **Info** pane, click the button corresponding to the change you want to make.

To sort and filter files in the Photo Gallery window

→ In the **Navigation** pane, click **Tag**, **Date Taken**, or **Rating**.

To add tags to a files

1. Select the file or files you want to tag.
2. In the **Info** pane, click **Add Tags**. Then in the box that appears, type the tag you want to apply.

To change the Windows Media Player skin

1. In **Windows Media Player**, right-click a blank area of the bar at the top of the window or the **Player controls** area, and then click **Show Classic Menus**.

2. On the **View** menu, click **Skin Chooser**. For a broader selection, click **More Skins**. Scroll the list of skins, and follow the directions to download those you like; when you've finished downloading them, close the browser window.

3. In the **Skin Chooser** window, click the skin you want. Then click **Apply Skin**.

To burn a folder of picture files from Windows Explorer

1. In Windows Explorer, navigate to the folder containing the files you want to burn to CD or DVD. Select either the entire folder or individual files, and then on the toolbar, click **Burn**.

2. Insert a blank CD or DVD in the drive. Then in the **Burn a Disc** dialog box, enter a name in the **Disc title** box.

3. If you don't intend to burn more data to the disc or want to ensure that the disc is compatible with older operating systems and with CD or DVD players, click the **Show formatting options** button, and in the expanded **Burn a Disc** dialog box, select the **Mastered** option.

4. Click **Next**.

To burn music tracks to disc from Windows Media Player

1. Display Windows Media Player in full mode.

2. Click the **Burn** tab. Then drag the album, play list, or tracks you want to burn into the **Burn List** area of the **List** pane.

3. At the bottom of the **List** pane, click **Start Burn**. When prompted, insert a writable CD or DVD into your computer's disc burner.

To use Windows Photo Gallery to share your media files with other people on your network

1. On the Windows Photo Gallery toolbar, click the **File** button, and then click **Share With Devices**.

2. Under **Sharing settings** in the **Media Sharing** dialog box, select the **Share my media** check box, and then click **OK**.

3. In the expanded dialog box, click **Settings**.

4. If you want, in the **Share media as** box in the **Media Sharing – Default Settings** dialog box, change the name of the collection of media files you are sharing.

5. Select or clear the check boxes under **Media types**, **Star ratings**, and **Parental ratings** to include only the specific media files you want to share. Then click **OK** in each of the open dialog boxes.

13   Managing Computer Security

To create a new user account

1. In **Control Panel**, under **User Accounts and Family Safety**, click the **Add or remove user accounts** task.

2. In the **Manage Accounts** window, click the **Create a new account** task. In the **New account name** box, type a name for your account. Select the **Administrator** option, and then click **Create Account**.

To change an account type

1. In **Control Panel**, under **User Accounts and Family Safety**, click the **Add or remove user accounts** task.

2. In the **Manage Accounts** window, on the **Choose the account you would like to change** page, click the account you want to change, and then click the **Change the account type** task.

3. On the **Choose a new account type for** page, select the option you want, and then click **Change Account Type**.

To create a password for an account

1. In **Control Panel**, under **User Accounts and Family Safety**, click the **Add or remove user accounts** task.

2. Click the account for which you want to create a password, and on the **Make changes to account** page, click the **Create a password** task.

3. On the **Create a password for account** page, in the **New password** box, type the password you want, and then press ⇥ to move to the next field. In the **Confirm new password** box, retype your password, and in the **Type a password hint** box, type something that will help you remember your password.

4. Click **Create password** to save the password.

To delete an account

1. In **Control Panel**, under **User Accounts and Family Safety**, click the **Add or remove user accounts** task.

2. Click the account you want to delete, and on the **Make changes to account** page, click the **Delete the account** task.

3. Choose whether to keep the content of selected personal folders. If you decide to delete files, click **Delete Files**. Then on the confirmation page, click **Delete Account**.

To change a user account picture

1. In **Control Panel**, click **User Accounts and Family Safety**.

2. Under **User Accounts**, click the **Change your account picture** task.

3. In the **Change Your Picture** window, click any picture that you like, and then click **Change Picture**; or, click **Browse for more pictures**, navigate to the picture you want to use, and click the picture.

To create a password reset disk

1. Insert a USB flash drive or floppy disk into your computer.
2. In **Control Panel**, click **User Accounts and Family Safety**, and then click **User Accounts**.
3. In the **Tasks** list, click the **Create a password reset disk** task.
4. On the **Welcome** page of the **Forgotten Password** wizard, click **Next**.
5. On the **Create a Password Reset Disk** page, select the USB flash drive or floppy disk drive you want to use, and then click **Next**.
6. On the **Current User Account Password** page, enter the password you use to log on to Windows Vista, and then click **Next**. When the **Progress** bar displays *100% complete*, click **Next**. Then click **Finish**.

To adjust parental controls for another user on your computer

1. Display **Control Panel**, and under **User Accounts and Family Safety**, click the **Set up parental controls for any user** task.
2. In the **Parental Controls** window, click the user for whom you want to set up parental controls.
3. In the **User Controls** window, under **Parental Controls**, select the **On, enforce current settings** option.
4. Under **Windows Settings**, adjust the parental controls as you want, and then click **OK**.

To view an activity report for a user account that has parental controls applied

1. Display **Control Panel**, and under **User Accounts and Family Safety**, click the **Set up parental controls for any user** task.
2. In the **Parental Controls** window, click the user for whom you want to view an activity report.
3. In the **User Controls** window, with the **On, collect information about computer usage** option selected under **Activity Reporting**, click **View activity reports**.

To change Windows Firewall setting options

1. In **Control Panel**, click **Security**, and then under **Security Center**, click the **Check firewall status** task.
2. Select the **On** option or the **Off** option. If you select **On** and will be connecting to a less-secure network, select the **Block all incoming connections** check box.

3. Click the **Exceptions** tab. Then in the **Program or port** list, select the programs or ports you want Windows Firewall to allow unlimited access.

4. Click the **Advanced** tab, and select each individual network connection you want protected by Windows Firewall. Then click **OK**.

To change Windows Defender setting options

1. On the **Start** menu, click **All Programs**, and then click **Windows Defender**. Then on the Windows Defender toolbar, click **Tools**.

2. On the **Tools and Settings** page, set any options you want. Then in the **Settings** area, click **Options**. On the **Options** page, apply any settings you want.

3. In the **Automatic scanning** area, set the frequency and time for automatic scans to occur, select whether to perform a quick scan or full-system scan at that time, and click **Save**.

To check the security status of your computer

→ Display **Control Panel**, and then under **Security**, click the **Check this computer's security status** task. Make sure that all four settings are set to **On**. If any are not, click the corresponding **Find a program** button to locate and install the missing security application.

To set Internet Explorer security settings

1. In **Control Panel**, click **Security**, and then under **Internet Options**, click the **Change security settings** task.

2. In the **Internet Properties** dialog box, click **Default level**, or slide the control to the level you want.

3. If you want to customize the security options, click **Custom level** to display the **Security Settings** dialog box for the currently selected Internet zone. Make any changes you want, and then click **OK**. In the **Warning** message box prompting you to confirm your changes, click **Yes**.

4. In the **Select a zone** area, click **Restricted sites**. Then click **Sites**.

5. In the **Add this website to the zone** box of the **Restricted sites** dialog box, type any URLs you want to add, and click **Add**. Then close the **Restricted sites** dialog box, and click **OK** in the **Internet Properties** dialog box.

14   Optimizing Your Computer System

To adjust visual effects

1. In **Control Panel**, click **System and Maintenance**, and then click **Performance Information and Tools**.

2. In the **Tasks** list, click the **Adjust visual effects** task.

3. In the **Performance Options** dialog box, select the options you want, and then click **OK**.

To adjust power settings

1. In **Control Panel**, click **System and Maintenance**, and then click **Performance Information and Tools**.

2. In the **Tasks** list, click the **Adjust power settings** task.

3. In the **Power Options** window, under the **High Performance** option, click **Change plan settings**, and in the **Edit Plan Settings** window, change any settings you want.

4. Click **Change advanced power settings**, and in the **Power Options** dialog box, change any settings you want.

To turn Windows features on and off

1. In **Control Panel**, click **Programs**, and then under **Programs and Features**, click the **Turn Windows features on or off** task.

2. In the **Windows Features** dialog box, select the check box for any feature you want to install, or clear the check box for any feature you want to remove. Then click **OK**.

To view your temporary Internet files and associated settings

1. In **Control Panel**, click **Security**, and then under **Internet Options**, click the **Delete browsing history and cookies** task.

2. On the **General** tab of the **Internet Properties** dialog box, in the **Browsing history** area, click **Settings**. Then in the **Temporary Internet Files and History Settings** dialog box, click **View files** or **View objects**.

To run the Disk Cleanup utility

1. In **Control Panel**, click **System and Maintenance**, and then under **Administrative Tools**, click the **Free up disk space** task.

2. In the **Disk Cleanup Options** dialog box, click the option you want.

3. In the **Disk Cleanup** dialog box, select the check boxes of all the categories you want to delete, and click **OK**. Then click **Delete Files** to confirm that you want to delete the selected categories of files.

To schedule Disk Cleanup

1. In **Control Panel**, click **System and Maintenance**, and then under **Administrative Tools**, click the **Schedule tasks** task.

2. In the **Actions** pane, click **Create Basic Task**.

3. In the **Name** box of the **Create Basic Task** wizard, type a name for the task, and in the **Description** box, type a description. Then click **Next**.

4. On the **Trigger** page, select the frequency or condition that will cause the task to start, and then click **Next**.

5. If you selected the **Daily**, **Weekly**, **Monthly**, or **When a specific event is logged** option, enter the parameters associated with that option, and then click **Next**.

6. On the **Action** page, with the **Start a program** option selected, click **Next**.

7. On the **Start a Program** page, click **Browse**. Locate and select the program you want to schedule, and click **Open**. Then click **Next**.

8. On the **Summary** page, click **Finish** to create the new task and add it to your Windows schedule.

To schedule and then run Disk Defragmenter

1. In **Control Panel**, click **System and Maintenance**, and then under **Administrative Tools**, click the **Defragment your hard drive** task.

2. In the **Disk Defragmenter** dialog box, click **Modify schedule**.

3. In the **Disk Defragmenter: Modify Schedule** dialog box, click the **How often**, **What day**, and/or **What time** arrows, and in the respective lists, select the options you want. Then click **OK**.

4. Click **Defragment now**.

5. When the defragmentation process is complete, click **OK** to close the **Disk Defragmenter** window.

To locate information about the internal and external devices on your computer

1. In **Control Panel**, click **Hardware and Sound**, scroll the window if necessary, and then click **Device Manager**.

2. In Device Manager, click the plus sign to the left of any category to display information about it.

3. To update the device driver, disable or uninstall the device, or view and modify additional properties, right-click the device.

To examine the programs and processes running on your computer

1. In **Control Panel**, under **Programs**, click **Change startup programs**.
2. On the **Software Explorer** page of Windows Defender, scroll the list, and click the name of any program to see its details.
3. If you want to prevent a program that is on the list from starting automatically, click the program name, and then **Remove**.
4. In the lower-left corner of the **Windows Defender** window, click **Show for all users**.
5. In the **Category** list, click **Currently Running Programs**, and scroll the list that appears. Click any program that interests you to view information about it in the right pane.

To examine the system resource utilization

1. Start **Windows Task Manager**.
2. In **Windows Task Manager**, click the tabs to view information about programs running on your computer and the processes currently running in your Windows Vista session.
3. On the **Performance** tab, click the **Resource Monitor** button
4. Close **Windows Task Manager** so that it doesn't block your view of the **Resource Monitor** window, and then view the information charts in the **Resource Overview** section at the top of the **Resource Monitor** window.
5. Click the **Resource Overview** heading to hide the charts, and then click each of the resource area headings to view current and historical usage for that area.

15   Identifying and Solving Problems

To open Windows Help And Support and enable Windows Online Help And Support

1. On the **Start** menu, click **Help and Support**.
2. In the **Windows Help and Support** window, at the right end of the toolbar, click **Options**, and then in the list, click **Settings**.
3. In the **Help Settings** dialog box, ensure that the **Include Windows Online Help and Support** check box is selected. Then click **OK**.

To browse Windows Help And Support

→ In the **Windows Help and Support** window, on the toolbar, click the **Browse Help** button, and then click any topic you wish to explore.

To search Windows Help And Support

1. In the **Windows Help and Support** window, type the topic you want to search for in the **Search Help** box, and then click the **Search Help** button.
2. Click any topic link that interests you. Move between visited topics by clicking the **Back** and **Forward** buttons.

To display the Problem Reports And Solutions window

→ In **Control Panel**, click **System and Maintenance**, and then click **Problem Reports and Solutions**.

To turn off automatic reporting

1. In **Control Panel**, click **System and Maintenance**, and then click **Problem Reports and Solutions**.
2. In the **Tasks** list, click the **Change settings** task.
3. On the **Choose how to check for solutions to computer problems** page, select the **Ask me to check if a problem occurs** option, and then click **OK**.

To manually submit problem reports

→ In **Control Panel**, click **System and Maintenance**, click **Problem Reports and Solutions**, and then click the **Check for new solutions** task.

To locate Windows Vista newsgroups

→ On the **Start** menu, click **Help and Support**. Then in the **Windows Help and Support** window, under **Ask someone**, click **Windows communities**.

To request remote assistance

1. On the **Start** menu, click **All Programs**, click **Maintenance**, and then click **Windows Remote Assistance**.
2. On the **Windows Remote Assistance** page, click **Invite someone you trust to help you**.
3. If you have configured Windows Mail, Outlook, or another e-mail program on your Windows Vista computer, click **Use e-mail to send an invitation**, enter and confirm the password you want your remote assistant to use, and click **Next**; then skip to step 6. Otherwise, click **Save this invitation as a file**.
4. In the **Password** box, type a string of six or more characters you want your remote assistant to enter in order to gain access to your computer. Then click **Finish**.
5. Send the remote assistance invitation file to the person you want to assist you, as an attachment to an e-mail message. Then contact him or her separately with the remote assistance password.
6. After the invitation is accepted, click **Yes** to allow your remote assistant to view your screen and chat with you.
7. In the **Windows Remote Assistance** window, on the toolbar, click the **Chat** button, and from the chat box, tell your helper to take control of your computer.
8. In the message box asking you to share control of your computer, click **Yes**.
9. When you decide that you no longer want to share control of your computer, on the toolbar, click the **Stop sharing** button.
10. When you finish the Remote Assistance session, click the **Disconnect** button.

To display the Remote Assistance settings

→ In **Control Panel**, click **System and Maintenance**. Then under **System**, click the **Allow remote access** task.

To completely disable Remote Assistance

1. In **Control Panel**, click **System and Maintenance**. Then under **System**, click the **Allow remote access** task.

2. In the **Remote Assistance** area of the **System Properties** dialog box, clear the **Allow Remote Assistance connections to this computer** check box, and then click **OK**.

To limit Remote Assistance access

1. In **Control Panel**, click **System and Maintenance**. Then under **System**, click the **Allow remote access** task.

2. In the **Remote Assistance** area of the **System Properties** dialog box, click **Advanced**.

3. In the **Remote Assistance Settings** dialog box, set the access level, invitation duration, and access type as you want, and then click **OK**.

To back up a document to a removable storage device and schedule future backups

1. Log on to your computer as an administrator.

2. Display **Control Panel**, and then under **System and Maintenance**, click **Back up your computer**.

3. In the **Backup and Restore Center**, under **Back up files or your entire computer**, click **Back up files**.

4. Select the hard disk or other location where you want to save the backup, and then click **Next**.

5. In the **Back Up Files** wizard, select the categories you want to back up, and then click **Next**.

6. Adjust the **How often**, **What day**, and **What time** settings to the way you want them by clicking each one in turn and selecting from the list.

7. If you are backing up to a CD or DVD, insert a blank disk into your CD or DVD drive, and then click **Save settings and start backup**.

To restore files from a backup

1. In the **Backup and Restore Center**, under **Restore files or your entire computer**, click **Restore files**.

2. Select the restore option you want, and then click **Next**.

3. Click **Add files**. Navigate to the location of the file you want to restore, double-click its file name, and then click **Next**.

4. Select the options you want, and then click **Start restore**.

5. When Windows reports that the file has been successfully restored, click **Finish**, and close the **Backup and Restore Center**.

To create a manual restore point

1. In **Control Panel**, click **System and Maintenance**, and then click **System**.
2. In the **Tasks** list on the left side of the **System** window, click **System protection**.
3. In the **System Properties** dialog box, click **Create**, and then in the **System Protection** box, type a name for the restore point.
4. In the **System Protection** box, click **Create**.
5. After Windows Vista creates the restore point, click **OK**.

To restore your computer to a restore point

1. In **Control Panel**, click **System and Maintenance**, and then click **System**.
2. In the **Tasks** list, click **System protection**.
3. In the **System Properties** dialog box, click **System Restore**.
4. Select the **Choose a different restore point** option, and then click **Next**.
5. On the **Choose a restore point** page, click the restore point you want, and then click **Next**.
6. When asked to confirm your selected restore point, click **Finish**.

To transfer your files to another computer

1. Log on to your computer as an administrator.
2. On the **Start** menu, click **All Programs**, click **Accessories**, click **System Tools**, and then click **Windows Easy Transfer**.
3. Follow the instructions in the **Windows Easy Transfer** wizard to specify the transfer media or method, the information you want to transfer, and the password for re-covering that information.
4. If you are transferring files and settings via removable media, start Windows Easy Transfer on the second computer, and then click **Continue transfer in progress**.
5. Provide the information requested by the wizard. When prompted to do so, insert the transfer disk into the second computer, select the destination drive, enter the password, and then follow the wizard's instructions to complete the transfer.

Chapter at a Glance

Make your computer easier to use, **page 22**

Update Windows system files, **page 12**

End a computing session, **page 18**

1 Getting Started with Windows Vista

In this chapter, you will learn to:

✔ Log on to Windows Vista.

✔ Activate Windows.

✔ Update Windows system files.

✔ End a computing session.

✔ Make your computer easier to use.

Whether you have purchased a new computer with the Windows Vista operating system already installed on it or upgraded your computer's operating system from an earlier version of Windows, this chapter will help you quickly get started doing useful work.

Each time you turn on your computer, it goes through a process of starting up (also called *booting*) during which it loads the system files necessary for you to interact with your computer and for your computer to interact with other devices. After the startup process completes, you identify yourself to Windows Vista, and provide the information Windows Vista needs to present an individually tailored working environment. If your computer is part of a domain, logging on to Windows Vista also logs you on to the domain. The process might sound somewhat complicated, but in actual practice, it is quite simple.

When you first set up your computer, it is a very good idea to check for and install any available system updates, and to verify that Windows Vista is configured to update itself whenever necessary. By doing so, you can be sure that your computer system includes the most current features, tools, and security precautions.

When you finish working with your computer, you can either shut down the computer entirely, or you can leave it in running in various ways. For example, you can log off from Windows Vista, lock the computer, or put the computer into sleep mode to conserve resources.

See Also For information about the different editions of Windows Vista and how they are addressed in this book, see "Introducing Windows Vista," at the beginning of this book.

In this chapter, you will log on to Windows Vista and, if necessary, activate it. You will ensure that any available system updates are installed on your computer and that Windows Vista is configured to keep itself up to date by automatically checking for, downloading, and installing any available security and performance updates. Then you will explore different methods of logging off and shutting down your computer. We end with a discussion of the many accessibility features available as part of the Windows Vista operating system, and the ways in which you can adapt Windows Vista to make its features easier for you to use or to make the on-screen elements easier to see.

See Also Do you need only a quick refresher on the topics in this chapter? See the Quick Reference section at the beginning of this book.

> **Important** No practice files are required to complete the exercises in this chapter. For more information about practice files, see "Using the Companion CD" at the beginning of this book.
>
> For all the exercises, Windows Vista must already be installed on your computer and you must know your user name and password (if your user account requires one).

Logging On to Windows Vista

Your computer might be used by only you, or it might be used by several people. If only you use your computer, it needs only one configuration, or *user account*. If other people use your computer, each person should log on with his or her own account. By using separate accounts, each person can set up the Windows Vista environment to look and work the way he or she wants it, without interfering with another person's computing experience. Each account is associated with a *user profile* that describes the way the computer environment looks and operates (the *user interface*) for that particular user. This information includes simple things such as the color scheme, desktop background, fonts, and program shortcuts, as well as personal information that you want to keep confidential, such as saved passwords, site-specific cookies, links to favorite sites and folders, and your Internet browsing history. Each user profile includes a personal folder not accessible by other people using the computer, in which you can store documents, pictures, media, and other files you want to keep private.

> **Important** In the high-tech world, people who use computers are referred to collectively as *users*. Although we use that rather impersonal term throughout this book, we never forget that users are people too!

Each user account is designated as either an administrator account or a standard account. The first user account created on your computer is automatically an administrator account—every computer must have at least one—so if you are the first or only person using the computer you are probably operating as an administrator.

See Also For information about standard and administrator accounts and why it is more secure to operate as a standard user, see "Administering Windows User Accounts" in Chapter 13, "Managing Computer Security."

The process of starting a computer session is called *logging on*. When you start the computer, Windows displays a *Welcome screen* containing links to each of the computer's active user accounts. (If your computer is part of a domain, you might need to press Ctrl+Alt+Delete to display the Welcome screen.) You select your user account and, if your account is password protected, enter your password to log on to the computer. When logging on to a computer that is part of a domain, you will always enter your domain credentials.

Networks, Domains, and Workgroups

A *network* is a physical group of computers that communicate with each other through a wired or wireless connection. A network can be as small as two computers connected by a cable, or as large as the Internet. For the purpose of simplifying the process of authorizing access to networked resources, computers on a network are grouped in one of two ways:

- A *domain* is a logical (rather than physical) group of *resources*—computers, servers, and other hardware devices—on a network. The resources are centrally administered through Windows Server. Computers and users can connect to a domain. A computer connecting to the domain and validated by a *machine account* is visible as a domain resource; and a person logging on to the domain with a *user account* can access domain resources, from whatever computer she or he is working on. With the appropriate permissions, a domain user can connect to the computer of another domain user by entering the computer's *Universal Naming Convention (UNC)* address.

- A *workgroup* is a logical group of computers that is not centrally administered but communicates through a network. Individual users do not log on to a workgroup.

See Also For information about connecting your computer to a domain or workgroup, see Chapter 8, "Making Connections."

If you are not working on a domain and you enter your user account password incor-
rectly, Windows displays your password hint. If you still can't remember the password,
all is not lost. If you have taken the time to create a *password reset disk*, you can reset
the password by clicking the Reset Password link and then following the instructions
given by the Password Reset wizard. If you are working on a domain and you experience password problems, you will have to seek the help of your network administrator.

See Also For information about password reset disks, see the sidebar "Backing Up Your
Windows Password" in Chapter 13, "Managing Computer Security."

After you log on, Windows Vista loads your user profile and then displays your personalized working environment. The first time you log on to a computer, Windows also
prepares your desktop, which takes a few extra seconds.

In this exercise, you will log on to a computer that is not part of a domain. There are no
practice files for this exercise.

See Also If you are new to computing, see the section "Information for New Computer Users"
at the beginning of this book for an explanation of basic terminology you will encounter
throughout this book.

BE SURE TO know your user account name and password (if your account is password
protected) before beginning this exercise.

1. Start your computer.

   The computer goes through a complex process of identifying the system elements
   and allocating resources. Some of the process will be visible, although probably not
   very meaningful.

2. If the startup process ends by displaying the message **Press CTRL+ALT+DELETE or
   use the Windows Security button to log on**, press ⌷Ctrl⌷+⌷Alt⌷+⌷Del⌷ to start the process of logging on to a domain. Enter your domain name, user name, and password
   to log on, and skip to the end of this exercise.

   > **Troubleshooting** Certain editions of Windows Vista might bypass the Welcome
   > screen when only one user account is active on your computer and that account is not
   > password protected.

After the computer starts, the Welcome screen appears, displaying the names and pictures associated with all active user accounts.

3. If multiple user accounts are available, point to each in turn.

   A glow appears around the active user account picture as you point to it.

4. Click your user account name or the associated picture.

   See Also For information about changing your account picture, see "Managing Your Windows User Account" in Chapter 13, "Managing Computer Security."

Go

5. If access to your account is protected by a password, type your password in the **Password** box, and then click the **Go** button or press [Enter] to continue.

Your Windows Vista desktop appears, with the Windows Sidebar on the right side of the screen.

The desktop you see when you log on to Windows for the first time might be one of the many beautiful Windows Wallpapers; or, if you purchased the computer with Windows Vista already installed, the original equipment manufacturer (OEM) might have specified a brand-specific desktop. When you install Windows Vista yourself, you have the choice of several photographic desktop backgrounds. The default Windows Vista Service Pack 1 desktop background displays a colorful, modern design. (The default desktop for

> **Troubleshooting** Some editions of Windows Vista do not automatically display the Windows Sidebar. For information about displaying and working with this useful and fun feature, see "Using and Modifying Sidebar Gadgets" in Chapter 10, "Staying Organized."

the original release of Windows Vista was a picturesque scene of a lake and mountains.) You can change this to one of the many beautiful photographs or artistic renderings that comes with Windows Vista, to a blank colored background, or to one of your own photos or graphics. If your computer is running Windows Vista Ultimate, you can download Windows DreamScenes—video clips that run, in a continuous loop, as a desktop background. Most of the graphics in this book depict a plain, pale background so it doesn't detract from the screen element we're showing you.

See Also For information about desktop background options, see "Changing the Desktop Background" in Chapter 4, "Personalizing Windows Vista." For detailed information about the elements of the Windows Vista desktop, see Chapter 2, "Working Efficiently in Windows Vista."

Each time you log on to a new Windows Vista session, the Welcome Center opens. Don't confuse the Welcome Center (shown in the illustration on the opposite page) with the Welcome screen on which you clicked your user account—they are similarly named, but completely different. The top section of the Welcome Center displays information specific to your computer; clicking Show More Details displays the System window and information about your computer hardware, network settings, and licensing. The middle section includes links to basic computer administration options, and the bottom section includes links to training, services, add-ins, and other offers from Microsoft. Clicking Show All in either of these two sections displays additional links. If you would prefer to not to see the Welcome Center each time you log on, clear the Run At Startup check box in the lower-left corner of the Welcome Center.

Activating Windows

When you upgrade your computer's operating system to Windows Vista, or the first time you start a new computer, you are prompted to *activate* your copy of Windows.

Each copy of Windows Vista must be activated within 30 days of the first use. After that grace period expires, you will not be able to use all the functions of Windows. You can activate Windows over the Internet or by telephone, or it will activate itself after a few days, if you have an active Internet connection. You don't have to give any personal information about yourself or your computer during the activation process. (If you are asked to *register* after activating a product, the information you provide might be used to send you marketing materials.)

The goal of Windows Product Activation is to reduce a form of software piracy known as *casual copying* or *softlifting*, which is the sharing of software in a way that infringes on the software's *license terms*.

In this exercise, you will check whether Windows Vista has been activated, and manually activate it if necessary. There are no practice files for this exercise.

BE SURE TO log on to Windows Vista before beginning this exercise.

Start

1. At the left end of the taskbar, click the **Start** button.

   The Start menu opens.

   Your user account picture appears in the upper-right corner of the Start menu. A link to your personal folder, labeled with your user name, appears beneath the picture. The appearance of the Start menu will vary depending on the programs installed on your computer and any previous computing activities.

2. On the **Start** menu, click **Control Panel**.

You can access all the Windows Vista tools and settings by navigating through the Control Panel feature groups.

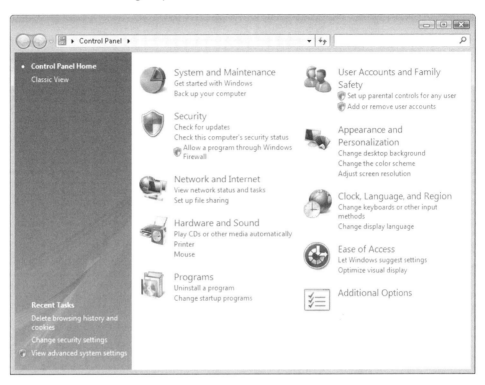

See Also For information about navigating through Windows Vista, see "Finding Your Way Around Your Computer" in Chapter 2, "Working Efficiently in Windows Vista," and "Navigating to Folders and Files" in Chapter 3, "Working with Folders and Files."

3. In **Control Panel**, click **System and Maintenance**. Then in the **System and Maintenance** window, click **System**.

The System window provides current information about your computer system. If your copy of Windows has been activated, "Windows is activated" appears in the Windows Activation area at the bottom of the window. Otherwise, the time remaining in the grace period appears. A Windows security icon appears to the left of the activation information to indicate that the action requires administrator permission.

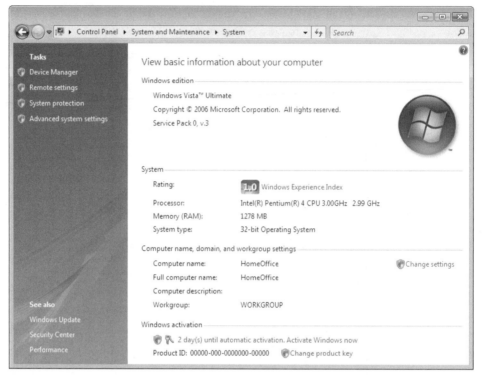

4. If Windows has not yet been activated, in the **Windows activation** area, click **Activate Windows now**.

5. In the **User Account Control** dialog box, if you are logged on as an administrator, click **Continue**. Otherwise, enter an administrator password and then click **OK**.

   See Also For information about User Account Control, see "Introducing Windows Vista" at the beginning of this book.

   The Windows Activation dialog box opens.

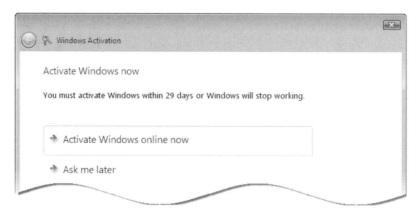

6. In the **Windows Activation** dialog box, click **Activate Windows online now**.

Windows Vista connects to the Internet, verifies that your copy of Windows is genuine, and activates it.

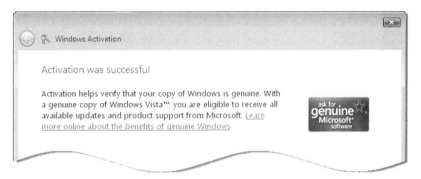

7. In the **Windows Activation** dialog box, click **Close**.

Identifying Genuine Windows Software

Counterfeit software floppy disks, CDs, DVDs, and packaging might look the same as or similar to the authentic software. A genuine individual copy of Windows Vista (one not acquired with the purchase of a computer or through the Microsoft Volume Licensing program) is distributed on a holographic CD. Each copy has a Certificate of Authenticity sticker on the top of the retail package and an orange product key label on the installation CD holder. The front of the CD features:

- A copper hologram with a clean, wavy outer edge.

- A high-resolution, three-dimensional hologram of the Windows logo, in which the flag appears to wave when you tilt the CD.

- A security patch located at the bottom of the CD, in which the word *Microsoft* changes to the word *GENUINE* when you tilt the CD.

The back of the CD features a detailed hologram on the inner mirror band, containing the words *Microsoft* and *GENUINE*.

See Also You can see samples of counterfeited software from around the world at *www.microsoft.com/resources/howtotell/*. To verify whether your copy of Windows Vista is genuine, run the Windows Validation Assistant from that same location.

Pirated software is often distributed with bundled software or through auction Web sites, spam e-mail messages, and downloads from Web sites other than those located within the microsoft.com domain. The easiest way to avoid counterfeit software is to purchase it from a reputable reseller.

The Perils of Piracy

Windows Product Activation is a security measure instituted by Microsoft to help prevent the use of unlicensed copies of Windows. *Software piracy*—the illegal reproduction and distribution of software applications—is a multi-billion dollar industry. The Fourth Annual BSA and IDC Global Software Piracy Study commissioned by the Business Software Alliance (*www.bsa.org*) concluded that "35 percent of the software installed in 2006 on personal computers worldwide was obtained illegally, amounting to nearly $40 billion in global losses due to software piracy."

The counterfeit software manufacturing industry stifles the potential growth of the high-tech industry and contributes to loss of tax revenue. Software piracy is also harmful to its users, for these reasons:

- Unlicensed software is not eligible for technical support or product upgrades. When you attempt to install a product update, security patch, or service pack from the Microsoft Web site, your system or software is tested to verify whether it is licensed.

- Abuse of software licenses can result in financial penalties and legal costs, as well as a bad reputation for you or your company. Individual company executives can be held criminally and civilly liable for the copyright infringements of individuals within their organizations.

- Pirated software can contain harmful viruses with the potential to damage individual computers or entire networks.

Windows Vista has a built-in piracy protection system—if certain conditions alert it to the possibility that you are running a pirated copy, most Windows Vista functionality will shut down, and you will be able to use only Windows Internet Explorer, for only one hour at a time. During that hour, you will be able to browse the Internet and receive security updates, but you won't be able to create or save any files until you activate your copy of Windows.

See Also For more information about software piracy, visit *www.microsoft.com/piracy/*.

Updating Windows System Files

When you first upgrade to Windows Vista or purchase a computer with Windows Vista already installed, the operating system files installed on your computer are the ones available to the manufacturer when your installation media or computer was manufactured.

From time to time, Microsoft releases updates to Windows Vista, either to provide additional functionality or to protect your computer from new security threats. It's important to install these updates as soon after their release as possible.

Windows Update is a utility that scans your computer, confers with the Microsoft Update online database, and recommends or installs any updates that are available for your operating system, your software programs, or your hardware. Quite apart from knowing that you have the "latest and greatest," by using Windows Update, you can be sure that your computer is updated whenever necessary. You can access Windows Update from the Start menu, Control Panel, and Windows Help And Support.

During the update process, Windows Update collects the version numbers of your operating system, Web browser, and other installed software, as well as information about the hardware devices that are connected to your computer. It then compiles a list of updates that are available for your system. Updates are classified as follows:

- **Important updates** increase the security or reliability of the operating system and Microsoft software products.
- **Recommended updates** address non-critical problems, and help enhance your computing experience.
- **Optional updates** do not address specific Microsoft software problems. These might include software add-ons or drivers for third-party hardware.

When the update process is complete, Windows Update discards the version and ID information that it collected from your computer.

During the Windows Vista installation process, you are asked to indicate whether you want Windows to automatically update your system as updates become available on the Windows Update site. Automatic updating is very convenient if you don't want to bear the responsibility of remembering to manually update your system, or if you want to be sure you have updates as soon as they become available.

If you chose not to update automatically when Windows Vista was installed, you can change your selected update option at any time through Control Panel. The options are to have Windows Vista do one of the following:

- Download and install updates automatically.
- Download updates and notify you when they are ready to be installed.
- Simply notify you when an update is available.

> **Important** If your computer is part of a domain, your network administrator might control the installation of updates.

In this exercise you will check update settings, install available updates, and set up the computer to periodically install critical updates. There are no practice files for this exercise.

> **BE SURE TO** log on to Windows Vista before beginning this exercise.

Start

1. Click the **Start** button, click **All Programs**, and then click **Windows Update**.

   Windows Update displays information about your computer's update history and settings. Depending on the edition of Windows Vista installed on your computer, additional information about Windows components might also be shown here.

Your current update settings

2. If a **View available updates** link appears below the **Install updates** button in the update status box, click it. Otherwise, skip to step 5.

   The View Available Updates list displays the updates that are available for your computer, grouped by subject (you can change the order by clicking any column header.) Some updates are specific to the hardware components of your system.

   Important updates are automatically selected for installation. You can choose to not install an update, but unless you have a very good reason to wait, we recommend that you install Important updates as soon as possible.

If administrator permission is required to install an update, the Windows security icon appears on the Install button.

3. Select the updates you want to install, and then click **Install**. In the **User Account Control** dialog box, if you are logged on as an administrator, click **Continue**. Otherwise, enter an administrator password, and then click **OK**.

A progress bar reports on the update activities as Windows downloads the selected update(s), creates a *restore point*, and then installs each update.

After installing the selected update(s), Windows Vista might prompt you to restart your computer. This is an indication that Windows is currently using some of the system files that need to be updated.

4. If Windows Vista prompts you to restart your computer, close any open files, and then click **Restart now**. After your computer restarts, log on, and then repeat step 1 to return to Windows Update.

5. In the left pane, click the **Change settings** task.

   The Change Settings window opens. You can change the frequency, time, type, and scope of automatic updates.

Microsoft recommends that you automatically install updates each day at 3:00 A.M. An obvious problem with this setting is that your computer might not be on in the middle of the night. You can change the update time and frequency by selecting from the lists.

6. If **Install updates automatically** is not already selected, select it now.

7. In the second **Install new updates** list, click a time at which your computer will usually be on and online.

   It's best to select a time outside your core work hours—say at the beginning or end of your workday—when connecting to the Internet and installing updates won't impact your ability to work by monopolizing your computer's resources.

> **Tip** If you prefer to have more control over the update process but still enjoy the benefit of automatic updates, select the Download Updates But Let Me Choose Whether To Install Them option. Windows Vista will then download available updates to your computer and displays a security icon in the notification area. You can click the icon to review and approve or reject the installation of each update.

8. With the **Include recommended updates** and **Use Microsoft Update** check boxes selected, click **OK**. In the **User Account Control** dialog box, if you are logged on as an administrator, click **Continue**. Otherwise, enter an administrator password, and then click **OK**.

   Windows Update displays your selected settings.

 CLOSE the Windows Update window.

Switching Quickly Among Users

Fast User Switching makes it possible for multiple people to be logged on to their user accounts on one computer at the same time. For example, if you want to read your e-mail or access a file stored in your *Documents* folder, but another person has been working on the computer you want to use, you can log on to your account without requiring that the other person close the programs and files she or he is working with. Fast User Switching was an optional feature in Windows XP but is always on in Windows Vista.

To log on to your user account while another account is active:

1. On the **Start** menu, click the **Shut Down Options** button, and click **Switch User**. The Welcome screen appears.

2. Click the user account you want to log on to, and enter the password if one is required.

Multiple user accounts can be logged on to a computer at one time without interfering with the activities of each other. If you want files to be available to all user accounts, store them in the Public folders rather than the folders within your user profile.

See Also For information about other Windows Vista security features, see Chapter 13, "Managing Computer Security."

Ending a Computing Session

If you are going to stop working with your computer for any length of time, you can safeguard your information and save power in a number of ways:

- If you want to prevent passersby from seeing what you're working, you can *lock* the computer, which displays the Welcome screen and requires that you log on to your account to resume. Locking is most effective when your user account is protected by a password; otherwise, anyone can click your user account picture to unlock the computer and access your information.

  You can have Windows lock itself by configuring a screen saver to start after a designated period of time and to display the logon screen when you resume your computing session.

  See Also For information about configuring a screen saver, see "Selecting and Managing a Screen Saver" in Chapter 4, "Personalizing Windows Vista."

- If you're finished working on a computer that you share with other people, you can end your Windows Vista session (but not affect other users' sessions) by *logging off*. You must save your files and shut down all running programs before you log off; if you don't, Windows Vista will close any open windows and exit programs, possibly losing unsaved data in the process.

- If you're going to be away from your computer, conserve power and protect your work by putting your computer into *Sleep mode*. This is one of the best features of Windows Vista—you simply click the Sleep button and within seconds, Windows Vista saves any open files, records their state and the state of any running programs in memory and on your hard disk, and then puts your computer into a power-saving mode. When you "wake" the computer, usually by pressing the Enter key or the power button, Windows Vista needs only a few seconds to restore your previous computer session exactly as it was when you left it. Now that we have Windows Vista, we realize just how Sleep-deprived we were with earlier versions of Windows!

  Putting your computer to sleep conserves power and keeps your work quickly available. When a desktop computer is sleeping, it uses approximately 10 percent of the power required to run normally. When a mobile computer is sleeping, it uses approximately 2 percent of its battery power per hour.

> **Troubleshooting** Some video card drivers do not support Sleep mode. If the Shut Down Options menu does not include the Sleep option, update your video driver or consult the video card manufacturer's Web site for driver information.

● If you need to turn off your computer entirely—for example, to install hardware or to move a desktop computer—you do so by *shutting down* the computer. Shutting down closes all your open applications and files, ends your computing session, closes network connections, stops system processes, stops the hard disk, and turns off the computer.

In this exercise, you will lock and unlock your computer, put it to sleep and wake it up, log off from Windows Vista, and then shut down the computer. There are no practice files for this exercise.

BE SURE TO log on to Windows Vista before beginning this exercise.

1. If no programs are currently running on your computer, click the **Launch Internet Explorer Browser** button on the **Quick Launch** toolbar or the **Internet Explorer** link in the upper-left corner of the **Start** menu.

   Later in this exercise, having a program running will make the effect of the different shutdown options more apparent.

Lock

2. On the **Start** menu, click the **Lock** button.

   Windows displays the Welcome screen with only your user account available. The word *Locked* appears under your user name.

3. If your account is password protected, enter your password in the **Password** box, and then press the ⎡Enter⎤ key. Otherwise, click your account picture.

   Your previous computing session resumes.

Sleep

4. On the **Start** menu, click the **Sleep** button.

   Windows saves your file and program information and then your computer goes into a power-saving state. The hard disk stops turning (the computer no longer makes any noise), but the power light on the computer itself is still on, either steadily or blinking slowly.

5. Depending on your specific hardware, either move the mouse, press ⎡Enter⎤, or press your computer's power button to wake up your computer.

> **Troubleshooting** If you don't know which method to use to wake up your computer, try them in the order given. If none of the given methods work, consult the computer's manual or the computer manufacturer's Web site.

The computer comes out of its power-saving state, and Windows Vista displays the Welcome screen.

6. If your account is password protected, enter your password in the **Password** box, and then press [Enter]. Otherwise, click your account picture to resume your previous computer session.

Shut Down
Options

7. On the **Start** menu, click the **Shut Down Options** button to display a list of ways you can pause or end your computing session.

The Shut Down Options list will vary depending on your computer's hardware configuration.

8. In the **Shut Down Options** list, click **Log Off**.

If no programs are running on your computer, Windows Vista logs you off. Otherwise, Windows Vista displays a list of running programs and open files.

9. If you don't have any unsaved work, click **Log off now** to complete the process and display the Welcome screen. Otherwise, click **Cancel** to return to your computing session; then save and close open files, shut down running programs, and click **Log Off** in the **Shut Down Options** list to complete the process.

> **Troubleshooting** If you have unsaved files but don't click Cancel within 30 seconds, Windows Vista shuts down the running programs and logs you off.

Shut Down

10. In the lower-right corner of the Welcome screen, click the **Shut Down** button.

> **Troubleshooting** If any other user accounts are logged on to the computer, Windows Vista gives you the opportunity to cancel the Shut Down process. If you shut down a computer while people are logged on to it, they could lose data in open files or running programs.

Windows Vista shuts down all the computer processes and turns off your computer.

> **Troubleshooting** If your computer seems to be operating unusually slowly, or you're experiencing technical problems that seem related to the operating system rather than to an application, try restarting your computer. Restarting clears the *system cache*—an area in memory where Windows Vista stores information it might need to access quickly—and frequently resolves minor issues. To restart your computer, click Restart on the Shut Down Options menu.

Making Your Computer Easier to Use

Are the words on the screen too small to read easily? Do you wish the icons were larger? Does it take you a while to locate the insertion point because it is so skinny? Windows Vista includes these *utilities* (small programs) to assist people with visual or auditory disabilities:

- *Audio Description* narrates videos as they play, if this feature is available within the video file.

- *High Contrast* changes the display of your screen from the usual muted Windows Vista colors to a starker color scheme that makes individual items stand out on the screen.

- *Magnifier* opens a magnification panel in which the screen under the mouse pointer is displayed, magnified up to nine times. You can adjust the size and location of the magnification panel.

- *Narrator* is a text-to-speech tool that works with Windows setup, the Windows desktop, Control Panel programs, Windows Explorer, Notepad, and WordPad. It reads menu commands, dialog box options, and other screen features out loud, telling you what options are available and how to use them. It also reads your keystrokes to you as you type them and tells you the pointer location as you move the mouse around.

- *Sound Sentry* flashes the screen element you specify (your choices are the active caption bar, active window, or desktop) every time the system's built-in speaker plays a sound.

You can turn off unnecessary animations and background images; specify how long notifications stay open (the default is seven seconds); and change the size of text, icons, the focus rectangle, the cursor, and the mouse pointer. Windows Vista also supports text captions for spoken dialogue and text narratives for videos, if they are available for the content you are working with.

See Also For information about using keyboard shortcuts, see "Information for New Computer Users" at the beginning of this book, and the "Keyboard Shortcuts" sections at the end of each chapter. For information about handwriting recognitions, see "Configuring Tablet PC Options" in Chapter 5, "Installing and Configuring Devices."

The traditional method of entering information into a computer document is by typing it using the keyboard. However, mobility problems can make typing difficult. Windows Vista includes a variety of tools to help with entering information, including the following:

- *Filter Keys* causes Windows to ignore brief or repeated keystrokes, or slows the repeat rate.
- *Mouse Keys* enables you to move the cursor around the screen by pressing the Arrow keys on the numeric keypad.
- *On-Screen Keyboard* displays a visual representation of a keyboard from which you can select individual keys by using your mouse, pen, or other device.
- *Speech Recognition* allows you to control Windows, control open programs, and dictate text by speaking into a microphone.
- *Sticky Keys* makes it easier to use the keyboard with one hand by making the Ctrl, Shift, and Alt keys "stick down" until you press the next key.
- *Toggle Keys* sounds an audio signal when you press the Caps Lock, Num Lock, or Scroll Lock key. A high-pitched sound plays when the keys are activated, and a low-pitched sound plays when the keys are deactivated.

You can also make the *keyboard shortcut* for a command more obvious by underlining the letter in the command name that corresponds to the shortcut key, and you can activate a window by pointing to it rather than clicking it. If your hardware supports handwriting recognition, you can write, draw, or otherwise record information within variety of programs, because Windows Vista includes the Tablet PC functions that were previously available only in Windows XP Tablet PC Edition.

You can turn on the High Contrast, Magnifier, Narrator, On-Screen Keyboard, Sticky Keys, or Filter Keys features before logging on to Windows Vista by clicking the Ease Of Access icon in the lower-left corner of the Welcome screen (or by pressing Windows logo key+U), selecting the options you want, and then clicking Apply or OK.

After logging on to Windows Vista, you can control the accessibility settings from the Ease Of Access Center. To open the Ease Of Access Center:

1. On the **Start** menu, click **Control Panel**.
2. In **Control Panel**, click **Ease of Access**, and then click **Ease of Access Center**.

When you first open the Ease Of Access Center, an audio guide reads aloud the text at the top of the screen, and provides mouse-free access to the Magnifier, Narrator, and On-Screen Keyboard utilities, or to switch to a high-contrast display.

You can turn off the audio guide and/or scan functions if you don't need them.

To optimize a specific type of element, you can select from the groups of settings at the bottom of the Ease Of Access Center.

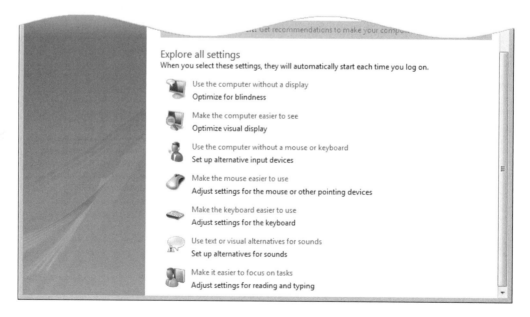

If you want Windows to help you determine what settings will improve your computing experience, click Get Recommendations To Make Your Computer Easier To Use near the center of the window to begin a simple, five-part questionnaire about your eyesight, dexterity, hearing, speech, and reasoning. (Don't worry; your results are private.) Based on the issues you indicate, Windows Vista recommends and describes adjustments that might be helpful. Some are accessibility features and others are simple adjustments to Windows settings.

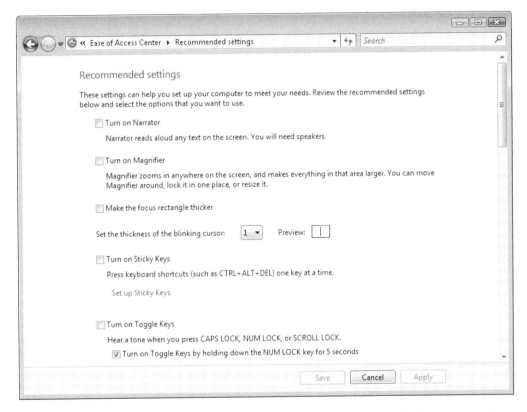

You can enact any suggested change by selecting its check box and clicking Apply or Save.

The tools available with Windows Vista provide only a minimum level of assistance for users with special needs. Most users with disabilities will need specialized programs with more advanced functionality for daily use.

Key Points

- You start a Windows Vista session by logging on, and end it by logging off. You can log off and leave the computer running, or you can log off as part of the process of shutting down.

- Each person who uses the computer logs on with his or her own user account. Your Windows Vista environment preferences are stored with your user account so that when you log on to Windows Vista, it looks and works the way you want.

- You must activate your copy of Windows Vista within 30 days of first use. After that period, you won't be able to create or save files until you activate Windows Vista.

- Windows Vista includes many alternative input and output options designed to make your computer more accessible.

- You can change the look of Windows Vista and the way your computer functions to make it easier for you to see or use the computer. You make these changes from the Ease Of Access Center as well as from the Welcome screen.

- It is important to keep your computer up to date with the most current upgrades and security updates. Windows Update makes it easy to do this automatically or manually.

- You can save power without closing files and exiting programs by putting your computer to sleep. This conserves more energy than shutting down the computer.

Keyboard Shortcuts

Press this	To do this
Ctrl+Esc or Windows logo key	Display the Start menu.
Windows logo key+L	Lock your computer.
Right Shift for eight seconds	Turn Filter Keys on or off.
Left Alt+left Shift+Print Screen	Turn High Contrast on or off.
Left Alt+left Shift+Num Lock	Turn Mouse Keys on or off.
Shift five times	Turn Sticky Keys on or off.
Num Lock for five seconds	Turn Toggle Keys on or off.
Windows logo key+U	Open the Ease Of Access Center.

Chapter at a Glance

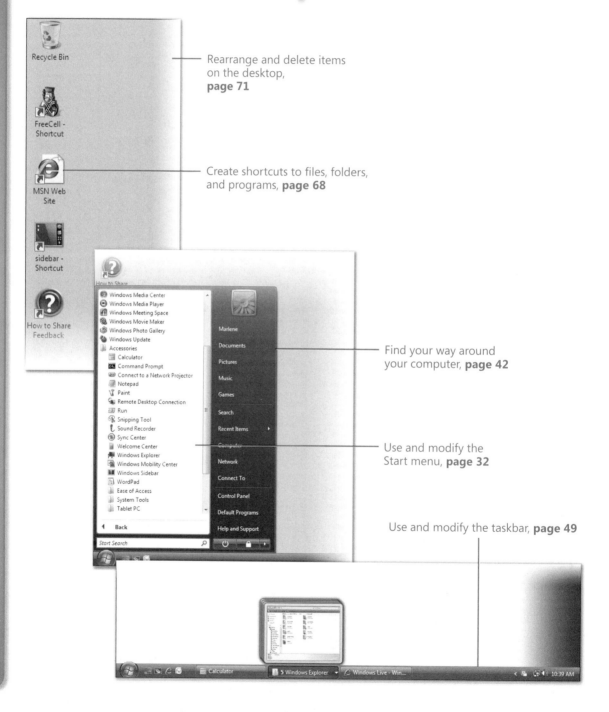

Rearrange and delete items on the desktop, **page 71**

Create shortcuts to files, folders, and programs, **page 68**

Find your way around your computer, **page 42**

Use and modify the Start menu, **page 32**

Use and modify the taskbar, **page 49**

2 Working Efficiently in Windows Vista

In this chapter, you will learn to:

- ✔ Find your way around the Windows desktop.
- ✔ Use and modify the Start menu.
- ✔ Find your way around your computer.
- ✔ Use and modify the taskbar.
- ✔ Control your computer by using voice commands.
- ✔ Create shortcuts to files, folders, and programs.
- ✔ Rearrange and delete items on the desktop.

Working in the Windows environment is a lot like working in a real-world office environment. You have a desktop on which you can organize all your work tools, and you have folders in which to organize all your files. Windows incorporates all these elements into its user interface, which is the means by which you and your computer interact.

The most basic element of the Windows Vista user interface is a background screen called the *desktop*. All the programs you run on your computer open on top of this background screen. At the bottom of the screen, the *taskbar* displays buttons you can click to run programs, utilities, and commands, as well as buttons representing the windows of open programs and files. The new *Windows Sidebar* displays useful *gadgets* that provide constantly updated information, such as the time.

In this chapter, you will explore some of the elements of the Windows Vista user interface and the various ways in which you can look at the information on your computer. You will then see how to tailor some of these elements to suit the way you work.

See Also Do you need only a quick refresher on the topics in this chapter? See the Quick Reference section at the beginning of this book.

> **Important** No practice files are required to complete the exercises in this chapter. For information about practice files, see "Using the Companion CD" at the beginning of this book.

Finding Your Way Around the Windows Desktop

Windows Vista presents its tools, commands, and structure through a *graphical user interface (GUI)*. Graphical user interfaces include the following types of components:

- **Desktop.** The basic display area against which you can manipulate icons representing programs, folders, and files.

- **Icons.** Visual representations of programs, folders, files, or other objects or functions.

- **Pointing device.** A device such as a mouse that controls a pointer with which you can select objects displayed on the screen.

- **Windows.** A framework within which you can run a program or display a folder or file.

- **Menus.** Lists from which you can give instructions by running commands.

- **Dialog boxes.** Boxes in which you refine instructions by typing information or selecting from the available options.

See Also For information about how to work with the components of a GUI, see the section "Information for New Computer Users" at the beginning of this book. For information about Windows Sidebar, see "Using and Modifying Sidebar Gadgets" in Chapter 10, "Staying Organized."

Depending on your Windows Vista settings and the programs installed on your computer, there might be one or more *icons* on your desktop, each representing a file, folder, link, or shortcut to a specific item. Windows Vista assigns an icon to every item you see on your computer. The icon might represent a file type (such as a document, a text file, or a database) or storage component (such as a folder, hard disk drive, or CD drive), or it might indicate the default program for opening a file. This visual representation can make it easier to find a file or program you're looking for. When an icon represents a *shortcut* to an item stored somewhere other than the folder you are viewing, an arrow appears in its lower-left corner.

You can save or move programs and files directly to your desktop, which is represented in your computer's storage hierarchy as a folder. For example, if you download a program or other file from the Internet that you will need to use only once, you might save it to your desktop so you can quickly find it, use it, and then delete it. When you install a program on your computer, a link to the program is added to the Start menu, and you usually have the option of creating a *desktop shortcut*. (Some installation programs automatically create a desktop shortcut, but others give you the courtesy of choice.) You can create your own shortcuts to programs, to specific folders or files, to network locations, or to Web sites, on the desktop or in any other folder. You delete an item from the desktop as you would from any other folder. When you delete a shortcut, however, you aren't actually deleting the program, folder, or file to which it points—only the pointer to that item.

When you purchase a new computer, the *original equipment manufacturer (OEM)* might already have installed programs—either trial or full versions—on it as part of a computer system. To make these programs discoverable, the manufacturer might place shortcuts to the programs on the desktop (in addition to those on the Start menu), along with links to "offers" (advertisements) for products and services you can purchase. It wouldn't be unusual to purchase a new computer and find 20 shortcuts already on its desktop the first time you start it up. If you upgrade to Windows Vista from a previous version of Windows, your existing desktop shortcuts and links will still be available.

One of the icons Windows places on the desktop is a link to the *Recycle Bin*, which is where Windows temporarily stores files you delete. When the Recycle Bin is empty, the icon depicts an empty trash can; after you delete items (and until you empty the Recycle Bin), the icon depicts pieces of paper in the trash can. You can recover deleted files from the Recycle Bin, or you can empty the Recycle Bin and permanently delete the files to free up space on your hard disk.

See Also For information about managing the Recycle Bin, see "Creating, Renaming, and Deleting Folders and Files" in Chapter 3, "Working with Folders and Files."

Below each icon on the desktop is the name of the element it represents. If the name is too long, it is truncated by an ellipsis (...) when not selected and displayed in full when you click it. Pointing to an icon (positioning the mouse pointer over it) displays a box, called a *ScreenTip*, containing identifying information. You can start a program, open a folder or file, or jump to a network location or Web site by double-clicking the associated icon or desktop shortcut.

At any time, you can click the Show Desktop button on the Quick Launch toolbar to minimize all open windows so that you can access your desktop icons and shortcuts.

Show desktop

Using and Modifying the Start Menu

The *Start menu* is a list of options that is your central link to all the programs installed on your computer, as well as to all the tasks you can carry out with Windows Vista. You open the Start menu by clicking the Start button at the left end of the taskbar, or by pressing the Windows logo key found to the left of the Spacebar on most keyboards. The Start menu on a Windows Vista computer looks similar to the Windows XP version, but its functionality has been streamlined.

Pinned programs area

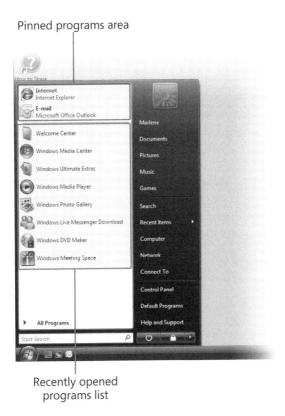

Recently opened
programs list

> **Tip** If you are accustomed to the *Windows Classic* Start menu found in Windows 2000 and
> earlier versions, you might find that the change takes a little getting used to. If you are un-
> able to adjust, you have the option of changing back to the Classic version. However, the new
> menu is designed to increase efficiency, so we recommend that you at least give it a try!

You can quickly access your favorite programs by inserting shortcuts to them in a special
area at the top of the left side of the Start menu called the *pinned programs area*. Links
to your default Web browser and e-mail program are pinned here by default. You can
rearrange pinned programs by dragging them into whatever order you want.

Below the first horizontal line (the menu separator) on the left side of the Start menu are links to the last nine programs you started. (You can adjust that number, or remove the list entirely.) When you first start Windows Vista, this *recently opened programs list* displays links to some of the programs that come with Windows Vista, including Windows Media Player, Windows Photo Gallery, and Windows Meeting Space, as well as links to a Web site from which you can download Windows Live Messenger (the replacement for Windows Messenger and MSN Messenger) and to other programs, depending on the edition of Windows Vista running on your computer.

Below the recently opened programs list, the All Programs link provides access to a list of most of the programs installed on your computer. You display the list by clicking or pointing to All Programs. You can find and start almost any installed program from this list. (Most program setup utilities put a link to the program on the Start menu.)

> **Tip** A right-pointing arrow next to a link or menu item indicates that clicking it, or simply pointing to it for a few seconds, will display a list of options.

The right side of the Start menu is divided by menu separators into three sections:

- The top section displays your user account picture and a link to your personal folder, as well as links to the folders where you are most likely to store your files.

- The middle section displays links to the Search Results window; to the 15 files you most recently opened; to a window that displays the contents of your computer; to a window that displays the computers, programs, folders, and files you can access on your network; and if you have created network connections, to those connections.

- The bottom section displays links to Control Panel, from which you can access all the Windows Vista settings; to the default settings for opening various types of files and media; and to Windows Help And Support, where you can find a variety of information and troubleshooting resources.

At the bottom of the Start menu are the Start Search box and the commands you use to log off from or shut down your computer.

You can customize the Start menu and change the way things work. For example, you can:

- Display or hide lists of recently used programs and files, and control the number of programs (up to 30, depending on your screen resolution) shown.

- Display or hide links to the Computer, Control Panel, and Games windows, as well as to your *Documents*, *Favorites*, *Personal*, and *Pictures* folders. By default, clicking a link displays the contents of the item in the associated window or folder. Alternatively, you can display its contents as a menu from which you can make a choice. (This can be more efficient than clicking items within windows.)

● Display or hide the Administrative Tools and Favorites menus.

● Display or hide links to the Connect To, Default Programs, Help, Network, Printers, and Search windows. These links aren't available as menus because they don't contain other groups or folders.

● Control the items and areas available for the Search function.

● Change the size of the icons that appear on the Start menu, activate the display of context menus when you right-click a Start menu item, rearrange Start menu items by dragging them, highlight newly installed programs, open submenus by pointing to them rather than clicking, and arrange the All Programs list in alphabetical order.

> **Tip** Don't worry if you don't understand what some of these customization options are right now. By the time you have worked your way through this book, you will know whether making adjustments to these options is appropriate for the way you work.

In this exercise, you will hide and redisplay the recently opened programs list and change the number of programs it shows. Then you will start a program from the Start menu. You will also add shortcuts to the pinned programs area, rearrange them, and remove them. There are no practice files for this exercise.

> **BE SURE TO** log on to Windows Vista before beginning this exercise, and if the Welcome Center is open, close it.

Start

1. Click the **Start** button to display the **Start** menu, and note the programs that appear in the recently opened programs list.

> **Tip** If your recently opened programs list is empty, you can still follow along with this exercise so that you know how to clear the list later.

2. Right-click the **Start** button, and then click **Properties**.

The Taskbar And Start Menu Properties dialog box opens, displaying the Start Menu tab.

On this tab, you have the option to change to the Windows Classic Start menu, or to remove lists of recent files and programs from the Start menu.

3. With **Start menu** selected, click **Customize**.

The Customize Start Menu dialog box opens.

4. Scroll through the list to view the ways in which you can customize the menu, but don't change any of the default settings at this time.

5. In the **Start menu size** area, type or select (by clicking the arrows) 0 to clear the list of recently opened programs. Then click **OK**.

6. In the **Taskbar and Start Menu Properties** dialog box, click **Apply**.

7. Click the **Start** button.

   The recently opened programs list is empty, and the horizontal line separating it from the pinned programs area is no longer visible.

8. With the **Start** menu open, click the **Start** button to close the menu and return to the **Taskbar and Start Menu Properties** dialog box. Then click **Customize**.

9. In the **Start menu size** area, type or select 6, and then click **OK**.

10. In the **Taskbar and Start Menu Properties** dialog box, click **OK** to put your change into effect and close the dialog box. Then click the **Start** button.

    Six programs appear in the recently used programs list. Note that removing the list did not clear its contents; it only hid them.

11. On the **Start** menu, click **All Programs**.

    The All Programs list appears in the left pane of the Start menu, displaying your currently installed programs.

Programs you have recently installed might be highlighted.

12. In the **All Programs** list, click **Accessories**.

The folder expands, pushing items at the top and bottom of the list out of view. All the programs in this folder come with Windows Vista.

You can still access the hidden parts of the All Programs list by using the scroll bar on the right.

See Also For information about scrolling, see "Information for New Computer Users" at the beginning of this book.

13. At the top of the **Accessories** list, click **Calculator**.

The Start menu closes, the Calculator program starts and displays a representation of a calculator on the screen, and a Calculator button appears on the taskbar.

14. Display the **Start** menu, and then on the right side, click **Games**.

> **Troubleshooting** In certain editions of Windows Vista, the Games link on the Start menu and the contents of the *Games* folder do not appear by default. You can complete this exercise by substituting any other window.
>
> If you want to add the Games link, follow steps 2 and 3 of this exercise, and in the Customize Start Menu dialog box, under Games, click the Display As A Link option, and then click OK. To populate the *Games* folder, see "Turning Windows Features On and Off" in Chapter 14, "Optimizing Your Computer System."

When you point to Games, the icon at the top of the Start menu changes from your user account picture to a representation of a deck of cards. Then the Games window opens on top of the Calculator, and a Games button appears on the task-bar. The Games taskbar button appears pressed to indicate that it is the active window.

15. In the **Games** window, right-click **Solitaire**, and then click **Pin to Start Menu**.

See Also For information about the performance ratings shown on the right side of the Games window, see "Improving Your Computer's Performance" in Chapter 14, "Optimizing Your Computer System."

16. Display the **Start** menu.

The pinned programs area now includes a link to the Solitaire game.

> **Tip** You can also pin programs to the Start menu by dragging them from the All Programs list. You can delete a link from the pinned programs area by right-clicking the link and then clicking Remove From This List.

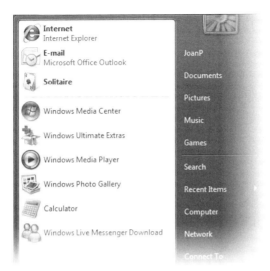

17. On the **Start** menu, drag **Calculator** from the recently opened programs list to the pinned programs area, and drop it above **Solitaire**.

    While you are dragging the link, a thick black line indicates where it will appear if you release the mouse button.

18. In the pinned programs area, right-click **Calculator**, and then click **Unpin from Start Menu** to return Calculator to the recently opened programs list.

19. In the pinned programs area, right-click **Solitaire**, and click **Unpin from Start Menu**.

    The Solitaire link disappears from the pinned programs area and (because it was never on the recently opened programs list) from the Start menu.

20. Click away from the **Start** menu to close it.

21. On the Windows taskbar, click the **Games** taskbar button to minimize the Games window, and then click the **Calculator** taskbar button to minimize the Calculator.

    You will learn more about windows and taskbar buttons later in this chapter.

 BE SURE TO reset the links displayed on the Start menu to the number you want.

Finding Your Way Around Your Computer

Programs, tools, and information are available on your computer in a hierarchical structure. Information is stored in files that are organized in folders on hard disk drives and other storage devices (such as a CD, DVD, or USB flash drive). You can look at a representation of this storage structure by displaying the contents of the disks in the available drives.

The tools available to you in each folder window vary based on the folder's contents, but all include these basic features:

- The *Address bar* reflects your navigation *path*, beginning with the Windows symbol representing the overall Windows storage structure. The arrow after each folder name links to a list of its subfolders.

> **Tip** The path of a folder or file gives the address where the folder or file is stored on your hard disk. A typical path starts with the drive letter and lists the folders and subfolders, separated by backslashes (\), you have to navigate through to get to the folder or file.

- The *toolbar* presents menus and buttons specific to the content of the current window. When more buttons are available than can be shown, chevrons (>>) appear at the right end of the toolbar; clicking the chevrons displays a list of other commands.

- The *Navigation pane* displays your personal folders and (when you expand the Folders list) displays a hierarchical view of the entire storage structure of your computer. To display the contents of a personal folder, click the folder name. To expand a folder in the Folders list, point to the folder, and then click the white arrow that appears to its left. (Click the black arrow to hide the subfolders.)

- The *Content pane* displays files and folders stored in the currently selected folder or storage device.

Each drive is identified by a letter, and in some cases by a description. Your computer's primary hard drive (the one where the operating system is installed) is almost always identified by the letter C. (By tradition, the letters A and B are reserved for floppy disk drives, which have been superseded by higher capacity storage media and are rarely installed in computers these days.) If your computer has additional hard drives, they are assigned the next sequential letters, followed by any drives for removable media. You can navigate through the folder hierarchy on each drive, displaying the contents of folders within folders until you find the file you want. This navigation process is called *browsing*.

> **Tip** You can assign a drive letter to a specific computer or shared folder on your network by *mapping a drive* to that folder. This is commonly done to create a constant connection to a *network share* (a folder on a different computer on your network) but can also be used to maintain a connection to an Internet location.

However, you don't have to browse to find the programs, tools, and information you need in your daily work. You don't even have to know precisely where things are stored, because Windows Vista provides a system of links that you can use to navigate directly to Windows Vista settings and tools, to programs, and to certain "buckets" of information. You have already seen evidence of this link system with the icons on the desktop and the links on the Start menu, but it is also used in other key components of Windows Vista, which we will explore here and in other topics of this book.

See Also For more information about browsing drives and networks, see "Navigating to Folders and Files" in Chapter 3, "Working with Folders and Files."

When Windows Vista was installed on your computer, it created three *system folders*:

- **Program Files.** Most programs (including the programs and tools that come with Windows Vista) install the files they need in subfolders of the *Program Files* folder. During installation, you are given the opportunity to designate a different folder. Thereafter, you shouldn't move, copy, rename, or delete the folders and files; if you do, the program will probably not run, nor will you be able to uninstall it.

- **Users.** The first time a user logs on to the computer, Windows Vista creates a user profile containing 12 subfolders: *AppData*, *Contacts*, *Desktop*, *Documents*, *Downloads*, *Favorites*, *Links*, *Music*, *Pictures*, *Saved Games*, *Searches*, and *Videos*. All but one of these folders is available from your *personal folder*, which you open by clicking your user name at the top of the Start menu. You can save documents, spreadsheets, graphics, and other files in your personal folder. As you work on your computer and personalize Windows, it saves information and settings specific to your individual user profile in this folder.

> **Tip** If you log on to your computer with more than one user name, Windows creates a user profile folder for each name. If you want to make files on the computer available regardless of how you log in, save them in the *Public* profile folder.

The *Users* folder also contains a *Public* profile folder, the contents of which are accessible to anyone logged on to the computer. By default, the *Public* folder contains five subfolders: *Public Documents*, *Public Downloads*, *Public Music*, *Public Pictures*, and *Public Videos*. Computers running Windows Vista editions that support Windows Media Center also have a *Recorded TV* folder.

> **Tip** You can make the *Public* folder available to other computers on your network by selecting that option in the Network And Sharing Center. For more information, see "Sharing Drives and Folders" in Chapter 8, "Making Connections."

- **Windows.** Most of the critical operating system files are stored in this folder. You can look, but unless you really know what you are doing, don't touch! Most Windows Vista users will never need to access the files in the *Windows* folder.

> **Troubleshooting** If you upgraded your computer from an earlier version of Windows, the *Windows* folder from the earlier version might still remain on your computer. However, it will have been renamed to Windows.old during the upgrade process to avoid confusion.

In this exercise, you will explore the storage structure of your computer, and locate basic Windows Vista settings and tools, while learning different ways of getting to the information stored on your computer. There are no practice files for this exercise.

 BE SURE TO log on to Windows Vista before beginning this exercise.

Start

1. Click the **Start** button, and then on the right side of the **Start** menu, click **Computer**.

   When you point to Computer, the Start menu icon changes from your user account picture to a representation of a computer system. Then when you click Computer, the Computer window opens.

   > **Troubleshooting** The contents of your Computer window will correspond with the number and types of drives your computer can access, and will probably not be identical to those shown here. If you have used the Computer window before, the Folders list might be expanded. If the items you see in your Computer window are represented by words or icons in a different way than shown here, take a minute to adjust the view. On the toolbar, click the Views arrow, and then in the list, click Tiles. If the Folders list is expanded, click the Folders header to hide the list.

Address bar   Toolbar

Navigation pane   Content pane

2. In the **Computer** window, double-click **Local Disk (C:)** to display the contents of drive C.

   Icons identify each item in the window. For example, the icon on the hard disk drive with the Windows logo above it identifies the drive on which Windows Vista is installed.

3. If your Folders list is already displayed, skip to step 4. Otherwise, at the bottom of the **Navigation** pane, click **Folders** to display the Folders list.

Personal folders

Folders list

From this window, you can navigate through the storage structure of the selected drive in three ways: by double-clicking folders in the Content pane, by expanding folders in the Folders list, or by clicking locations in the Address bar.

> **Important** The folders and files stored directly on a drive are said to be stored in that drive's *root directory*. The root directory often contains system files that should not be modified or moved in any way.

4. In the **Folders list**, under **Local Disk (C:)**, point to **Users**, and then click the arrow that appears to the left of the folder name.

   The folder expands to display a list of user accounts on the computer.

5. In the **Folders list**, under **Users**, click your own user name.

   Your personal folders appear in the window.

6. In the **Address** bar, click the arrow to the right of **Users**, and then in the list, click **Public**.

The folders available to all users appear in the window.

Minimize, Maximize, and Close buttons

Maximize

7. To quickly experiment with window-management techniques, click the **Maximize** button in the upper-right corner of the open window.

The window expands to completely fill your screen, and if your display is set to Windows Aero, the title bar changes from gray to black to provide a quick visual indicator of the window size. A Restore Down button replaces the Maximize button; clicking this button will return the window to its previous size.

> **Tip** You can manually resize a window by positioning the mouse pointer over the window's frame and, when the pointer changes to a double-headed arrow, dragging the frame to make the window smaller or larger. You cannot manually resize a maximized window; you must first restore the window to its non-maximized state.

Minimize

8. In the upper-right corner of the window, click the **Minimize** button.

   The folder disappears behind its taskbar button.

Close

9. Click the **Public** taskbar button once to redisplay the window. Then click its **Close** button.

10. On the **Start** menu, click **Control Panel**.

    When you point to Control Panel, your user account picture changes to a represen-tation of a touch-screen. Then the Control Panel window opens.

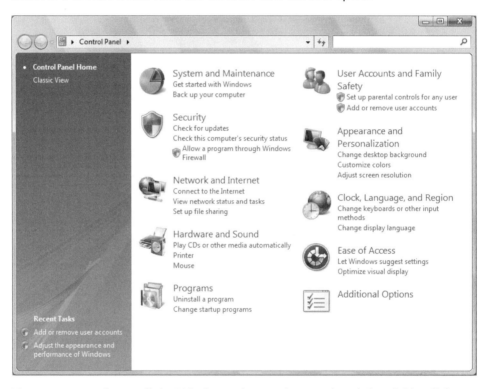

You can access almost all the Windows Vista settings and tools by clicking links within Control Panel. If you know the specific setting or tool you're looking for, you can type it in the Search box in the upper-right corner. Control Panel then displays only the settings and tools containing or tagged with your search term. We discuss the features available from Control Panel throughout this book.

See Also For information about the excellent search features of Windows Vista, see "Finding Specific Information" in Chapter 3, "Working with Folders and Files."

Using and Modifying the Taskbar

The taskbar that appears across the bottom of your screen (your primary display, if you have more than one) is your link to current information about what is happening on your Windows Vista computer. In addition to the Start button, the taskbar displays the Quick Launch toolbar, taskbar buttons, and notifications. You can hide the Quick Launch toolbar and the notifications, but not the Start button and taskbar buttons.

Preview of grouped windows

Quick Launch toolbar   Taskbar buttons   Notification area

> **Troubleshooting** If the Quick Launch toolbar is not visible, right-click an empty area of the taskbar, point to Toolbars, and then click Quick Launch.

The *Quick Launch toolbar* displays single-click links to programs and commands. Windows Vista installs links to Windows Internet Explorer and to the Show Desktop and Switch Between Windows commands on the Quick Launch toolbar. You can add more program links at any time by dragging a program icon or shortcut icon onto the toolbar. You can also adjust its width or remove it from the taskbar entirely. When the toolbar contains more links than can be shown in the space allocated to the toolbar, chevrons appear at its right end. Clicking the chevrons displays a list of the hidden links, in which you can click the one you want.

A *taskbar button* represents each open window, file, or program (but not dialog boxes, message boxes, warnings, or the Windows Sidebar). When more than one file is open in a program, Windows might group the taskbar buttons by program to avoid taking up space on the taskbar with a button for each window. When windows are grouped, a number following the *program icon* on the button indicates the number of open windows represented by the button.

Pointing to a taskbar button displays a thumbnail of the window (or windows) it represents. Clicking the button activates the window. When multiple windows are grouped under one taskbar button, you can:

● Display one window by clicking the taskbar button and then in the list, clicking the window you want to display.

● Display all the windows in the group by right-clicking the taskbar button and then clicking the arrangement you want:

● Click Cascade to display the windows on top of each other, with the title bar of each window visible and the contents of only the top window visible.

● Click Show Windows Stacked to display the content of all the windows arranged in a grid, with more windows stacked vertically than horizontally. For example, eight windows are arranged in two columns of four.

● Click Show Windows Side By Side to display the content of all the windows arranged in a grid, with more windows stacked horizontally than vertically. For example, eight windows are arranged in four columns of two.

In every arrangement, the open windows are the same or similarly sized, regardless of their size before you minimized them.

● Minimize all the windows in the group by right-clicking the taskbar button and then clicking Minimize Group.

● Close all the windows in the group by right-clicking the taskbar button and then clicking Close Group. Windows Vista will prompt you to save or discard any unsaved changes.

Taskbar buttons change size so that they fit on the taskbar as you open and close programs. The maximum number of buttons that can fit on the taskbar varies depending on your monitor and display settings. When you exceed the maximum, Windows either tiles the buttons or displays a scroll bar, depending on the current taskbar configuration.

The *notification area* displays information about the status of programs, including those running in the background (programs you don't need to interact with), as well as links to certain system commands. Some notification icons are hidden by default, and you can choose to hide others that you don't actively want to monitor.

When the Show Hidden Icons button appears at the left end of the notification area, you can click it to temporarily display all the notifications. Icons appear temporarily in the notification area when activities such as the following take place:

- The printer icon appears when you send a document to the printer.
- A message icon appears when you receive a new e-mail message.
- The Windows Security icon appears if you need to install an update, or if an element of your security system (such as antivirus software) is missing or fails.
- Network connections and Windows Live Messenger icons appear when those features are in use. (Inactive connections are indicated by the presence of a red X on the icon.)

A digital clock at the right end of the notification area displays the current system time. You can display more date and time information by pointing to the clock or by increasing the space available.

The taskbar displays one row of buttons and is *docked* at the bottom of the desktop, but you can control its size and position:

- You can dock the taskbar at the top, bottom, or on either side of the desktop by dragging it to the edge of the screen against which you want to dock it.
- When the taskbar is docked at the top or bottom, you can expand it to be up to half the height of your screen by dragging its border down or up.
- When the taskbar is docked on the left or right, you can expand it to be up to half the width of your screen by dragging its border right or left.
- You can stipulate that the taskbar should be hidden when you're not using it, or that it should always stay on top of other windows so that its tools are always available.

> **Troubleshooting** By default, the taskbar is locked so that you can't move it or change its properties. To unlock the taskbar, right-click an empty area of the taskbar, and then click Lock The Taskbar. A check mark indicates when this option is selected.

In this exercise, you will display, hide, and move between multiple windows by using the taskbar. You will then change the taskbar appearance and the links that appear on it.

> **USE** the Calculator and Games windows you opened earlier in this chapter. If you didn't complete that exercise or closed the windows, open and minimize them now.

Launch Internet
Explorer Browser

1. On the **Quick Launch** toolbar, click the **Launch Internet Explorer Browser** button.

Internet Explorer starts, and a button appears on the taskbar. The button label is preceded by an Internet Explorer icon to indicate what type of window it represents.

2. Repeat step 1 nine times so that ten browser windows are open.

> **Troubleshooting** If your screen resolution is so high that opening 10 windows doesn't cause their taskbar buttons to group, continue opening browser windows until they do.

On the taskbar button, the number to the left of the Internet Explorer icon indicates the number of windows represented by that button.

3. Click the **Games** taskbar button, and then the **Calculator** taskbar button.

The Games and Calculator windows open on top of the browser windows.

4. Click the **Internet Explorer** taskbar button, and then in the list, click the first (from the bottom) **Windows Internet Explorer** link.

The first browser window you opened comes to the top of the stack.

Switch between
windows

5. On the **Quick Launch** toolbar, click the **Switch between windows** button.

A visual representation of the open windows appears.

What you see at this point will vary depending on the video card installed in your computer and your display settings. Each window might be represented by a three-dimensional version displaying its exact content, with all the windows stacked on top of each other. Or it might be represented by its program icon in a box on top of the current display.

6. Press the → and ← keys to move through the display of windows. Then click the representation of any browser window.

The selected window comes to the front and the display returns to normal.

Show desktop

7. On the **Quick Launch** toolbar, click the **Show desktop** button.

All the open windows minimize.

8. Right-click the **Internet Explorer** taskbar button, and then click **Show Windows Stacked**.

The 10 Internet Explorer windows appear, arranged in a grid.

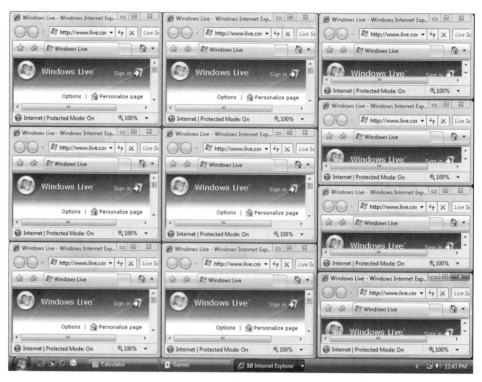

9. Click the **Close** buttons of any three of the visible Internet Explorer windows. Then repeat step 8 to display the windows first stacked, and then side by side.

10. Investigate other arrangements, and then click the **Show desktop** button to minimize all the open windows.

11. Right-click an empty area of the taskbar, and then, if a check mark appears to the left of **Lock the Taskbar**, click it.

    Three columns of dotted lines appear at each end of the Quick Launch toolbar to indicate that the taskbar is unlocked. You can now change the size and location of the taskbar, and the size of the Quick Launch toolbar.

12. Point to the top border of the taskbar. When the pointer changes to a double-headed arrow, drag the border up until the taskbar is three rows high.

    Notice that although there is enough space for all the buttons to display individually, they remain grouped.

13. Right-click an empty area of the taskbar, and then click **Properties**.

    The Taskbar And Start Menu Properties dialog box opens, displaying the Taskbar tab.

14. Review the options for customizing the appearance of the taskbar. Then clear the **Group similar taskbar buttons** and **Show Quick Launch** check boxes.

The taskbar preview above the list of options reflects your change.

15. Click the **Notification Area** tab.

16. Review the options for modifying the notification area. Then in the **System icons** area, clear the **Clock** check box, and click **Apply**.

The taskbar reflects your changes, and the dialog box remains open. You can indi-vidually hide or display notification icons by clicking the Customize button, clicking the behavior for the icon you want to change, and then selecting the behavior you want (Hide When Inactive, Hide, or Show) from the list.

17. In the **Taskbar and Start Menu Properties** dialog box, click the **Toolbars** tab.

You can display the Quick Launch toolbar from this tab, as well as from the Taskbar tab and from the context menu that appears when you right-click the taskbar. You can also display a number of useful toolbars that might help streamline your com-puting activities.

18. Select the **Address** check box, and then click **OK**.

The Address bar appears on the taskbar, and the dialog box closes.

You can type a folder path or a *Uniform Resource Locator (URL)* in the Address bar and then press Enter to open the target destination in a new window.

CLOSE all open windows.

BE SURE TO return the taskbar to its original state by displaying the Quick Launch tool-bar, grouping similar taskbar buttons, displaying the clock, hiding the Address bar, reducing the height of the taskbar to one row, and then locking it before continuing.

Controlling Your Computer by Using Voice Commands

People working in the legal, medical, and other industries are accustomed to dictating information—either to another person, or to a voice recorder—for other people to transcribe. Similarly, executives frequently find it faster to dictate letters and memos for an assistant to type, rather than type the documents themselves. Most of us can speak faster than we can type.

Dictation naturally evolved into the development of speech recognition software. For some years now, specialized programs have been available to record information dictated in a normal speaking voice as text. Windows Vista takes speech recognition a step further, providing a means by which you can control your computer by voice, rather than by using a keyboard and mouse. You can free yourself from the keyboard and mouse, so your hands are available for other tasks. Frequent computer users might find that this provides a welcome relief from the physical discomfort that typing and mousing can cause on wrists, elbows, and shoulders.

Different people speak faster, slower, louder, softer, more or less clearly, and with different accents. You can increase the accuracy with which the Speech Recognition engine recognizes your individual speech pattern by creating and refining an individual speech profile. You might also want to create specific speech profiles for different environments. For example, if you are going to use speech recognition with your mobile PC both in a relatively noisy work environment and in a relatively quiet home environment (or perhaps the other way around, if you have young children), creating separate profiles will help to ensure that the ambient noise is handled appropriately.

After you set up your microphone, a tutorial guides you through a series of six sessions that teach you how to give commands while training the Speech Recognition engine to recognize your voice. After you complete the tutorial, other training sessions are available to further increase the accuracy of the Speech Recognition engine.

See Also If you experience difficulty setting up the microphone for speech recognition, see "Setting Up a Microphone" in Chapter 5, "Installing and Configuring Devices."

In this exercise, you will configure your Windows Vista computer to recognize your voice, and you will create a simple text document without using the keyboard or mouse. There are no practice files for this exercise.

BE SURE TO have a microphone available before beginning this exercise.

Start

1. Click the **Start** button, type speech recognition in the **Start Search** box, and then press Enter .

> **Tip** You can display the Start menu by pressing the Windows logo key, if your keyboard includes one. This key, which is labeled with the waving flag of the Windows logo, is usually found to the left of the Spacebar.

The Set Up Speech Recognition wizard starts.

> **Tip** You can browse to the Set Up Speech Recognition wizard by opening Control Panel and then clicking Ease Of Access, Speech Recognition Options, and Start Speech Recognition.

2. Read the information on the **Welcome to Speech Recognition** page, and then click **Next**.

3. Select the option for the type of microphone you are using, and then click **Next**.

4. On the **Set up your microphone** page, read the instructions, and then click **Next**.

5. On the **Adjust the microphone volume** page, read the microphone test paragraph aloud in your normal speaking voice. Click **Next**, and then on the page confirming that your microphone is set up, click **Next** again.

> **Tip** The accuracy of speech recognition depends on the quality of your microphone, the way you speak, and the amount of ambient noise. If you are serious about using this technology, invest in a good headset microphone, preferably a USB headset.

6. Read the information on the **Improve speech recognition accuracy** page, and then with **Enable document review** selected, click **Next**.

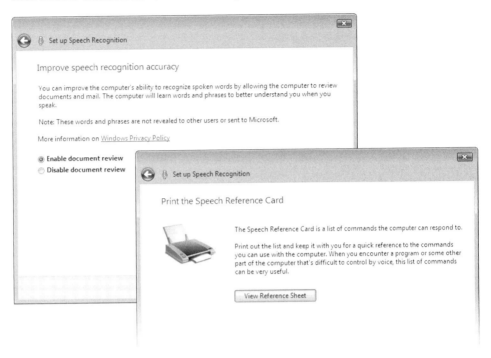

7. On the **Print the Speech Reference Card** page, click **View Reference Sheet**.

   Windows Help And Support displays the Common Commands In Speech Recognition topic.

   See Also For your convenience, you can find the speech recognition commands in the sidebar "Speech Recognition Command Reference," later in this chapter.

8. Close the **Windows Help and Support** window, and then on the **Print the Speech Reference Card** page, click **Next**.

   After you set up speech recognition, it will automatically start each time you log on to Windows Vista.

9. If you do not want speech recognition to start automatically, clear the **Run Speech Recognition at startup** check box. Then click **Next**.

Speech recognition is now set up as part of your user profile. Next, you will take a short lesson in controlling your computer by using speech commands.

10. If you are already comfortable with speech commands, click **Cancel**, and then skip to step 13. Otherwise, click **Start Tutorial**.

11. Remove your hands from the keyboard and mouse. Then follow along with the instructions given in the tutorial, using only voice commands.

    The tutorial is divided into six sections—Welcome, Basics, Dictation, Commands, Working With Windows, and Conclusion—and takes approximately 45 minutes to complete.

    The tutorial is hosted in a simulated environment—you aren't actually control-ling your own computer while working through the tutorial. You can't stray from the bounds of the tutorial—it reacts only when you do exactly as it instructs. But while you work through the tutorial, Windows Vista Speech Recognition learns your speaking style so that it will react more accurately to speech commands you give when interacting with your computer.

12. On the final page of the tutorial, click **Finish**.

   The Speech Recognition command bar appears at the top of your screen, and the Speech Recognition icon appears in the notification area.

13. To test your newfound skills in the real world, say Start listening.

   The speech recognition status changes from Sleeping to Listening. You can now give any speech commands to your computer that you want.

14. Say Start Internet Explorer.

   Windows Internet Explorer starts, displaying your default home page. You are controlling your computer by using your voice alone.

15. Experiment further with the speech recognition technology. When you finish, say Stop listening, or click the microphone on the Speech Recognition command bar. If you want to stop Speech Recognition, click the **Close** button on the command bar.

 BE SURE TO click the Close button on the Speech Recognition command bar to exit speech recognition, if you do not want to use it.

Tip Working through the tutorial acclimated Windows Vista to your voice and speech pattern, but you will undoubtedly find that the recognition is not yet entirely perfect. You can complete additional voice-training tutorials by clicking Train Your Computer To Better Understand You in the Speech Recognition Options window.

Speech Recognition Command Reference

This sidebar includes reference information from Windows Help And Support. The verbal commands for interacting with Windows Vista Speech Recognition are listed here in seven tables. Throughout, words in italic font indicate that you can say many different things in place of the example word or phrase and get useful results.

Frequently Used Commands

To do this	Say this
Click any item by its name	*File*; *Start*; *View*
Click *item*	Click *Recycle Bin*; click *Computer*; click *File*
Double-click *item*	Double-click *Recycle Bin*; double-click *Computer*; double-click *File*
Switch to an open program	Switch to *Paint*; switch to *WordPad*; switch to *program name*; switch *application*
Scroll *direction*	Scroll up; scroll down; scroll left; scroll right
Insert a new paragraph or new line in a document	New paragraph; new line
Select a word in a document	Select *word*
Select a word and start to correct it	Correct *word*
Select and delete specific words	Delete *word*
Show a list of applicable commands	What can I say?
Update the list of speech commands that are currently available	Refresh speech commands
Make the computer listen to you	Start listening
Make the computer stop listening	Stop listening
Move the Speech Recognition microphone out of the way	Move speech recognition
Minimize the microphone bar	Minimize speech recognition

Troubleshooting Using Speech Recognition to press keyboard keys will work with only Latin alphabets.

Commands for Clicking the Screen

To do this	Say this
Show the mouse grid	Mouse grid
Move the mouse pointer to the center of any mouse grid square	*number—or numbers—of the square*; 1; 7; 9; 1, 7, 9
Click any mouse grid square	Click *number of the square*
Select an item to drag with the mouse grid	*number—or numbers—of the square* where the item appears; 3, 7, 9 (followed by) mark
Select an area where you want to drag the item with the mouse grid	*number—or numbers—of the square* where you want to drag; 4, 5, 6 (followed by) click

Commands for Using Common Controls

To do this	Say this
Click any item by saying its name	*File*; *Edit*; *View*; *Save*; *bold*
Click any item	Click *File*; click *bold*; click *Save*; click *Close*
Double-click any item	Double-click *Computer*; double-click *Recycle Bin*; double-click *Folder name*
Right-click any item	Right-click *Computer*; right-click *Recycle Bin*; right-click *Folder name*
Minimize all windows to show your desktop	Show Desktop
Click something you don't know the name of	Show numbers (numbers will appear on the screen for every item in the active window)
Click a numbered item	19 OK; 5 OK
Double-click a numbered item	Double-click 19; double-click 5
Right-click a numbered item	Right-click 19; right-click 5

Commands for Keyboard Keys

To do this	Say this
Press any key on the keyboard	Press *keyboard key*; press *a*; press *capital b*; press *SHIFT plus a*; press *CTRL plus a*
Press certain keyboard keys without saying "Press" first	*Delete*; *Backspace*; *Enter*; *Page Up*; *Page down*; *Home*; *End*; *Tab*

> **Tip** You can also use the ICAO\NATO phonetic alphabet to say the keyboard keys to press. For example, you can say "Press alpha" to press "a" or "Press bravo" to press "b."

Commands for Working with Text

To do this	Say this
Insert a new line in the document	New line
Insert a new paragraph in the document	New paragraph
Insert a tab	Tab
Insert the literal word for the next command; for example, you can insert the word "comma" instead of the punctuation mark	Literal *word*
Insert the numeral form of a number	Numeral *number*
Put the cursor before a specific word	Go to *word*
Put the cursor after a specific word	Go after *word*
Do not insert a space before the next word	No space
Go to the start of the sentence that the cursor is in	Go to start of sentence
Go to the start of the paragraph that the cursor is in	Go to start of paragraph
Go to the start of the document	Go to start of document
Go to the end of the sentence that the cursor is in	Go to end of sentence
Go to the end of the paragraph that the cursor is in	Go to end of paragraph
Go to the end of the current document	Go to end of document
Select the word in the current document	Select *word*
Select the word range in the current document	Select *word range*; Select *word* through *word*
Select all text in the current document	Select all
Select the *1-20* words before the location of the cursor	Select previous *1-20* words; select previous *10* words
Select the *1-20* words after the location of the cursor	Select next *1-20* words; select next *10* words
Select the last text you dictated	Select that
Clear the selection on the screen	Clear selection
Capitalize the first letter of the word	Caps word

To do this	Say this
Capitalize all the letters of the word	All caps word
Make all the letters in the word lowercase	No caps word
Change the next *number of* words to uppercase	Change next *number of* words to uppercase
Change the next *number of* words to lowercase	Change next *number of* words to lowercase
Delete the previous sentence	Delete previous sentence
Delete the next sentence	Delete next sentence
Delete the previous paragraph	Delete previous paragraph
Delete the next paragraph	Delete next paragraph
Delete the selected or last dictated text	Delete that

Commands for Punctuation Marks and Special Characters

To make this appear	Say this	To make this appear	Say this
,	Comma	[	Open bracket; open square bracket
;	Semicolon	]	Close bracket; close square bracket
.	Period; dot; full stop; decimal point	|	Vertical bar
:	Colon	:-)	Press smiley face
"	Open double quote; open quote; open inverted commas	:-(	Press frowny face
"	Close double quote; close quote; close inverted commas	;-)	Press winky face
'	apostrophe	™	Trademark sign
'	Open single quote	¾	Three quarter sign
'	Close single quote	¼	One quarter sign
>	Greater than sign	½	One half sign
<	Less than sign	£	Pound sterling sign; pound; pound sign

To make this appear	Say this	To make this appear	Say this
/	Forward slash	&	Ampersand; and sign
\	Backslash	*	asterisk
~	Tilde	//	Double slash
@	At sign	`	Back quote
!	Exclamation mark; exclamation point	<	Open angle bracket
?	Question mark	>	Close angle bracket
#	Number sign; pound sign; hash sign	±	Plus or minus sign
$	Dollar sign	«	Open angle quote
%	Percent sign	»	Close angle quote
^	Caret	×	Multiplication sign
(	Open parenthesis; open paren	÷	Division sign
)	Close parenthesis; close paren	¢	Cent sign
_	Underscore	¥	Yen sign
-	Hyphen; minus sign; dash	§	Section sign
–	En dash	©	Copyright sign
—	Em dash; double dash	®	Registered sign; registered trademark sign
=	Equal sign	°	Degree sign
+	Plus sign	¶	Paragraph sign
{	Open brace; open curly bracket	…	Ellipsis; dot dot dot
}	Close brace; close curly bracket	ƒ	Function sign

Commands for Working with Windows and Programs

To do this	Say this
Open a program	Open *Paint*; open *WordPad*; open *program name*
Switch to an open program	Switch to *Paint*; switch to *WordPad*; switch to *program name*; switch *application*
Close a program	Close that; close *Paint*; close *Documents*; close *Internet Explorer* (works only with the active window)
Restore	Restore that; restore *Paint*; restore *Internet Explorer* (works only with the active window)
Minimize	Minimize that; minimize *Paint*; minimize *Internet Explorer* (works only with the active window)
Maximize	Maximize that; maximize *Paint*; maximize *Internet Explorer* (works only with the active window)
Cut	Cut that; cut
Copy	Copy that; copy
Paste	Paste
Delete	Delete that; delete
Undo	Undo that; scratch that; undo
Scroll *direction*	Scroll up; scroll down; scroll right; scroll left
Scroll an exact distance in pages	Scroll down 2 pages; scroll up 10 pages
Scroll an exact distance in other units	Scroll up 5; scroll down 7
Go to a field in a form or a program	Go to *field name*; go to *Subject*; go to *Address*; go to *Cc*

Creating Shortcuts to Files, Folders, and Programs

Shortcuts are icons on your desktop, on the Quick Launch toolbar, or on the Start menu that are linked to programs, folders, and files in other locations. Many programs give you the option of creating one or more shortcuts during installation, or in some cases, they create the shortcuts without asking.

You can create your own shortcuts on the desktop, and you can add a shortcut to the Quick Launch toolbar by dragging it from the desktop to the toolbar. You can also delete any shortcut you don't want. Deleting a shortcut does not delete the program, folder, or file that the shortcut is linked to.

In this exercise, you will create one desktop shortcut to a program and another to a Web site. There are no practice files for this exercise.

> **BE SURE TO** minimize any open windows before beginning this exercise.

1. Right-click an open area near the center of the desktop, point to **New**, and then click **Shortcut**.

   The Create Shortcut wizard starts.

   > **Tip** *Wizards* consist of a series of pages (similar to dialog boxes) that walk you through the steps necessary to accomplish a particular task. In this case, the wizard will prompt you for the information necessary to create a desktop shortcut.

2. Click **Browse**. In the **Browse for Files or Folders** dialog box, click the arrow to the left of **Computer** to expand the folder. Then expand **Local Disk (C:)** and **Program Files**.

Most programs create their own subfolder in the *Program Files* folder and then install most of the files they need to run in that subfolder.

3. In the **Select the target** box, expand the *Windows Sidebar* folder, click the **sidebar** file, and then click **OK**.

The path to the selected file appears in the Type The Location Of The Item box.

4. In the **Create Shortcut** wizard, click **Next**. On the wizard's second (and final) page, click **Finish** to create a shortcut with the same name as the selected file.

> **Tip** You can change the name that appears below the shortcut by replacing the text in the Type A Name box with the name you want. After you create the shortcut, you can change its name by clicking its icon, clicking its name to select it for editing, and then typing the new name.

A shortcut to the Windows Sidebar appears on the desktop in approximately the place you originally right-clicked. The shortcut icon matches the Windows Sidebar program icon.

> **Tip** You can change the size of your desktop icons by right-clicking the desktop, pointing to View, and then clicking Large Icons or Classic Icons. (The default selection is Medium Icons.)

5. If the Windows Sidebar is displayed on the right side of your screen, right-click it (don't right-click a gadget), and click **Close Sidebar**. Then double-click the **sidebar** shortcut to test that it works.

   The Windows Sidebar opens.

6. If you want, close the Windows Sidebar again. Then right-click another open area near the center of the desktop, point to **New**, and click **Shortcut**.

7. In the **Create Shortcut** wizard, in the **Type the location of the item** box, type http://www.msn.com. Then click **Next**.

8. In the **Type a name for this shortcut** box, replace *New Internet Shortcut* with MSN Web Site. Then click **Finish** to close the dialog box and create another shortcut.

   The Internet Explorer icon represents the Web site shortcut.

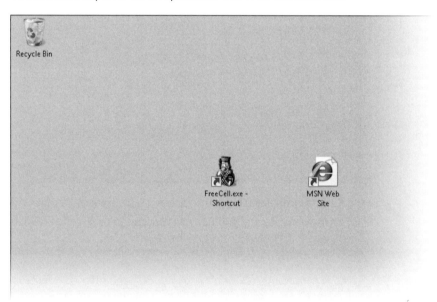

9. Double-click the **MSN Web Site** shortcut to open the MSN Web site in your default Web browser.

10. Click the Web browser window's **Close** button to close the window.

 BE SURE TO retain the two shortcuts for use in the next exercise.

Rearranging and Deleting Items on the Desktop

After you have installed several programs and created shortcuts to put the programs, folders, and files you use most often at your fingertips, your desktop might start to get pretty messy. To cope with the clutter, some people like to line up their icons and shortcuts in regimented rows, some like to arrange them as a sort of frame around the perimeter of their screen, and others like to group them by type in various discrete locations. You can organize your icons and shortcuts manually, or if you are happy with simple arrangements, you can have Windows Vista arrange them for you.

In this exercise, you will rearrange the items on your desktop, and then delete a shortcut from your desktop.

 USE the desktop shortcuts you created in the previous exercise. If you did not complete that exercise you can do so now, or use any desktop shortcuts of your own.

1. Drag your desktop shortcuts to random positions on the desktop.

Notice that as you drop the desktop shortcuts, they align to an invisible grid.

2. Right-click an empty area of the desktop, point to **View**, and then click **Auto Arrange**.

> **Tip** A check mark indicates when the Auto Arrange option is selected.

Windows Vista neatly arranges your shortcuts and icons on the left side of the desktop.

3. Now try to drag a shortcut to a different position on the desktop.

   You can move the shortcuts up and down, but not away from the left edge of the screen.

4. If you don't like the Auto Arrange feature, right-click an open area of the desktop, point to **View**, and then click **Auto Arrange** to turn it off.

5. Right-click the **MSN Web Site** shortcut, click **Delete**, and then in the confirmation message box, click **Yes**.

Key Points

- The Windows Vista user interface is designed to provide simple and intuitive access to the tools and information you need to do useful work.
- Files are organized on your computer in a folder structure. You can locate files by navigating through folders, or by entering file information in the Start Search box.
- You can locate Windows Vista settings and tools by clicking links in Control Panel or by entering search terms in the Control Panel Search box.
- The Start menu tracks recently opened files and programs so that you can easily reopen them.
- You can create and rearrange shortcuts to programs, folders, and files so that you can open them directly from the Start menu, desktop, or Quick Launch toolbar.
- You can customize the Windows desktop, including the Start menu, taskbar, and Quick Launch toolbar, to help you work most efficiently.

Keyboard Shortcuts

Press this	To do this
Ctrl+Esc or Windows logo key	Open or close the Start menu.
Windows logo key+D	Display the desktop.
Windows logo key+M	Minimize all windows.
Windows logo key+Shift+M	Restore all minimized windows.
Windows logo key+E	Open the Computer window.
Alt+Tab	Switch between open items.
Windows logo key+Tab	Cycle through programs by using Windows Flip 3-D.
Alt+Esc	Cycle through items in the order in which they were opened.

Chapter at a Glance

Navigate to folders and files, **page 76**

Create, rename, and delete folders and files, **page 97**

View information about a folder or file, **page 93**

Find specific information, **page 105**

View folders and files in different ways, **page 84**

3 Working with Folders and Files

In this chapter, you will learn to:

- ✔ Navigate to folders and files.
- ✔ View folders and files in different ways.
- ✔ View information about a folder or file.
- ✔ Create, rename, and delete folders and files.
- ✔ Move and copy folders and files.
- ✔ Find specific information.

To simplify the way you work with files on your computer, the Windows Vista interface uses a hierarchical storage system to organize information on your computer in the way you would organize information in an office. Instead of organizing paper files in paper folders in filing cabinets, you organize electronic files in electronic folders on the storage disks accessible to your computer.

There are many different types of files, but they fall into these two basic categories:

- **Files used or created by programs.** These include *executable files* and *dynamic-link libraries (DLLs)*. These files are usually installed to a program-specific subfolder of the *Program Files* folder on your primary hard disk drive. Some files may be hidden (not shown in a standard folder view) to protect them.

  > **Tip** Hidden files can't be selected or deleted; a folder might appear empty, but if it contains one or more hidden files, you cannot delete it. You can unhide files from the Folder Options dialog box discussed in "Viewing Files and Folders in Different Ways" later in this chapter.

- **Files created by you.** These include documents, spreadsheets, graphics, text files, slide shows, audio clips, video clips, and other things that you can open, look at, and change by using one or more programs.

The files installed with a program and those it creates for its own use are organized the way the program expects to find them, and you shouldn't move or remove them. You do, however, control the organization of the files you create (such as documents and spreadsheets), and knowing how to manage these files is essential if you want to be able to use your computer efficiently.

No matter how organized you are, there will be times when you can't remember where you stored a particular file. No problem! Windows Vista includes a powerful new search feature that can help you almost instantly locate files and other information on your computer.

In this chapter, you will use the Windows Vista navigation tools to explore the file storage structure on your computer. You will experiment with different ways of displaying information and learn how to find information. You will also create, edit, delete, move, and rename files, and search for files in various ways.

See Also Do you need only a quick refresher on the topics in this chapter? See the Quick Reference section at the beginning of this book.

Important Before you can use the practice files in this chapter, you need to install them from the book's companion CD to their default location. See "Using the Companion CD" at the beginning of this book for more information.

Navigating to Folders and Files

You view all the drives, folders, files, and peripherals that are part of your computer system, as well as those on any computers you are connected to through a network, in Windows Explorer. There are several ways to do this. For example, you can:

- Click a folder link on the Start menu to open that folder, and then:
  - Click Computer or Network to display an overview of all the hard disk drives and storage devices accessible to your computer.
  - Click your user name to open your personal folder, or click *Documents*, *Pictures*, or *Music* to open those subfolders directly.
- Point to All Programs on the Start menu, click Accessories, and then click Windows Explorer (or press Windows logo key+E) to display the contents of your *Documents* folder.
- Right-click a folder on the Start menu or desktop, and then click Explore.

The latter two options display the folder contents with the Folders list expanded in the Navigation pane.

Windows Explorer provides the means to manipulate folders and files in a variety of ways. For now, we will focus on the elements of the window that you use to navigate through the folder structure on your computer. In addition to the Address bar, Navigation pane, and Content pane discussed earlier in the book, these elements include the following:

● **Back button and Forward button.** Click these to display the contents of folders you have already viewed in the Content pane.

● **Recent Pages button.** Click this button to see a list of folders you have viewed so that you can select the one you want to display.

See Also For an introduction to the Windows Explorer window elements, see "Finding Your Way Around Your Computer" in Chapter 2, "Working Efficiently in Windows Vista."

In this exercise, you will navigate among folders in various ways.

> **USE** the practice folders and files located in the *Documents\Microsoft Press\ WindowsVistaSBS_Dlx\Files* folder.
> **BE SURE TO** log on to Windows Vista before beginning this exercise.

Start

1. Click the **Start** button, and then on the **Start** menu, click **Computer**.

In the window that opens, the Content pane displays information about the storage devices and locations accessible to your computer.

The Navigation pane displays the Favorite Links list and the Folders list.

2. If the Folders list is closed as shown above, expand it as shown below by clicking the **Folders** heading at the bottom of the **Navigation** pane.

> **Tip** Your Windows Explorer display depends on the storage structure of your computer and whether you have explored its contents before. As a result, it will be different than the one shown in our graphics, but you will still be able to follow the steps in this exercise.

The Favorite Links list displays links to:

- Your user profile–specific folders
- A virtual folder containing files you have recently worked with
- A folder containing dynamically updating links to past searches and standard search groups
- The *Public* folders on your computer

You can add items to the Favorite Links list by dragging them to the list.

The Folders list displays a hierarchical view (also called a *tree view*) of disks and folders. You can also access network resources, Control Panel tools, and the Recycle Bin from the Folders list.

3. In the **Content** pane, double-click the icon for your drive **C** (called *Local Disk (C:)* in the preceding graphic).

   The Content pane displays the folders and files stored on this disk. The Address bar reflects the fact that you are now looking at the contents of one of the drives accessible to your computer.

4. In the **Content** pane, double-click **Users**.

   The Content pane displays all the user profile folders currently set up on your computer.

5. In the **Content** pane, double-click your user profile folder.

   The Content pane displays your 11 personal content folders.

The currently displayed folder is also selected in the Folders list so that you can see your position within the overall storage hierarchy.

In some of these folders, such as *Documents*, you will store files; others, such as *Contacts*, will contain information you save through Windows Vista or Windows Internet Explorer.

See Also For information about Windows Contacts, see "Keeping Track of Contacts" in Chapter 10, "Staying Organized."

6. In the **Favorite Links** list, click **Documents**.

> **Tip** You can add any folder to the Favorite Links list by selecting it in the Content pane and dragging it to the list. A black bar indicates where the new link will appear when you release the mouse button.

The Address bar indicates that the contents of your *Documents* folder are currently displayed in the Content pane. At the top of the hierarchy in the Folders list, the link to the *Documents* folder within your personal folder is selected.

You can use the links in Favorite Links and the links at the top of the Folders list to jump quickly to the folders you will probably use most, without having to navigate through the storage structure to find them.

> **Troubleshooting** The *Microsoft Press* folder will appear in your *Documents* folder only if you installed the practice files for this book (or for another Microsoft Press book) in the default location. You can follow the steps in this exercise and the other exercises in this chapter using your own files, but to see the results shown, you need to install the practice files. Refer to "Using the Companion CD" at the beginning of this book for more information.

7. In the **Folders** list, point to **Documents**, and then click the white arrow to the left of the folder name. In the list of subfolders, click the white arrow to the left of *Microsoft Press*. Then click the white arrow to the left of *WindowsVistaSBS_Dlx*.

   Each time you click, the arrow turns black and the folder expands to show its contents. As the structure indents to the right with each click, the Folders list adjusts itself in the Navigation pane, scrolling up or down or to the left or right to give you the best view of the current items. By clicking the arrows in the Folders list rather than the folders in the Content pane, you expose the hierarchical structure without changing the display in the Content pane or the path in the Address bar.

8. In the **Folders** list, click *Files* to display that folder's contents in the Content pane.

   The Address bar changes to reflect the path of the displayed files.

Accessing Your Entire Network

If you are connected to a network, you can use Windows Explorer to navigate not only to drives and resources on your own computer, but also to drives and re- sources across your entire network. To display an overview of network resources, click Network on the Start menu.

If you want to access a particular network drive or resource on a regular basis— for example, if you regularly connect to a specific server—you can *map* the drive in Windows Explorer to make it more easily available. When you map a drive, you assign it a *local* drive letter so that it appears along with other available storage devices and locations when you view the contents of your computer. You can map a drive temporarily or instruct Windows to reconnect to that drive every time you log on.

To map a drive:

1. On the **Start** menu, click **Computer**.

2. On the toolbar above the Content pane, click **Map network drive**.

3. In the **Map Network Drive** window, specify the drive letter you want to use for this drive.

4. Click **Browse**, navigate to the drive or folder you want to map, and then click **OK** to return to the Map Network Drive window with the path entered in the Folder box.

5. If you want to connect to this location only until the end of the current Windows session, clear the **Reconnect at logon** check box.

6. Click **Finish**.

   The network drive opens in a new window.

To disconnect from a mapped drive or folder, right-click it, and then click Disconnect.

9. In the **Address** bar, click the arrow to the right of *Files*.

A list shows the subfolders within the *Files* folder.

10. In the list, click *Presentations* to display the files stored in that folder.

> **Tip** To close a list without making a selection, press the Esc key.

11. In the **Address** bar, click the arrow between *Files* and *Presentations*, and then in the subfolder list, click *Videos*.

By clicking the arrows between folders you can easily navigate to other folders in the same folder path.

Back

12. In the upper-left corner of the window, click the **Back** button to return to the most recently displayed folder, *Presentations*.

Notice that the Back button takes you back through your browsing history rather than back up the folder path.

13. In the **Folders** list, point to *Documents*, and then click its black arrow to collapse the hierarchical structure without changing the Content pane.

> **Tip** You might have to wait until *Documents* moves to the right in the Folders list to see its arrow.

Forward

14. Point to the **Forward** button to display a ScreenTip telling you where clicking the button will take you. Then click the **Forward** button to redisplay the *Videos* folder.

Recent Pages

15. To the right of the **Back** and **Forward** buttons, click the **Recent Pages** button.

The Recent Pages list displays the folders you have opened since opening the Computer window, in reverse order.

16. In the **Recent Pages** list, click **Computer** to return to your starting point.

17. Experiment with the Windows Explorer navigation features until you feel comfortable moving through your computer's storage structure in various ways.

Close

18. In the upper-right corner of the window, click the **Close** button to close Windows Explorer.

Viewing Folders and Files in Different Ways

The Windows Explorer window is dynamic and changes to reflect the content you are viewing. You can also customize the window to suit the way you work. The Back and Forward buttons, the Address bar, the Search box, the toolbar, and the Content pane are always displayed, but you can display or hide other elements by clicking Organize on the toolbar, clicking Layout, and then clicking the element. These optional elements include the following:

- **Navigation pane.** When you become accustomed to navigating from the Address bar, you might want to turn off the Navigation pane to provide more space for the Content pane.

- **Details pane.** This pane at the bottom of the window provides information about the displayed content, such as the number of items in a folder, or the file type of a selected file. This information might or might not be useful, depending on the Content pane view.

- **Menu bar.** If you prefer working with menus and commands rather than toolbar buttons, you can display the Menu bar above the toolbar.

- **Preview pane.** This pane on the right side of the window displays a preview of the content of a selected file so that you can see what it contains.

- **Search pane.** When you search for information on your computer, you can display this pane above the toolbar to refine the search.

In the Content pane, you can view folders and files in different ways by making a selection from the Views list on the toolbar. You can set the view for each folder, or you can set a default view for all folders. Available views include the following:

- **Icons.** The four Icon views (Extra Large, Large, Medium, and Small) display an icon and file name for each file or folder in the current folder. In all but Small Icons view, the icons display either the file type, or in the case of graphic files (including Microsoft Office PowerPoint slides) the actual file content. Folder icons display the contents of the folder.

- **List.** This view is similar to Small Icons view in that it shows the names of the files and folders accompanied by a small icon representing the file type.

- **Details.** This view displays a list of files or folders and their properties. The properties shown by default for each file or folder are Name, Date Modified, Type, Size, and Tags. You can hide any of these properties, and you can display a variety of other properties that might be pertinent to specific types of files, including Author and Title.

> **Tip** Although the Content pane always displays column headings, they are pertinent only to Details view.

- **Tiles.** This view displays a medium-size icon and the name, type, and size of each file or folder in the selected folder.

You can display the properties of a folder or file in the Details pane by selecting the folder or file in any view. You can further refine the display of files and folders by changing the settings in the Folder Options dialog box, which you can display by clicking Organize on the toolbar and then clicking Folder And Search Options. You can also change how you browse folders and whether you click or double-click to navigate in this dialog box.

For example, you can specify whether Windows Explorer and all Windows programs should display file name extensions, which are hidden by default. All file names have an extension, separated from the name itself by a period, that designates the file's type or the program in which it was created. If you often need to know the type of a file, it might be easier to turn on the display of file name extensions so that they are visible in all views than to have to constantly switch to Tiles or Details view to see the file type.

In this exercise, you will adjust the display of the Windows Explorer window and view the contents of a folder in different ways. You will also explore the Folder Options dialog box.

USE the *Presentations* subfolder and the practice files located in the *Documents\Microsoft Press\WindowsVistaSBS_Dlx\Files* folder.

1. On the **Start** menu, click **Computer**.

   The Computer window opens.

2. On the toolbar, click **Organize**, point to **Layout**, and then in the list, click **Details Pane** to hide the pane.

   > **Troubleshooting** If Details Pane does not have a blue border around it on the Organize list, it is already hidden, and you can skip step 2; otherwise, clicking Details Pane will display the pane instead of hiding it.

3. Display the **Organize** menu, point to **Layout**, and then click **Navigation Pane** to hide the pane.

   The Content pane now occupies the entire area below the toolbar.

   > **Tip** If you have changed the default folder view, your window might look different from this one.

4. In the **Address** bar, click the arrow to the left of **Computer**, and then click your personal folder.

5. In the **Content** pane, double-click *Documents*, double-click *Microsoft Press*, double-click *WindowsVistaSBS_Dlx*, double-click *Files*, and then double-click *Presentations*.

The *Presentations* folder contains two files, which are currently displayed in Details view.

6. On the toolbar, click the **Views** button (not the arrow) four times to cycle through the four most common views: Tiles, Large Icons, List, and Details.

7. In the **Address** bar, click *Files* to display the contents of that folder. Then if the folder is not displayed in Details view, click the **Views** button to switch to that view.

8. On the toolbar, click the **Views** arrow.

A list appears, showing the available view options. The slider on the left indicates which view is currently selected.

9. In the list, drag the slider up and down without releasing the mouse button, pausing to see the effect on the display in the Content pane.

10. Release the button when the slider is to the left of **Medium Icons**.

> **Tip** You can also switch views by clicking the view you want in the list.

Notice that the graphic files are represented by thumbnails, and the folders and other files are represented by type icons.

11. Display the **Views** list, and then click **Details**.

12. Point to each of the five column headings in turn (*Name*, *Date Modified*, *Type*, *Size*, and *Tags*).

    As the pointer passes over each heading, the heading changes color to indicate that it is selected, and an arrow appears at the heading's right end. You can click the arrow to filter the contents in various ways.

13. Click the **Size** heading (not its arrow).

    The files are sorted in descending order by file size, as indicated by the downward-pointing arrow above the *Size* heading.

14. Click **Size** again.

    The files are re-sorted in ascending order by file size, and the arrow changes direction to indicate the change of order.

15. Right-click anywhere in the column headings.

A list of attributes that might be attached to a file or folder appears; those currently displayed in Details view are indicated by check marks. *Name* is unavailable (gray) because the file name must be displayed.

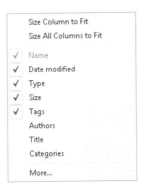

16. In the attributes list, click **Authors**.

A new *Authors* column is displayed, and the names of the people who created the files are listed.

17. Right-click anywhere in the column headings, and then in the attributes list, click **More**.

The Choose Details dialog box opens. The currently displayed properties appear at the top of the list.

18. Scroll through the list to see the approximately 240 file attributes you can display in Details view. Then clear the **Authors** check box, and click **OK**.

    The *Authors* column disappears from the window.

19. Click the **Name** column header to return to the default order. Then in the **Views** list, click **Tiles**.

    Tiles view displays a thumbnail or icon for each item, along with its name, file type, and file size.

20. On the **Organize** menu, click **Folder and Search Options**.

    The Folder Options dialog box opens, displaying the General tab. On this tab, you can change the basic way that Windows Explorer works.

> **Important** If you change any of the settings in the Folder Options dialog box, the instructions in this book might not work for your computer. We recommend that only experienced users of Windows Explorer change these options.

21. In the **Folder Options** dialog box, click the **View** tab.

    On this tab, you can set the default view for all folders, and you can change specific view settings.

    > **Tip** When you first start working in Windows Vista, the default view for each folder is determined by its type. If you apply the current folder view to all folders and then change your mind, you can click Reset Folders to restore the type-based default views. For information about folder types, see "Viewing Information About a Folder or File" later in this chapter.

22. Scroll the **Advanced settings** list, and note the ways you can change the Windows Explorer display.

    Notice that by default, Windows Vista system folders and files that have been assigned a hidden attribute are not shown. Also notice that extensions for known file types are hidden.

    If you don't want to view files in Details or Tiles view to ascertain their file types, you can clear the Hide Extensions For Known File Types check box to display file names with their extensions; for example, *cat.jpg*. Then the file name identifies the type of each file.

23. Click **Cancel** to close the dialog box without changing any settings.

> **BE SURE TO** redisplay the Navigation pane if you want to be able to use it to move around your computer.
>
> **CLOSE** the Files window.

Viewing Information About a Folder or File

Every file or folder has a variety of information associated with it, including its name, size, and author. You can view this information in several ways:

● Display the files and folders in Details view.

● Select a specific file or folder, and view some items of information in the Details pane.

● Point to a file to display a ScreenTip with some items of information.

● Right-click a file or folder, and click Properties to view all the available information in the Properties dialog box.

You can add a title to a file in the Details pane, and you can add and edit other information in the Properties dialog box.

In this exercise, you will view file information in the Details pane and add a title to a file. Then you'll display the Properties dialog box and add other information.

USE the *Videos* subfolder and the practice files located in the *Documents\Microsoft Press\ WindowsVistaSBS_Dlx\Files* folder.

BE SURE TO display your *Documents* folder before beginning this exercise.

1. Navigate to the *Microsoft Press\WindowsVistaSBS_Dlx\Files* folder, and display the contents in **Tiles** view.

2. If the **Details** pane isn't open, point to **Layout** on the **Organize** menu, and then in the list, click **Details Pane**.

   The Details pane indicates that there are 35 items in the *Files* folder.

3. In the **Content** pane, click the *Costs* worksheet.

   The Details pane displays the file's icon, name, type, authors, size, and date modified, with placeholders to a title and tags.

4. In the **Details** pane, click **Add a title**.

   The Title box becomes editable.

5. In the **Title** box, type Disorganization, and then click **Save**.

   After Windows Vista updates the file properties, the title appears in the Details pane.

6. In the **Content** pane, point to *Costs*.

A ScreenTip displays several items of information about the file, including the title you just created. The modification date and time given reflect the date and time you added the title to the file properties.

7. Right-click *Costs*, and then click **Properties**.

> **Tip** You can also display a file's properties by selecting the file and then clicking Properties on the Organize menu.

The Costs Properties dialog box opens. The General tab gives overview information about the file; the Security tab gives information about who can use the file; and the Previous Versions tab lists previous versions that you can restore if you need to.

> **Tip** As long as a file is stored in a subfolder of your personal folder, other people cannot access it unless they know your user account credentials. However, if you work on a network with shared folders, or if you need to store a file in the *Public* folder so that it is accessible to other users of your computer, you might want to limit who can do what with the file. You cannot set a password for a file or folder in Windows but you can assign permissions to specific users or groups of users on the Security tab of the file's Properties dialog box. On that tab, you can click the Learn About Access Control And Permissions link to display a detailed Help topic.

8. In the **Costs Properties** dialog box, click the **Details** tab.

This tab displays all the file's properties. If you can change a property, pointing to its right displays a box where you can enter or edit the information.

9. On the **Details** tab, point to the right of **Tags**, click the box that appears, and type
    e. Then wait a few seconds.

    A list appears, displaying tags beginning with the letter *e* that are assigned to files
    in this folder (in this case, there are two—*efficiency* and *Excel*).

10. Select the *efficiency* check box to insert that tag.

    Now when you search for all files associated with *efficiency*, this file will be part of
    the search results, even though that word doesn't appear in the file.

    See Also For information about searching for files, see "Finding Specific Information"
    later in this chapter.

11. Click **OK** to close the dialog box.

12. In the **Content** pane, double-click the *Videos* folder.

    The folder contents appear in Details view. The Type column indicates that the one
    item in this folder is a Windows Media Audio/Video file.

13. Right-click a blank area of the **Content** pane, and then click **Properties**.

The Videos Properties dialog box opens. The General, Security, and Previous Versions tabs provide the same information as the corresponding tabs in a file's Properties dialog box. You can use the options on the Sharing tab to share this folder with colleagues on a network.

See Also For information about sharing folders, see "Sharing Drives and Folders" in Chapter 8, "Making Connections."

14. In the **Videos Properties** dialog box, click the **Customize** tab.

This folder is assigned the Documents type.

15. Click the **Use this folder type as a template** arrow, and in the list, click **Pictures and Videos**. Then click **OK**.

The folder contents now appear in Large Icons view, because that view is more suited to quickly identifying pictures and videos. The toolbar now has a Slide Show button, which you can click to see a full-screen view of the files in the folder.

 CLOSE the Videos window.

Tip You can quickly remove the properties from a file you have created (but not from a folder) by selecting the file and then clicking Remove Properties on the Organize menu. In the Remove Properties dialog box, you can then select the properties you want to remove.

Creating, Renaming, and Deleting Folders and Files

With each program you use on your computer, you create files of a particular type. For example, with Microsoft Office Word 2007, you create documents (*.docx* files); with Microsoft Office Excel 2007, you create workbooks (*.xlsx* files); and with Microsoft Office PowerPoint 2007, you create presentations (*.pptx* files). Windows Vista also provides programs—Notepad, WordPad, and Paint—that you can use to create and edit simple text documents and graphics.

See Also For information about WordPad and Paint, see Chapter 11, "Working with Graphics and Documents."

With most programs, the files you create are only temporary until you save them to your hard disk or to another location, such as a USB flash drive. (Certain programs that create more complex files, such as Microsoft Office Access, must save a file or file structure to a specific location when creating a new file.) Each program may have a default location for saving new files—for example, to your *Documents* folder or to a program-specific folder within the *Program Files* folder on your primary hard disk drive.

As you create files, you will also want to create folders in which to organize the files for easy retrieval. Often you will need to rename a folder or file to accurately reflect its content. And periodically you will want to delete folders and files you no longer need. For safety reasons, removing a file from your computer is a two-step process: You first delete the file, which moves it to the Recycle Bin—a holding area on your hard drive from which is it possible to restore an item if you realize you need it. Then you periodically empty the Recycle Bin, which permanently erases its contents.

> **Tip** The contents of the Recycle Bin take up space on your hard disk. If you need this space, and are absolutely positive you will never need to restore a deleted file, you can instruct Windows to erase items immediately when you delete them. To do so, right-click the Recycle Bin, click Properties, and click Do Not Move Files To The Recycle Bin.

When you buy a computer these days, it likely comes with a hard disk that will store several *gigabytes (GB)* of information. A gigabyte is 1 billion *bytes*, and a byte is a unit of information that is the equivalent of one character. Some of your files will be very small—1 to 2 *kilobytes (KB)*, or 1000 to 2000 characters—and others might be quite large—several *megabytes (MB)*, or several million characters. The small ones are easy to copy and move around, but large files or large groups of files are easier to copy and move from one place to another, or to send by e-mail, if you *compress* them. You can compress files you created, program files, or even other folders into a compressed folder that is identified by a zipper on its folder icon.

In this exercise, you will create a new folder and two new files: a text document and a picture. After renaming one of the files, you will compress the two files and then delete all the files and folders you created in the exercise. There are no practice files for this exercise.

BE SURE TO display your *Documents* folder and the Details pane before beginning this exercise.

1. Navigate to the *Documents\Microsoft Press\WindowsVistaSBS_Dlx\Files* folder, and display its contents in **Tiles** view.

2. On the **Organize** menu, click **New Folder**.

   A new folder appears in the Content pane, with the name *New Folder* selected so that you can change it.

3. Press the [Home] key, type My followed by a space, and then press [Enter].

4. Press [Enter] again to open the empty folder.

5. Right-click anywhere in the **Content** pane, point to **New**, and then click **Text Document**.

   A new text document is created, with the name *New Text Document* selected so that you can change it.

6. Double-click **New**, type My followed by a space, and then press [Enter].

   The file name, date, type, and size are displayed to the right of the file's icon. Because the file is empty, the size is 0 KB.

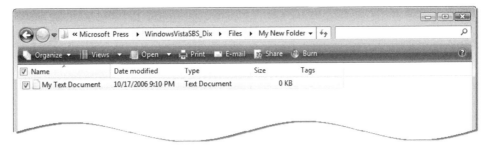

7. Press Enter again to open the file.

   The text document opens in the Microsoft Notepad program, a text-editing program that comes with Windows Vista.

   > **Troubleshooting** If the document opens in a different program, that program has been designated as your default text editor. You can follow the next two steps in that program.

8. Type This is a text file.

Close

9. Click the **Close** button to close the file, and click **Save** when prompted to save your changes.

   The file size reported in the Content pane is 1 KB because the size is rounded up to the nearest whole kilobyte. However, the size reported in the Details pane is the actual size of 20 bytes.

File size rounded to nearest kilobyte

Actual file size

10. Right-click a blank area of the **Content** pane, point to **New**, and then click **Bitmap Image**.

A new graphic file is created, with the name *New Bitmap Image* selected so that you can change it.

11. Change the name of the file to My Bitmap Image, and then press Enter.

When you rename the file, it moves to the top of the file list to maintain the alphabetical sort order.

> **Tip** *Bitmap* images represent images as dots, or *pixels*, on the screen and are saved in the bitmap (*.bmp*) format.

12. Right-click the graphic file, and then click **Edit**.

The blank graphic file opens in the Microsoft *Paint* program, a simple graphics program that comes with Windows Vista.

> **Troubleshooting** If the image opens in a different program, that program has been designated as your default graphics editor. You can follow the next step in that program.

13. Experiment with the Paint tools while creating a picture of any kind. (Click a tool, move the pointer over the blank canvas, and drag the pointer to use the tool.) When you're done, click the **Close** button to close the file, and click **Save** when prompted to save your changes.

In the Content pane, the Size column reflects the size of the graphic. The Details pane displays a thumbnail of the graphic you created, and reports the file's dimensions as well as its size. If you want, you can switch to an icon view to see an image of the graphic.

14. With *My Bitmap Image* selected, point to *My Text Document*, and then add it to the selection by selecting the check box that appears to its left.

> **Troubleshooting** Check boxes are turned on by default in certain editions of Windows Vista, and not in others. If you don't see a check box when you point to a file or folder in the Content pane, display the View tab of the Folder Options dialog box, select the Use Check Boxes To Select Items check box in the Advanced Settings list, and then click OK.

The Details pane indicates that two items are selected and reports the total size of the selection. Because the file sizes in the Content pane are rounded up, the total in the Details pane might be less than the sum of the individual file sizes.

15. Right-click the selection, point to **Send To**, and then click **Compressed (zipped) Folder**.

A compressed folder named for one of the selected files is created. The folder name is selected so that you can change it.

16. Type My Compressed Folder, and then press Enter.

17. Double-click the compressed folder to open it.

The Content pane now displays the files that have been compressed into the zipped folder. The Extract All Files button on the toolbar and the zipped folder icon in the Details pane indicate that you are viewing a compressed folder rather than a standard folder.

18. Point to the right border of the Name column heading, and when the pointer changes to a bar with opposing arrows, double-click. Then double-click the right borders of the other column headings to see all the information available in Details view.

File-compression information

Compressed folder icon

19. In the upper-left corner of the window, click the **Back** button to redisplay the contents of the *My New Folder* folder.

Back

Because you created a graphic in this folder, it has been assigned the Pictures And Video type, with a default view of Large Icons.

20. Click *My Bitmap Image* to select it, hold down the ⌨Ctrl key, and click *My Text Document* to add it to the selection. Then press the ⌨Del key, and click **Yes** to confirm the deletion.

> **Tip** You can also delete a file or folder by selecting it and then clicking Delete on the Organize menu. You cannot delete a file by pressing the Backspace key.

21. If the **Navigation** pane is not displayed, point to **Layout** on the **Organize** menu, and then click **Navigation Pane**. Scroll to the bottom of the **Navigation** pane, and then click **Recycle Bin**.

The Recycle Bin contains all the files you have deleted. The toolbar displays the Empty The Recycle Bin and Restore All Items buttons so that you can quickly perform those tasks.

22. Right-click *My Text Document*, and then click **Restore**.

The file is moved from the Recycle Bin back to the location from which it was deleted.

23. Scroll up in the **Navigation** pane, and click the *My New Folder* subfolder of the *Files* folder to see the restored file.

CLOSE the My New Folder window.

Moving and Copying Folders and Files

When you have accumulated enough files that you need to organize them in some way, you can easily move files and folders from one location to another. The methods of copying, pasting, moving, and renaming are the same for both files and folders.

One of the ways you might want to organize your files is by type. As you saw in "Viewing Information About a Folder or File" earlier in this chapter, Windows Vista includes four types of folders that are designed to hold files of a certain type: Documents, Pictures and Videos, Music Details, and Music Icons. When you display the contents of the folder, buttons on the toolbar provide easy access to features appropriate for that type of file, such as playing music or viewing photographs.

> **Tip** To easily share files with other people using your computer or with other computers in a workgroup, store them in the *Public* folder.

In this exercise, you will make copies of files and folders and then move files between folders.

USE the *Narrations* and *Photographs* subfolders and the practice files located in the *Documents\Microsoft Press\WindowsVistaSBS_Dlx\Files* folder.

BE SURE TO display your *Documents* folder, the Details pane, and the Navigation pane before beginning this exercise.

1. Navigate to the *Documents\Microsoft Press\WindowsVistaSBS_Dlx\Files* folder.

2. With the contents of the *Files* folder displayed in the Content pane in **Details** view, click the *Introduction* audio file to select it. Then on the **Organize** menu, click **Copy**.

   Nothing seems to happen.

3. Right-click the *Narrations* folder, and then click **Paste**.

   The folder's modification date changes to reflect when the folder was modified.

4. Double-click the *Narrations* folder to verify that it now contains a copy of the *Introduction* file.

   A Play All button appears on the toolbar so that you can play the audio file if you want.

Back

5. Click the **Back** button, select the *Introduction* file, and delete it, clicking **Yes** when prompted to confirm the deletion.

6. In the **Content** pane, right-click *Cat*, and click **Cut**. Then right-click the *Photographs* folder, and click **Paste**.

   The *Cat* image moves to the *Photographs* folder.

7. Click the **Type** column heading to sort the files by type.

8. Click *Crow* (the first JPEG image file in the list), hold down the [Shift] key, and click *Frog*. Then on the **Organize** menu, click **Cut**.

9. Right-click the *Photographs* folder, and then click **Paste**.

   The selected JPEG image files move to the folder.

10. In the **Content** pane, drag the *MusicBox* file to the *Photographs* folder, but don't release the mouse button.

    The *Photographs* folder is highlighted, and a ScreenTip appears with the instruction *Move to Photographs*.

11. Release the mouse button to move the file.

    > **Tip** To copy a file by dragging it, point to the file, hold down the Ctrl key, and then drag the copy to its new location, releasing first the mouse button and then the Ctrl key.

12. In the **Navigation** pane, click *Photographs* to display its contents in the Content pane.

    Because this folder has been designated as a Picture And Video folder, the toolbar includes a Slide Show button. .

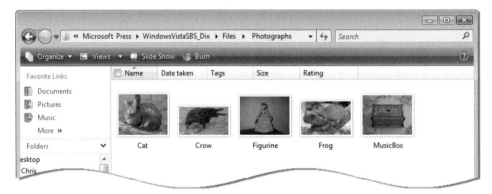

13. Click the first image in the file (*Cat*), and on the toolbar, click **Slide Show**.

    The *Cat* graphic is displayed full-screen. After a few seconds, the next graphic appears.

14. After the slide show has cycled through all the graphics in the folder, press the [Esc] key to end the slide show.

CLOSE the Photographs window.

Finding Specific Information

As far as we are concerned, the awesome new search capabilities of Windows Vista are one of its three best features. (The others are Sleep mode and the amazing graphic capabilities—for those people with video cards capable of supporting them.)

With Windows Vista, you can find files, messages, and message attachments on your computer almost instantly. You don't need to know the name of the file or item you want to find; simply type a word or phrase in the Start Search box on the Start menu or the Search box in the upper-right corner of a Windows Explorer window to display a list of matching items. If you want to find information on the Internet, click the Search The Internet link that appears above the Start Search box on the Start menu to open the Windows Live Search site displaying links to sites related to the term you typed.

How does Windows Vista find items so quickly? Behind the scenes, Windows Vista maintains an index of all the key words in and associated with the data files on your computer—documents, music, videos, graphics, local copies of e-mail messages, Web pages stored in your recent history or Favorites list, and so on. (It does not include the system or program files; such an index would be huge and would slow down the search process.) When you type a search term, Windows looks for it in the index instead of searching your hard disk. You shouldn't ever need to worry about the index, but after you have some experience with searching, you might want to check Windows Help And Support for information about index locations and settings.

> **Tip** After a lot of file moving or renaming, your search results might seem inaccurate because the index is out of date. Just be patient. If you have a lot of files stored on your computer, it can take Windows several hours to update its index. If you need to force Windows Vista to update the index, you can open Control Panel, click System And Maintenance, and then click Indexing Options. In the Indexing Options dialog box, click Advanced, and then in the Advanced Options dialog box, click Rebuild.

If a simple search in the Start Search or Search box doesn't locate the item you are looking for, you can perform more advanced searches in the *Search Results* folder. Your search criteria can include the date a file was created, its size, part of its name or title, its author, and any tags you might have listed as properties of the file.

In this exercise, you will quickly locate items on your computer and on the Internet. You will then use advanced criteria in the *Search Results* folder to look for other files and will open the Preview pane to help identify the correct file.

USE the practice files located in the *Documents\Microsoft Press\WindowsVistaSBS_Dlx\ Files* folder.

1. Click the **Start** button.

Start

The Start menu opens with the insertion point blinking in the Start Search box at the bottom.

2. In the **Start Search** box, type bamboo.

As you type, Windows filters the programs, files, folders, and e-mail messages stored on your computer and displays a list of items (only as many as will fit on the Start menu) related to your search term.

Tip If your search returns more results than can be shown, you can display the entire list in the Search Results window by clicking See All Results.

3. Point to each file in the search results in turn to display a ScreenTip with the file's properties.

If you get in the habit of entering properties for your files, this handy trick can help you quickly identify the file you want.

4. At the bottom of the **Start** menu, click the **Search the Internet** link.

Your Web browser starts, displaying the results of a Windows Live Search for *bamboo*.

5. Close your Web browser.

6. On the **Start** menu, click **Search**.

The *Search Results* folder opens in a window.

7. In the upper-right corner of the window, in the **Search** box, type bamboo.

The *Search Results* window displays the files that match the search term. You can change the view and sort the files the same way you would with any folder.

See Also For information about changing views and sorting files, see "Viewing Folders and Files in Different Ways" earlier in this chapter.

8. On the **Search** toolbar, to the right of **Show only**, click **Picture**.

The Picture filter hides any file in the search results that is not a graphic, and the view switches to Large Icons so that you can see thumbnails of the graphics.

9. Double-click the word **bamboo** in the **Search** box, and then type statue.

No items match this search term.

10. At the right end of the **Search** toolbar, click the **Advanced Search** arrow.

The Search pane opens at the top of the window.

When a simple search term fails to find the file you are looking for, you can use the options in this pane to supply more information about the file.

11. Click the **any** box to the right of **Date taken**, and then in the list, click **is before**. Then click the date box to the right, and use the calendar to set the date to **December 31, 2006**.

12. Delete the word **statue** from the **Search** box. Then in the **Tag** box, type statue*, and click **Search**.

You have specified that you want to find a picture created before December 31, 2006 that has some variation of the word *statue* (perhaps *statues* or *statuette*) in the title. The Search Results window displays two files that match these criteria.

> **Tip** In searches, the asterisk (*) is a *wildcard character* that represents any number of characters (including zero). The question mark (?) represents one character. For example, enter *.txt* to search for any text file; enter *s*.txt* to search for any text file with a file name that begins with the letter *s*; and enter *s??.txt* to search for any text file that has a three-letter file name beginning with the letter *s*.

13. Click the **is before** box to the right of **Date taken**, and then in the list, click **any**. Then click the **Advanced Search** arrow to close the Search pane.

> **Troubleshooting** If you don't reset the date criteria, the date setting will be applied to future searches.

14. To the right of **Show only** on the **Search** toolbar, click **All**. Then select the contents of the **Search** box, and type tag.

The Search Results window displays any file that has *tag* in its file name or in its text. In this case, you are looking for a file containing an announcement from Lucerne Publishing about a new book series called *The Taguien Cycle*.

15. On the **Organize** menu, point to **Layout**, and then click **Preview Pane**.

The Preview pane opens on the right side of the window.

16. Click the first file in the search results to view its contents in the Preview pane.

17. Press the ↓ key to preview each file in turn.

CLOSE the Search Results window.

Key Points

- Windows Explorer provides several ways to move around your computer. Becoming familiar with them will increase your ability to quickly find specific files.

- Displaying the folders and files in different ways can help you identify them more easily.

- Windows Vista displays graphic representations of the files and folders on your computer. Different file types are represented by different graphic icons, so you can differentiate between them at a glance.

- In addition to its name, properties such as size, author, and date of creation or modification are stored with each file. You can view and change this information in the file's Properties dialog box.

- To organize folders and files in a logical structure, you can rename, move, copy, and delete them.

- You can quickly locate information on your computer by using a search term, or you can use the Search pane to set up search criteria with whatever information you have available.

Keyboard Shortcuts

Press this	To do this
F3 or Windows logo key+F	Search for a file or folder.
Windows logo key+E	Open the Computer window.
Ctrl+Windows logo key+F	Search for computers on a network.

Press this	To do this in Windows Explorer
Ctrl+C	Copy the selection.
Ctrl+X	Cut the selection.
Ctrl+V	Paste the selection.
Delete	Delete the selected item and move it to the Recycle Bin.
Shift+Delete	Delete the selected item without first moving it to the Recycle Bin.
F2	Rename the selected item.
Shift+Arrow key	Select more than one item in a window.
Ctrl+A	Select all items in a window.
Alt+Enter	Display properties for the selected item.
F4	Expand the Address bar list.
Alt+Up Arrow	View the folder one level up.
End	Display the bottom of the active window.
Home	Display the top of the active window.
Left Arrow	Collapse the current selection (if it is expanded), or select the parent folder.
Alt+Left Arrow	View the previous folder.
Right Arrow	Display the current selection (if it is collapsed), or select the first subfolder.
Alt+Right Arrow	View the next folder.

Chapter at a Glance

Change the desktop
background, **page 126**

Optimize visual effects,
page 118

Manage your system
date and time, **page 133**

4 Personalizing Windows Vista

In this chapter, you will learn to:

✔ Change the the look of Windows Vista on your screen.

✔ Optimize visual effects.

✔ Change the desktop background.

✔ Select and manage a screen saver.

✔ Manage your system date and time.

✔ Change your computer's name.

The way programs look on your computer screen and the way you use them are to a large extent determined by the Windows Vista user interface. Some elements of the interface, such as the graphics, fonts, and colors, might seem merely cosmetic but they can affect the way you work. You can personalize almost any aspect of your computer's appearance and functionality to suit your needs and preferences.

In this chapter, you will change the appearance of Windows Vista by working with themes, color schemes, and backgrounds. You will also select a screen saver, update the system date and time, and change the name by which your computer is identified on a network.

See Also Do you need only a quick refresher on the topics in this chapter? See the Quick Reference section at the beginning of this book.

Important Before you can use the practice files in this chapter, you need to install them from the book's companion CD to their default location. See "Using the Companion CD" at the beginning of this book for more information.

Changing the Look of Windows Vista on Your Screen

You can easily change the look of the Windows interface by applying a different *theme*. A theme usually includes a desktop background color or picture; a color scheme that affects title bars and labels; specific fonts that are used on title bars, labels, and buttons; sounds that are associated with specific actions; and other elements. Previous versions of Windows came with a long list of available themes, and additional themes could be downloaded from the Internet. Windows Vista has simplified the theme-selection process by offering only two themes—Windows Vista and Windows Classic. You can search for other themes online, or possibly purchase theme packs from software retailers.

In this exercise, you will switch between the Windows Vista and Windows Classic themes. If you want, you can explore the online options on your own at a later time. There are no practice files for this exercise.

BE SURE TO log on to Windows Vista and display Control Panel before beginning this exercise.

1. In **Control Panel**, click **Appearance and Personalization**.

   The Appearance And Personalization window opens.

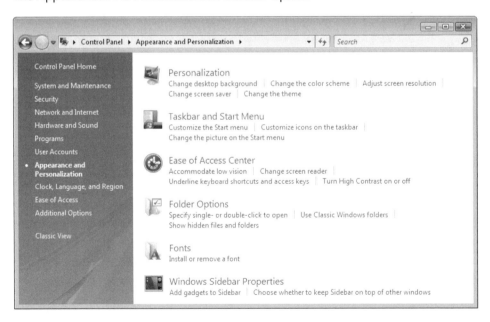

2. Under **Personalization**, click the **Change the theme** task.

   The Theme Settings dialog box opens, displaying a preview of the current theme.

3. Click the **Theme** arrow, and then in the list, click **Windows Classic**.

   The Sample box changes to reflect your selection. You might recognize this theme if you previously used a computer running Windows 2000.

4. Click **OK** to close the dialog box and apply your settings.

   The left pane of the Appearance And Personalization window now has a white background. The font, title bar, and buttons have changed, and if you were displaying the Windows Aero interface, you'll notice even more changes, such as the absence of transparency in the window frames.

5. In the **Appearance and Personalization** window, point to **Personalization** to view the Windows Classic item selection indicator.

Minimize

6. In the upper-right corner of the **Appearance and Personalization** window, click the **Minimize** button.

   The solid blue Windows Classic desktop looks quite dull compared to the Windows Vista desktop. The taskbar has changed from blue to gray; the Start button from round to rectangular; and Windows Sidebar, if it is displayed, from translucent to solid gray.

7. On the taskbar, click the **Control Panel\Appearance and Personalization** taskbar button to redisplay the window.

8. Under **Personalization**, click the **Change the theme** task to redisplay the **Theme Settings** dialog box.

9. In the **Theme** list, click **Windows Vista**.

   The Sample box displays the Windows Vista default desktop. Regardless of the desktop background you were displaying before beginning this exercise, the default desktop depicting a lake and mountain scene is shown.

10. In the **Theme Settings** dialog box, click **OK**.

Your desktop, Start button, taskbar, Sidebar, and open windows now have the default Windows Vista look and feel.

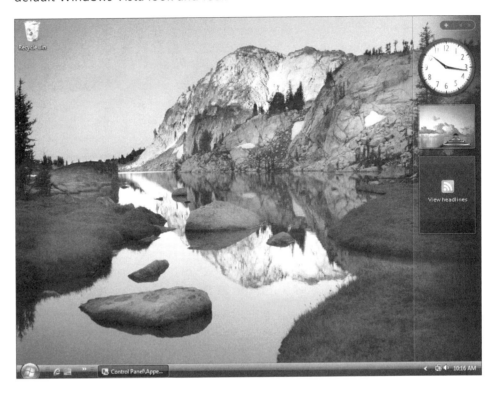

> **Tip** You'll be working with the desktop background in the next exercise, so there is no need to reset your desktop background before continuing.

 CLOSE the Appearance And Personalization window.

Optimizing Visual Effects

In the previous exercise, you set the desktop theme, which selected the Windows Vista background, sounds, icons, buttons, windows shape, and so on. These options provide a pleasant user interface and are available on any computer running Windows Vista. However, the pinnacle of the Windows Vista visual experience is Windows Aero, which is identified within Windows Vista as a color scheme, but is so much more than simply colors. It is truly a thing of beauty, incorporating soft edges, shadows, transparent window frames, animated window transitions, active previews of hidden windows from the taskbar, and a three-dimensional rotating stack display. In short, all the bells and whistles! Unfortunately, Windows Aero works only on systems that have the necessary hardware configuration, which includes:

- 1 GHz 32-bit (x86) or 64-bit (x64) processor
- 1 GB of RAM
- 128 MB graphics adapter
- DirectX 9-class graphics processor that supports a Windows Display Driver Model Driver, Pixel Shader 2.0, and 32 bits per pixel

If you purchased your computer before 2006, it is unlikely that it meets these requirements (unless your computer is set up for gaming or professional graphics production). You might be able to upgrade your system by purchasing more RAM and a new graphics card. If your hardware does meet the minimum requirements, you will have the pleasure of the Windows Aero experience when running these Windows Vista editions:

- Windows Vista Home Premium
- Windows Vista Ultimate
- Windows Vista Business
- Windows Vista Enterprise

> **Tip** Don't know which edition of Windows Vista is installed on your computer? Click System And Maintenance in Control Panel, and then click Welcome Center. The edition is reported at the top of the Welcome Center window.

If you purchased a Windows Aero-qualified computer system with Windows Vista already installed, Windows Aero was probably turned on when you first started the computer. If you upgraded your hardware or upgraded to Windows Vista from a previous version of Windows, you might need to make some adjustments.

In this exercise, you will check your hardware configuration to see whether it meets Windows Aero requirements, set the monitor colors and refresh rate to the levels necessary to support Windows Aero, and then configure the Windows Aero color scheme, including window frame transparency. There are no practice files for this exercise.

Tip The screens shown in other exercises in this book are captured with Windows Aero and font smoothing turned off, because those features do not present as clearly on the printed page.

OPEN Control Panel.

1. In **Control Panel**, click **System and Maintenance**, and then click **System**.

   The System window opens.

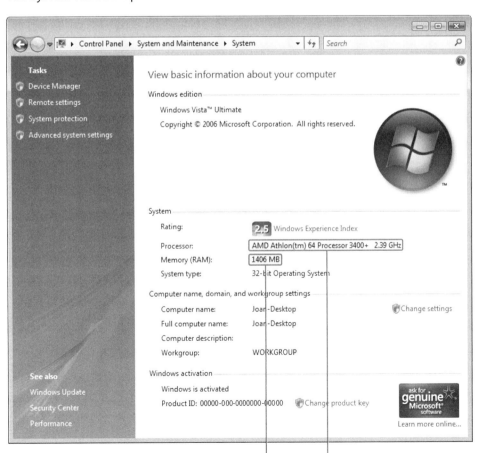

RAM   Processor speed

Your processor speed and installed RAM are shown under System. You need a processor speed of at least 1.0 GHz, and at least 1 GB (1024 MB) of RAM to display Windows Aero features.

2. In the **Address** bar, click the arrow to the right of **Control Panel**, and then in the list, click **Appearance and Personalization**.

3. In the **Appearance and Personalization** window, click **Personalization**.

The Personalization window opens. From this window, you can customize any aspect of the Windows Vista user interface.

> **Tip** You can display the Personalization window by right-clicking the desktop and then clicking Personalize.

4. In the **Personalization** window, click **Display Settings**. Then in the **Display Settings** dialog box, click **Advanced Settings** to display information about your graphics adapter.

Graphics adapter memory

Windows Aero features require 128 MB of dedicated video memory.

5. In the **Advanced Settings** dialog box, click the **Monitor** tab. In the **Monitor Settings** area, click the **Screen refresh rate** arrow to display a list of valid refresh rates for the selected monitor.

> **Tip** The screen refresh rate, which varies from monitor to monitor, determines the number of times per second your monitor redraws the image. At lower refresh rates, the monitor may appear to be flickering rather than displaying a constant picture, and this can lead to eyestrain. A refresh rate of 70 Hertz (Hz) or above is considered to be flicker-free.

6. Select a screen refresh rate of at least 10 Hertz, preferably 70 or over. Then click **OK**.

7. If your computer system includes multiple monitors on the same graphics adapter or multiple enabled graphics adapters, select the other monitors in turn, click **Advanced Settings**, confirm the available graphics memory, select an appropriate refresh rate, and click **OK**.

8. In the **Display Settings** dialog box, click the **Colors** arrow to display the available color qualities.

9. Set the color quality to at least **32 bit**. Then click **OK**.

10. In the **Personalization** window, click **Window Color and Appearance**.

   If the Window Color And Appearance page opens, then Windows Aero is already selected as your color scheme; skip to step 15 to continue. Otherwise, the Appearance Settings dialog box opens.

11. In the **Color scheme** list, click **Windows Aero**. Then click **Effects**.

> **Troubleshooting** The Windows Aero option appears only if your hardware supports it.

12. In the **Effects** dialog box, select the **Use the following method to smooth edges of screen fonts** check box if it is not already selected, and in the list, click **ClearType**. Then click **OK** in each of the two open dialog boxes.

Windows Vista applies the Windows Aero interface. One effect you might immediately notice regardless of other settings is the change in the appearance of the Personalization window; the title bar takes on a subtle pattern, and if transparency is already enabled, you can see right through the window frame to whatever is behind the window.

> **Troubleshooting** Screens shown in the remainder of this exercise depict the full Windows Aero user interface; this interface is beautiful on screen, but might not display as well on the printed grayscale page of this book, so you'll need to rely on what you see on screen for a true representation.

13. Point to the **Personalization** taskbar button.

A thumbnail representation of the window appears. This is another effect of Windows Aero.

Thumbnail preview

14. In the **Personalization** window, click **Window Color and Appearance**.

When the Windows Aero color scheme is in effect, clicking this link opens the Window Color And Appearance page.

15. Click each of the eight color icons at the top of the page in turn.

The current selection is immediately previewed in the frame of the Window Color And Appearance page. The subtle pattern in the window frame might be more apparent against darker colors. You can tailor any of the colors to your liking by clicking Show Color Mixer and then adjusting the Hue, Saturation, and Brightness.

16. Select the **Enable transparency** check box, or if it is already selected, clear it and then reselect it.

Notice the subtle change between the transparent and solid window frames.

17. With the **Enable transparency** check box selected, drag the active window around the screen so that its title bar passes over another screen element such as a picture on the desktop background, the Sidebar, or a desktop icon.

You can see through the top, bottom, and both sides of the window frame, although the transparency is most noticeable in the title bar. The Default color provides the most transparency.

Transparent title bar

18. On the **Window Color and Appearance** page, click **OK**.

CLOSE the Personalization window.

Changing the Desktop Background

If the default Windows Vista desktop background doesn't appeal to you or if you want to change the background for another reason, you can do so at any time. Your choice of background usually reflects your personal taste—what you like to see when your program windows are minimized or closed. Some people prefer simple backgrounds that don't interfere with their desktop icons, and others like photos of family members, pets, or favorite places.

Windows Vista comes with over 35 desktop backgrounds to choose from, including photographs, paintings, and computer art. You can preview each background on your desktop before actually applying it. If you prefer, you can opt for a plain background and then set its color. You can also choose from the 15 sample photos that come with Windows Vista or any digital image of your own.

In this exercise, you will preview the available desktop background options, and display a photograph as your background. Then you will switch to a plain, solid color background.

> **USE** the images located in the *Documents\WindowsVistaSBS_Dlx\Backgrounds* folder.
> **OPEN** Control Panel.

1. In **Control Panel**, under **Appearance and Personalization**, click the **Change desktop background** task.

   The Desktop Background page opens, with Windows Wallpapers selected in the Picture Location list, and thumbnails of the available wallpapers grouped in categories in the box below, scrolled to the category containing your current desktop.

   > **Troubleshooting** If your desktop background is currently set to something other than one of the Windows Wallpapers, that category is selected in the Picture Location list and shown in the box.

> **Tip** If Use Check Boxes To Select Items is selected in your Folder Options dialog box, a check box with a check mark appears in the corner of the current desktop background thumbnail. Otherwise, the current background is indicated by a gray box. For more information, see "Moving and Copying Folders and Files" in Chapter 3, "Working with Folders and Files."

2. With **Windows Wallpapers** selected in the **Picture Location** list, scroll through the available wallpapers, and click any thumbnails that interest you.

When you click a thumbnail, a preview of the wallpaper appears on the desktop behind the window.

3. Click the **Picture Location** arrow, and then in the list, click **Sample Pictures**.

   The 15 sample pictures displayed come with Windows Vista. These pictures are stored in the *Public Pictures\Sample Pictures* folder. (You can also find a link to that folder in your personal *Pictures* folder.) They are also displayed by default in other Windows Vista features such as the Photos screen saver and the Sidebar slide show.

4. In the **Picture Location** list, click **Pictures**.

   The Picture Location box displays the contents of your *Pictures* folder.

5. Click **Browse**. Then in the **Browse** dialog box, navigate to the *Documents\Microsoft Press\WindowsVistaSBS_Dlx\Backgrounds* folder, and double-click the *Arizona02* image.

   The selected picture appears as your desktop background, the Picture Location list shows the path to the practice file folder, and the entire contents of the folder appear in the Picture Location box.

6. Below the **Picture Location** box, select the **Center** option.

On your desktop, the picture changes to its actual dimensions. If your monitor is set to a screen resolution of 1024×768, this might result in blank space above and below the picture; a higher resolution might display blank space on all four sides.

> **Troubleshooting** Results can vary depending on your hardware.

7. Click **Change background color**. In the **Color** dialog box that opens, click any color you like, and then click **OK**.

   The blank space around the picture changes to the selected color.

8. In the **Picture Location** list, click **Solid Colors**.

   The window now displays 39 thumbnails of plain, solid colors.

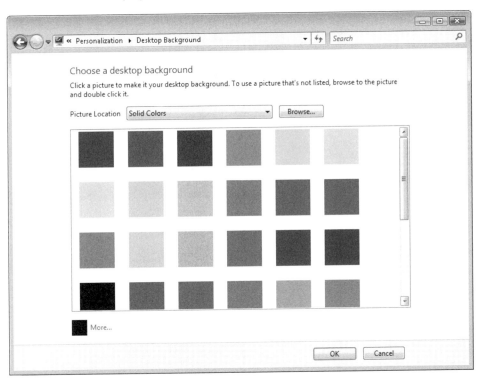

> **Tip** If none of these suit your needs, you can click the More link to display the Color dialog box from which you can select any color.

9. Click the light gray color (third row of the second column, when the window is sized to display six thumbnails across), and then click **OK** to apply your background selection.

 CLOSE Control Panel.

BE SURE TO adjust the desktop background to suit your preferences before moving on. We retained the pale gray background to make the graphics in this book easier to see.

Selecting and Managing a Screen Saver

Screen savers are static or moving images that are displayed on your computer after some period of inactivity. The original concept behind screen savers was that they prevented your computer's monitor from being permanently "imprinted" with a specific pattern when it was left on for too long without changing. Modern monitors are not as susceptible to this kind of damage, but it is still a good idea to use a screen saver or to have your monitor automatically use power-saver mode after a period of inactivity.

Another reason for using a screen saver is to protect your computer from prying eyes when you are away from your desk. To further protect your data, you can require that your password be entered to unlock the screen saver after it is set in motion.

The default screen saver is a Windows Vista logo that moves around on a black background. Windows Vista comes with eight additional animated screen savers. You can choose any of these, display a slide show of the images and/or videos in a specific folder as a screen saver, download other animated screen savers from the Internet, or display no screen saver at all.

> **Tip** To quickly locate additional screen savers online, visit *search.microsoft.com*, type *screen savers* in the Search Microsoft.com For box, and then click the Search button.

In this exercise, you will preview available screen savers and then select a screen saver that consists of a slide show of photographs.

USE the images located in the *Documents\WindowsVistaSBS_Dlx\Backgrounds* folder.
OPEN Control Panel, and then click Appearance And Personalization.

1. Under **Personalization**, click the **Change screen saver** task.

The Screen Saver Settings dialog box opens.

2. Click the **Screen saver** arrow, and then in the list, click **Photos**.

The preview screen displays a slide show of the 15 pictures in the *Public Pictures\ Sample Pictures* folder.

> **Troubleshooting** If you have pictures in your own *Pictures* folder, you might see those pictures instead of the samples in the public *Sample Pictures* folder.

3. Click **Settings**.

The Photo Screen Saver Settings dialog box opens.

4. To the right of **Use pictures and videos from**, click **Browse**.

5. In the **Browse For Folder** dialog box that opens, browse to the *Documents\ Microsoft Press\WindowsVistaSBS_Dlx\Backgrounds* folder, and then click **OK**.

> **Tip** If you have a folder of your own favorite photos on your computer, feel free to browse to that folder instead.

6. Adjust the slide show speed if you want, and then click **Save**.

   In the Screen Saver Settings dialog box, the slide show preview cycles through the pictures in the selected folder. You can click Preview to see the full-screen slide show as it will appear when in action; move the mouse or press the Esc key to return to the dialog box.

   > **Tip** To use a password to return to your regular desktop in Windows Vista, select the On Resume, Display Logon Screen.

7. Choose the screen saver option you want to use on your computer, and then click **OK**.

 CLOSE the Appearance And Personalization window.

Managing Your System Date and Time

Your computer has an internal clock that keeps track of the date and time, even when it is turned off. By default, Windows Vista displays the *system time* in the notification area at the right end of the taskbar. When you point to the time, the *system date* is displayed as a ScreenTip. The system time controls a number of behind-the-scenes settings and is also used by Windows and your programs to maintain an accurate record of happenings on your computer.

> **Tip** If you prefer to not display the time, right-click a blank area of the taskbar, click Properties, click the Notification Area tab, and then clear the Clock check box in the System Icons area of the Taskbar And Start Menu Properties dialog box.

You can set the system date, system time, and time zone manually, or, if your computer is connected to the Internet, you can synchronize your system date and time with an Internet-based *time server*. If you have a continuous Internet connection, you can program your computer to synchronize itself on a regular schedule. If your computer is on a domain, the time is centrally controlled from the domain server and you can change it only temporarily (until the next time the server synchronizes the domain clock).

In this exercise, you will manually reset your system time and then connect to an Internet time server for an automatic update. There are no practice files for this exercise.

 BE SURE TO have an active Internet connection available before beginning this exercise.

1. Close any open programs to display the Windows desktop.

   The notification area displays the current system time.

   > **Tip** If your taskbar is vertical, or is more than one row high, the notification area displays the time and the date. For information about changing the taskbar, see "Using and Modifying the Taskbar" in Chapter 2, "Working Efficiently in Windows Vista."

2. Point to the clock to display the current system date as a ScreenTip. Then click the clock to display the date, a calendar, and the time in both analog and digital formats.

3. Click **Change date and time settings**.

   The Date And Time dialog box opens, displaying the Date And Time tab. This tab displays your current system date, time, and time zone. The system time appears in analog and digital formats, with both clocks changing in one-second increments.

Tip If you want to keep track of the time in a different time zone, you can activate up to two additional clocks. On the Additional Clocks tab of the Date And Time dialog box, select a Show This Clock check box, select the time zone, enter a display name, and click OK. The additional clock is displayed in the ScreenTip that appears when you point to the clock in the notification area.

4. Click **Change date and time**. In the **User Account Control** dialog box, if you are logged on as an administrator, click **Continue**. Otherwise, enter an administrator password, and then click **OK**.

5. In the **Date and Time Settings** dialog box, position the insertion point in the hours (or drag the mouse pointer over the hour displayed in the digital clock to select it), and then click the up arrow to the right of the clock once, to change the hour.

The analog clock reflects your change, and both clocks stop advancing. You can also use this technique to change the minutes, seconds, and AM/PM setting.

6. In the **Date and Time Settings** dialog box, click **OK**.

The clock on the taskbar changes to reflect the new time.

7. In the **Date and Time** dialog box, click the **Internet Time** tab.

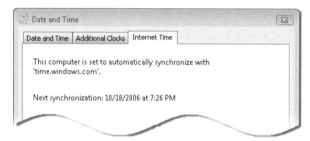

> **Troubleshooting** If your computer is on a domain, the contents of the tab will appear dimmed and the Internet Time Synchronization feature will not be available. If this occurs, skip to the end of this exercise.

8. Click **Change settings**. In the **User Account Control** dialog box, if you are logged on as an administrator, click **Continue**. Otherwise, enter an administrator password, and then click **OK**.

The Internet Time Settings dialog box opens.

9. With the **Synchronize with an Internet time server** check box selected, click the **Server** arrow. In the list, click the server you want to use, and then click **Update now**.

> **Tip** The four servers in the list with *nist* in their names are maintained by the National Institute of Standards and Technology at various locations around the U.S. The time.nist.gov server is at the National Center for Atmospheric Research in Boulder, Colorado; time-nw.nist.gov is at Microsoft in Redmond, Washington; and time-a.nist.gov and time-b.nist.gov are at NIST in Gaithersburg, Maryland.

Your computer connects to the selected time server via the Internet, and updates your system time.

 CLOSE the Internet Time Settings dialog box and the Date And Time dialog box.

Changing Your Computer's Name

When Windows Vista was installed on your computer, the person doing the installation provided a name by which the computer is identified. If you installed Windows Vista yourself, you might have chosen a name that was meaningful or helpful to you, such as *TabletPC* or *Accounting1*. If you purchased the computer with Windows Vista already installed, the name might be only a series of numbers and characters. If you have administrator permissions, you can change the computer name.

To view the computer name:

→ On the **Start** menu, click **Computer**.

The *Computer* folder name appears in the Address bar, and the name assigned to your computer appears in the Details pane at the bottom of the window.

To change the computer name:

1. On the **Start** menu, right-click **Computer**, and then click **Properties**.

The System window opens.

2. Under **Computer name, domain, and workgroup settings**, click **Change settings**. In the **User Account Control** dialog box, if you're logged on as an administrator, click **Continue**. Otherwise, enter an administrator password, and then click **OK**.

3. On the **Computer Name** tab of the **System Properties** dialog box, click **Change**.

4. In the **Computer Name/Domain Changes** dialog box, replace the existing computer name with the name you want, and then click **OK**.

5. Click **OK** to acknowledge that the name change won't take effect until you restart your computer, and then close the **System Properties** dialog box.

6. In the **Windows** message box, click **Restart Now**, or if it isn't convenient to restart your computer at this time, click **Restart Later**.

Changing the Name of the Computer Folder

By default, the link to your *Computer* folder is called *Computer*. If you want, you can change this name to match your computer name (or any other name, but that might be confusing). To change the link name:

1. On the **Start** menu, right-click **Computer**, and then click **Rename**.

2. With *Computer* selected for editing, type the name you want to appear, and then press `Enter`.

   The link name can't contain a slash (/ or \), colon (:), asterisk (*), question mark (?), double quotation mark ("), less than sign (<), greater than sign (>), or pipe (|). Some symbols, such as an exclamation point (!), at symbol (@), pound sign (#), dollar sign ($), percent symbol (%), caret (^), ampersand (&), and underscore (_) are valid, as are uppercase and lowercase letters, numbers, spaces, commas, periods, and parentheses. Windows displays up to two lines of characters (if separated by a space) on the Start menu.

Key Points

- You can easily personalize Windows Vista interface elements such as colors, fonts, and the desktop background.

- If your computer hardware meets the minimum requirements, you can enjoy the ultimate Windows Vista visual experience by implementing the Windows Aero color scheme.

- You can choose from a number of screen savers that come with Windows Vista, download others from the Web, and display your own pictures as a screen saver.

- The date and time shown on your computer can be automatically updated from an Internet time server.

- If your computer was assigned an impersonal string of letters and numbers as its name, you can easily change it. In no time, *SQ003GG8* can become *Heidis-Helper*.

Keyboard Shortcuts

Press this	To do this
Windows logo key+D	Display the desktop.
Ctrl+Esc	Open the Start menu.
Windows logo key	Open or close the Start menu.

Press this	To do this in a dialog box or task pane
Spacebar	Select or clear the check box if the active option is a check box.
Arrow keys	Select a button if the active option is a group of option buttons.
Ctrl+Tab	Move forward through tabs.
Ctrl+Shift+Tab	Move back through tabs.
Tab	Move forward through options.
Shift+Tab	Move back through options.

Chapter at a Glance

Configure Tablet PC options, **page 160**

Install and share a local printer, **page 166**

Configure your system for multiple monitors, **page 147**

Change the way your mouse works, **page 151**

5 Installing and Configuring Devices

In this chapter, you will learn to:

- ✔ Display more on your monitor.
- ✔ Configure your system for multiple monitors.
- ✔ Change the way your mouse works.
- ✔ Change the keyboard input language.
- ✔ Configure Tablet PC options.
- ✔ Install and share a local printer.
- ✔ Connect to a remote printer.
- ✔ Set up speakers and a microphone.

People discuss computers in terms of *hardware* and *software*. As you probably know, physical items such as computers and monitors are hardware, and all the programs that you use to do things with that hardware are collectively known as software.

Whether you're working in an office or at home, you will eventually want to install one or more bits of extra hardware, called *peripheral devices*, on your computer. Some devices, such as the keyboard, monitor, and mouse, usually come with the computer, but you will purchase others separately. The most common devices are speakers and a printer. Other popular devices include scanners, storage devices such as Zip drives, and fax machines. Depending on your interests and use of the computer, you might also have a microphone, camera, biometric identification device, joystick, or drawing tablet.

Peripheral hardware devices fall into two categories:

- ● *External peripherals.* You can install these devices by connecting them to ports without having to open up your computer. Examples are your computer's monitor, keyboard, mouse, and speakers.

  Many external peripherals that connect to your computer through a USB port fall into a category called *Plug and Play*, which quite literally means that you can plug them in and use them. When you connect such a device to your computer, Windows Vista communicates with it and configures the necessary settings. Other external peripherals might require a specific *device driver* in order to work properly. Device drivers are bits of code that enable peripheral devices to "talk" to your computer, but they are unfortunately not universal. To hook up a printer, for example, you might need a driver that is not only specific to the printer but also specific to Windows Vista. If you purchased the peripheral before the release of Windows Vista, you might need to download updated drivers for it.

Some devices come with software you can install to take full advantage of its capabilities. For example, you might connect an all-in-one printer/scanner/fax/copy machine to your computer and be able to print, fax, scan to a file, and copy without installing additional software, but to be able to send scanned pages as e-mail messages or to edit them as text files, you will need to install the software provided with the machine.

● *Internal peripherals.* You have to install these devices inside your computer's case. The internal component might be in the form of a card that provides a new connection at the back of the computer, or it might be a new hard disk drive, DVD drive, or tape backup drive that is accessed from the front of the computer. Probably the most common internal devices people install themselves are RAM (random access memory) sticks, because increasing the RAM in a computer increases its speed and performance.

See Also For information about increasing the speed of your computer, see "Improving Your Computer's Performance" in Chapter 14, "Optimizing Your Computer System."

To install an internal device, you need to remove the cover from your computer and delve into its innards. Be sure to shut down the computer and disconnect it from its power source before attempting to install any internal component. Then follow the installation instructions provided by the manufacturer of the device.

The point of all these devices, of course, is to make your computing experience more productive, more enjoyable, and hopefully, simpler (although it might not seem that way when you need to use a half dozen hardware devices in order to write a letter).

In this chapter, you will work with a computer's most common external peripherals—the monitor, keyboard, mouse, printer, speakers, and microphone. You will adjust your screen resolution to provide the largest possible working area, and if your computer supports dual monitors, configure the primary and secondary displays as you want them. You will change keyboard and mouse settings and see how to configure Tablet PC options. You will install a printer for your own use and make it available for other people to connect to, and then you will learn how to locate and connect to printers on your network. You will also set up speakers and a microphone.

See Also Do you need only a quick refresher on the topics in this chapter? See the Quick Reference section at the beginning of this book.

> **Important** No practice files are required to complete the exercises in this chapter. For more information about practice files, see "Using the Companion CD" at the beginning of this book.

Need More Ports?

Most computers come equipped with a standard set of *ports* with which you connect a keyboard, mouse, monitor, or printer. If your computer has a sound card and a network card, you also have audio and network ports. All modern desktop and laptop computers have *Universal Serial Bus (USB)* ports through which many peripheral devices connect. (A USB connection provides both power and data transfer capabilities to a peripheral device.) Many computers also have *IEEE 1394* ports for the high-speed transfer of audio and video data.

If you want to install several peripheral devices on the same computer, you might find that you don't have enough ports to connect them all. All is not lost! Here are three options for expanding your connection capacity:

- **Install extra ports.** You can purchase a card with more ports in almost any computer store. After turning off your desktop computer and removing its cover, you insert the card into one of the available *expansion slots*. When you turn the power back on, Windows Vista detects and installs the new ports without further ado.

- **Daisy-chain multiple devices.** Many devices that connect to the computer via its *parallel port* can be "daisy-chained" together to form a linked network of devices. For example, you might connect a Zip drive to your computer's parallel port and then connect a printer to the parallel port on the Zip drive. Data you send to the printer will pass through the Zip drive.

- **Use a hub or switch box.** You can connect a single multi-port *hub* to your computer and then connect multiple devices to the hub, enabling all the devices to share that single connection. Hubs are available for network, parallel, and USB devices. If you want to physically connect multiple peripheral devices but you don't need to use more than one at a time, you can use a *switch box*, which looks similar to a hub but allows only one active connection at a time.

Displaying More on Your Monitor

When you purchase a computer monitor, one of the things you consider is its size, or display area, which is measured like a television screen: diagonally in inches. More important than the physical size, though, is the *screen resolution* it supports, which is measured in *pixels* and is expressed as the number of pixels wide by the number of pixels high. Pixels are the individual dots that make up the picture displayed on your screen. Each pixel displays one color; depending on your screen resolution, the images you see on screen might consist of 500,000 to 1,000,000 individual dots of color.

When personal computers first became popular, most computer monitors were capable of displaying only 640 pixels horizontally and 480 pixels vertically (a screen resolution of 640×480). Now most display at 800×600 pixels and 1024×768 pixels, and some can display at 2048×1536 pixels (or perhaps by the time this book is published, even higher). In effect, as the screen resolution increases, the size of each pixel decreases, and more information can be shown in the same display area. The graphics in this book were captured on a monitor set to a screen resolution of 1024×768.

> **Tip** The maximum resolution is the lower of the resolution supported by your monitor or the resolution supported by the graphics card installed in your computer. As you change the screen resolution, the Colors setting might also change. Lower resolutions might support higher color quality.

Most computer users have a choice of at least two different screen resolutions, but you might have many more choices. Some people prefer to work at 800×600 because everything on their screen appears larger; others prefer to fit more information on their screen with a 1024×768 (or higher) display. Recent statistics indicate that approximately 80 percent of Internet users have their screen resolution set to 1024×768 or greater—up from 79 percent in 2006, 60 percent in 2004 and 42 percent in 2001.

Many monitors and mobile PCs have widescreen displays with resolutions such as 1280×768, intended to improve the experience of viewing movies on the computer by displaying them at the correct *aspect ratio*. These resolutions may be available on your computer regardless of the aspect ratio of your actual monitor. Windows Vista includes desktop background graphics specifically designed for widescreen displays.

In this exercise, you will change your screen resolution to the maximum and minimum sizes supported by your computer. There are no practice files for this exercise.

> **Troubleshooting** Screen resolution capabilities are hardware-specific. The settings available on your computer may be different from those shown or specified in this exercise.

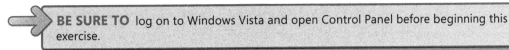

BE SURE TO log on to Windows Vista and open Control Panel before beginning this exercise.

1. In the **Control Panel** window, click **Appearance and Personalization**, and then click **Personalization**.

> **Tip** You can open the Personalization window directly by right-clicking the Windows Vista desktop and then clicking Personalize.

2. In the **Personalization** window, click **Display Settings**.

The Display Settings dialog box opens.

Resolution setting markers

Selected screen resolution

3. If you have more than one monitor installed, select the monitor you want to change. Then drag the **Resolution** slider all the way to the left to switch to the minimum resolution.

> **Tip** You can easily determine which monitor is which by clicking the Identify Monitors button. A large number corresponding to the icons in the preview pane flashes on each monitor.

The change is reflected in the preview area, but not on your screen.

4. In the **Display Settings** dialog box, click **Apply**. Then in the **Display Settings** message box that appears, click **Yes**.

> **Tip** You have 15 seconds to decide whether to retain the changed resolution. If you click Yes, the resolution is retained; if you click No or don't click either button, the resolution returns to its previous setting.

Your display changes to the lowest resolution supported by your system. Unless your monitor was already set to the minimum resolution, everything shown on the screen—the taskbar, Personalization window, Display Settings dialog box, and any other open windows and dialog boxes—appears much larger.

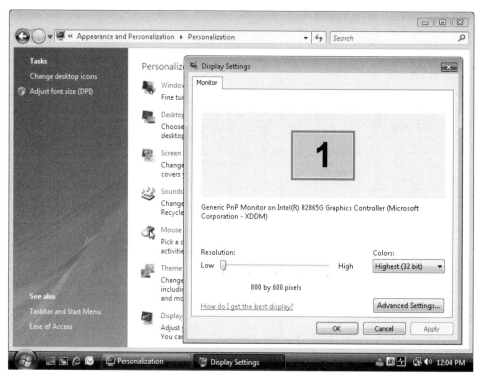

5. In the **Display Settings** dialog box, click the slider bar above the right-most resolution marker to change to the maximum resolution supported by the selected monitor.

You can either drag the slider to a marker or click above the marker you want.

6. Click **Apply**, and then in the **Display Settings** message box, click **Yes**.

Your screen resolution changes to the maximum supported by your system.

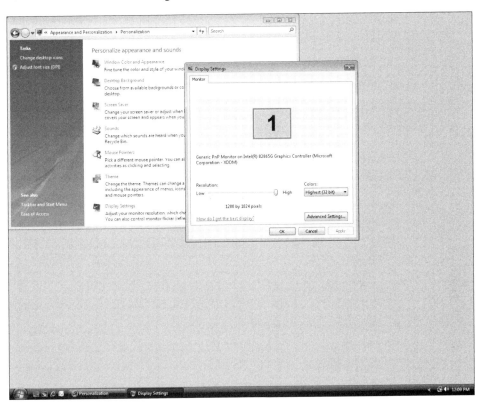

7. Experiment with the available screen resolutions. Apply the one you like best, and then in the **Display Settings** window, click **OK**.

 CLOSE the Personalization window.

Configuring Your System for Multiple Monitors

If you often work with multiple programs or with large-format files (such as spreadsheets) that are difficult to see on your monitor because of their width, you might want to extend your desktop by adding one or more monitors. Or if you deliver presentations through a projector attached to your computer, you might find it convenient to configure your desktop to display on two screens so that you can work privately on your computer screen while displaying information publicly through the projector. Windows Vista makes it easy to configure up to 10 display devices attached to your computer.

To add a second monitor, you must have one of the following:

● A video card that supports multiple monitors. If you do, there will be two video ports on the back of your computer for connecting your monitors.

● More than one video card.

● A dual monitor adaptor.

After connecting your monitors and restarting your computer, you might be prompted to install additional video drivers, as directed in the instructions that came with your monitor.

When you connect your computer to a secondary display, Windows Vista detects the device and prompts you to specify how you want to display information on it:

● **Mirrored.** The same content appears on both displays. This is useful when you are giving a presentation and are not facing the screen (for example, when standing at a podium facing an audience) or want to have a closer view of the content you are displaying.

● **Extended.** Your desktop expands to cover both displays. The Windows taskbar appears only on the screen you designate as the primary display.

● **External display only.** Content appears only on the second display. This is useful if you are working on a mobile PC running on battery power. When connected to a second display, you can conserve battery power by turning off the mobile PC screen.

To configure your computer to display your Windows desktop across two monitors:

1. Open the **Display Settings** dialog box by right-clicking the desktop, clicking **Personalize**, and then clicking **Display Settings** in the Personalization window.

   If a second monitor is connected to your computer but not active, it appears in the preview area but is screened.

2. In the preview area, click Monitor **2**, select the **Extend the desktop onto this monitor** check box, and then click **Apply**.

   Your desktop expands across both display devices.

When working on a computer connected to two display devices, Windows appoints one the *primary display* and the other the *secondary display*. The Welcome screen and task-bar always appear on the primary display, as do most application windows when they first open. You can then drag selected windows to the secondary screen.

> **Troubleshooting** You can't move a maximized window between screens; you must first reduce the size of the window either by clicking the Restore Down button on the window's title bar or by double-clicking the title bar.

To ascertain which monitor or other display device is the primary display, point to either monitor representation in the Display Settings dialog box. A ScreenTip appears, displaying the monitor's role (primary or secondary) and in the case of the secondary monitor, its position in relation to the primary monitor.

To change the primary monitor:

1. In the preview area of the **Display Settings** dialog box, click the secondary display.

2. Select the **This is my main monitor** check box, and then click **Apply**.

By default, Monitor 2 appears immediately to the right of Monitor 1. When you move the cursor horizontally from screen to screen, it should leave the right edge of the left screen and enter the left edge of the right screen at vertically the same point. If your monitors are not physically the same size, are set to different screen resolutions, or are not placed level with each other, you can change the alignment of the displays so that the cursor moves cleanly between them.

To adjust the relationship of the displays to each other:

→ In the preview area of the **Display Settings** dialog box, drag Monitor **2** to the location you want it to be in relationship to Monitor **1**.

As you move the monitor representation, a ScreenTip displays the position in pixels of the upper-left corner of Monitor 2 in relation to the upper-left corner of Monitor 1. Monitor 1 is always at 0,0.

Expanding Your Laptop with Peripheral Devices

Laptop computers are useful when you want to be able to move around with your computer—from room to room, from work to home, or from city to city. Although laptops can offer fast computing and large hard-disk storage and many now offer a widescreen display, you usually have to deal with a smaller monitor, a smaller keyboard, and a touchpad or joystick mouse instead of a standard mouse. It is also possible that your laptop computer came without an internal CD or DVD drive.

In addition to the frustration caused by these basic differences between laptop and desktop computing, you might find that your wrists become tired because you can't rest them on the keyboard, or you accidentally tap the touchpad when you're typing and move the insertion point without realizing it—which can result in inadvertent errors in your documents.

Although carrying a full-size monitor, keyboard, and mouse when you travel with your laptop is not convenient, expanding your laptop computer with full-size peripherals is a great way to improve your computing experience whether you're in your office or at home. If you use a laptop because you need it both at home and at work, you can set up a monitor, keyboard, and mouse at each location for a relatively small sum of money. You then have the best of both worlds—portable computing and a full-size setup.

You connect peripheral devices to your laptop in the same manner that you would connect them to a standard desktop computer. You might find that your laptop has a limited number of ports, or that it has only a USB port and not a parallel port; inexpensive adaptors are available to help you increase the available ports as required. Some newer USB keyboards also incorporate a USB port into the keyboard, so you can plug the keyboard into the laptop and the mouse into the keyboard.

If you attach a full-size monitor to your laptop, you might at first see the same display on both monitors, or the display might appear only on the laptop. To change the monitor displaying your desktop, look at the function keys at the top of the laptop's keyboard—one of them (usually F5, sometimes F4) includes a graphic representation of a monitor. Hold down the Alt key, and then press the appropriate function key to switch among three options: laptop display and external display, external display only, and laptop display only.

> **Tip** If the monitor-switching key is not obvious, consult your laptop manual or the manufacturer's Web site for further information.

Changing the Way Your Mouse Works

In the beginning, a computer mouse consisted of a shell with one button to click with and a rubber ball on the bottom that correlated your mouse movements with a pointer on the screen. Nowadays, mice come in many shapes and sizes, employing a variety of functions, buttons, wheels, and connection methods.

Windows Vista offers enhanced wheel support that allows for smooth scrolling both vertically (as is traditional) and horizontally (on the newer mice that support this). Check the manufacturer's documentation to see if your mouse is able to take advantage of this technology. But even if your mouse is not of the latest generation, you can still customize your mouse settings in various ways to optimize the way it works with Windows.

To change the way the mouse buttons work:

1. In the **Control Panel** window, under **Hardware and Sound**, click **Mouse**.

   The Mouse Properties dialog box opens, displaying the Buttons tab.

2. On the **Buttons** tab, in the **Button configuration** section, select the **Switch primary and secondary buttons** check box to change the default primary button from left to right.

   This setting is useful if you are left-handed, you injure your right hand, or switch mousing hands to decrease wrist strain.

3. In the **Double-click speed** area, drag the slider to the speed you want. Explore and change the other options on this page, and then click **OK**.

To change how the mouse pointer looks and works:

1. Open the **Mouse Properties** dialog box, and then click the **Pointers** tab.

2. In the **Scheme** list, click one of the 21 available system schemes to change the pointer set.

   Experiment with some of the more-interesting system schemes, such as Conductor, Dinosaur, and Hands. The Customize list displays the pointers associated with that scheme.

3. In the **Customize** list, click any pointer, and then click **Browse**.

4. In the **Browse** dialog box displaying the contents of the *Cursors* folder, double-click any cursor to replace the selected pointer.

> **Tip** Feel free to experiment with the shapes of pointers; you can restore the pointers to the original scheme defaults at any time by clicking Use Default.

5. Click the **Pointer Options** tab, set the pointer speed, movement, and visibility options, and then click **OK**.

To change how the mouse wheel works:

1. Open the **Mouse Properties** dialog box, and then click the **Wheel** tab.

2. To control how much of the screen scrolls as you turn the mouse wheel, in the **Vertical Scrolling** area, either select the **The following number of lines at a time** option and then type or click the arrow keys to set the number of lines you want to scroll, or select the **One screen at a time** option.

   The default setting is to scroll three lines at a time, but if you frequently use the mouse to scroll through lengthy documents or Web pages, you might find it more convenient to scroll by screen rather than by line. Windows Vista sets the scrolling distance based on the size of the window you are scrolling in.

   > **Tip** You can move forward and backward between visited Web pages by holding down the Shift key and then scrolling the wheel vertically.

3. If your mouse supports horizontal scrolling, in the **Tilt the wheel to scroll the following number of characters at a time** box, enter the number of characters you want to scroll horizontally when you tilt the mouse wheel to the left or right.

Changing the Keyboard Input Language

Keyboards come in a variety of language-specific versions that incorporate special alphabet characters used in those languages. Your desktop or laptop computer might have a keyboard configured for American English, UK English, French, Canadian French, German, Swedish, Danish, Belgian, Dutch, Spanish, Italian, Portuguese, Arabic, Chinese, Hebrew, Russian... the list goes on, and includes some specialized languages such as Gaelic, Inuktitut, and Maori. Some keyboards, such as the Japanese keyboard, depict two alphabets.

When you first set up your Windows Vista computer, you choose an *input language* that matches your keyboard, and Windows Vista programs itself to correctly recognize the keys that you press to match the letters, numbers, characters, or commands depicted on each key.

Under some circumstances, you might want to use a keyboard configured for a different language, or you might want to instruct Windows to treat your keystrokes on your existing keyboard as if you were using a different-language keyboard. For example, if your computer is set up to recognize a U.S. English keyboard and you frequently correspond with customers in a language—such as French, German, or Swedish—that uses characters not included in the English alphabet—such as ç, ä, or å—you will need to enter letters that don't exist on the U.S. English keyboard. You can enter those characters in a Microsoft Office Word document by selecting them from the Symbol dialog box, and in most programs by pressing Alt and then a specific number combination on the numeric keypad, if you have one. (The symbol is inserted when you release the Alt key.) Or to save yourself that trouble, you can connect a language-specific keyboard to your computer. All the letters of that language appear on the keyboard and you simply press the keys to enter them.

> **Tip** When you attach a different-language keyboard to your laptop, both keyboards are available to you.

If you are familiar with the layout of a language-specific keyboard but don't want to physically switch keyboards to enter the keystrokes in that language, you can configure your computer to recognize keystrokes as though you were using the different-language keyboard. You switch between input languages by using the tools on the Language bar that appears on the Windows taskbar.

In this exercise, you will configure your computer to enter keystrokes as though you are typing on a Swedish keyboard. There are no practice files for this exercise.

Tip If you are already working with a Swedish keyboard, substitute another language in this exercise.

OPEN Control Panel.

1. In **Control Panel**, click **Clock, Language, and Region**. Then under **Regional and Language Options**, click the **Change keyboards or other input methods** task.

   The Regional And Language Options dialog box opens, displaying the Keyboards And Languages tab.

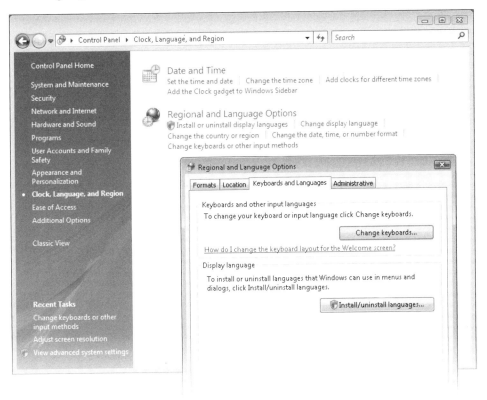

2. Click **Change keyboards**.

The Text Services And Input Languages dialog box opens, displaying your current input language and the input devices configured for that language, as well as any other languages you have installed.

3. Click the **Default input language** arrow to expand the list of available languages.

   Only the original input language appears in the list. To accept input from another language-specific keyboard, you must first install the language.

4. In the **Installed services** area, click **Add**.

   The Add Input Language dialog box opens.

5. Browse through this dialog box, noting the available languages. Expand a few of the languages and their Keyboard lists.

   Notice that each language does not have its own keyboard, but some have more than one associated keyboard.

Expand

6. In the list, click the **Expand** button to the left of **Swedish (Sweden)**, and then click the **Expand** button to the left of **Keyboard**.

The standard keyboard options for this language are Swedish and US.

7. In the **Keyboard** list, select the **Show More** check box.

The list expands to include all the available language keyboards.

8. Scroll the list to see the amazing variety of available keyboards.

Some languages have up to six available keyboards, each with different keyboard layouts or alphabets. You can enter the selected language (Swedish) from any of these keyboards.

9. In the expanded **Keyboard** list, select the check box of the keyboard that is connected to your computer. Then click **Preview**.

> **Troubleshooting** If you are working on a standard U.S. English keyboard, you will notice that there are six layouts available. If you don't know which yours is, select US.

A diagram of the selected keyboard appears.

10. Click **Close**. Then in the **Keyboard** list, select the **Swedish** check box, and click **Preview**.

A diagram of the Swedish keyboard appears.

Notice the three Swedish letters to the left of the Enter key: Å, Ä, and Ö. These are the last three letters of the Swedish alphabet. The characters in these three positions on your own keyboard have been rearranged to make room for them.

11. Close the **Keyboard Layout Preview** window and, provided the first keyboard preview displayed a keyboard layout matching your own, click **OK** in the **Add Input Language** dialog box.

> **Troubleshooting** If the US keyboard did not match your own keyboard, repeat step 9 until you locate one that does match.

The Default Input Language list and Installed Services area now include both your original keyboard language and keyboard layout, and Swedish with two keyboard layouts. Your original language is still selected as the default, as indicated in the Default Input Language list.

Note that each language in the Installed services box is represented by a specific two-letter combination in a small blue square. The two-letter abbreviation for Swedish is SV, short for *Svensk—Swedish* in Swedish.

12. In the **Text Services and Input Languages** dialog box, click **OK**.

To the left of the notification area on the Windows taskbar, the Language bar appears, displaying the two-letter abbreviation of the default input language.

> **Tip** The contents of the Language bar vary depending on what language-specific capabilities are configured. You can change the location and appearance of the Language bar from the Language Bar tab of the Text Services And Input Languages dialog box.

13. On the **Language** bar, click the input language button. Then in the input language list, click **Swedish (Sweden)**.

The input language button label changes to SV, and a keyboard button appears to its right.

14. Click the keyboard button.

The keyboard list displays the two keyboards you chose for Swedish input: Swedish and your own.

Keyboard list

Language bar

15. In the keyboard list, click **Swedish**.

Start

16. To confirm that the input language has changed, click the **Start** button, and then with the insertion point in the **Start Search** box, press the single quote (') key to the left of the Enter key.

The letter ä, which appears to the left of the Enter key on the Swedish keyboard, appears in the Search box.

17. Experiment with the input languages if you want. Then redisplay the **Keyboards and Languages** tab of the **Regional and Language Options** dialog box, and click **Change keyboards**.

18. In the **Installed services** area, click **Swedish (Sweden)**, and then click **Remove**.

CLOSE the Regional And Language Options dialog box and the Clock, Language, And Region window.

Configuring Tablet PC Options

A variety of new and improved features for working with a Tablet PC are built in to Windows Vista—you don't have to purchase a different edition of the operating system for a laptop than you would for a desktop PC. The most visible improvement is the updated Input Panel, which is readily available as a tab at the edge of the screen. Tap the tab, and the Input Panel opens, ready to receive your written input. This input is more likely to be interpreted accurately if you take a little time to train the handwriting recognition program.

You can enter information into a Tablet PC with a pen and, if your computer supports touch input, with your finger. You can configure options to support pen and finger flicks as a means of navigating in documents and other files.

In this exercise, you will explore the Tablet PC configuration options, as well as those for your pen and the Input Panel. There are no practice files for this exercise.

> **Troubleshooting** The instructions in this exercise assume you are working on a Tablet PC. You can work through the exercise on a desktop computer by following the alternative instructions provided.

 BE SURE TO open Control Panel before beginning this exercise.

1. In the **Control Panel** window, tap **Mobile PC**. Then in the **Mobile PC** window, tap **Tablet PC Settings**.

   > **Troubleshooting** If your Control Panel does not include the Mobile PC category, click Hardware And Sound, and then click Tablet PC Settings.

   The Tablet PC Settings dialog box opens. On the General tab, you can indicate whether you are right-handed or left-handed, and you can calibrate the screen for better pen tracking.

2. Tap the **Handwriting Recognition** tab.

   On this tab, you can set options that will allow the handwriting recognizer to progressively "learn" about your style of writing.

3. Tap the **Display** tab, and then tap the **Orientation** arrow. In the list, tap the **Primary** option that is not your current orientation, and then tap **Apply**.

   The screen orientation changes. If you do not want to keep this orientation, switch it back before continuing.

   > **Tip** If your Tablet PC has tablet buttons, you can tap the Change button and set up the orientation sequence for a button.

4. Tap the **Other** tab.

   This tab provides access to options for configuring your pen and the Input Panel.

5. Tap the **Go to Pen and Input Devices** link.

The Pen And Input Devices dialog box opens. The Pen Options tab displays a list of the pen equivalents of various mouse actions. You can adjust the settings for each pen action other than single-tapping to conform to the way you use the pen. You can change the size of the gesture required to start Input Panel, the speed and duration of the pen equivalent of right-clicking, and the speed and location variance that constitute a double-tap. (You cannot change the single-click action.)

6. Tap the **Press and hold** action, and then click **Settings**.

   In the Press And Hold Settings dialog box, you can turn the press and hold for right-clicking action on or off, and you can set the speed and duration of the action.

7. Tap **Cancel**, and then in the **Pen and Input Devices** dialog box, tap the **Pointer Options** tab.

   The options on this tab control the feedback you receive in response to pen actions.

8. Tap the **Flicks** tab.

On this tab, you can set whether you can navigate and edit content with a flick of the pen.

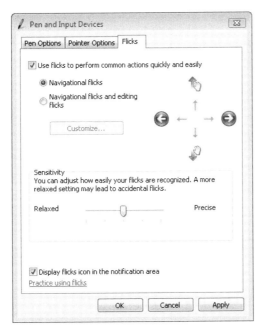

You cannot customize navigation flicks, but you can customize editing flicks.

9. Experiment with the options on this tab, and then tap **Cancel** to close the **Pen and Input Devices** dialog box.

10. On the **Other** tab of the Tablet PC Settings dialog box, tap the **Go to Input Panel Settings** link.

The Options dialog box opens, with the Settings tab active. On this tab, you can specify the location and functionality of the Insert button that appears when you are writing in the Input Panel. You can also turn the AutoComplete feature on or off and restore the default Input Panel settings.

> **Tip** You can also open this dialog box from the Input Panel, by tapping Tools and then Options.

11. Tap the **Opening** tab.

On this tab, you can choose how to open the Input Panel and where its tab and icon appear on the screen.

12. Explore the other tabs of the **Options** dialog box. Then close the dialog box and the Mobile PC window.

13. Locate the **Input Panel** tab on your screen, point to it to open the tab, and then tap it to open the Input Panel.

    By default, the Input Panel floats on the screen and can be dragged to any convenient location.

14. On the **Input Panel**, tap **Tools**, and then in the list, tap **Dock at Top of Screen**.

    The Input Panel stretches to the width of the screen and anchors itself at the top.

 BE SURE TO restore the default Float setting, and then close the Input Panel.

Installing and Sharing a Local Printer

To print from a computer that is not part of a network, you must physically connect a printer to your computer, usually through either a USB port or a parallel port. A printer that is connected directly to your computer is called a *local printer.* The software to run the printer is installed on and run from your computer. When you connect a printer to your computer and then turn on the printer, Windows Vista recognizes that a device has been connected and identifies the type of device. It then searches through its database of drivers to locate the appropriate software to run the printer. If Windows Vista doesn't have the current driver for your particular printer, it asks you to provide the driver.

> **Troubleshooting** Many printers come with a CD containing installation files and drivers that were current at the time the printer was manufactured. If you don't have the current *printer drivers,* you can usually locate them on the printer manufacturer's Web site.

If your computer is connected to a network, you can share your local printer with the entire network or with a select group of people. When you share your printer, you assign it a name. This name might be based on the manufacturer or model of the printer (such as *HP LaserJet*), some special feature (such as *Color*), or perhaps the physical location of the printer (such as *Front Office*). Regardless, simple names work best because they are more likely to be easily identified by everyone who needs to use your printer.

> **Tip** Some printers suggest their own printer name during the sharing process. You can either accept the suggested name or replace it with one you choose.

In this exercise, you will install a local printer, test the installation by printing a test page, and then share the printer for use by other people. There are no practice files for this exercise, but if you are logged on to the computer with a standard user account, you need to have an administrator password available to share the printer.

> **Important** You do not need to be connected to a network to complete this exercise; you can share your printer even if no one but you will ever need to use it.

BE SURE TO have a printer and the appropriate connection cable available before beginning this exercise.

Tip If you already have a working connection to your printer, skip to step 14 to learn how to share it.

1. Connect the printer to the appropriate port on your computer.

2. Connect the printer to a power outlet, and then if necessary, turn it on.

   If your computer connects to the printer through a USB port, Windows Vista recognizes the device and displays an alert while it configures the necessary settings and drivers.

3. If Windows Vista does not recognize the printer, skip to step 5. Otherwise, click the alert to display the progress of the printer installation.

4. After Windows declares the printer ready to use, close the **Driver Software Installation** window, and skip to step 14. If the installation did not complete successfully, continue with step 5.

5. Open **Control Panel**, and under **Hardware and Sound**, click **Printer**.

6. On the toolbar of the Printers window, click **Add a printer**.

7. On the first page of the **Add Printer** wizard, click **Add a local printer**.

8. On the **Choose a printer port** page, select the port to which your printer is connected from the **Use an existing port** list, and then click **Next**.

Troubleshooting It is likely that the correct port will already be selected. If not, the installation instructions from your printer manufacturer will tell you which port you should use. Some manufacturers supply helpful drawings to guide you.

Tip While working through the wizard, you can return to a previous page by clicking the Back button in the upper-left corner.

9. If you have an installation CD for your printer, insert it in the appropriate drive, click **Have Disk**, and follow the instructions on the screen to install your printer. Otherwise, in the **Manufacturer** list, click the brand name of your printer.

Important Your installation CD must contain updated drivers that are compatible with Windows Vista. If your drivers are out of date, you might need to download current drivers from the printer manufacturer's Web site.

The Printers list changes to reflect a list of the printer drivers that come with Windows Vista for the selected manufacturer.

> **Tip** Updated drivers are often available through Automatic Updates.

10. In the **Printers** list, click the model of your printer (which you can usually find printed on the top or front of the printer). Then click **Next**.

> **Troubleshooting** If the Printers list doesn't include your specific model, select a model with a similar name. Alternatively, download the necessary drivers from the manufacturer's Web site, return to the Install The Printer Driver page, and click Have Disk to install the printer manually.

11. On the **Type a printer name** page, change the printer name if you want to, or accept the default name. If you want Windows and any programs you install, such as Microsoft Office Word, to print to this printer when you click the Print button, select the **Set as the default printer** check box. Then click **Next**.

> **Tip** You can change your default printer at any time. To do so, display the Printers window, and double-click the printer you want to set as the default. Then on the Printer menu of the printer's management window, click Set As Default Printer.

12. On the wizard's confirmation page, click **Print a test page**.

After Windows Vista sends the test page to the printer, a confirmation message box appears.

13. In the confirmation message box, click **Close**. Then in the **Add Printer** wizard, click **Finish**.

Your local printer appears in the Printers window.

14. In the **Printers** window, right-click the icon representing your printer, and then click **Sharing**.

The printer's Properties dialog box opens, displaying the Sharing tab.

15. Click **Change sharing options**. In the **User Account Control** dialog box, if you are logged on as an administrator, click **Continue**. Otherwise, enter an administrator password, and then click **OK**.

16. Select the **Share this printer** check box. Then in the **Share name** box, type a simple name for the printer (or leave the default).

17. In the **Properties** dialog box, click **OK**.

In the Printers window, the printer's icon now indicates that it is shared.

 CLOSE the Printers window and Control Panel.

Connecting to a Remote Printer

A *network printer* is a printer that is not connected directly to your computer but is available through a network. It might be a free-standing networked printer, or it might be accessible through someone else's computer, through a print server, or through a printer hub.

If the printer you are connecting to is available to everyone on the network, you will not need specific permission to connect to it. If the printer has been made available only to specific people or groups, you will have to ask the printer's "owner" or your network administrator to make the printer available to you.

In this exercise, you will connect to a network printer. There are no practice files for this exercise.

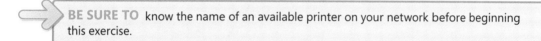
BE SURE TO know the name of an available printer on your network before beginning this exercise.

1. Open **Control Panel**, and under **Hardware and Sound**, click **Printer**.
2. On the toolbar of the Printers window, click **Add a printer**.
3. On the Add Printer wizard's first page, click **Add a network, wireless, or Bluetooth printer**.

   Windows Vista searches your network and then displays a list of available printers.

4. On the **Select a printer** page, click the printer you want to connect to, and then click **Next**.

> **Troubleshooting** If the printer you want to connect to isn't in the list, click The Printer That I Want Isn't Listed. Then on the Find A Printer By Name Or TCP/IP Address page, in the Select A Shared Printer By Name box, type \\ followed by the name of the computer to which the printer is attached, and the printer name, in the format shown, and then click Next. If not everyone on your network is allowed to use this printer, you might be prompted to enter your user account name and password to complete the connection.

Windows attempts to connect to the selected printer. If the drivers required by that printer aren't already installed on your computer, Windows Vista requests permission to install them.

5. In the **Printers** message box, click **Install driver**. In the **User Account Control** dialog box, if you are logged on as an administrator, click **Continue**. Otherwise, enter an administrator password, and then click **OK**.

After connecting to the printer, you can give it a name other than the one assigned by the printer's "owner."

6. On the **Type a printer name** page, change the printer name if you want to, or accept the default name. If you want Windows and any programs you install, such as Word, to print to this printer when you click the Print button, select the **Set as the default printer** check box. Then click **Next**.

You can print a test page, and print to the network printer just as you normally would.

7. In the **Add Printer** wizard, click **Finish**.

The network printer appears in the Printers window. You can print to it as you would to a local printer.

 CLOSE the Printers window and Control Panel.

Updating Device Drivers

Device drivers are files containing information that Windows needs to communicate with your printer, fax machine, scanner, camera, or other device. Drivers can be specific to an individual device or to a family of devices (such as all HP LaserJet printers), and they are often specific to a certain version of Windows.

Device drivers can be found on the Web site of the device manufacturer or on certain Web sites that centralize driver information. (Be aware when you visit these unaffiliated sites that they might require a subscription, or they might be trying to sell tools that can detect your drivers and suggest updates.)

Setting Up Speakers

Computer systems that are equipped with *sound cards* usually come with a set of external speakers so that you can listen to music and other audio files. Some monitors come with built-in speakers that take the place of external speakers. If you're a real audiophile, you might want to purchase fancy surround-sound speakers for your computer. Or if you want to listen to audio output privately, you can connect headphones directly to your computer or (if your speakers have a headphone jack) through the external speakers.

Most standard speaker systems consist of two speakers with one cord that connects them to each other, another that connects them to the computer, and a power cord that connects them to the power source. One speaker might have a volume control (independent of the computer's volume control) and a headphone jack.

Your desktop computer will have an audio output jack (usually found on the back of the computer case) and may also have a dedicated headphone jack (either on the front or on the back of the case). On a desktop computer case that features standard component color-coding, the audio output jack will be indicated by pale green coloring and the headphone jack by pale orange coloring.

In this exercise, you will connect speakers to your Windows Vista computer and adjust the audio output levels. There are no practice files for this exercise.

> **BE SURE TO** have a set of computer speakers available before beginning this exercise.

1. Remove the speakers from their packaging, if you have not already done so.

   > **Tip** If you are using an alternate audio configuration, such as a headset microphone, connect the input and output cables appropriately and then skip to step 6.

2. If necessary, link the two speakers by using the connector cable provided.

3. Position the speakers to the left and right of your monitor to provide stereo sound quality.

4. Connect the speakers to the audio output jack on your computer by using the connector cable provided.

> **Tip** The audio output jack might be indicated by a small speaker icon, an arrow symbol, or the words *Audio* or *Audio/Out*.

5. Connect the speakers to a power outlet by using the AC adapter cord provided.

6. Open **Control Panel**, and then click **Hardware and Sound**.

   The Hardware And Sound window opens.

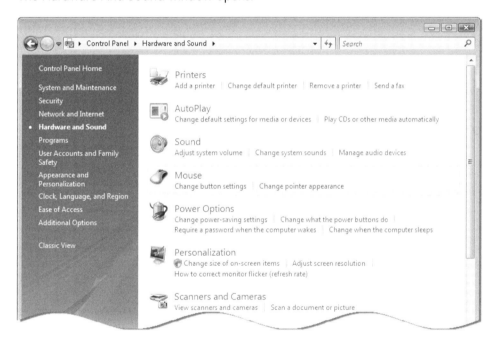

7. In the **Hardware and Sound** window, click **Sound**.

   The Sound dialog box opens.

8. Click each of the tabs, and explore the available options.

9. On the **Playback** tab, click your speakers, and then click **Configure**.

   The Speaker Setup wizard starts.

10. On the **Choose your configuration** page, select the appropriate audio channel, and then click **Test**. Test each of the channels to hear the different options, select the channel you want, and then click **Next**.

    If you choose any configuration other than Mono, the Select Full-Range Speakers page appears next. You can enable, disable, and test speakers from this page.

11. If the **Select full-range speakers** page appears, click **Next** to complete the configuration, and then on the **Configuration complete** page, click **Finish**.

 CLOSE the Sound dialog box and the Hardware And Sound window.

Setting Up a Microphone

With the rapid evolution of Internet-based communications, digital video, and speech-to-text technologies, microphones are being used more commonly with business and home computer systems. Microphones come in a variety of options, such as the following:

- Freestanding microphones
- Microphones that attach to your computer
- Headset microphones with built-in headphones that allow more private communication and consistent recording quality
- Boom microphones with a single headset speaker

If you will be recording a lot of speech or using the Speech Recognition feature, it is worth investing in a good-quality microphone. Buy anything less than the best you can afford, and you are likely to find yourself making a return trip to the store. To get the highest quality, it is critical that you choose the type of microphone that best fits your needs. Headset and boom microphones maintain a constant distance between the microphone and your mouth, which helps to maintain a more consistent sound level than a stationary microphone. The headphones built into headset and boom microphones provide the same privacy as a telephone, because the audio output is heard only by the wearer.

On a desktop computer case that features standard component color-coding, the audio input jack will be indicated by pink coloring.

In this exercise, you will connect a microphone to your Windows Vista computer and adjust the audio input levels. There are no practice files for this exercise.

> **BE SURE TO** have a microphone available before beginning this exercise.

1. Remove the microphone from its packaging, if you have not already done so.

> **Troubleshooting** If you are using a USB microphone, ensure that you are logged in as an administrator before connecting the microphone to the USB port. If you connect the microphone while logged in as a standard user, the device installation might not succeed, but no obvious indicator of the problem appears.

2. Plug the microphone connector cable into the audio input jack on your computer, or into a USB port, depending on the connection type.

> **Tip** The audio input jack might be indicated by a microphone icon or the word *Mic* or *Microphone*.

3. Open **Control Panel**, and then click **Ease of Access**.

4. In the **Ease of Access** window, under **Speech Recognition Options**, click **Set up a microphone**.

   The Microphone Setup Wizard starts.

5. Select the option for the type of microphone you are using, and then click **Next**.

6. On the **Set up your microphone page**, read the instructions, and then click **Next**.

   The Adjust The Microphone Volume page appears.

7. On the **Adjust the microphone volume** page, read the microphone test paragraph aloud in your normal speaking voice. Or just for fun, you might try singing a couple of lines from your favorite song!

As you speak (or sing), the volume gauge moves in response to your voice, and the microphone settings (which you can't see here) adjust to your natural speaking volume.

> **Troubleshooting** If the volume gauge does not move, your microphone might be incorrectly connected, or it might not be compatible with your computer. If this happens, hold the microphone close to your mouth and speak loudly—if the recording meter moves slightly, the connection is good, and the problem is between your microphone and your computer. You might be able to solve this problem by downloading new device drivers from the microphone manufacturer's Web site, or it might be simpler to replace the microphone.

8. When you finish reading the paragraph, click **Next**. Then click **Finish** to complete the wizard.

 CLOSE the Ease Of Access window.

Key Points

- To fit more or less content on your screen, you can change the size at which your monitor displays information.

- You can output information from your computer to two (or more) screens, either displaying the same content on both screens or doubling the size of your desktop.

- Windows Vista automatically locates the drivers necessary to install USB devices, so you can connect a device and start using it without further effort.

- You can configure your computer to receive input from multiple language-specific keyboards and to send keystrokes from your keyboard as if it were a different-language keyboard.

- A variety of options allow you to tailor your mouse to suit the way your work.

- New Tablet PC functionality makes it easier to write and move around efficiently by using a pen or your finger.

- You can print to a printer that is connected directly to your computer, or to a printer that is connected to another computer on your network.

- You can increase the quality of audio output and input if you connect external speakers and a microphone to your computer.

Keyboard Shortcuts

Press this	To do this
Ctrl+Esc	Open the Start menu.
Ctrl+Tab	Move forward through dialog box tabs.
Ctrl+Shift+Tab	Move back through dialog box tabs.
Esc	Cancel the current task.
Enter	Replace clicking the mouse for many commands.
F1	Display Help.

Chapter at a Glance

Display Web sites in Internet Explorer 7, **page 190**

Find, save, and return to Web sites, **page 202**

Discover and subscribe to RSS feeds, **page 210**

6 Safely and Efficiently Accessing the Internet

In this chapter, you will learn to:

- ✔ Connect to the Internet.
- ✔ Display Web sites in Internet Explorer 7.
- ✔ Block pop-up windows.
- ✔ Change your home page.
- ✔ Change the appearance of Web content.
- ✔ Find, save, and return to Web sites.
- ✔ Print Web pages.
- ✔ Send Web pages and links to other people.
- ✔ Discover and subscribe to RSS feeds.
- ✔ Restrict objectionable content.

The Internet is a worldwide network consisting of millions of smaller networks that exchange information. Originally constructed and used by governments and large organizations for the exchange of text-based data, the Internet evolved almost overnight with the implementation in 1990 of a prototype for the World Wide Web, known simply as the *Web*, by Tim Berners-Lee. While combining the existing concept of *hypertext* with the Internet, Berners-Lee developed the system of hyperlinks and Uniform Resource Identifiers, also known as Uniform Resource Locators (URLs) that paved the way for the global exchange of information we take for granted today.

Browsing the Internet (also known as *surfing the Web*) has become an entertainment medium in itself, as well as a simple and powerful research solution that puts a world of information at your fingertips, literally. Students, scholars, business people, shoppers, gamers, and others can now find almost any information or entertainment they want on the Web. Many television programs are now available for viewing on the Internet, because their producers recognize that people are looking for entertainment on their computers rather than turning on the television.

Moreover, the Web is no longer a one-way information highway for individual computer users. The advent of personal Web spaces called *Web logs*, or *blogs*, means that anyone can post anything on the Web for family, friends, and complete strangers to view and respond to. Blogs range from personal diaries and ways for communities to keep in touch to sources of information on a specific topic that are replacing traditional media in importance. They can provide on-the-spot news about current events, and because they are not constrained by printing and production processes, they can "scoop" other media with late-breaking news. They are also uncensored and largely unregulated, meaning that viewers need to bear in mind that their information is not necessarily unbiased or correct.

Windows Vista includes Windows Internet Explorer 7, a *Web browser* with which you can easily find, view, search, print, and save Web pages while shielding your computer and the people who use it from exposure to malicious or objectionable content. Internet Explorer provides a framework in which you can view Web pages, and an engine with which you can perform basic tasks.

In this chapter, you learn how to configure Internet Explorer 7 to best fit your needs and how to use some of the great features not available in previous versions of Internet Explorer. You will personalize the Internet Explorer browser window and content display, and specify the amount of objectionable language, nudity, sex, and violence users of your computer are able to see.

See Also Do you need only a quick refresher on the topics in this chapter? See the Quick Reference section at the beginning of this book.

> **Important** No practice files are required to complete the exercises in this chapter. For more information about practice files, see "Using the Companion CD" at the beginning of this book.
>
> The exercises in this chapter assume that Internet Explorer 7 is your default Web browser. If it is not, you might have to vary the exercise steps slightly, but you will still be able to follow along with the exercises.

Connecting to the Internet

In the past, many employers were concerned that giving employees access to the Internet from their work computers would mean a loss of productivity, because people could receive and send personal e-mail messages, indulge in surreptitious Web surfing, or download objectionable content. These days, more and more employers are coming to the conclusion that Internet access can actually enhance the productivity of people in some jobs, and many provide organization-wide access.

In addition, Internet access is fast becoming one of the primary reasons for buying a home computer. Setting up a connection from your computer to the Internet is easier than ever with Windows Vista. The most difficult part of the process will likely be finding out what types of connections are available from Internet service providers (ISPs) in your area and deciding which one you want to use.

To use the Internet, you must connect to a computer or network of computers that acts as a go-between, by using one of the following types of connections:

- *Local area network (LAN)*. If you connect to the Internet through a LAN, you are actually connecting to a computer on your network that has been set up to provide Internet access; connections to upstream providers are handled for you by that computer.

- *Cable*, *ISDN*, **or** *DSL*. If you are connecting through a dedicated cable, ISDN (integrated services digital network), or DSL (digital subscriber line) connection—one that doesn't require a user account name or password—you will connect your computer to a *router* (usually one leased or purchased from your service provider). After following the service provider's instructions to set up the router for the first time, Windows Vista will automatically handle the connection process.

- *Dial-up connection*. If you are connecting through a dial-up connection, you are making a connection from your computer to another computer using two *modems* and an ordinary telephone line. The remote computer usually belongs to the *Internet service provider (ISP)* with whom you have set up your user account.

Whichever type of connection you use, the Windows Vista Network And Sharing Center can help you with the necessary setup work.

To create an Internet connection through an ISP, you need to first set up a user account. The ISP will then provide the information you will need to provide to complete the connection process in the Network And Sharing Center, such as:

- The specific *IP address* or the address of the *DHCP server*

- *DNS* addresses and domain names

- *POP3* or IMAP settings for incoming e-mail

- *SMTP* settings for outgoing e-mail

In this exercise, you will use the Network And Sharing Center to connect to the Internet through a broadband or dial-up connection. There are no practice files for this exercise.

BE SURE TO log on to Windows Vista and have your Internet connection information available before beginning this exercise. If you are connecting through a dial-up connection, you must have the name and access number of your ISP and your dial-up user account name and password.

Start

1. Click the **Start** button, click **Control Panel**, and then in **Control Panel**, click **Network and Internet**.

2. Under **Network and Sharing Center**, click the **Connect to a network** task.

   The Connect To A Network wizard starts, displaying all available network connections. If you have several connections available, you can filter the list by clicking the Show arrow and then clicking Dial-up And VPN or Wireless.

3. At the bottom of the page, click the **Set up a connection or network** link.

4. On the **Choose a connection option** page, click **Connect to the Internet**, and then click **Next**.

> **Tip** You can return to a previous page of the wizard at any time by clicking the Back button in the upper-left corner of the window.

5. On the **How do you want to connect** page, click either **Broadband** or **Dial-up**, and then click **Next**.

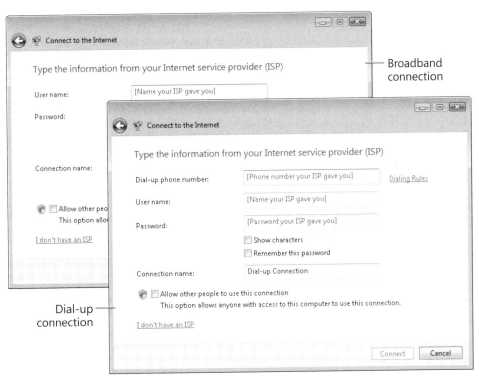

Broadband connection

Dial-up connection

6. Enter the requested connection information, and then click **Connect** to close the window and create the connection.

CLOSE the Network And Internet window.

> **Tip** To connect to an existing network connection, click Connect To on the Start menu. Then in the Connect To A Network wizard, click the connection you want to use, and click Connect.

Displaying Web Sites in Internet Explorer 7

Whether or not Internet Explorer 7 is your default browser, you can start it from the Windows Vista Start menu and use it to explore the Web. With all browsers, you navigate to a specific Web site by typing its address, or Uniform Resource Locator (URL), in an address box and then clicking *hyperlinks* to move to specific Web pages.

In the past, you needed to open your Web browser multiple times if you wanted to view multiple Web pages at the same time. Although you can still do that with Internet Explorer 7, you will usually want to display multiple Web sites on separate *tabs* within one Internet Explorer program window. *Tabbed browsing* is convenient because it takes far less time to open a new tab than it does to start a new instance of Internet Explorer, and it's much easier to move between open sites by selecting from the tabs at the top of one window than by selecting from taskbar buttons that don't display as much information. When you have several pages open, you can display thumbnails or a list of all the open pages and then click the page you want to view. When the open tabs exceed the available space, navigation buttons appear to the right or left of the tabs.

For the duration of the session (until you close the tab), Internet Explorer keeps track of the pages you visit within each tab. You can move backward and forward between those pages.

While you are working in Internet Explorer, you might want or need to interact with other programs—for example, to edit an HTML file you are working with, or to send a Web page or link by e-mail. You can tell Internet Explorer which program to open for a specific task on the Programs tab of the Internet Options dialog box. Select an HTML editor from the list of those installed on your computer, and then if you want Internet Explorer to use different default programs for other tasks than those set in Windows, click Set Programs to open the Windows default program settings and make your changes.

See Also For more information about choosing a default Web browser, e-mail client, media player, contact management system, and other programs, see "Specifying the Default Program for a Type of File" in Chapter 7, "Working with Programs."

In this exercise, you will start Internet Explorer and use various methods to open new, bookmarked, and linked Web sites and pages. You will open pages in the same window, on a new tab in the same window, and in a new window. You will navigate between sites and pages, close some sites, and then close them all. There are no practice files for this exercise.

> **BE SURE TO** have an active Internet connection before beginning this exercise.

1. In the upper-left corner of the **Start** menu, click **Internet**.

   > **Troubleshooting** The name of your default Internet browser appears below the word *Internet*. If Internet Explorer is not your default browser, point to All Programs on the Start menu, and then click Internet Explorer.

   Internet Explorer starts, displaying your current home page.

   See Also For information about changing the site that opens when you start Internet Explorer, see "Changing Your Home Page" later in this chapter.

Go

2. Click once in the **Address** box to select the URL of the currently displayed page. Type http://www.microsoft.com, and then click the **Go** button or press [Enter].

   The Microsoft Web site replaces your home page.

3. In the **Address** box, replace *microsoft* with msn. Then press [Alt] + [Enter].

   > **Tip** You don't have to type a full Web site URL to move to a different site or a different page within the same site. You can change as much or as little of the URL as necessary.

   The MSN site opens on a new tab.

4. Click the **Start** button (or press the 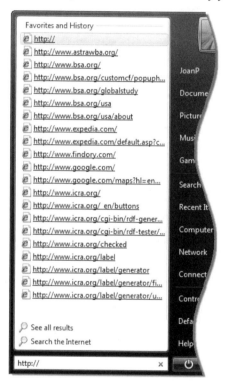 key).

When the Start menu opens, the insertion point is already in the Start Search box in the lower-left corner of the menu.

5. In the **Start Search** box, type http://.

Windows filters all the indexed information on your computer and displays a list of items containing the characters you've typed; in this case, items from your Favorites and History lists, as well as the entry you're currently typing.

You can click any Web site or page in the list to open it in Internet Explorer.

> **Tip** Internet Explorer records the Web sites you visit in your History list, so you can easily locate a site you have previously been to. Favorites are sites or locations that you save so you can return to them later.

6. In the **Start Search** box, complete the URL by typing money.msn.com. Then press Enter .

As you type, Windows continues to filter the item list shown on the Start menu. When you press Enter, the home page of the MSN Money site opens in a new tab, in the existing Internet Explorer window.

7. On the page, below the MSN Money title, click one of the links to other pages of the MSN Money site.

   The selected page replaces the home page you were viewing.

8. Right-click another of the page links to display a menu of options for working with that page.

Page links

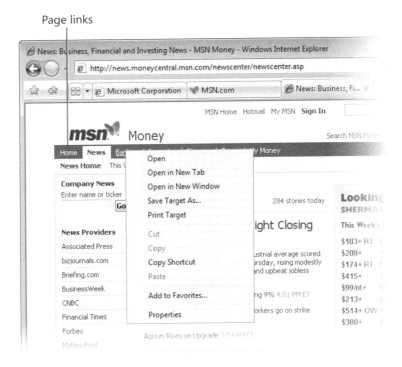

9. On the context menu, click **Open in New Tab**.

   The selected page opens in a *background tab*, so that the tab displaying the page you linked from is still on top of the others.

   > **Tip** Clicking Open In New Window starts an entirely new instance of Internet Explorer.

10. In the tab area, click the new tab to bring it to the front. (If you followed the instructions exactly so far, it is the fourth of four tabs.)

Back

11. Click the original MSN Money tab (the third tab), and then to the left of the **Address** box, click the **Back** button.

You return to the MSN Money home page. Because you have visited only two pages on this tab, either the Back button or the Forward button is active at any one time.

Recent Pages

12. To the right of the Back and Forward buttons, click the **Recent Pages** button.

A list of the pages visited on this tab appears, with a check mark indicating the current page.

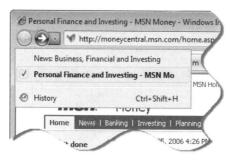

13. In the list, click the page that doesn't have a check mark next to it, to return to that page.

14. On the **Command** bar, click **Tools**. Then on the **Tools** menu, click **Internet Options**.

The Internet Options dialog box opens, displaying the General tab.

15. In the **Tabs** area, click **Settings**.

The Tabbed Browsing Settings dialog box opens.

16. Review the types of changes you can make, and change any settings that you want. Then click **OK** in the **Tabbed Browsing Settings** dialog box and again in the **Internet Options** dialog box.

Close Tab

17. In the browser window, click any one of the middle tabs, and then click the **Close Tab** button that appears.

The tab closes, and the tabs to its right slide over to take its place.

Close

18. On the Internet Explorer window title bar, click the **Close** button.

Because more than one tab is open, Internet Explorer prompts you to confirm that you want to close them all. (This is one of the settings you can change in the Tabbed Browsing Settings dialog box.)

19. In the message box, click **Show Options**.

You can have Internet Explorer reopen the current set of tabs the next time you start it, or you can disable the warning. This warning actually does come in handy sometimes while making the transition to tabbed browsing—it can be easy to forget that closing the window affects more than one site.

20. In the message box, click **Close tabs** to close all the tabs and exit Internet Explorer.

> **Tip** From time to time, Microsoft releases a new version of Internet Explorer. If you have configured Windows Vista for automatic updates, you will be informed of all the updates when they happen. You can always find the latest version of Internet Explorer at *www.microsoft.com/windows/ie/.*

Protecting Personal Information

Microsoft and MSN are licensees of the TRUSTe Privacy Program, which means that every Microsoft or MSN Web site contains a link to a privacy statement that must inform you of the following:

- The types of personal, identifying information that are collected from you through the Web site
- The name of the organization that is collecting the information
- How the information is used
- With whom the information might be shared
- Your choices regarding collection, use, and distribution of the information
- The kind of security procedures that are in place to protect against the loss, misuse, or alteration of your information
- How you can correct inaccuracies in the information

For more information about TRUSTe, you can visit *www.truste.org*. If you have concerns about the protection of your personal information while using MSN Explorer, you can send an e-mail message to *MSNPrivacy@msn.com*.

Blocking Pop-Up Windows

Pop-up windows (or just *pop-ups*) are the small Web browser windows that open on top of (or sometimes below) the Web browser window when you display a Web site or click an advertising link. Pop-ups frequently display annoying advertisements, adware (fake warning messages containing links to product sites), spyware (malicious software that can collect personal information from your computer), or other types of content you did not invite and probably don't want. Some types of pop-ups are valid; these might appear when you click a link for more information or when you log on to a secure site.

The Internet Explorer Pop-up Blocker is a feature through which you can prevent unwanted pop-ups from displaying. The Pop-up Blocker is turned on by default. When a pop-up tries to open, an audio alert sounds, and the *Information Bar* appears at the top of the Internet Explorer content pane, notifying you that a pop-up has been blocked. If you want to display the pop-up, you can click a link on the Information Bar to configure specific pop-up options for that site. You have the option of turning off the audio alert and/or Information Bar notifying you when a pop-up is blocked.

You can allow all pop-ups that appear when you are viewing a specific site by adding the site to either the Pop-up Blocker list of allowed Web sites or your Trusted Sites list. You can temporarily allow pop-ups from a site you are visiting, and configure the filter level to allow pop-ups from secure sites or to block most or all pop-ups.

To modify Pop-up Blocker settings:

→ On the Internet Explorer **Tools** menu, point to **Pop-up Blocker**, and then click **Pop-up Blocker Settings**.

To turn off Pop-up Blocker:

1. On the **Tools** menu, point to **Pop-up Blocker**, and then click **Turn off Pop-up Blocker**.

2. In the **Pop-up Blocker** message box requesting confirmation, click **Yes**.

Changing Your Home Page

Each time you open a new instance of Internet Explorer without specifying a target Web page, the browser window opens and displays your *home page*. This is generally the main page of a site to which you often refer, such as MSN for general information, your company's home page for internal news, or a financial Web site for tracking your investments. If you prefer, you can select a blank (Internet Explorer–generated) page as your home page and display a specific Web site only when you choose to visit one.

In this exercise, you will change your home page, add a second home page, and then set a blank home page. There are no practice files for this exercise.

BE SURE TO have an active Internet connection before beginning this exercise.

1. On the **Start** menu, click **Internet**.

> **Troubleshooting** If Internet Explorer is not your default browser, point to All Programs on the Start menu, and then click Internet Explorer.

Internet Explorer starts, displaying your current home page on the default tab.

When you purchase a new computer or upgrade your operating system, the computer or software manufacturer usually sets your home page as part of that process.

2. Replace the URL in the **Address** box with http://www.microsoft.com, and then press Enter.

The Microsoft home page replaces your default home page on the current tab.

Home

3. On the **Command** bar, click the **Home** arrow, and then in the list, click **Add or Change Home Page**.

The Add Or Change Home Page dialog box opens, displaying the current URL.

4. In the dialog box, click **Use this webpage as your only home page**, and then click **Yes**.

Launch Internet
Explorer Browser

5. Close the browser window. Then on the **Quick Launch** toolbar, click the **Launch Internet Explorer Browser** button.

   Internet Explorer restarts, displaying the Microsoft Web site home page as your default home page.

6. In the **Address** box, replace *microsoft* with msn, and then press Enter.

   The MSN home page opens on the current tab.

7. In the **Home** list, click **Add or Change Home Page**. Then in the dialog box, click **Add this webpage to your home page tabs**, and click **Yes**.

8. Click the **Home** button.

   Internet Explorer displays the two home pages you have set, on separate tabs.

9. In the **Home** list, point to **Remove**, and then click **Remove All**. Then in the **Delete Home Page** dialog box, click **Yes**.

10. Click the **Home** button.

    Internet Explorer displays your blank home page.

 BE SURE TO set your home page or pages as you want them before continuing.

Changing the Appearance of Web Content

Some Web sites set the formatting, such as fonts, font sizes, and text and background colors, used in their pages in order to control the way the site looks on your screen. Others don't. In the latter case, you can change the appearance of content displayed in the Internet Explorer browser window by changing the formatting. You might make these changes for personal preference or for readability if, for instance, you have trouble distinguishing certain colors or find it difficult to read small text on a computer monitor.

To change the size of the text on Web pages that don't specifically set the text size:

→ On the Internet Explorer **Page** menu, point to **Text Size**, and then click the size you want: **Smallest**, **Smaller**, **Medium** (the default), **Larger**, or **Largest**.

To change the text and background colors used on Web pages that don't specifically set the color:

1. On the Internet Explorer **Tools** menu, click **Internet Options**.

2. On the **General** tab of the **Internet Options** dialog box, in the **Appearance** section, click **Colors**.

3. In the **Colors** dialog box, clear the **Use Windows colors** check box.

4. Click the **Text, Background, Visited**, or **Unvisited** color button, select the color you want to use for that feature, and then click **OK** in each open dialog box.

To change the font size, text colors, and background color of all Web pages (even Web pages that specify those elements):

1. Complete the previous steps to change font sizes and set custom colors.

2. On the **General** tab of the **Internet Options** dialog box, in the **Appearance** section, click **Accessibility**.

3. In the **Formatting** area of the **Accessibility** dialog box, select the **Ignore colors specified on webpages** check box and the **Ignore font sizes specified on webpages** check box.

4. Click **OK** to effect your changes.

To change the fonts used on Web pages and in documents that don't specifically set a text font, follow the same procedures, but click Fonts to change the fonts, and then select the Ignore Font Styles check box in the Accessibility dialog box.

Finding, Saving, and Returning to Web Sites

To increase the efficiency with which you can move among sites you are currently viewing or have viewed in the past, and to make it easier to find sites that contain the information you need, Internet Explorer offers the following navigation tools, which put Web site information at your fingertips:

- **Live Search.** With this feature, you can perform plain-text searches on the Web, or search the files and folders on your computer.

- **Favorites Center.** This window contains links you have saved to Web sites, folders, and files; links to RSS feeds you have subscribed to; and a record of your Internet browsing history. You can display the Favorites Center as a multi-page window or pin it as a pane in the browser window.

- **Quick Tabs.** This feature displays screenshots of all Web pages currently open.

- **Tab List.** Clicking this button displays a submenu of the open Web pages.

Favorites Center
displaying
browsing history

Quick Tabs display

In this exercise, you will conduct a simple search, expand the available search resources, save a page to your Favorites Center, and return to a page from your History list. There are no practice files for this exercise.

BE SURE TO start Internet Explorer before beginning this exercise.

Search

1. In the **Live Search** box at the right end of the Navigation bar, type a plain-text query, and then click the **Search** button.

Live Search searches the Web for pages containing content and keywords related to your question, and displays the results in the browser window. You can display any listed site by clicking its title, which is underlined to indicate that it is formatted as a hyperlink.

Search Options

2. At the right end of the **Live Search** box, click the **Search Options** arrow.

Depending on the programs installed on your computer, Live Search may be the only search provider listed.

3. In the **Search Options** list, click **Find More Providers**.

The Internet Explorer Web site appears, displaying links to two dozen search providers you can make available to the search utility. Adding a provider from this list makes it available in the Search Options list. To conduct a search through that provider, enter your search term, click the Search Options arrow, and then in the list, click the provider you want to use.

Add to Favorites

4. On the toolbar, click the **Add to Favorites** button, and then in the list, click **Add to Favorites**.

You can create additional folders within your Favorites Center by clicking New Folder.

5. In the **Add a Favorite** dialog box, click **Add** to make the current page available from your Favorites Center.

Favorites Center

6. On the toolbar, click the **Favorites Center** button.

The Favorites pane expands, displaying the page (Favorites, Feeds, or History) you most recently viewed.

7. If the Favorites page is not displayed, click **Favorites** to verify that the Add Search Providers page is there. Then click the **History** arrow, and in the list, click **By Site**.

The History page displays an alphabetical list of the sites you have visited in the last 20 days. You can click any site in the History list to open it in Internet Explorer.

Tip On the General tab of the Internet Options dialog box, you can clear the History list or change the number of days (0 to 999) Internet Explorer retains your browsing history.

Pin the Favorites
Center

8. In the upper-right corner of the **Favorites Center**, click the **Pin the Favorites Center** button to convert the temporary window to a pane.

9. In the **History** list, click **By Date**, click **Today**, click **search.live (search.live.com),** and then click **Live Search: What plants grow on volcanoes?** to return to your original search results.

Close

10. Experiment with other aspects of the Favorites Center. When you finish, click the **Close** button in the upper-right corner of the Favorites Center.

> **Tip** To clear your Internet Explorer history, click Delete Browsing History on the Tools menu.

 CLOSE the Internet Explorer window.

Printing Web Pages

While you're browsing the Web, Internet Explorer makes it easy to print the Web page you're viewing, either on paper, to a file, or if you have Microsoft Office OneNote 2007 installed on your computer, to your OneNote notebook. Before printing the page, you can preview it and adjust settings such as the paper size, the orientation, and the margins.

> **Tip** You can quickly send the contents of a Web page and a link to that page to your default OneNote notebook by clicking Send To OneNote on the Internet Explorer Tools menu. You must have previously started OneNote at least one time before you can send information to it from Internet Explorer.

In this exercise, you will preview and print a Web page. There are no practice files for this exercise.

 BE SURE TO install a printer before beginning this exercise.

1. On the **Start** menu, type http://www.otsi.com in the **Start Search** box, and then press Enter.

The home page of our company Web site opens. The size and orientation of the page content is defined so that the content is in a horizontal format.

Print

2. On the **Command** bar, click the **Print** arrow, and then click **Print Preview**.

The OTSI home page appears in a Print Preview window, in the default portrait (vertical) orientation. Because the page content is restricted to a horizontal format, accepting these default settings will result in a small version of the Web page at the top of the printed page. Around the page, four Adjust Margin icons indicate the page margins; you can change the left, right, top, or bottom margin by dragging the appropriate Adjust Margin icon.

Adjust Margin icon

Landscape

3. On the Print Preview window toolbar, click the **Landscape** button.

In landscape (horizontal) orientation, the content fits more appropriately on the page.

View Full Width

4. On the toolbar, click the **View Full Width** button.

The page expands to fill the width of the window.

Print Document

5. Experiment with other adjustments. Then on the toolbar, click the **Print Document** button.

The Print dialog box that opens is similar to the Print dialog box that opens when you print a document from another program, such as Microsoft Office Word. Rather than having their own printing capabilities, programs that you run on your computer simply use the built-in Windows printing function.

6. Select the printer you want to use, and then click **Print** to print the page exactly as shown in the Print Preview window. (Or if you would prefer to not actually print the page, click **Cancel**.)

The Print dialog box and Print Preview window close, and your document is printed, with the Web page title and page number at the top of each page and the URL and date of printing at the bottom of each page.

CLOSE the Internet Explorer window.

Sending Web Pages and Links to Other People

Sharing information from Web pages can be very useful—for example, when you're re-
searching information (such as travel plans) on behalf of a group, or come across an article
that you know would be of interest to a co-worker, friend, or family member. To share the
information, or to simply keep a copy of it handy in an easily accessible electronic format,
you can send a static copy of the page (to someone else or to yourself) embedded in an
e-mail message. Alternatively, you can send the page URL in a message, and the recipient
can click the URL to link to the "live" Web page.

In this exercise, you will first send a Web page in an e-mail message, and then send a link
to a Web page. There are no practice files for this exercise.

> **BE SURE TO** configure a working e-mail account on your computer before beginning this
> exercise.

1. Start Internet Explorer to display your default home page.

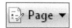

2. On the **Command** bar, click the **Page** button to display a menu of actions you can
   perform with the current Web page.

3. On the **Page** menu, click **Send Page by E-mail**. Then in the **Internet Explorer**
   Security message box that appears, click **Allow**.

   A new e-mail message opens in your default e-mail program. A copy of the currently
   displayed page is embedded in the message, not as a graphic, but as individual HTML
   and graphic elements. You can click any text or graphic in the embedded page and
   work with it as you would work with other e-mail message content.

4. Change the size of the message window, and notice that the content changes to fill the space.

5. Address the e-mail message to yourself, and then send it. (Or if you prefer, close the message window without sending the message.)

   You can work with the message you receive as you would with any other—you can view it, delete it, save it for later reference, or forward it to someone else.

6. On the **Page** menu, click **Send Link by E-mail**.

   The message created this time contains only the URL of the current Web page. Notice the variation in the message subject.

7. Address the e-mail message to yourself, and then send it. (Or if you prefer, close the message window without sending the message.)

 CLOSE the Internet Explorer window.

Discovering and Subscribing to RSS Feeds

Really Simple Syndication (RSS) is a technology with which Web sites and blogs can send information to you, so that you don't have to visit the site. You can subscribe to an RSS feed from any site that offers one. Although RSS is a recent technology, RSS feeds are available for thousands of Web sites.

In the past, you had to install a newsreader program on your computer to subscribe to and view RSS feeds. Now you can subscribe to feeds directly from Internet Explorer 7. When you visit a site that has one or more RSS feeds, the RSS button on the Command bar becomes active (orange); a star-like symbol in the upper-right corner indicates new content. You can click the button to view the default feed, or click its arrow to display a list of feeds available from the site. You can also choose to have Internet Explorer play an audio alert when it finds an available feed on a Web page.

Web-based newsreaders and many other sites, such as the MSN Syndicated Content (RSS) Directory at *rss.msn.com* offer directories of RSS feeds. You simply click the link next to a site you like to subscribe to it.

Subscribing to an RSS feed adds it to the Feeds page of your Internet Explorer Favorites Center. You can return to it at any time to view up-to-date article synopses, and click any headline that interests you to display the article. RSS feeds can include the publisher's recommendation for how often subscribers will receive updates. You can stipulate the minimum update frequency for the feeds you subscribe to from Internet Explorer 7. To control the feed settings, display the Content tab of the Internet Options dialog box, and then in the Feeds area, click Settings.

Your Favorites Center is available to you only on the computer it is stored on. If you want to access your newsfeeds from any computer, you can connect to a Web-based newsreader such as one of the following:

- My MSN, a home page you can personalize with the elements you want to see when you start your Web browser, accepts RSS feeds. To use this site, you need to register an e-mail address as a Microsoft .NET Passport or Windows Live ID. (You might already have done this for another purpose.) For more information, visit

  my.msn.com

- Google Reader displays all your RSS feeds without all the extra information that might be on your My MSN page. To use this reader, you need a Google account. For more information, visit

  www.google.com/reader/

- My Yahoo! also supports RSS feeds. To use this reader, you need a Yahoo! account. For more information, visit

  my.yahoo.com

Web-based RSS readers do not require that you install any software on your computer. To locate other readers, search the Internet for *RSS reader*.

Restricting Objectionable Content

In addition to the basic ways you can tailor your Web-browsing experience, Internet Explorer includes settings that protect your privacy and offer peace of mind regarding the types of content that can be viewed on your computer. The Content Advisor feature controls the types of content that Internet Explorer may display by monitoring Web sites in accordance with the Internet Content Rating Association, an independent organization that catalogs Web sites within rating categories that cover:

- Content that creates feelings of fear or intimidation, sets a bad example for young children, or encourages children to perform or imitate dangerous or harmful behavior

- Depictions of gambling or of the use of weapons, alcohol, tobacco, or other drugs

- Depictions of discrimination or encouragement to engage in discriminatory behavior

- Offensive language including profanity, expletives, terms for bodily functions, anatomical references, obscene gestures, explicit sexual references, and otherwise vulgar, discriminatory, or crude language

- Partial, frontal, or full nudity, revealing attire, and provocative displays

- Mild or explicit sexual activity, passionate kissing, and clothed or non-explicit sexual touching

- Violence, including aggressive, natural, or accidental violence; fighting in which creatures are injured or killed or damage is inflicted on realistic objects; injuring or killing of humans or non-threatening creatures; injuring or killing of humans with blood and gore; or wanton and gratuitous violence

- User-generated content, such as chat rooms, that is not controlled by a site owner and might or might not be moderated

You can add other rating systems such as SafeSurf (*www.safesurf.com*) to Content Advisor, to increase your level of control. Web site authors and owners who are aware of Internet rating systems voluntarily submit their sites for rating. You can allow only sites with a certain rating, and you can block the display of unrated sites (although this might result in a lot of sites being blocked because their owners don't know about the program).

> **Tip** For information about the Internet Content Rating Association and tips for ensuring safe Web browsing for kids, or to apply for an ICRA label for a Web site you control, visit *www.icra.org.*

For each of the content categories, you can specify the level of that type of content Internet Explorer may display: None, Limited, Some, or Unrestricted.

Protecting Children's Privacy

In November 1998, the U.S. Congress passed the Children's Online Privacy Protection Act (COPPA), which requires that operators of U.S.-based online services or Web sites obtain parental consent prior to the collection, use, disclosure, or display of the personal information of children under the age of 13. COPPA went into effect on April 21, 2000, and is governed by regulations established by the Federal Trade Commission.

More information about COPPA, including guides for parents, teachers, and Web site operators, is available at *www.ftc.gov/bcp/menus/consumer/data/child.shtm.*

In this exercise, you will configure the Content Advisor settings, and then see Content Advisor in action. There are no practice files for this exercise.

BE SURE TO start Internet Explorer before beginning this exercise.

1. On the Internet Explorer **Tools** menu, click **Internet Options**. Then in the **Internet Options** dialog box, click the **Content** tab.

2. In the **Content Advisor** area, click **Enable**.

3. In the **User Account Control** dialog box, if you're logged on as an administrator, click **Continue**. Otherwise, enter an administrator password, and then click **OK**.

> **Troubleshooting** Repeat step 3 each time the User Account Control message box appears while completing the remaining steps of this exercise.

The Content Advisor dialog box opens, displaying the Ratings tab.

4. In the **Select a category** list, click each category in turn and move the slider located below the category list to display descriptions of each restriction level.

   Some categories have three levels of restriction and others have four.

5. Set the restriction level for each category as you want it, and then click the **Approved Sites** tab.

   You can allow or deny the display of specific sites regardless of their content, by entering the site URL in the Allow This Website box and then clicking the Always button or the Never button.

   Troubleshooting Don't be misled by the names of the tab and text box—you can block sites as well as allow them by entering their information here.

6. Add any sites you want to this list, and then click the **General** tab.

If you activate Content Advisor without selecting the Users Can See Websites That Have No Rating check box, Internet Explorer blocks the display of any site that hasn't been submitted for rating by ICRA or another rating organization you specify, or whose site administrator hasn't added the rating code to the Web site's pages.

7. For the purposes of this exercise, leave the **Users can see websites that have no rating** check box cleared, and the **Supervisor can type a password** check box selected. Then in the **Supervisor password** area, click **Create password**.

If you don't proactively create a password, Content Advisor prompts you to do so the first time you activate it.

8. In the **Create Supervisor Password** dialog box, type P@ssw0rd in the **Password** and **Confirm password** boxes, and click **OK**. Then click **OK** in the message box confirming that the password was successfully created.

You can display the Internet Explorer Web page that lists currently available rating systems by clicking Find Rating Systems in the Rating Systems area.

9. In the **Content Advisor** dialog box, click **OK**. Then click **OK** in the message box confirming that Content Advisor has been enabled.

In the Internet Options dialog box, the buttons in the Content Advisor area change to Disable and Settings.

10. Close the **Internet Options** dialog box, and then close the **Internet Explorer** window.

    The Content Advisor settings are applied to all windows opened after this point. If you try to open a site that does not meet your criteria, Internet Explorer displays a dialog box restricting access to the site.

    You must enter the supervisor password to access sites that don't meet the established criteria. You can browse the Web to see if you come across a site restricted by Content Advisor. Keep in mind that only sites that include their ratings within the page code are filtered by Content Advisor.

11. Click the **Start** button, type http://www.microsoft.com in the **Start Search** box, and then press ⌊Enter⌋.

    Internet Explorer starts and displays the Microsoft Corporation Web site home page. Content Advisor displays a warning that the page has been rated by a rating system that you don't have installed.

> **Troubleshooting** In fact, the RSACi rating system used by the Microsoft Web site has been merged into the ICRA rating system, but at the time we wrote this book, Content Advisor wasn't aware of that. Perhaps it will be by the time you work through this exercise.

12. Select the **Always allow this website to be viewed** option, type P@ssw0rd in the **Password** box, and then click **OK**.

13. Click any of the links in the **Product Families** list.

Content Advisor again restricts you from displaying the page. Obviously, this type of constant restriction can be quite irritating. After you view a few other Web sites with your criteria in place, you might want to make adjustments to the Content Advisor settings to fine-tune the way it works.

14. To disable Content Advisor, click **Internet Options** on the **Tools** menu, and on the **Content** tab of the **Internet Options** dialog box, click **Disable**.

To prevent other people from changing the restrictions you have set on your computer, after activating Content Advisor, you must enter the supervisor password to change its settings or disable it.

15. In the **Supervisor Password Required** message box, type P@ssw0rd in the **Password** box, and then click **OK**. If a message box notifies you that Content Advisor has been turned off, click **OK**. Then close the **Internet Options** dialog box.

 CLOSE the Internet Explorer window.

Tip On the Advanced tab of the Internet Options dialog box are many settings that affect various aspects of Internet Explorer, such as accessibility, browsing, printing, and searching. For the most part, you are unlikely to need to change these options. However, if you find yourself wishing that some aspect of Internet Explorer worked a different way, you might want to display the Advanced tab to see if one of its options will do the trick.

Key Points

- The Windows Internet Explorer 7 tabbed browsing interface lets you open multiple Web sites in a single instance of Internet Explorer. You don't clutter up the taskbar, and it's faster and easier to open and switch between sites.

- If you want to quickly return to a site you've already visited, you can locate and open it from the Start menu.

- Not only can you change the home page that opens when you start Internet Explorer, but you can open multiple home pages.

- You can personalize the look of the browser window as well as the way content appears and performs within the window.

- Windows Vista incorporates safeguards that shield computer users from objectionable Internet content. What you see is up to you: You can specify the level of protection you want for yourself and for other users of your computer.

Keyboard Shortcuts

Press this	To do this in Internet Explorer 7
Ctrl+click	Open links in a new tab in the background.
Ctrl+Shift+click	Open links in a new tab in the foreground.
Ctrl+T or double-click an empty	Open a new tab in the foreground space on the tab row.
Ctrl+Tab or Ctrl+Shift+Tab	Switch between tabs.
CTRL+W or ALT+F4	Close current tab (or current window when there are no open tabs).
Alt+Enter	Open a new tab in the foreground from the Address bar.
Ctrl+n (where *n* is a number	Switch to a specific tab number between 1 and 8.
Ctrl+9	Switch to the last tab.
Ctrl+Alt+F4	Close other tabs.
Ctrl+Q	Open Quick Tabs (thumbnail view).

Chapter at a Glance

Install and remove programs, **page 222**

Manage hard disks, **page 227**

Specify the default program for a type of file, **page 232**

7 Working with Programs

In this chapter, you will learn to:

- ✓ Install and remove programs.
- ✓ Manage hard disks.
- ✓ Start programs automatically.
- ✓ Specify the default program for a type of file.
- ✓ Recover from software errors.
- ✓ Play games.

Nowadays you can purchase a computer, plug it in, and start working without installing any additional software. New name-brand computers usually come with the operating system (in this case, Windows Vista) already installed. They often also include software packages that provide the programs you need to carry out specific tasks, such as word processing. Sooner or later, however, you will want to install additional programs, from a CD, a network server, or a Web site.

Most programs place a link on the Start menu. You can start the program by clicking that link or by opening a file of a type that is associated with the program. For example, double-clicking an image file in Windows Explorer starts Windows Photo Gallery and then displays the graphic. You can change the program associated with a file type. For example, if you are more likely to want to work with photographs in an image-editing program, you can instruct Windows to open any file with a *.jpg* extension in that program when you double-click it. To save time, you can have Windows start programs for you, when you log on to the computer. You can easily change a few settings to make working with programs more efficient.

When you are ready, you will want to explore the programs that come with Windows Vista. Some of these programs are in the form of *gadgets* displayed on Windows Sidebar that keep tools such as a calculator or notepad immediately available. Others are stand-alone programs that provide tools to help you perform common tasks, such as scheduling appointments, keeping track of contact information, communicating via e-mail, or collaborating with co-workers. Previously you might have had to purchase a special software program to provide these functions that now come already installed. Although you still have that option, these built-in programs can provide invaluable time-saving support by putting specialized tools at your fingertips.

In this chapter, you will learn about installing new programs on your computer and re-moving programs you no longer need. You will set up a program to start automatically when you turn on your computer, and you will specify which program will open files of a particular type when you double-click them. Finally, you will take a tour of some of the programs that come with Windows Vista, and you will experiment with Sidebar.

See Also Do you need only a quick refresher on the topics in this chapter? See the Quick Reference section at the beginning of this book.

Important Before you can use the practice files in this chapter, you need to install them from the book's companion CD to their default location. See "Using the Companion CD" at the beginning of this book for more information.

Installing and Removing Programs

With so many programs available to help save you time, increase your productivity, broaden your knowledge base, or simply entertain you, one of your first tasks with a new computer system is usually installing programs. When you upgrade from a previous version of Windows, your installed programs remain available. If you regularly use several different programs, not having to reinstall them on your new system can save you a lot of time. When you purchase a new name-brand computer it might come with several programs pre-installed that you are not interested in using. If you no longer use a program—it didn't live up to your expectations, your interests changed, you replaced it with something better, and so on—and you don't intend to ever use it again, you should remove it to avoid taking up valuable disk space.

Installing Programs

You can install programs from a variety of sources, including physical media that you can hold in your hand—such as a CD, DVD, or floppy disk—and less tangible sources such as a file stored on your computer, on your network, or on a Web site. Regardless of the source of the installation files, you install almost all programs by running an executable file, which is often named *Setup.exe*. However, the precise installation process varies from program to program.

Here is what you might expect to encounter when installing from various sources:

- **CD or DVD installation.** Many software manufacturers use an *autorun file*, which is located in the *root* directory of the CD or DVD. When you insert a disc in a drive, Windows Vista looks for an autorun file and, if one is available, starts it automatically. The autorun file in turn starts an executable file that either leads you through a setup process or simply starts the program stored on the CD or DVD. Autorun files take the guesswork out of the setup process, because they don't require you to browse to a specific location, find a specific file, run a specific program, or make decisions about how to install the program.

- **Network installation.** If you work for a company that keeps the most current versions of its licensed software on one or more servers rather than distributing it on CD to its employees, you will likely install programs directly from a network server. Your network administrator will give you instructions for locating and installing these programs.

- **Internet installation.** Many companies supply free software or software upgrades that you can download or install from a Web site. To install a program over the Internet, click the link that is provided. If your Internet browser security settings allow file downloads and are set to prompt you for permission, you will have two options—to run the installation file from its current location on the Internet, or to download the installation file to your computer and run it from there. If you have a high-speed Internet connection through a DSL modem or a cable modem, and the installation file is small, it is simplest to run the installation file from the Internet. If you have a slower or less reliable connection, or the installation file is large, it is a good idea to download the file and run it locally.

Depending on the program you are installing, you might have to enter a unique registration code, called a *product key* or *CD key*, during the setup process. Product keys are issued by the software manufacturer, either physically or electronically:

- If you are installing the program from a CD or DVD, the product key is usually located on a sticker on the back of the jewel case.

- If you are installing the program from a network server, your network administrator will be able to supply the product key.

- If you are installing the program from the Internet, the software owner will supply you with a product key when you pay for it; free software might not require a product key, but the software supplier might request or require you to register with the company before installing the software. The information you provide might be used to register your interest in the product for support purposes, for statistical purposes, or so that the supplier can follow up with marketing materials and other information.

> **Tip** In the United States, the E-mail User Protection Act (HR 1910) requires that companies provide you with a means to remove yourself from mailing lists, and you can generally find a removal link or instructions at the bottom of the e-mail messages you receive from the company if you would prefer not to receive further messages.

Product keys are one of the methods software manufacturers use to try to prevent software piracy. A program that requires a product key for installation can't be installed without it. If you lose your product key, you won't be able to install the program in the future, unless you have registered your copy of the software and can successfully appeal to the software manufacturer for a replacement product key.

See Also For information about software piracy, see the sidebar "The Perils of Piracy" in Chapter 1, "Getting Started with Windows Vista."

Most software companies require that you read and acknowledge a license agreement before you can install their software. You might be tempted to just click I Agree so that you can move on, but bear in mind that the license agreement is a legal contract. As with any contract, it is a good idea to read the agreement before consenting to it and installing the software.

> **Troubleshooting** With Windows Vista, only a user with *administrative privileges* can install some types of programs on your computer. If you do not have administrative privileges for the computer on which you want to install a new program, or if you are logged in with a Standard account (which we recommend for security), Windows prompts you to enter an administrative password to continue.

Many programs offer multiple installation options, such as *typical*, *complete*, or *custom*. Some programs that you install from a CD or DVD offer the option of copying large files to your computer or accessing them from the CD or DVD when needed. To save space on your hard disk for the features you will use most, you might have the option of waiting to install rarely used program features until the first time you need them. When choosing your installation type, consider the way in which you will use the program, the amount of space it requires, and how much space is available on your hard disk. Also think about whether the installation source will be available to you later, in case you need to reinstall the program or access features that weren't installed initially. In most cases, the default (typical) installation fits the needs of the average user and is the best choice.

When you start the installation process, most programs offer you the opportunity to accept or change the installation location, which is usually a product-specific sub-folder within the *Program Files* folder on your drive C. Unless you have a very specific reason for doing so, there is no need to change this default location; accepting it guarantees that the program and Windows know where to find program files. While actively installing files, the installation program might display a progress bar to keep you informed about what is going on during the installation process, and you might be informed of specific actions and file installations as they occur.

When the installation process is complete, you might be required to restart your computer. Restarting the computer allows the installation program to replace older versions of files that are in use and to clean up after itself.

> **Tip** If you would prefer not to restart your computer after installing a program, you can close the dialog box by clicking its Close button. The final setup tasks will then be completed the next time you start or restart the computer.

Removing Programs

Most commercial programs have many components—executable files, reference files, theme or graphic files, shortcuts, registry settings, and so on—and each component has to reside in a specific location for the program to work correctly. If you want to remove a program from your hard disk, it would be tedious—and with some large programs, virtually impossible—to track down and delete all its components. To ensure that a program is removed completely, instead of deleting the program's files and folders directly, you should always uninstall the program through Control Panel, as described in the following steps.

1. Display **Control Panel**, and under **Programs**, click the **Uninstall a program** task.

   The Programs And Features window opens.

2. In the list of installed programs, select the one you want to remove.

Uninstall and Change buttons appear on the toolbar.

> **Tip** If you want to change the setup of a program after you have installed it—for example, to install parts of the program that weren't included in the original installation—you can click the Change button on the toolbar to re-run the program setup from files installed on your computer.

3. On the toolbar, click **Uninstall**.

Simple programs might be deleted immediately, and you can then simply close Control Panel. For programs with multiple components, the process is a little more complicated. A message box asks you to confirm that you want to proceed.

4. In the message box, click **Yes**. In the **User Account Control** dialog box, if you're running as an administrator, click **Continue**. Otherwise, enter an administrator password, and then click **OK**.

The uninstall program gathers information from your computer, including information about any shared components (files that are commonly required by many programs) used by the program you are removing. Then it deletes the files, shortcuts, and registry entries associated with the program.

> **Tip** The uninstall program should not remove any documents or other personal files you created by using the program. Nevertheless, it is a good idea to back up any information you don't want to lose.

If the program you are removing makes use of shared components, it might be necessary to restart your computer to complete the process. If a restart is necessary, a message box appears, and you have the opportunity to save files and exit programs before continuing.

5. After saving and closing files, click **Yes** to restart your computer now, or click **No** to complete the uninstall process when you next restart or start your computer.

If you click No, the program will remain in the list in the Programs And Features window until the next time you start or restart your computer.

Managing Hard Disks

Each program that you install and each file you create or save on your computer requires a certain amount of space on the hard disk allocated for that purpose. By default, most programs install to the *Program Files* folder on drive C. With most setup programs, you can choose a different location during the installation process, but there is rarely a reason to do so.

If you have a small hard disk drive, or if your hard disk is partitioned and the primary drive is smaller than ideal for the amount of data you want to store on it, you might need to take steps to clean up its contents from time to time.

You can monitor and manage your hard disks from the Disk Management area of the Computer Management console. To display information about the storage disks connected to your computer:

1. On the **Start** menu, right-click **Computer**, and then click **Manage**. In the **User Account Control** dialog box, if you're running as an administrator, click **Continue**. Otherwise, enter an administrator password, and then click **OK**.

   The Computer Management console starts.

2. In the left pane, expand **Storage**, and then click **Disk Management**.

Disk Management displays information about your computer's disk configuration, including hard disk drives, CD-ROM and DVD-ROM drives, and removable storage drives (regardless of whether they contain media). At a glance, you can see information about each disk, such as the file system, capacity, amount and percentage of free space, and status.

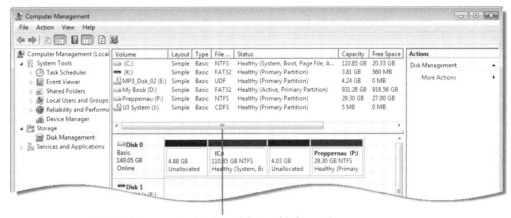

Scroll this pane to display additional information.

Clicking the More Actions link in the Actions pane displays additional options for working with the element currently selected in the Disk Management pane.

You can add volumes to a disk or change the disk type, and create new volumes from unallocated space. You can change the drive letter assigned to a volume, format the volume, increase its size by adding space from other disks, decrease its size, or delete it.

In the Settings dialog box, you can specify the color and pattern for the various regions of a disk (including unallocated and free space, partition types, and volume types) and set the display proportions for disk and disk regions, to make the information you want to see immediately available.

> **Tip** With extended use, files stored on your computer can become fragmented—divided into multiple chunks stored in non-contiguous locations on the disk. This can lead to slow performance. For information about repairing fragmented files, see "Improving Your Computer's Performance" in Chapter 14, "Optimizing Your Computer System."

It is not advisable to make changes to the format and allocation of your disks unless necessary; some changes are difficult to undo. Windows Vista includes a substantial amount of information that will help you to make decisions about the disk management for your computer.

To display the Disk Management Help file, open the Disk Management snap-in and then click the Help button on the Computer Management console toolbar.

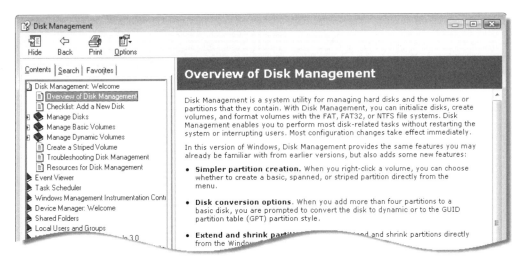

Starting Programs Automatically

If you use certain programs every day, you can have Windows start them for you whenever you log on to your account. For example, many people start their e-mail programs first thing in the morning; other people might work all day in a particular accounting program. You might open your organization's intranet site each morning to look for announcements or open a news Web site to stay up to date on the headlines.

To specify that a particular program should start automatically, you place a shortcut to the program in your *Startup* folder. Each user has his or her own *Startup* folder, and there is also a *Startup* folder that applies to all users, so you can choose to make a program start automatically for everyone, or just for yourself.

> **Tip** If the program you're starting requires a user account name and password, you will be prompted to enter that information when Windows starts the program.

You can access your *Startup* folder or the *Startup* folder that belongs to all users of your computer through the Start menu or through Windows Explorer. You cannot access another user's *Startup* folder.

In this exercise, you will specify that a program start automatically when anyone logs on to your computer. This example uses Microsoft Paint, but you can substitute any other program. There are no practice files for this exercise.

BE SURE TO log on to Windows Vista before beginning this exercise.

1. On the **Start** menu, point to **All Programs**. Scroll the **All Programs** list if necessary, right-click the *Startup* folder, and then click **Explore All Users**.

> **Tip** Clicking Explore opens your own *Startup* folder.
>
> If you only want to check the contents of the *Startup* folder and not change them, you can click Open All Users to open Windows Explorer with the Folders list closed.

Windows Explorer opens with the *Startup* folder for all users displayed in the Content pane. (Whether or not the folder contains any files depends on your installation.) Even if you usually work in Windows Explorer with the Navigation pane or the Folders list closed, choosing Explore All Users opens Windows Explorer with them both open.

2. Under **Programs** in the **Folders** list, click **Accessories** to display the contents of that folder in the Content pane.

> **Troubleshooting** If the Navigation pane and Folders list aren't open, open them now.

3. If necessary, scroll the **Navigation** pane until the *Startup* folder is visible.

4. In the **Content** pane, point to the shortcut to the **Paint** program, hold down the secondary mouse button, and drag the program to the *Startup* folder in the **Navigation** pane, releasing the mouse button when you see the *Move to Startup* ScreenTip.

   When you release the mouse button, a context menu (also called a shortcut menu) appears.

> **Troubleshooting** The context menu appears because you used the secondary mouse button to drag the file, rather than the primary mouse button. If you use the primary mouse button, the Paint shortcut simply moves to the folder, and you don't see the context menu. You would then need to copy it back into the *Accessories* folder.

5. On the context menu, click **Copy Here**. In the **User Account Control** dialog box, if you're running as an administrator, click **Continue**. Otherwise, enter an administrator password, and then click **OK**.

   A copy of the shortcut is created in the *Startup* folder for all users of your computer. Paint will start automatically for each user as she or he logs on to Windows.

6. In the **Folders** list, click the *Startup* folder to display your new shortcut.

Shut Down
Options

7. On the **Start** menu, click the **Shut Down Options** button, and then click **Log Off**. Then log on again.

   After Windows starts, a new Paint window opens.

> **CLOSE** the Paint window.
>
> **BE SURE TO** delete the Paint shortcut from the *Startup* folder if you don't want Paint to start every time you open Windows.

Specifying the Default Program for a Type of File

Usually you have just one program of a particular type installed on your computer—one word processor, one spreadsheet program, one database program, and so on. In each program, you create files of a specific type, identified by the file name extension. For example, the documents you create and save in Microsoft Office Word 2007 have the *.docx* extension appended to their file names. By default, these extensions are hidden from your view, and you never have to type them when you assign a name to a file. But they are there nevertheless.

One of the functions of the file name extension is to identify programs that can open the file. If you double-click the file in Windows Explorer and the default program associated with the file's extension is installed on your computer, Windows Vista starts the program, and that program then opens the file. This system is all well and good as long as each extension is "owned" by a single program.

> **Tip** When you double-click a file with an extension for which Windows has no program association, or if the associated program is not installed on your computer, Windows displays the Open With dialog box so that you can select the program you want to use. You might be able to open the file in a different program that creates similar files. For example, you can often use Microsoft Office Excel to open older spreadsheet files with the *.wks* extension, which were probably created in either Microsoft Works or Lotus 1-2-3.

However, the system breaks down if a file name extension represents a format that more than one installed program can work with. The classic example of file-type conflict arises with graphics files. The extensions of these files represent the format of the file rather than the program that created it. By design, most graphics programs can open and create files in several different graphics formats, because different formats are suited for different types of output. For example, one format might produce superior results in print, and another might be great for on-screen viewing. Of the files suited to viewing on a computer, some might produce high-quality images but also large file sizes; whereas others might produce acceptable quality with smaller sizes that are faster to download from the Web.

Until you install a graphics program on your computer, double-clicking a graphics file in Windows Explorer displays the graphic in Windows Photo Gallery. When you install a different graphics program, its installation program might lay claim to all graphics file formats. Then if you double-click a file with any of those extensions, Windows Vista calls upon that program to open the file. Or it might not. Double-clicking a file might continue to open it in Windows Photo Gallery, when you really want to work with the file in your new graphics program.

You can right-click a file and then click Open With to display the dialog box from which you can select the program you want to use. If you always want to open all files of a certain type with a different program than the one Windows Vista currently calls on for that task, you can change the default program for the type.

In this exercise, you will change the default program for a bitmap graphic from Windows Photo Gallery to Paint.

USE the *MusicBox* graphic. This practice file is located in the *Documents\Microsoft Press\ WindowsVistaSBS_Dlx\Programs* folder.
OPEN the practice file folder.

1. In the **Content** pane, double-click the *MusicBox* image.

   Unless the default program for opening bitmap files has changed, the image opens in Windows Photo Gallery

   See Also For information about Windows Photo Gallery, see "Viewing and Cataloging Pictures" in Chapter 12, "Working with Digital Media."

2. Close the **Windows Photo Gallery** window. Then in the **Content** pane, right-click the *MusicBox* image, point to **Open With**, and click **Choose Default Program**.

   The Open With dialog box opens, displaying the different programs you have installed that will open this type of file.

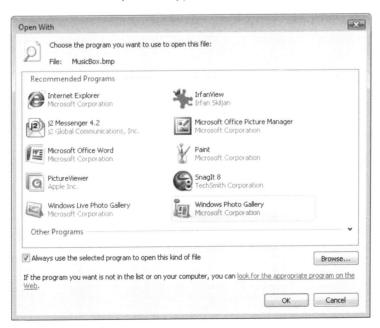

3. Under **Recommended Programs**, click **Paint**, and then click **OK**.

> **Tip** If you don't want to use any of the recommended programs, you can click Browse and navigate to the program you want to use.

Paint starts and opens the graphic file. Any files with the .bmp extension that you open after this will open in Paint, unless you change the default program to something else.

CLOSE the Paint window.

BE SURE TO reset the default program for bitmap graphics if you don't want them to continue opening in Paint.

Recovering from Software Errors

From time to time, you will inevitably experience a problem while running a software program. The problem might be due to a fault in the program, to a corrupt file, or to computer or network resource issues. If a program stops responding—commonly known as *crashing*—you will be unable to exit or restart from within the program window. When this happens, you can exit the program from the Windows Task Manager.

To start Windows Task Manager:

1. Press Ctrl+Alt+Del (once only; pressing this key combination twice will restart the computer).

2. On the screen that appears, click **Start Task Manager**.

Windows Task Manager includes tabs on which you can monitor:

- Applications, processes, and services running on your computer
- CPU usage, physical memory usage, and network utilization
- Users currently logged on to the computer

To exit a program, display the Applications tab, click the program you want to exit, and then click End Task.

Changing Your Default Middleware Programs

Middleware is software that connects two or more otherwise separate programs, which could be applications or system programs. Common types of middleware include transaction processing monitors and terminal emulation, messaging, and database access programs. Many middleware applications are Web-based. Because middleware is merely a connector and not part of the programs being connected, middleware programs are interchangeable. For example, you might choose to use Windows Internet Explorer or Firefox to browse the Internet, and you might choose to use Microsoft Office Outlook or Windows Mail to send e-mail messages from within those programs.

Windows Vista comes with a standard set of Microsoft middleware programs (Windows Media Player, Windows Internet Explorer, and Windows Mail). On a new computer, the original equipment manufacturer (OEM) might have installed and selected other middleware programs as the defaults. However, the Microsoft middleware programs are available as part of the Windows Vista installation, and you can select one or more of them as the default at any time.

To change the default settings:

1. On the **Start** menu, click **Default Programs.**

   The Default Programs window opens to the Choose The Program That Windows Uses By Default page.

2. Click the **Set program access and computer defaults** task. In the **User Account Control** dialog box, if you're running as an administrator, click **Continue**. Otherwise, enter an administrator password, and then click **OK**.

   In the Set Program Access And Computer Defaults dialog box, you have three choices:

   - *Microsoft Windows* sets all the standard Microsoft middleware programs as the defaults.

   - *Non-Microsoft* sets the current Web browser, e-mail program, media player, and instant messaging program as the defaults.

   - *Custom* sets the defaults for each of the five middleware options to your choice of either the Microsoft middleware program or the current program.

3. Make any necessary changes to your default middleware programs, and then click **OK**.

Playing Games

Windows Vista Service Pack 1 comes with 10 games of varying difficulty to entertain you when you have a few spare minutes:

- **Chess Titans.** A three-dimensional chess game with colored squares to guide you.

- **FreeCell.** A version of solitaire with all the cards visible. New look in Windows Vista.

- **Hearts.** A card game where having hearts and the queen of spades is bad and having the jack of diamonds is good. New look in Windows Vista.

- **InkBall.** Pinball for the Tablet PC, where bouncing balls are controlled by ink strokes.

- **Mahjong Titans.** A solitaire-like version of the classic Chinese game, played with tiles instead of cards.

- **Minesweeper.** A board game involving hidden mines and number clues. New look in Windows Vista.

- **Purble Place.** Three children's games in one: Comfy Cakes, Purble Shop, and Purble Pairs. New in Windows Vista.

- **Solitaire.** The classic card game, whose goal is to reorder randomly displayed cards by suit and rank. New look in Windows Vista.

- **Spider Solitaire.** A two-deck version of solitaire. New look in Windows Vista.

With the Business and Enterprise editions of Windows Vista, the *Games* folder and the games that come with Windows Vista are not installed by default. If a Games link does not appear on the right side of the Start menu, you can display it by following these steps:

1. Right-click the **Start** button, click **Properties**, and on the **Start Menu** tab of the Properties dialog box, click **Customize**.

2. Scroll the list in the **Customize Menu** dialog box, and under **Games**, click **Display as a link**. Then click **OK** in each of the open dialog boxes.

   A link to the *Games* folder now appears on the right side of the Start menu.

If the folder that opens when you click the Games link is empty, you need to turn on the display of Games from the Windows Features dialog box.

See Also For information about making games available, see "Turning Windows Features On and Off" in Chapter 14, "Optimizing Your Computer System."

To play a game, you double-click it in the *Games* folder. Clicking a game icon displays information about the game's publisher, developer, and genre (type) in the Details pane at the bottom of the folder window and information about how well it will perform on your computer in the Preview pane on the right side.

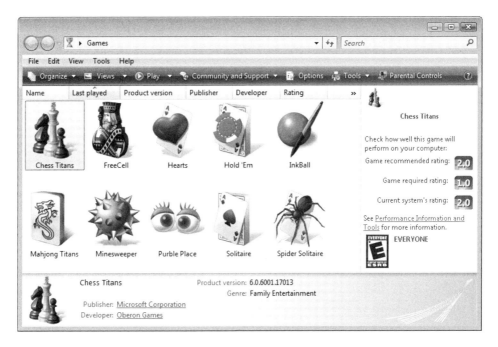

You might also want to while away some time playing games other than those that come with Windows Vista. You can find thousands of games in stores and online for purchase, and many are available for free download.

Installing a game adds a link to the game to your *Games* folder so that you can easily start all games from one central location.

Key Points

- When installing new programs, you can usually answer a few setup questions and then leave most of the details to Windows Vista. Similarly, Windows Vista provides a safe way of completely removing programs you no longer use.

- You can instruct Windows Vista to automatically start a program when you log on to your computer.

- You can choose the program Windows Vista starts when you double-click a file of a particular type.

- You can monitor applications, processes, and services running on your computer from the Windows Task Manager.

- You can monitor and manage the storage disks on your computer from the Disk Management area of the Computer Management console.

Keyboard Shortcuts

Press this	To do this
Windows logo key	Open or close the Start menu.
Ctrl+Esc	Open the Start menu.
Shift+F10	Display the shortcut menu for the selected item.
Windows logo key+Spacebar	Bring all gadgets to the front and select Windows Sidebar.
Windows logo key+G	Cycle through Sidebar gadgets.
Tab	Cycle through Sidebar controls.

Chapter at a Glance

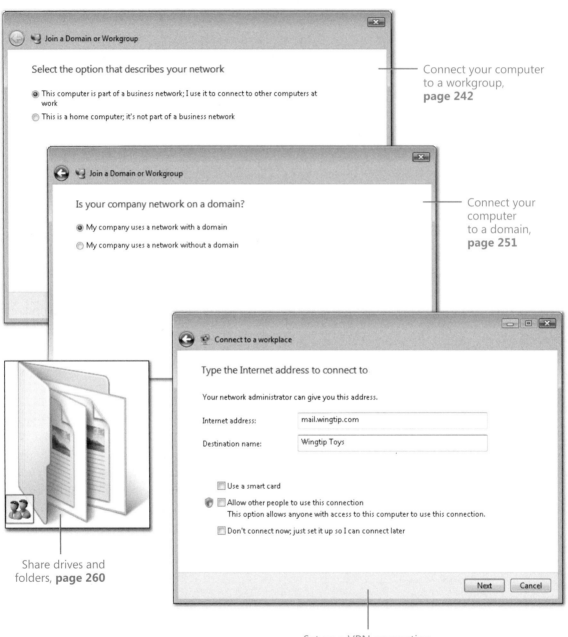

Connect your computer to a workgroup, **page 242**

Connect your computer to a domain, **page 251**

Share drives and folders, **page 260**

Set up a VPN connection, **page 245**

8 Making Connections

In this chapter, you will learn to:

✔ Connect your computer to a workgroup.

✔ Set up a VPN connection.

✔ Connect your computer to a domain.

✔ Access your domain computer remotely.

✔ Share drives and folders.

Every Windows Vista computer is set up to connect to a network through either a domain or a workgroup. If your computer is part of a domain, you are probably well aware of it—most networked computers within commercial office environments are on a domain. If your computer is part of a workgroup, you might not be aware of it—if your computer is the only one in your office or home, for example, you might not realize that your computer is the basis of its own network.

See Also For information about domains and workgroups, see the sidebar "Networks, Domains, and Workgroups" in Chapter 1, "Getting Started with Windows Vista."

There are various ways to connect to a network. When you are in the office or at home, you connect by means of a network cable or wireless network adapter. If you have a user account on a domain, and your network administrator has configured the system to allow *virtual private network (VPN)* connections, you can access domain resources when you are away from the office by setting up a VPN connection from a remote computer to the domain, over the Internet. If you set up your domain computer to allow Remote Desktop connections, you can not only access the information stored on it, but also log on to it remotely, and work on it as though you were working directly on it at the office.

In this chapter, you will learn how to join your computer to a new or existing work group, and how to set up your computer to log on to a domain. You will set up a VPN connection to a domain from an off-network location, and explore how to access domain resources. You will configure your computer to allow Remote Desktop connections, and then connect to a computer by using Remote Desktop. Finally, you will explore ways of sharing drives and folders on your computer with other network users.

See Also Do you need only a quick refresher on the topics in this chapter? See the Quick Reference section at the beginning of this book.

Important Before you can use the practice files in this chapter, you need to install them from the book's companion CD to their default location. See "Using the Companion CD" at the beginning of this book for more information.

Connecting Your Computer to a Workgroup

If you have several computers in your household and have set up a home network so that you can share resources such as printers, the computers are probably part of a workgroup. If there are fewer than 20 networked computers in your office, they might be part of a workgroup or they might be part of a domain. (If you have more than 20 networked computers, they are almost certainly part of a domain.) The main difference between the two is in how the network resources are managed. In a workgroup:

- No computer has control over any other.
- User accounts for each computer are administered individually; you need a user account on a specific computer to log on to that computer.
- All computers must be on the same local network (wired or wireless).

All the computers in a workgroup must be on the same network, but a network can include multiple workgroups. Windows Vista automatically joins your computer to a workgroup during installation. During a new installation, Windows Vista uses the default workgroup; during an upgrade, it retains the existing workgroup setting. You can change the workgroup you're joined to at any time, and you can create a new workgroup for specific resource-sharing purposes.

Tip You can reconfigure a workgroup-joined computer to connect to a domain; for example, if you take your personal laptop to the office, or want your home computer to be visible to other domain users.

In this exercise, you will join your computer to a new workgroup that you will create for the purpose of sharing resources. There are no practice files for this exercise.

> **BE SURE TO** start Windows Vista and display Control Panel before beginning this exercise.

1. In **Control Panel**, click **System and Maintenance**, and then click **System**.

   The System window opens, displaying information about your computer.

2. Under **Computer name, domain, and workgroup settings**, click **Change settings**. In the **User Account Control** dialog box, if you're logged on as an administrator, click **Continue**. Otherwise, enter an administrator password, and click **OK**.

   The System Properties dialog box opens, displaying the Computer Name tab.

3. To the right of **To use a wizard to join a domain or workgroup**, click **Network ID**.

   The Join A Domain Or Workgroup wizard starts.

4. With **This computer is part of a business network** selected, click **Next**.

> **Troubleshooting** It might seem logical to click This Is A Home Computer, but that option does not allow you to create a new workgroup.

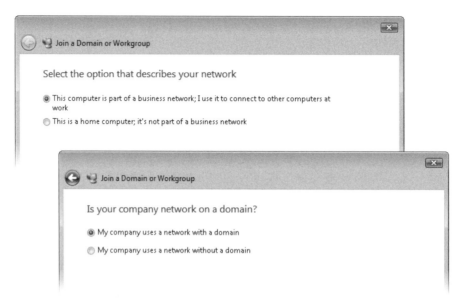

5. Click **My company uses a network without a domain**, and then click **Next**.

6. In the **Workgroup** box, type a descriptive name for the new workgroup. (No matter how you type it, the name appears in all capital letters.) Then click **Next**.

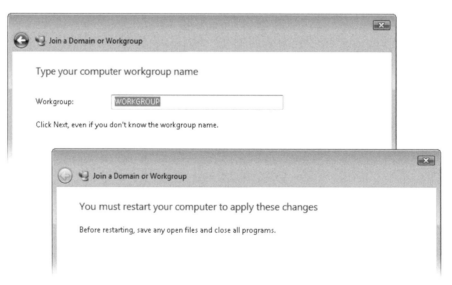

7. On the wizard's final page, click **Finish**.

8. In the **System Properties** dialog box, click **OK**.

   You must restart your computer for the change to take effect.

9. Close any open files, and exit any running programs. Then in the message box, click **Restart Now**.

10. After restarting, display the **System** window, and verify that your computer is now joined to the new workgroup.

 CLOSE the System window.

Setting Up a VPN Connection

Virtual private network (VPN) connections are becoming increasingly common in the corporate world. With a VPN connection, a domain user can access a private (corporate or institutional) network via the Internet, thus extending the private network so that she or he is virtually, if not physically, part of it.

If your organization has set up a *remote access server*, you can create a VPN connection to your domain over the Internet. Using this connection, you have full access to network resources while you are away from the office, which is extremely useful when you are traveling or working from home.

The speed of your VPN connection is limited by the speed of your Internet connection. If you are connecting to a VPN through a dial-up connection, you might run out of patience while waiting for your computer to access common network resources. However, if you are connecting through a broadband connection, access speeds can be nearly as good as being physically there.

In this exercise, you will create a VPN connection over the Internet. There are no practice files for this exercise.

Troubleshooting If your organization does not have a remote access server, you cannot complete this exercise.

 BE SURE TO have the host name or IP address of your organization's VPN server and your domain user account name and password available before beginning this exercise.

1. Display **Control Panel**, and then click **Network and Internet**.

The Network And Internet window opens.

2. Under **Network and Sharing Center**, click the **Connect to a network** task, and then at the bottom of the **Connect to a network** window, click the **Set up a connection or network** task.

The Connect To A Network wizard starts.

3. Scroll to the end of the **Choose a connection option** list, click **Connect to a workplace**, and then click **Next**.

4. On the **How do you want to connect** page, click **Use my Internet connection (VPN)**. The Type The Internet Address To Connect To page opens.

5. In the **Internet address** box, type the remote access server's host name or IP address, and in the **Destination name** box, type a name for the connection (for example, the company name).

6. Specify whether you want to make the connection available to other users of your computer or keep it to yourself, and then click **Next**.

7. On the **Type your user name and password** page, enter your network credentials.

Notice that you can display the characters of your password to confirm it before proceeding. If you select this option, your password will be visible only on this page, not during the actual logon process.

8. Click **Connect**.

You connect to the network. The network verifies your user account name and password, and then logs you on.

While your computer is connected to the network, a network icon appears in the notification area, and you can connect to the same network resources as you could if you were sitting at your desk at work.

Network icon

9. In the **Connect to a workplace** wizard, click **Close**.

   The first time you connect to the network, Windows Vista might prompt you to specify whether it is a private or public network.

10. If the **Set Network Location** window appears, click **Work**. Then in the **User Account Control** dialog box, if you're logged on as an administrator, click **Continue**. Otherwise, enter an administrator password, and click **OK**.

 CLOSE the Network And Internet window.

> **Tip** To disconnect from a VPN connection, right-click the network icon, point to Disconnect From, and then click the VPN connection.

Creating an Ad Hoc Wireless Network

If you want to share information stored on your computer with other people nearby and everyone's computer has a wireless network adapter, a simple method of sharing is to set up an ad hoc wireless network. In spite of the fact that members must be within 30 feet of each other, this type of network presents a lot of possibilities. For example, you might consider establishing an ad hoc network at a meeting of mobile computer users so that you can share information with other attendees on their own screens rather than an overhead projector. (After establishing the network, you can do this by using Windows Meeting, a really cool new feature of Windows Vista.)

See Also For information about Windows Meeting, see "Conducting Online Meetings" in Chapter 9, "Communicating with Other People."

Ad hoc networks are by definition temporary; they cease to exist when members disconnect from them, or when the computer from which the network was established moves beyond the 30-foot effective range of the others.

You can share an Internet connection through an ad hoc network, but keep in mind that the Internet connection is then available to anyone logging on to a computer that is connected to the network, and thus is likely not very secure.

To set up an ad hoc network:

1. On the **Start** menu, click **Connect To**.

2. In the **Connect to a network** window, click the **Set up a connection or network** task.

3. On the **Choose a connection option** page, click **Set up a wireless ad hoc (computer-to-computer) network**, and then click **Next**.

   > **Troubleshooting** The Set Up An Ad Hoc Network option appears only on computers that have wireless adapters.

4. Read the ad hoc network information, and then click **Next**.

5. Provide a network name, select whether the network is open or requires authentication, provide a security phrase if necessary, and then click **Next**.

After Windows Vista sets up the ad hoc network, you have the option of sharing your Internet connection.

To disconnect from an ad hoc network, display the Connect To A Network window, click the ad hoc network, and then click Disconnect.

Connecting Your Computer to a Domain

If you work in an organization that has a domain, you probably have a desk with a computer on it that you identify as your own. But as far as the domain is concerned, there is no connection between that computer and you as a domain user.

Logging on to a domain requires a password-protected domain user account. Domain user accounts (not to be confused with Windows user accounts) are administered centrally and are not associated with any particular computer. As a result, any domain user can log on to any computer on the domain.

For a computer to be visible to other domain computers, a network administrator must create a machine account for the computer. The machine account is linked to the computer name; no two computers on any one domain can have the same name. Changing the name of a domain-connected computer may require an update to the machine account information. However, you can replace a computer with another that has the same name and connect that computer to the domain by using the original machine account.

> **Tip** You can connect to a domain from a computer that doesn't have a machine account on that domain. Other domain users will not see the computer when browsing the domain, but they can connect to shared folders on it if they know the computer name.

In this exercise, you will connect a computer for which a machine account has already been created to a domain. There are no practice files for this exercise.

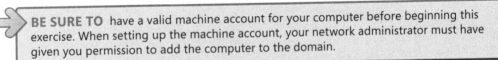

BE SURE TO have a valid machine account for your computer before beginning this exercise. When setting up the machine account, your network administrator must have given you permission to add the computer to the domain.

1. Connect your computer to your corporate network, either physically or through a VPN connection.

2. Display **Control Panel**, click **System and Maintenance**, and then click **System**.

3. In the **System** window, under **Computer name, domain, and workgroup settings**, click **Change settings**. Then in the **User Account Control** dialog box, if you're logged on as an administrator, click **Continue**. Otherwise, enter an administrator password, and click **OK**.

4. In the **System Properties** dialog box, click **Network ID**.

5. In the **Join a Domain or Workgroup** wizard, with **This computer is part of a business network** selected, click **Next**.

6. With **My company uses a network with a domain** selected, click **Next**.

   The wizard displays a list of the information you need to have before proceeding.

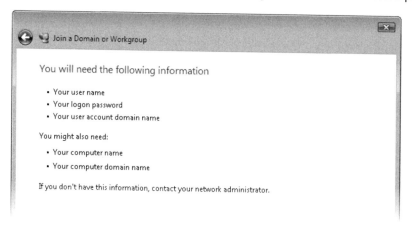

7. Make sure you have all the necessary information, click **Next**, and then enter your user name, password, and domain name.

   No matter how you type it, the domain name is displayed in all capital letters.

8. Click **Next**.

   Windows Vista searches the specified domain for a machine account with the same name as your computer and displays a message if it finds one.

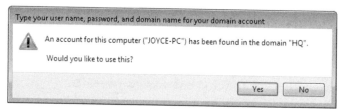

9. Click **Yes**.

Windows Vista asks whether you want to enable the user account on the computer.

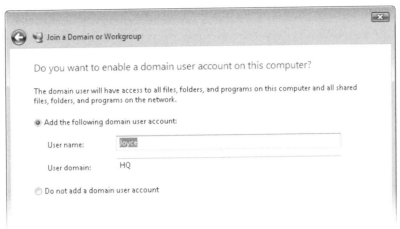

10. If you want to enable your user account, click **Next**. Otherwise, click **Do not add a domain user account**, and then click **Next**.

Windows Vista asks whether you want to have administrator privileges on this computer. Unless you are the domain's network administrator, it is safest to accept the default Standard Account option.

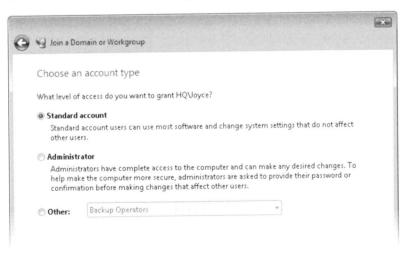

Troubleshooting Removing a computer from a domain requires Administrator privileges. Any administrator can enter his or her credentials to allow Windows Vista to complete that task. But if you plan to frequently switch between domains or between a domain and a workgroup, it might be more convenient to click Administrator.

11. Click **Next**, and then click **Finish**.

12. In the **System Properties** dialog box, click **OK**.

     A message box tells you that you must restart your computer for the change to take effect.

13. Close any open files, and exit any running programs. Then in the message box, click **Restart Now**.

14. When your computer restarts, press [Ctrl]+[Alt]+[Del] to display the Welcome screen. Then enter your domain credentials, and press [Enter] to log on to the domain.

Accessing Your Domain Computer Remotely

If you frequently travel with a mobile computer, or if you work from locations such as a central office, branch office, and home office, you don't need to have all your programs and data files on all the computers you work with. You can use the computer you have at hand to work virtually on your own computer by using *Remote Desktop*. If the computer is not on the same network as your own computer, you can use this handy feature only if you first establish a VPN connection to the domain.

Before you can connect to your own computer, you need to configure it to allow remote access. You can allow access via Remote Desktop from computers running a previous version of Windows or only from computers running Windows Vista. Restricting access to computers running Windows Vista provides a greater level of security because of its method of authentication (user verification).

> **Important** This level of security goes both ways. You can use Remote Desktop from your Windows Vista computer to connect to a computer running a previous version of Windows, but you will be asked to acknowledge that the Windows Vista security features will not be in effect for that connection.

After connecting to the remote computer, you see its desktop on your local computer's monitor. You use your computer's keyboard and mouse to start programs, move around, and work just as if you were sitting at the remote computer. Even the sound from the remote computer plays on your local system. You can select other local resources that you want to have available, such as printers, from the tab in the Remote Desktop Connection window.

During a remote session, the Connection bar (a yellow tab) appears at the top of the remote desktop. With the Connection bar buttons, similar to the window-management buttons found in the upper-right corner of a window, you can minimize or shrink the remote desktop to work on your local computer, while maintaining the connection to the remote computer. You can hide the Connection bar by clicking the thumbtack icon on its left edge, and display it again by pointing to the top of the remote desktop.

When you are ready to disconnect from a remote session, do not close the remote desktop or shut down the remote computer. Instead, you must log off from the remote computer by clicking the Shut Down Options button on that computer's Start menu, and then clicking Log Off (or if connected remotely to a computer running Windows XP, clicking Log Off on that computer's Start menu). If you shut down the remote computer, it will actually turn off, and you won't be able to access it again until you or someone else physically restarts it.

> **Important** Logging off from a remote desktop connection does not close files or exit programs in the way that logging off from a local computer session does. Unless you want them to remain open while you are disconnected from the remote computer, you should always close files and exit programs manually before logging off.

See Also For more information, search for *Remote Desktop* in the Help And Support Center.

In this exercise, you will set up your computer so that it can be accessed via Remote Desktop. Then you will connect to a computer configured for Remote Desktop from another computer. There are no practice files for this exercise.

> **BE SURE TO** display Control Panel before beginning this exercise.

1. In **Control Panel**, click **System and Maintenance**, and then under **System**, click the **Allow remote access** task. Then in the **User Account Control** dialog box, if you're logged on as an administrator, click **Continue**. Otherwise, enter an administrator password, and click **OK**.

The System Properties dialog box opens, displaying the Remote tab.

2. In the **Remote Desktop** area, to allow Remote Desktop connections from any other Windows computer, click **Allow connections from computers running any version of Remote Desktop**. To restrict connections to computers running Windows Vista, click **Allow connections only from computers running Remote Desktop with Network Level Authentication**.

3. If your computer is set up to go to sleep after a specific period of non-use, a **Remote Desktop** message box advises you that you won't be able to connect through Remote Desktop while the computer is in sleep mode. Click **OK** to close the message box.

See Also For information about managing your computer's power plan, see "Improving Your Computer's Performance" in Chapter 14, "Optimizing Your Computer System."

> **Tip** Any administrator of your computer is by default authorized as a remote user. If you want to authorize additional remote users, click Select Users, and then in the Remote Desktop Users dialog box, click Add. You can add individual users or groups of users.

4. In the **System Properties** dialog box, click **OK**.

5. From another computer on the domain, on the **Start** menu, point to **All Programs**, click **Accessories**, and then click **Remote Desktop Connection**.

The Remote Desktop Connection opens.

6. If the **Remote Desktop Connection** dialog box does not display the multi-tabbed area, click **Options**.

> **Tip** You can control the availability of your computer's resources during a remote session by selecting options on the Local Resources tab.

7. In the **Computer** box, type the name of the remote computer you want to access, and then click **Connect**.

> **Tip** If you don't know the computer name, you can click the Computer arrow, click Browse For More in the list, locate the computer you want to connect to in the Browse For Computers dialog box, and then click OK.

The Windows Security dialog box opens.

8. Enter your computer or domain credentials and, if you will be connecting to the remote computer from this computer on a regular basis, select the **Remember my credentials** check box. Then click **OK**.

> **Tip** To connect to a computer on a domain, enter your domain user name in the User Name box, in the format *DOMAIN\user name*. The domain shown below the Password box updates to reflect whether you are using computer or domain credentials.

A new window opens on your screen, displaying the desktop of the remote computer.

9. Explore the remote computer, and then when you are ready, log off from it.

BE SURE TO repeat steps 1 through 4 to turn off remote access, if you do not want to allow access from now on.

Storing and Managing Network Passwords

When you connect to a domain remotely, Windows Vista automatically stores your user name and password (collectively, your *credentials*) on the computer. You can change a password even if your computer is not connected to the domain. You can also remove passwords that you no longer use. If you change the credentials stored on your computer, Windows Vista passes the new credentials to the domain the next time you connect.

To store a network password:

1. In **Control Panel**, click **User Accounts and Family Safety**, and then click **User Accounts**.

2. In the **Tasks** list, click **Manage your network passwords**.

3. In the **Stored User Names and Passwords** dialog box, click **Add**.

   The Stored Credential Properties dialog box opens.

4. In the **Log on to** box, enter the server, Web site, or program for which you want to store credentials.

5. In the **User name** and **Password** boxes, enter your credentials for the server or Web site.

6. Under **Credential type**, select the type of entity for which you are storing credentials. Then click **OK**.

Sharing Drives and Folders

Whether you work on your computer in an office environment or a home environment, you might need to share files with other people on your domain or in your workgroup. Rather than sending copies of files to everyone who might need them, you can place the files on a *shared drive* or in a *shared folder* from which other people can access them.

> **Tip** A shared drive might be the entire contents of a hard disk or of another internal or external storage device, such as a CD drive or USB flash drive.

You control which drives and folders on your computer are shared. By default, when you share a drive or a folder, any other user on the network can access the files stored there whenever your computer is turned on. They can see the contents of the drive or folder, open files, save changes, create new files on the drive or in the folder, and delete files from the drive or folder. You can limit access so that only selected people or groups of people can work with the contents, and you can limit the types of access granted to each person or group.

> **Tip** A shared drive or folder is indicated by an icon that includes the head-and-shoulders images of two people.

The Windows Vista user profile structure includes a *Public* user profile folder that contains the *Public Documents*, *Public Downloads*, *Public Music*, *Public Pictures*, and *Public Videos* folders. The contents of these shared folders are available to anyone using the computer, meaning that multiple users of the same computer can share files with each other by placing the files in these folders.

> **Tip** If you collaborate with a team of people on a document and you want to avoid the risk of one person overwriting another person's changes, you need to use a system with version control. If your organization has a collaboration site built with Microsoft SharePoint products and technologies, such as Microsoft Office SharePoint Server 2007, you can store the document in a document library so that only one person at a time can check out and work on the document.

In this exercise, you will share a folder on your computer with everyone else on your domain or in your workgroup.

 USE the files located in the *Documents\Microsoft Press\WindowsVistaSBS_Dlx\Connections* folder.

1. Display your *Documents* folder. Then browse to the *MicrosoftPress\ WindowsVistaSBS_Dlx* subfolder.

2. In the **Content** pane, click the *Connections* folder, and on the toolbar, click **Share**.

   The File Sharing wizard starts.

3. Click the arrow to the right of the empty box, click **Everyone**, and then click **Add**.

   Any person with a user account and password for this computer will now have read-only access to the *Connections* folder. You can change the access level from Reader to Contributor or Co-owner by clicking the Permission Level arrow and then clicking the type of access you want to allow.

4. Click **Share**. Then in the **User Account Control** dialog box, if you're logged on as an administrator, click **Continue**. Otherwise, enter an administrator password, and click **OK**.

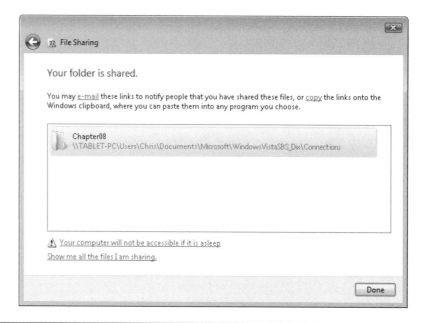

Restricting Permission to a Shared Folder

By default, a shared drive or folder is available to everyone on your network. You can limit access to specific people or groups by removing Everyone from the permitted user list and adding only the people or groups you want.

To customize permissions for a shared folder:

1. Open the shared folder's **Properties** dialog box.

2. On the **Sharing** tab, click **Advanced Sharing**. Then in the **User Account Control** dialog box, if you're logged on as an administrator, click **Continue**. Otherwise, enter an administrator password, and click **OK**.

3. In the **Advanced Sharing** dialog box, select the **Share this folder** check box, and then click **Permissions**.

4. In the **Permissions** dialog box, with **Everyone** selected, click **Remove**. Then click **Add**.

5. In the **Select Users or Groups** dialog box, enter the Windows user account names or domain user account names of the people you want to have access to the shared folder, and then close the four open dialog boxes.

5. After the folder is shared, click **Done**.

In the Folders list and Content pane, the folder icon changes to reflect that the folder is shared.

 CLOSE the Connections window.

Key Points

- Every Windows Vista computer is part of either a workgroup or a domain. You can share resources with other computers through either of these networks. You can change your network configuration and switch between workgroup and domain connections.

- If your domain supports VPN connections, you can connect your computer to a domain over the Internet, from any location.

- You can connect to a domain computer from another computer and work on it as though you were sitting in front of it, by using Remote Desktop.

- You can connect over the Internet to a remote computer and interact with it directly as though it were your own desktop.

Keyboard Shortcuts

Press this	To do this
Ctrl+Esc	Open the Start menu.
Alt+Up Arrow	View the folder one level up in Windows Explorer.
F1	Display Help.
Windows logo key+Break	Display the System Properties dialog box.

Chapter at a Glance

Set up Windows mail, **page 266**

Send and receive e-mail messages, **page 277**

Fax and scan documents, **page 284**

Conduct online meetings, **page 287**

9 Communicating with Other People

In this chapter you will learn to:

✔ Set up Windows Mail.

✔ Send and receive e-mail messages.

✔ Fax and scan documents.

✔ Conduct online meetings.

With computer communications, the world has become a much smaller place. It used to take months for a letter to travel from one side of the world to the other; it now takes seconds for an electronic letter to make the same trip. And with instant messaging, real-time electronic conversations between people who are miles apart are becoming commonly accepted as a comfortable, secure form of communication.

Windows Vista provides tools you can use to manage your online communications. You can do the following:

● Send, receive, store, and manage e-mail messages by using Windows Mail.

● Send, receive, store, and manage facsimile messages (faxes) by using Windows Fax.

● Manage real-time information-sharing sessions with Windows Meeting.

> **Tip** Your organization might support an enterprise messaging program such as Microsoft Office Outlook, or utilize Microsoft Office Communicator for internal messaging. These programs require specific server technology and are primarily used by larger businesses.

In this chapter, you will venture beyond your own computer and communicate with other people by using the tools provided with Windows Vista.

See Also Do you need only a quick refresher on the topics in this chapter? See the Quick Reference section at the beginning of this book.

> **Important** No practice files are required to complete the exercises in this chapter. For more information about practice files, see "Using the Companion CD" at the beginning of this book.

Setting Up Windows Mail

If your company or organization processes e-mail messages through Microsoft Exchange, you probably use Microsoft Office Outlook to manage your e-mail. If you don't have a more-sophisticated program such as Outlook, or if you want to access your e-mail from a computer on which Outlook or another commercial e-mail program is not installed, you can use Windows Mail. Windows Mail, formerly called Microsoft Outlook Express, comes with Windows Vista. You can quickly and easily configure Windows Mail to connect to any HTTP, IMAP, or POP3 e-mail account. Windows Mail does not support Web-based e-mail services, so you cannot use it to connect to a Hotmail account. If you want to connect to a Hotmail account, you can upgrade from Windows Mail to Windows Live Mail, which is available as a free download. More information about Windows Live Mail is available at *get.live.com/wlmail/overview/*.

The first time you start Windows Mail, you are prompted to set up an account by entering information provided by your Internet service provider (ISP) or network administrator. Thereafter, starting Windows Mail displays your Inbox with any messages downloaded from your mail server.

You can download e-mail from your server and work either *online* or *offline*. If you work offline, you can direct Windows Mail to connect to your server to send and receive e-mail messages at regular intervals. You can also block junk mail senders or other people or companies from whom you do not want to receive e-mail messages.

Windows Mail does not include a built-in address book. Instead, it interfaces with the Windows Contacts program, in which you can keep track of information about people such as friends, family members, co-workers, and customers.

See Also For information about Windows Contacts, see "Keeping Track of Contacts" in Chapter 10, "Staying Organized."

Within your mailbox, your e-mail messages are stored in a series of folders. The folder structure varies depending on the type of e-mail account you have. Windows Mail includes these default folders:

- **Inbox.** Your new messages are delivered to this folder.
- **Outbox.** Messages that you have sent, but that have not yet been delivered to the mail server, are held in this folder. If you are working offline, messages are held here until the next time you connect to the server.

- **Sent Items.** After you send a message, a copy of it is stored in this folder. Depending on the e-mail account type, you might have to stipulate that you want to save your sent messages.

- **Deleted Items.** Deleted messages are stored here until you purge the folder. This is the Windows Mail equivalent of the Windows Recycle Bin.

- **Drafts.** While you are preparing your message, but before it has been sent, Windows Mail periodically saves a copy of the message in the Drafts folder. If Windows Mail suddenly closes, or if you want to close the message and send it later, you can open the most recent version from this folder.

In addition to these standard folders, you can create your own folders in which you can organize your e-mail messages as you like. For example, you might create a folder for each project you're working on and then move messages to the appropriate folders as they arrive. Folders help to keep your Inbox less cluttered and make it easier to find specific messages later.

When you're using Windows Mail, you can choose whether you want to see all your e-mail folders and whether you want to *synchronize* your Windows Mail folders with the folders on your e-mail server. When you synchronize your folders, Windows Mail compares the folder on your computer to the folder on the server and updates both folders to the current status, downloading new messages to your computer and removing messages that have been deleted from either version.

> **Tip** At any time after you set up the program, clicking Options on the Tools menu displays a multi-tabbed dialog box, where you can tailor the way the program operates to meet your needs.

Mail Server Addresses for Popular Providers

If you have an e-mail account from AOL, Gmail, or Yahoo!, you can configure Windows Mail to connect to that account by using the following incoming/outgoing mail server addresses:

E-mail service	Incoming mail server	Outgoing mail server
AOL	imap.aol.com	smtp.aol.com
Gmail	pop.gmail.com	smtp.gmail.com
Yahoo!	pop.mail.yahoo.com	smtp.mail.yahoo.com

E-Mail Concepts

An in-depth discussion about e-mail technology is beyond the scope of this book, but to work with Windows Mail, you should understand the following concepts:

E-mail administration is managed through one or more *e-mail servers*—computers that manage your *mailbox* and send, receive, and distribute e-mail messages. E-mail servers operate under specific rules set by the server administrator. These rules govern such factors as the maximum size of each e-mail message you can send and receive, as well as the amount of space available for your individual mailbox.

Incoming messages are handled by a server running one of three *protocols*: *Hypertext Transfer Protocol (HTTP)*, *Internet Message Access Protocol (IMAP)*, or *Post Office Protocol 3 (POP3)*. Each of these protocols has a different set of rules for handling e-mail messages; your network administrator or ISP will be able to tell you which protocol your server uses. Outgoing messages are handled by a server running *Simple Mail Transfer Protocol (SMTP)*.

E-mail servers can do their jobs because every mailbox has a unique *e-mail address*. This address has two parts—the *alias* and the *domain*—separated by an at sign (@). For example, the e-mail address *someone@microsoft.com* represents a user named *someone* who has an e-mail account on the *microsoft.com* domain (in other words, the person works at Microsoft). Business e-mail aliases generally consist of a person's first and last name or initials. The domain name that follows is also where you'll find that business's Web site—simply replace the alias and the @ sign with *www* and a period, and you have the URL. Exceptions are ISP and Web-based e-mail accounts, where the domain name leads to the service provider's home page.

In this exercise, you will set up Windows Mail to connect to your existing e-mail account. Then you will learn about the Windows Mail user interface and ways you can customize it. There are no practice files for this exercise.

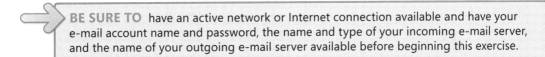

BE SURE TO have an active network or Internet connection available and have your e-mail account name and password, the name and type of your incoming e-mail server, and the name of your outgoing e-mail server available before beginning this exercise.

1. On the **Start** menu, click **All Programs**, and then click **Windows Mail**.

   Windows Mail starts. If this is the first time you've started the program, it prompts you to provide information about the e-mail account you want to connect to.

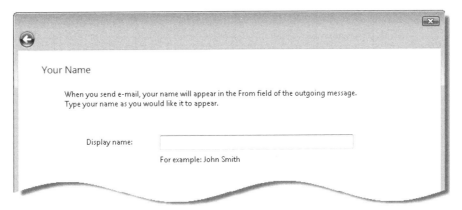

> **Troubleshooting** If the screen shown does not appear automatically, or if you want to configure Windows Mail to connect to a second account, click Accounts on the Tools menu. Then in the Internet Accounts dialog box, click Add, and click Mail.

> **Tip** If you see a message asking whether you want Windows Mail to be your default e-mail client, click Yes or No according to your preferences.

2. Enter your name as you want it to appear to recipients of e-mail messages from you, and then click **Next**.

3. On the **Internet E-mail Address** page, enter the e-mail address you want to set up Windows Mail for.

4. Click **Next** to display the **Set up e-mail servers** page. In the **Incoming e-mail server type** list, click the type of server that handles your incoming mail—HTTP, IMAP, or POP3—and then enter the names of your incoming and outgoing mail servers in the boxes.

5. If your outgoing e-mail server requires authentication, select the check box. Then click **Next**.

> **Troubleshooting** If you don't know whether your outgoing e-mail server requires authentication, do not select the check box at this time. After you complete the account configuration, send a test message; if the message can't be sent, change this setting.
>
> To make changes to the configuration of an existing account, click Accounts on the Tools menu. In the Internet Accounts dialog box, click the account you want to config-ure, and then click Properties. The outgoing mail server settings are on the Servers tab of the account Properties dialog box.

6. On the **Internet Mail Logon** page enter your e-mail account name and password.

If you clear the Remember Password check box, Windows Mail will prompt you for your password each time you start the program.

7. Click **Next**, and then click **Finish**.

Windows Mail connects to your e-mail server using the information you provided, and downloads your existing mail, maintaining any folder structure that has been set up on the server.

The Windows Mail user interface closely resembles that of other e-mail messaging programs.

Menu bar   Toolbar   Views bar   Search bar

Folder List   Message pane   Preview pane   Status bar

Depending on the type of e-mail account and number of accounts configured in Windows Mail, your messages appear either in the Local Folders Inbox or in the Inbox of another folder (named for the mail server). In either case, the Inbox is accessible from the Folder List. The message *headers* appear in the message pane, and the contents of the selected message appear in the preview pane.

Blocking Unwanted Messages

Windows Mail includes a junk e-mail filter that moves suspected spam to a separate folder, and anti-phishing technology that quarantines messages that might contain dangerous code. When a message that meets the criteria for one of these filters is received, a warning box appears.

You can close the warning box if you want to deal with the warning later. In some cases, you have the option of viewing additional information or accessing relevent program settings from the warning box. Unless you stipulate otherwise, Windows Mail does not make active content in suspected phishing messages available; instead, it flags the messages with security warning icons.

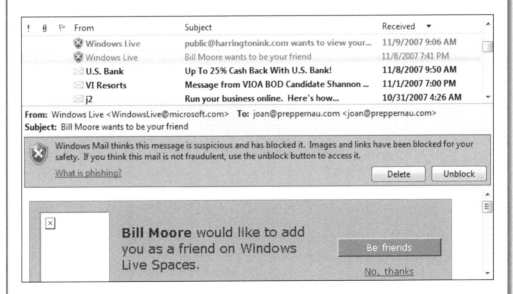

You can tailor the junk e-mail and phishing filter options to suit your preferences, setting the level of junk e-mail protection and specifying lists of senders Windows Mail should always or never allow messages from.

8. On the **View** menu, click **Layout**.

The Window Layout Properties dialog box opens.

From this dialog box, you can control which areas and tools appear in the Windows Mail program window.

9. Experiment with selecting and clearing check boxes and then clicking **Apply** to view the results of the change in the program window. For example, you can enlarge your work area by clearing the **Folder List** check box, or you can move the preview pane. When you finish, return the settings to those shown above or, if you make a change you like, press **OK** to keep it. (If you do make changes, your program window will look different from those shown in the next exercise.)

10. In the **Local Folders** list, click **Inbox**. Then in the **Search** box, type welcome.

As you type, Windows Mail filters the messages listed in the message pane to display only those containing the search term. It is not necessary to press Enter or click the Search button to start the search.

11. If the search finds multiple messages, click the **From** column header in the message pane to sort the filtered messages by sender. Then without clicking anything else, type mic to move the selection to messages from senders starting with that letter combination.

12. If the *Welcome to Windows Mail* message from the Microsoft Windows Mail Team is not selected, click that message to display its contents in the preview pane.

Click any column header to sort messages by that column.

13. In the preview pane, use the scroll bar to scroll through the contents of the welcome message, which contains a lot of helpful information about Windows Mail.

Notice that some of the message header information (the sender, recipient, and subject) are visible at the top of the preview pane.

14. In the message pane, double-click the message header to open the message in its own window.

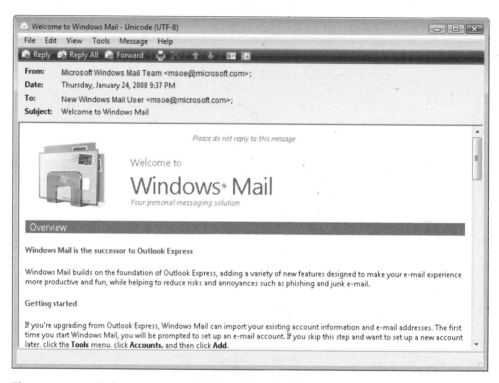

The message window contains additional header information (the date) as well as a menu bar and toolbar containing commands you can use to work with the open message.

15. In the message header, right-click **Microsoft Windows Mail Team** to display a menu of sender-specific commands.

16. On the context menu, click **Add to Contacts**.

A contact card form opens, displaying the Microsoft Windows Mail Team contact information. You will use this card in Chapter 10.

17. In the **Microsoft Windows Mail Team Properties** dialog box, click **OK** to save and close the contact card.

18. Close the message window. Then in the **Search** box, click the **Clear Search** button to redisplay all the messages in the Inbox.

Clear Search

Sending and Receiving E-Mail Messages

Windows Mail is a rich e-mail program with many sophisticated features and customizable options. Although an in-depth tutorial on Windows Mail is beyond the scope of this book, it is certainly worth investigating the main capabilities of the program on your own.

With Windows Mail, you can send and receive professional-looking e-mail messages with most of the features that are available in more-sophisticated programs such as Microsoft Office Outlook. For example, you can use *stationery*, customize fonts, create personal *signatures*, request *read receipts*, and check the spelling of your messages. You can send fancy messages in *Hypertext Markup Language (HTML)* or simple messages in plain-text format. You can also send and receive files that are sent with messages as *attachments*.

To send a new message, you click the Create Mail button on the toolbar to open a New Message window, where you can enter the address of the recipient and any people to whom you are sending courtesy copies. After typing a subject and the text of the message, you can format the message in almost any way you like, including using backgrounds, different fonts, and colors. You can check its spelling and attach files to it before clicking the Send button to send it on its way.

You can create a personalized signature to automatically finish off each of your e-mail messages with a professional touch, or you can send an electronic business card, either in Windows Contact format or as a *vCard*, to give a recipient all your contact information. If the recipient uses Windows Contacts, Outlook, or Windows Mail, he or she can drop your Windows Contact card or vCard into his or her electronic address book. If your contact information changes, you can send an updated card to all your contacts.

You can change the way Windows Mail sends and receives message, change the default message font, create a signature, turn on automatic spell-checking, and make other adjustments to Windows Mail from the Options dialog box. To open this dialog box, click Options on the Tools menu.

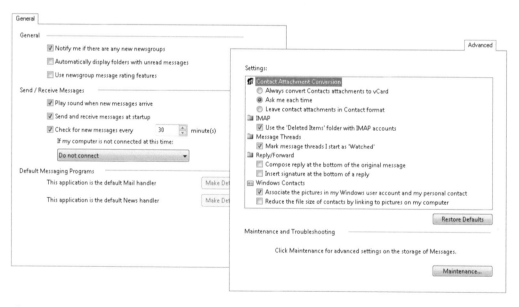

If you will be using Windows Mail, take the time to look over the extensive range of options you can set on the tabs of the Options dialog box (some of which are shown here). You will then know where to go to modify the way the program works to suit your preferences.

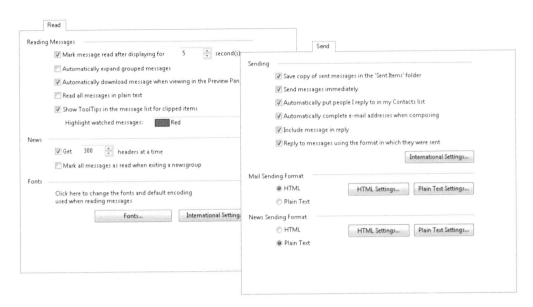

After you receive a message, you can click the message header in the message pane to display its contents in the preview pane, or you can double-click the message header to open it in its own window. You can respond to a message either from the open message window or from the program window by clicking buttons on the toolbar to reply to the sender, reply to the sender and anyone else who received the message, or forward the message to someone else.

Each e-mail message displayed in the message pane is represented by one or more icons indicating the message type, priority, and status. The most common icons include:

Icon	Represents
	The message has not been opened or activated in the preview pane.
	The message has been opened or activated in the preview pane.
	You sent a response to the message.
	You forwarded the message.
	The message sender marked this message as high priority.
	The message sender marked this message as low priority.
	You flagged the message for follow-up.
	The message has one or more file attachments.

In this exercise, you will send, receive, reply to, and delete e-mail messages.

BE SURE TO start Windows Mail before beginning this exercise.

1. On the toolbar, click the **Create Mail** button.

A New Message window opens.

2. In the **To** box, type your own e-mail address (the one you used to configure this account).

3. In the **Subject** box, type Test Message.

As you type, the text of the subject line appears in the message window title bar.

4. Click to place the insertion point in the message body area.

The commands on the toolbar above the message body become active. Most of these commands relate to formatting characters and paragraphs.

5. Type This is a test of sending a new e-mail message.

Your message is displayed in the font selected in the Font box above the body of the message. This is the default font for all messages.

6. In the message window, on the toolbar, click the **Send** button.

Windows Mail sends the new message and, after the message is processed by your mail servers, receives it in the Inbox.

> **Tip** If the message doesn't arrive promptly, click the Send/Receive button on the program window toolbar.

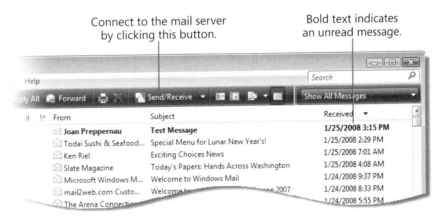

7. Double-click the message to open it in its own window.

8. On the message window toolbar, click the **Reply to Sender** button.

> **Tip** Always check to see whether anyone else appears on the To line or on the Cc line of the e-mail messages you receive. If you want to send your reply to everyone who received the original message, click the Reply All button instead of the Reply button.

A new message window opens, and the original window closes. The message form is set up so that you can respond to the message you received. The e-mail address of the original sender has been entered in the To line, followed by a semicolon to separate this recipient from any other you want to add. The original message subject is preceded by *Re:* in the Subject box and in the message window title bar to indicate that this is a response. A vertical line in the message body indicates the original message text.

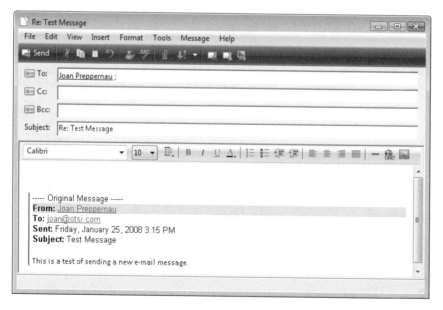

9. In the message body, type This is a test of replying to an e-mail message. Then click the **Send** button.

Windows Mail sends your response and, after the message is processed by your outgoing and incoming mail servers, receives it in the Inbox.

10. In the message pane, click the original message header, hold down the [Ctrl] key, and then click the reply message header to select the two messages.

11. On the toolbar, click the **Delete** button.

The e-mail messages are moved from the Inbox to the Deleted Items folder.

> **Troubleshooting** With IMAP accounts, the messages are still visible, but are "crossed out" to indicate that they have been deleted. If you have an IMAP account, click the chevrons at the right end of the toolbar to display all the options, and then click the Purge button to remove the deleted messages from your Inbox.

CLOSE Windows Mail.

Joining a Newsgroup

In addition to using Windows Mail to send and receive e-mail messages, you can configure it to connect to newsgroups. *Newsgroups* are moderated or unmoderated "message boards" on which people communicate about a specific subject. If people are talking about it, there is probably a newsgroup for it. Although this mode of communication has been somewhat eclipsed by blogs, which incorporate the graphics and pizzazz typical of a Web page, newsgroups are nevertheless an important resource. You can subscribe to a newsgroup by clicking Newsgroups on the Tools menu of the Windows Mail window.

Instant Messaging

Instant messaging (IM) is a real-time electronic communication system that allows you to "chat" with contacts by typing in a window on your computer screen. Windows Vista does not come with its own instant messaging program. However, you can click Windows Live Messenger Download on the All Programs menu to start your Web browser and display the Windows Live Services Web page, from which Windows Live Messenger is available as a free download. This page also describes the features of the program and the many things you can do with it in addition to chatting.

Faxing and Scanning Documents

With Windows Fax And Scan, you can send and receive faxes through an analog phone line and a modem, or through a fax server. After ensuring that the internal or external modem is correctly installed and turned on and that the phone line is plugged in, you need to set up a fax account to tell Windows how you will send and receive faxes. (If you want to send a fax via a fax modem but do not want to receive faxes, you don't have to set up an account.)

> **Troubleshooting** Windows Fax And Scan is a "Windows feature" that you can turn on and off. If the program does not appear on the All Programs menu, follow the process described in "Turning Windows Features On and Off" in Chapter 14, "Optimizing Your Computer System," to turn on Windows Fax And Scan from the Windows Features dialog box.

To send a fax from Windows Fax And Scan:

1. On the **Start** menu, click **All Programs**, and then click **Windows Fax and Scan**.

2. At the bottom of the **Navigation** pane, click **Fax**.

3. On the toolbar, click the **New Fax** button.

4. In the **New Fax** window, enter the receiving phone number (or the contact to whom you are sending the fax) and a subject.

5. Compose the fax or a cover sheet, and if you want, attach a file or insert a picture or scanned document.

6. Click **Send**.

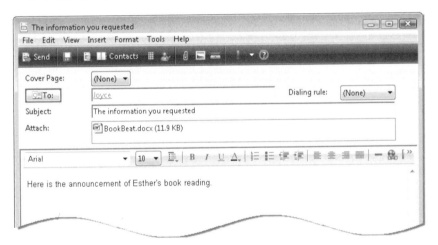

Received faxes appear in your Inbox in the Windows Fax And Scan window and can be viewed in much the same way as an e-mail message in an e-mail program.

If a scanner is connected to your computer, you can also use Windows Fax And Scan to scan text documents and graphics to your computer as digital files that you can send as faxes or e-mail message attachments. Most modern scanners are Plug and Play devices that you can simply plug into an appropriate port on your computer.

To scan a printed document:

1. Turn on the scanner, and insert the document you want to scan.

2. Start **Windows Fax and Scan**, and then at the bottom of the **Navigation** pane, click **Scan**.

3. On the toolbar, click the **New Scan** button, and adjust the settings in the **New Scan** window.

4. Click **Preview** to see how the scanned document will look.

5. If you are satisfied with the preview, click **Scan**.

   Windows Fax And Scan scans the document and displays the scanned image. You can then send it directly by clicking the Forward As Fax or Forward As E-Mail button on the toolbar, or you can click the Save As button to save it as a file on your computer.

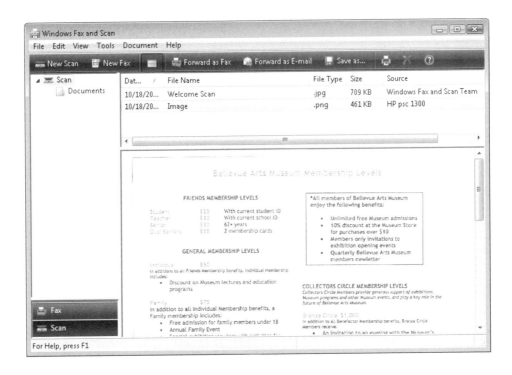

Conducting Online Meetings

No matter what type of job you have, you probably attend your fair share of meetings. In the past, meetings almost always involved sitting down in an office or conference room for a face-to-face discussion. Although advances in telephony have created the possibility of teleconferencing, this type of meeting is unsatisfactory if documents or supporting information need to be exchanged and discussed. That's where Web conferencing comes in. This latest evolution of the traditional meeting allows people in dispersed locations to meet, share content and ideas, collaborate on documents, and communicate using their computers.

With Windows Meeting Space, which comes with Windows Vista, you can set up an on-screen meeting for up to ten people. (You might want to supplement the meeting with a conference call or instant messaging.) The first time you start the program, you will be prompted to provide information for the People Near Me utility, so that Windows Vista can identify you to other Windows Meeting Space users. You can modify your People Near Me settings, and sign in or out of the service, at any time.

> **Troubleshooting** Windows Meeting Space is a "Windows feature" that you can turn on and off. If the program does not appear on the All Programs menu, follow the process described in "Turning Windows Features On and Off" in Chapter 14, "Optimizing Your Computer System," to turn on Windows Meeting from the Windows Features dialog box.

To open People Near Me:

→ In **Control Panel**, click **Network and Internet**, and then click **People Near Me**.

On the Settings tab of the People Near Me dialog box, you can set your user name; choose whether to allow invitations from anyone, from only trusted contacts, or not at all; and choose whether to sign into People Near Me each time you log on.

On the Sign In tab of the People Near Me dialog box, you can sign in or out of People Near Me.

After you configure People Near Me, you can join an existing meeting or start a new one. There are two methods of joining a meeting to which you have been invited.

If you received an invitation file and a password:

1. On the **Start** menu, click **All Programs**, and then click **Windows Meeting Space**.

2. On the **Windows Meeting Space** home page, click **Open an invitation file**.

3. In the **Open** dialog box, navigate to the invitation file. Click the file, and then click **Open**.

> **Tip** Windows Meeting Space invitation files have names corresponding to the meeting name, with the file name extension .wcinv.

4. On the meeting entry page, enter the password, and then click the **Join a meeting** button (the arrow in the green circle).

If you received only a password:

1. Start Windows Meeting Space. On the **Windows Meeting Space** home page, click **Join a meeting near me** to display a list of active meetings.

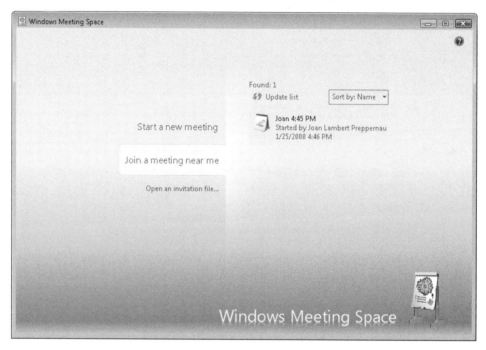

2. Click the meeting you want to join.

3. On the meeting entry page, enter the password, and then click the **Join a meeting** button.

You can invite people to a Windows Meeting session by sending an electronic invitation. If you want to make the meeting available to an entire group of people, you can make it visible through a local network to people near you so that they can join the meeting. As participants join the meeting, their names appear in the Windows Meeting window.

To initiate a meeting:

1. Start Windows Meeting Space. On the **Windows Meeting Space** home page, click **Start a new meeting**.

2. Assign the meeting a name and password (which you'll distribute to meeting attendees).

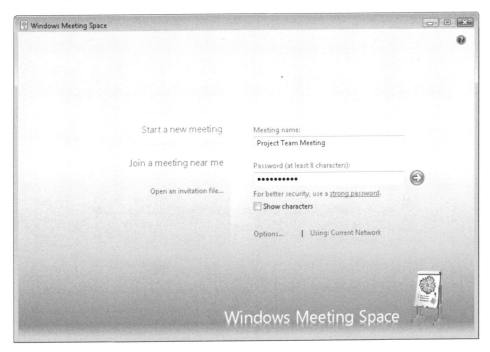

You can display the password characters to double-check it.

3. Click the **Create a meeting** button (the arrow in the green circle).

You can share a file such as a schedule or budget with participants by clicking Share A Program Or Your Desktop and then browsing to and double-clicking the file. It opens on your computer for editing, but all participants can see it. You can give control of the file to another participant so that she or he can edit the file on his or her computer. You can also share your entire desktop in a way that is similar to Remote Assistance.

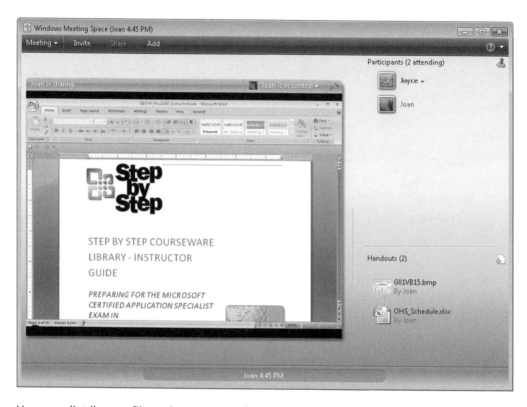

You can distribute a file such as an agenda to participants by clicking Add A Handout and then browsing to and double-clicking the file to make it available from the Windows Meeting Space window. Each participant then double-clicks the handout in the window to open a copy on his or her computer. One at a time, participants can make changes that are reflected in all the open copies of the handout file.

Privacy and security are maintained in a meeting because of the precautions taken when inviting people and because all communications are encrypted.

Key Points

- Windows Vista includes tools you can use to communicate with others, including Windows Mail, Windows Fax And Scan, and Windows Meeting.
- Windows Mail includes security features that protect you from spam and from phishing messages.
- You can easily personalize your e-mail communications to reflect your personality.

- With Windows Fax And Scan, you can send and receive faxes through a modem or a fax server.

- With Windows Meeting Space, you can conduct online meetings for up to 10 people. Each meeting attendee can share files or a view of his or her computer screen, and can collaboratively edit shared files.

Keyboard Shortcuts

Press this	To do this in Windows Mail
Ctrl+N	Create a new message.
Ctrl+R	Reply to a message.
Ctrl+Shift+R	Reply to all recipients of a message.
Ctrl+F	Forward a message.
Ctrl+Shift+E	Create a folder.
Alt+Enter	View the properties of a message.
Ctrl+Shift+V	Move a message to another folder.
Ctrl+Q	Mark a message as read.
Ctrl+T	Mark all messages in a conversation as read.
Ctrl+Shift+A	Mark all messages in a folder as read.
Ctrl+>	Move to the next message.
Ctrl+U	Move to the next unread message.
Ctrl+Y	Move to another folder.
Ctrl+Shift+C	Open Windows Contacts.
Ctrl+Shift+L	Open Windows Calendar.
Ctrl+W	Access newsgroups.

Press this	To do this in Windows Meeting Space
Alt+N	Start a new meeting.
Alt+M	Join a nearby meeting.
Alt+O	Open an invitation file.
Alt+U	Update the meeting list.
Alt+N	Invite an attendee to an active meeting.
Alt+S	Share your desktop in an active meeting.
Alt+A	Add a handout to an active meeting.

Chapter at a Glance

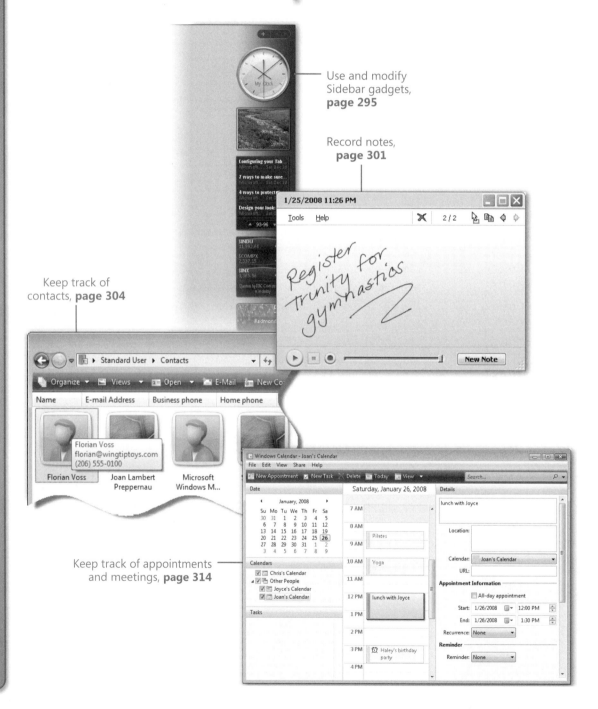

Use and modify
Sidebar gadgets,
page 295

Record notes,
page 301

Keep track of
contacts, **page 304**

Keep track of appointments
and meetings, **page 314**

10 Staying Organized

In this chapter, you will learn to:

✔ Use and modify Sidebar gadgets.

✔ Record notes.

✔ Keep track of contacts.

✔ Keep track of appointments and meetings.

Windows Vista includes several very useful programs that were not available with previous versions of Windows. These programs provide much of the functionality of a full-featured communication-management program, without any additional investment. (If you have Windows Vista, you already have these programs.)

In this chapter, you will learn about Windows Sidebar, Sticky Notes, Windows Contacts, and Windows Calendar. Together, these programs provide a set of tools you can use to keep information organized in a convenient, accessible manner.

> **Important** No practice files are required to complete the exercises in this chapter. For more information about practice files, see "Using the Companion CD" at the beginning of this book.

Using and Modifying Sidebar Gadgets

Windows Sidebar is a cool new feature introduced with Windows Vista. Sidebar displays a number of small programs called *gadgets* that provide dynamic content (up-to-date information or entertainment) on a transparent vertical bar. Initially, Sidebar displays a large analog clock, a newsreader, and a slide show of the contents of your Pictures folder. (If you purchased a new computer with Windows Vista already installed, the OEM might have added other gadgets to Sidebar.) You can move, change, resize, or delete any of the default gadgets, and you can add other gadgets that come with Windows or new gadgets that you download from the Internet.

Sidebar opens by default in certain editions of Windows Vista and must be manually started in others.

In this exercise, you will change the appearance of the analog clock, display news headlines and open an article, and then add a gadget to Sidebar. There are no practice files for this exercise.

> **BE SURE TO** display the Windows Vista desktop before beginning this exercise.

1. If Sidebar is not open on your desktop, click **All Programs** on the **Start** menu, click **Accessories**, and then click **Windows Sidebar**.

   Sidebar opens on the right side of your screen, displaying the default gadgets.

Gadget controls

2. Point to the **Clock** gadget to display the gadget controls, and then click the **Options** button, labeled with a wrench icon.

   The Clock dialog box opens, displaying an example of the current clock.

Next

3. In the preview area, click the **Next** button.

A different clock style appears in the preview area.

4. View the six other clock style options, and then display the one you like best.

5. In the **Clock name** box, type My Clock. Select the **Show the second hand** check box if you want the analog clock to display the passing of seconds, and then click **OK**.

Your personalized clock appears on Sidebar.

6. If headlines aren't already shown in the Feed Headlines gadget, click **View Headlines** to load current news headlines.

News headlines cycle through the Feed Headlines gadget four at a time. You can move backward or forward through the headlines by clicking the arrows at the bottom of the gadget.

7. Click any headline that interests you.

A window displays a synopsis of the associated article. You can view the entire article by clicking the headline at the top of the synopsis window.

8. On the Sidebar control at the top of Sidebar, click the **Add** button (labeled with a plus sign).

Sidebar control

The Gadgets window opens, displaying the available gadgets. (Your Gadgets window might include more than those shown here.)

9. Drag a couple of gadgets you think might be useful from the **Gadgets** window to Sidebar. Then close the **Gadgets** window.

For the purposes of this exercise, we chose the Stocks gadget, which you can use to quickly check stock prices, and the Weather gadget, which displays the current temperature and a photographic representation of the current weather conditions for any area you choose. Feel free to choose any other gadget that interests you. If you're feeling adventurous, you can click Get More Gadgets Online, in the lower-right corner of the window, browse the gadget gallery on the Microsoft Web site, and download any gadgets you want.

> **Important** Hundreds of gadgets are available from the Windows Vista gadget gallery. Very few of these were created by Microsoft, and therefore Microsoft does not offer guarantees or provide product support for any of them.

10. Right-click the **Slide Show** gadget, and then click **Detach from Sidebar**.

    The slide show moves to the upper-left corner of your screen and appears in a larger window.

11. Point to the **Slide Show** gadget to display controls to its right and on the gadget itself. On the gadget, click the **View** button (the right-most button, which has a magnifying glass icon).

    The currently displayed picture opens in Windows Photo Gallery. The slide show continues behind the photo gallery.

12. Close the **Windows Photo Gallery** window.

13. Right-click the **Slide Show** gadget, and click **Attach to Sidebar**. Then drag the reattached gadget to the bottom of Sidebar.

    The other gadgets move up to make room for the slide show.

14. Right-click an empty area of Sidebar, and then click **Properties**.

    The Windows Sidebar Properties dialog box opens.

15. Experiment with the Sidebar properties, clicking **Apply** to see the effects of different settings. When Sidebar is configured the way you want it, click **OK**.

> **Tip** You can make Sidebar available at all times by selecting the Sidebar Is Always On Top Of Other Windows check box in the Windows Sidebar Properties dialog box. Then when you maximize other windows, they won't overlap Sidebar. To remove Sidebar from the Windows desktop, right-click Sidebar, and then click Close Sidebar.

Recording Notes

Sticky Notes allows you to quickly record notes on an electronic note pad (resembling a Post-It pad) right on the Windows Vista desktop. This feature was designed primarily for use on Tablet PCs, but it can also be used on other types of computers.

Sticky Notes supports the following content:

● Handwritten notes, written either with a Tablet PC pen or with the mouse pointer.

● Voice notes, if your computer has a built-in or external microphone.

Each time you begin recording a note, whether written or verbal, Sticky Notes records the date and time and displays them in the title bar of that note.

You can't change the ink color or line size as you can with other Tablet PC programs, nor can you change the color of the sticky notes. You can, however, resize the Sticky Notes window.

If you want to keep Sticky Notes handy, you can set the Sticky Note window to remain on top of any open programs by pointing to Options on the Tools menu and then clicking Always On Top. If you do this, you might want to make the window smaller and move it to an out-of-the way location, such as at the edge of the display. If you work on a computer system with two (or more) monitors, you can keep the Sticky Notes window open on one monitor and work in program windows on the other.

> **Tip** Windows Sidebar includes a notepad-like gadget, which you can display on Sidebar or drag to your desktop.

You can share sticky notes with other people in two ways:

- **By pasting an individual note into another program.** You can use the Drag and Drop handle on the Sticky Notes toolbar to drag written notes to other programs (for example, Microsoft Office Word or Microsoft Office Outlook). You can copy and paste written or voice notes by clicking the Copy button on the Sticky Notes toolbar, switching to the other program, and then clicking the Paste button in that program. Depending on the application you paste the sticky note into, the note will appear either as an icon or as an image.

- **By exporting a stack of notes to a file.** You can click Export on the Tools menu and then name and save the file. (Sticky Notes files have the file extension .*snt*.) You can send the exported file to another person or copy it to another computer. The file can then be imported into another Sticky Notes installation, where it can either be added to the existing notes or replace the existing notes. (Exporting notes does not remove them from your Sticky Notes pad.)

In this exercise, you will record written and voice notes by using the Sticky Notes feature. There are no practice files for this exercise.

> **BE SURE TO** configure an internal or external microphone on your computer system before beginning this exercise.

1. On the **Start** menu, click **All Programs**, click **Accessories**, click **Tablet PC**, and then click **Sticky Notes**.

Or, if you are working on a Tablet PC:

On the **Start** menu, click **All Programs**, and then click **Sticky Notes**.

> **Troubleshooting** The Sticky Notes program is part of the group of optional Tablet PC features that you can turn on and off. If the Tablet PC folder does not appear in the Accessories folder on the All Programs menu, or if the Tablet PC folder is empty, follow the process described in "Turning Windows Features On and Off" in Chapter 14, "Optimizing Your Computer System," to turn on Tablet PC Optional Components from the Windows Features dialog box.

The Sticky Notes window opens.

2. With the Tablet PC pen or by dragging the mouse pointer, write a short note to yourself.

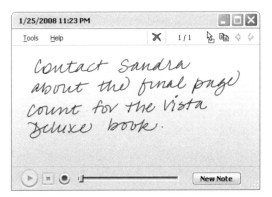

3. In the lower-right corner of the **Sticky Notes** window, click **New Note**.

A blank note appears, and the note counter on the toolbar changes to reflect that this is the second of two notes.

Record

Stop

4. If a microphone is installed on your computer, click the **Record** button at the bottom of the **Sticky Notes** window. Speaking into the microphone, dictate additional information about the note. When you finish, click the **Stop** button.

The note counter indicates the position of this note among the total number of notes.

An active Play button indicates that a voice note is available.

Play

Previous Note

5. If you recorded a voice note, click the **Play** button to hear it.

6. On the toolbar, click the **Previous Note** button to return to the first note.

CLOSE the Sticky Notes window.

Keeping Track of Contacts

Windows Contacts, the contact-tracking program that comes with Windows Vista, can be used as a stand-alone electronic address book, or it can be used in conjunction with Windows Mail, Windows Calendar, and Windows Fax And Scan to provide ready access to your contact information. With Windows Contacts, you can:

- Store e-mail addresses, street addresses, phone numbers, and personal information about a contact. You can attach a picture to each *contact record*.

- Create *contact groups* so that you can send e-mail messages to the entire group. For example, you might create a group for each project you're working on, or you might create a group for family members.

- Import contact information from several types of files, including CSV (Comma Separated Values), LDIF (LDAP server), vCard (VCF file), and Windows Address Book file (Outlook Express contacts).

- Export contact records as CSV files and vCards.

● Send and receive electronic business cards containing contact information in a format that can easily be merged into other people's contact databases.

● Print contact information in a variety of formats so that you can carry it with you when you don't have access to your computer or handheld electronic organizer.

Unlike contact records in electronic address books, such as an Outlook address book, each Windows Contact is an actual file stored in the *Contacts* folder of your Windows Vista user account. You can create contact records from scratch, or you can import existing contact information exported from another program.

To import contacts from a file:

1. Display the *Contacts* folder, and then on the toolbar, click **Import**.

2. In the **Import to Windows Contacts** dialog box, select the format of the file you are importing, and then click **Import**. If you are importing a CSV file, click **Browse** in the **CSV Import** dialog box.

3. In the **Open** dialog box, navigate to the source file, and then click **Open**.

4. Select the fields you want to import and, if necessary, map the source file fields to the Windows Contacts fields. Then click **Finish**.

To export all contacts to a file or files:

1. Display the *Contacts* folder, and then on the toolbar, click **Export**.

2. In the **Export Windows Contacts** dialog box, select the format you want to export contacts to, and then click **Export**.

3. If you are exporting to a CSV file:

   a. Click **Browse** in the **CSV Export** dialog box.

   b. In the **Save As** dialog box, navigate to the folder in which you want to save the exported file, enter the file name you want in the **File name** box, and click **Save**.

   c. In the **CSV Export** dialog box, click **Next**. Select the fields you want to export, and then click **Finish**.

   If you are exporting to vCard files, in the **Browse For Folder** dialog box, navigate to the folder in which you want to save the exported file(s), and then click **OK**.

5. In the **Windows Contacts** message box confirming the export, click **OK**. Then in the **Export Windows Contacts** dialog box, click **Close**.

> **Tip** The export operation exports all contacts, but not contact groups, from your *Contacts* folder. There is not an option to export only selected contacts.

After you create contact records, you can view and organize them in various ways, in the same way that you view and organize files in any folder in Windows Explorer.

Windows Mail and Windows Calendar rely on Windows Contacts to provide contact information for sending messages or meeting requests. You can open the *Contacts* folder directly from both of these programs. If you frequently send messages or meeting requests to specific groups of people, you can create a contact group that contains all the group members. Then rather than entering all the individual e-mail addresses in the message or meeting request, you can simply enter the contact group name, and the message or request will be addressed to all the group members.

In this exercise, you will create contact records and a contact group, and then test the contact group by sending an e-mail message.

USE the contact record you created in "Setting Up Windows Mail" in Chapter 9, "Communicating with Other People," if you completed that exercise.

1. On the **Start** menu, click **All Programs**, and then click **Windows Contacts**.

   Your *Contacts* folder opens. This folder is specific to your Windows Vista user account.

Contacts folder toolbar

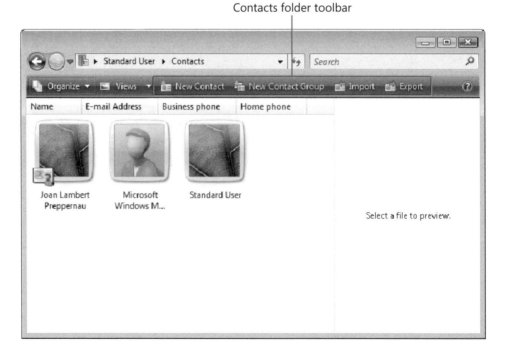

At the very least, the folder will contain a contact record specific to your user account. If you use Windows Mail and have not changed the default options, contact records have also been created for the senders of any messages to which you have responded. If you completed the exercise in "Setting Up Windows Mail" in Chapter 9, "Communicating with Other People," the folder will contain a contact record for the Microsoft Windows Mail Team.

2. Take a moment now to look at the *Contacts* folder toolbar indicated in the graphic on the facing page.

   If the folder isn't set to the correct folder type, some of the buttons shown will not be available. (None of the installations of Windows Vista I have worked with displayed the *Contacts* folder toolbar by default.)

3. If the **New Contact**, **New Contact Group**, **Import**, and **Export** commands are not visible on the toolbar, follow these steps:

   a. In the **Address Bar**, click your user name to move to your personal folder.

   b. Right-click the *Contacts* folder, and then click **Properties**.

   c. In the **Contacts Properties** dialog box, click the **Customize** tab.

   d. In the **Use this folder type as a template** list, click **Contacts**. Then select the **Also apply this template to all subfolders** check box.

   e. In the **Contacts Properties** dialog box, click **OK**. Then in your personal folder, double-click the *Contacts* folder to redisplay it.

   The toolbar now includes the New Contact, New Contact Group, Import, and Export buttons.

4. Click the **Microsoft Windows Mail Team** contact (or any other contact) to display in the **Preview** pane the information you have recorded for that contact.

> **Troubleshooting** If the Preview pane is not visible on the right side of the folder window, point to Layout on the Organize menu and verify that Preview Pane is selected. If the Preview pane is turned on but not visible, increase the width of the folder window (by dragging its edge) until the pane appears.

Additional toolbar commands for actions you can take with the selected contact record become available. Depending on your screen resolution, some of the commands might be hidden unless you view the *Contacts* folder at full-screen width.

Display additional commands

5. If the **Display additional commands** button appears at the right end of the toolbar, click it so you can see all the available commands.

The contact record–specific commands include Open, E-Mail, Edit, Delete, and Print.

6. On the toolbar, click **New Contact**.

   A blank Properties dialog box opens, featuring seven tabs on which you can record information about a contact.

7. On the **Name and E-mail** tab, enter the following information:

   - In the **First** box, type Florian.

     As you type the name, it appears in the dialog box title bar and in the Full Name box.

   - In the **Last** box, type Voss.

   - In the **Personal Title** box, type Mr.

   - Type florian@wingtiptoys.com in the **E-mail** box, and then click the **Add** button to its right.

The e-mail address is added to the list box. Because it is the only available address, it is designated as the preferred address.

8. On the **Work** tab, enter the following information:

- In the **Street** box, type 1234 Oak Street.
- In the **City** box, type Seattle.
- In the **State/Province** box, type WA.
- In the **Postal Code** box, type 10101.
- In the **Company** box, type Wingtip Toys.
- In the **Job Title** box, type Owner.
- In the **Phone** box, type (206) 555-0100.
- In the **Fax** box, type (206) 555-0101.
- In the **Website** box, type http://www.wingtiptoys.com.

> **Tip** You can click Go to test the URL in your default browser. This is a fictitious URL that redirects to the Microsoft Web site.

9. Click the **Home**, **Family**, **Notes**, **IDs**, and **IM** tabs, and review the types of information you can enter on each one.

   Windows Contacts is set up to record both business and personal information.

10. In the **Florian Voss Properties** dialog box, click **OK** to create the contact record.

    This information is now available from Windows Mail and Windows Calendar.

11. In the *Contacts* folder, point to the **Florian Voss** contact record.

    The contact information you need most frequently—Florian's telephone number and e-mail address—appears in a ScreenTip.

12. Click the **Florian Voss** contact record to display all the available contact information in the Preview pane.

13. Repeat steps 6 through 10, entering information about yourself to create a contact record with your own information. Be sure to enter your e-mail address.

14. On the toolbar, click **New Contact Group**.

    A blank Properties dialog box opens, featuring two tabs on which you can record information about a contact group.

15. On the **Contact Group** tab, in the **Group Name** box, type Vista Fans. Then click **Add to Contact Group**.

    The Add Members To Contact Group dialog box opens, displaying the contents of your *Contacts* folder.

16. Click **Florian Voss**, hold down the Ctrl key, and then click your own contact record.

Both names appear in the Selected Contacts box at the bottom of the dialog box.

17. In the **Add Members to Contact Group** dialog box, click **Add**.

The selected contacts appear on the Contact Group tab of the Vista Fans Properties dialog box.

> **Tip** If you want to add someone for whom you don't yet have a contact record to a contact group, you have two choices:
>
> - To add the person to the group and save a contact record at the same time, click Create New Contact, enter the person's contact information in the contact form, and then click OK.
> - To add the person to the group but not create a contact record, enter his or her name and e-mail address in the Contact Name and E-Mail boxes, and then click Create For Group Only.

18. Click the **Contact Group Details** tab to see the additional information you can enter for the group (address, telephone/fax numbers, notes, and Web site address). Then click **OK**.

    The Vista Fans contact group appears in the *Contacts* folder.

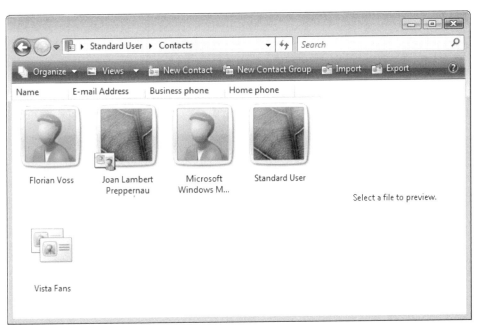

19. Click the **Vista Fans** contact group, and then on the toolbar, click **E-Mail**.

    If it isn't already running, Windows Mail (or your default e-mail program) starts and creates a new message addressed to Florian Voss and to you.

 CLOSE the message window and the *Contacts* folder.

Keeping Track of Appointments and Meetings

If you don't use Outlook, you can use the Windows Calendar program that comes with Windows Vista to schedule your time in an electronic calendar. Windows Calendar offers standard calendar functionality, such as appointments and events, and enables you to invite people to meetings and maintain a task list.

Appointments are blocks of time you schedule only for yourself, as opposed to *meetings*, to which you invite other people. *Events* are day-long blocks of time designated for things such as a holiday, birthday, payroll day, or anything else that occurs on a specific day but not at a specific time. In all other respects, events are identical to appointments.

Recurring appointments are appointments, meetings, and events that occur multiple times at a specific interval. Windows Calendar supports recurring appointments at daily, weekly, monthly, and yearly intervals. All the appointments in a recurring series are linked. When making changes to a recurring appointment, you can choose to update all occurrences or only an individual occurrence, depending on the type of change.

You can choose to display a *reminder* at a specified time before the start time of an appointment, meeting, or event. Windows Calendar supports reminder times from 0 minutes to 2 weeks in advance.

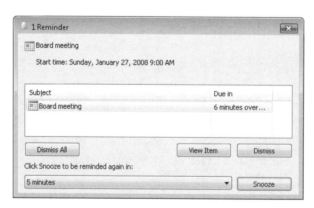

In your calendar, a recurring appointment is identified by a circling arrow icon, and an appointment for which a reminder is set is identified by a clock icon.

A reminder will appear prior to this appointment

This is a recurring appointment.

You can view your schedule for one day, one work week, one week, or one month. To view today's schedule, click the Today button on the toolbar.

> **Tip** To quickly display a calendar (but not your schedule) for the current month, clicking the clock in the Windows taskbar notification area.

Tracking Tasks

In addition to keeping track of your schedule, you can keep track of your tasks. Clicking the New Task button on the toolbar creates a new task in the Tasks pane in the lower-left corner of the Windows Calendar window. Type the name of the task, and fill in information in the Details pane.

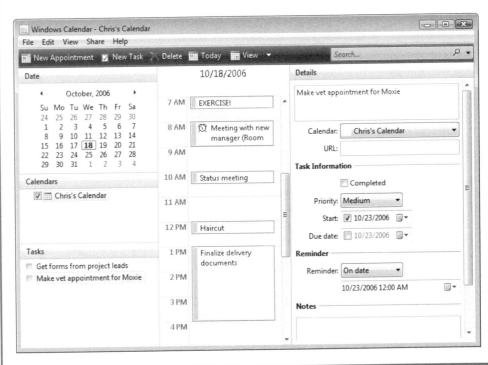

Changing Windows Calendar Defaults

From the Options dialog box, you can change the way Windows Calendar displays calendars, reminders, and time zones. You can also change the default settings for appointments and tasks. To display the Options dialog box, click Options on the File menu.

Your Windows Calendar is specific to your user account, and is not shared by other user accounts on the computer. There are two ways to share your calendar with other people:

- You can e-mail it as a file that the recipient can import.
- You can publish it to a server (for example, to an intranet site or Microsoft SharePoint site). Other people can subscribe to your published calendar. Both you and the other person must have permission to access the server.

Either method saves the calendar as an Internet Calendar (.ics) file.

You can create multiple calendars—for example, a business calendar and a personal calendar—and display one or more of them at the same time. You can also import a calendar file sent to you by someone else or subscribe to a calendar someone else has published.

When importing a calendar, you can create a new calendar separate from your own, or you can merge the imported calendar with yours. You can make changes to an imported calendar, but those changes are not communicated to the original calendar owner. When subscribing to a calendar, you can choose how often you want to receive updates and whether you want to see any published reminders and tasks. You cannot make changes to a subscribed calendar.

Group
An arrow on the
calendar icon indicates
a calendar subscription.

Appointments from
different calendars
appear in different colors.

Tip You can also subscribe to any of the thousands of Internet calendars available online. Click Subscribe on the Share menu, and in the Subscribe To A Calendar dialog box, click the Windows Calendar Website link. On the Internet Calendars For Windows Vista Calendar page, you can then click links to various Internet calendar providers.

When you create, import, or subscribe to a new calendar, Windows Calendar automatically changes the calendar color to one that is not already in use. When an appointment is not selected, you can change the name and color of any calendar you are displaying in Windows Calendar from the Details pane.

If you maintain several calendars, you might want to organize them in groups. You can display, hide, or delete an entire group of calendars or an individual calendar.

In this exercise, you will create appointments and invite yourself to a meeting. There are no practice files for this exercise.

BE SURE TO complete the previous exercise, or create a contact record for yourself in Windows Contacts, before beginning this exercise.

1. On the **Start** menu, click **All Programs**, and then click **Windows Calendar**.

Windows Calendar starts, displaying your calendar for today.

> **Tip** To display a different time period, click Day, Work Week, Week, or Month on the View menu.

2. On the toolbar, click the **New Appointment** button.

   A one-hour appointment appears on the calendar at approximately the current time. The appointment name is selected for editing.

3. Type Read Windows Vista Step by Step, and then press [Enter].

You have created an appointment that is happening right now. In the Details pane, you can change the start and end dates and times for the appointment, or you can drag the appointment to another location on the calendar.

> **Tip** To create an event, select the All-Day Appointment check box in the Appointment Information section. To create a recurring appointment, click the frequency in the Recurrence list. To set a reminder, click the time in the Reminder list.

4. Point to another timeslot on the calendar, and drag down or up to select three timeslots. Then type SBS Meeting, and press [Enter].

As you begin typing, the selected timeslots convert to a 90-minute appointment.

5. In the **Details** pane, click to position the insertion point in the **Location** box, and then type my house.

6. If necessary, scroll the **Details** pane to display the **Participants** section.

7. In the **Participants** section, click the **Attendees** button.

A Windows Calendar dialog box opens, displaying your Windows Contacts.

See Also For information about Windows Contacts, see "Keeping Track of Contacts" earlier in this chapter.

8. In the **Name** list, click your own contact record (the one you created in the previous exercise), and then click **To**.

> **Tip** To remove a name from the Attendees list, click the name and then press the Delete key.

9. Click **OK** to return to Windows Calendar.

Your name and e-mail address appear in the box to the right of the Invite button. An icon representing a group of people appears in the SBS Meeting item.

This icon indicates a meeting with invited attendees.

10. Click **Invite**.

Windows Mail or your default e-mail program starts, if it isn't already started, and creates an e-mail message containing the meeting invitation information in the form of an .ics file.

See Also For information about Windows Mail, see Chapter 9, "Communicating with Other People."

11. Send the message, and then display your e-mail Inbox. When the message arrives, open it.

The meeting request is attached to the message as an .ics file that you can import into your Windows Mail or Outlook calendar.

 CLOSE the message window and Windows Calendar.

Key Points

- Windows Sidebar is an innovative tool that displays real-time information on your Windows Vista desktop.

- You can record handwritten notes and voice notes on an electronic notepad using Sticky Notes.

- You can record business and personal contact information in Windows Contacts. The contact records and contact groups you create are available from Windows Mail and Windows Calendar.

- In Windows Calendar, you can track tasks, appointments, meetings, and events. You can import or link to other peoples' calendars as well as to Internet calendars.

Keyboard Shortcuts

Press this	To do this with Windows Sidebar
Windows logo key+Spacebar	Bring all gadgets to the front and select Windows Sidebar.
Windows logo key+G	Cycle through Sidebar gadgets.
Tab	Cycle through Sidebar controls.

Press this	To do this in Sticky Notes
Ctrl+N	Open a new note.
Ctrl+P	Play or pause a voice note.
Ctrl+R	Record a voice note.
Ctrl+S	Stop playback of a voice note.
Alt+Left Arrow	Go to the previous note.
Alt+Right Arrow	Go to the next note.
Alt+Space	Open the Sticky Notes shortcut menu.
Alt+F4	Close Sticky Notes.

Press this	To do this in Windows Calendar
Ctrl+N	Create an appointment.
Ctrl+T	Create a task.
Ctrl+P	Print the calendar for a specified date range.
Ctrl+Shift+1	Display a one-day view of the calendar.
Ctrl+Shift+2	Display a work-week view of the calendar.
Ctrl+Shift+3	Display a one-week view of the calendar.
Ctrl+Shift+4	Display a one-month view of the calendar.
Ctrl+G	Jump to a specific date.

Chapter at a Glance

Create simple graphics
page 326

Change the content, size, and orientation of graphics, **page 337**

Format words and paragraphs, **page 354**

Insert text and graphics, **page 358**

Create simple documents, **page 352**

11 Working with Graphics and Documents

In this chapter, you will learn to:

✔ Create simple graphics.

✔ Change the content, size, and orientation of graphics.

✔ Save graphic files in different formats.

✔ Print graphics.

✔ Create simple documents.

✔ Format words and paragraphs.

✔ Insert text and graphics.

✔ Print documents.

Many programs are available for creating and working with graphics. Some graphics programs are specifically suited for certain types of graphics, certain processes, or certain uses, and many of those programs are somewhat (or sometimes incredibly) expensive. Although these programs are excellent (and certainly necessary) for high-level graphics work, they can be quite difficult to learn and are excessive for the simpler purposes of the average computer user.

Similarly, several word processing programs also are available for creating and working with text documents. Again, these programs vary in their level of sophistication and price. The more complex the document, the more complex the program required to produce it, and the longer it takes to master all the features.

Windows Vista comes with programs that you can use to create and manipulate graphics and documents. You can use Microsoft Paint to create simple graphics or to edit more complex graphics. With Paint, you can open, view, print, edit, and save a variety of graphic file formats. You can use Microsoft WordPad to write a letter, a report, or even a novel—any reasonably straightforward document. You can apply simple formatting and insert a variety of elements in a WordPad document.

In this chapter, you will learn how to create, work with, and print graphics by using Paint. You will also learn how to create, work with, and print documents by using WordPad, as well as how to insert text and graphic files into your documents.

See Also Do you need only a quick refresher on the topics in this chapter? See the Quick Reference section at the beginning of this book.

Important Before you can use the practice files in this chapter, you need to install them from the book's companion CD to their default location. See "Using the Companion CD" at the beginning of this book for more information.

Creating Simple Graphics

Paint supplies a variety of tools that you can use to create and modify graphics, including ready-made shapes, such as squares and circles, and free-form drawing tools, such as pencils and brushes. Many of the tools, which are displayed in the toolbox, come in a variety of sizes and shapes. (For example, you can choose different thicknesses for the brush tool.) These options are displayed at the bottom of the toolbox.

The Paint toolbox includes the following tools:

- **Free-Form Select.** Use this tool to select an irregularly shaped part of a graphic.

    To use this tool: Click the Free-Form Select button, and then, in the options box at the bottom of the toolbox, click a background style (filled or transparent). Drag to outline the area you want to select. When you release the mouse button, the start and end points connect in a straight line. The resulting selection box is rectangular, but the actual selection follows the outline you drew.

● **Select.** Use this tool to select any square or rectangular part of the picture.

To use this tool: Click the Select button, and then, in the options box at the bottom of the toolbox, click the background style you want. Drag at an angle to define the outside edges of the selection area. To restrict the selection area to a square shape, hold down the Shift key while dragging.

● **Eraser/Color Eraser.** Use this tool to erase areas of your picture.

To use this tool: Click the Eraser button, and then, in the options box at the bottom of the toolbox, click the eraser size you want. Drag the Eraser over the area of the picture that you want to erase. Paint replaces the erased area with the current secondary color.

● **Fill With Color.** Use this tool to fill the entire picture or an enclosed shape with color.

To use this tool: Click the Fill With Color button, and then click inside a defined area to fill it with the primary color, or right-click inside a defined area to fill it with the secondary color.

● **Pick Color.** Use this tool to set the current foreground or background color.

To use this tool: Click the Pick Color button, and then click anywhere in the graphic to set the selected color as the primary color, or right-click to set the selected color as the secondary color.

● **Magnifier.** Use this tool to change the zoom level to settings in the range from 12.5 percent to 800 percent.

To use this tool: Click the Magnifier button. In the options box at the bottom of the toolbox, click or drag to select a zoom level; or click in the graphic to zoom and center that location.

● **Pencil.** Use this tool to draw thin, freeform lines or curves.

To use this tool: Click the Pencil button, and then drag to draw a line in the primary color, or right-drag to draw a line in the secondary color.

● **Brush.** Use this tool to paint thick or shaped freeform lines or curves.

To use this tool: Click the Brush button, and then, in the options box at the bottom of the toolbbox, click the brush shape you want. Click or drag to paint with the primary color; right-click or right-drag to paint with the secondary color.

- **Airbrush.** Use this tool to create a freeform spray paint effect.

  To use this tool: Click the Airbrush button, and then, in the options box at the bottom of the toolbox, click the spray pattern you want. Click or drag to paint with the primary color; right-click or right-drag to paint with the secondary color.

- **Text.** Use this tool to enter text or add labels to the picture.

  To use this tool: Click the Text button, and then, in the options box at the bottom of the toolbox, click the background style you want. Click to position the text insertion box and display the Fonts toolbar, and then type the text. While the text box is active, you can resize and move the text box, and change the font, font size, and text formatting. After you click away from the text box, you cannot edit its contents.

- **Line and Curve.** Use these tools to draw straight or curved lines.

  To use the Line tool: Click the Line button, and then, in the options box at the bottom of the toolbox, click the line width you want. Drag to draw a straight line in the primary color; or right-drag to draw a straight line in the secondary color. To restrict the angle of the line to any multiple of 45 degrees, hold down the Shift key while dragging.

  To use the Curve tool: Click the Curve button, and then, in the options box at the bottom of the toolbox, click the line width you want. Drag to draw a straight line from the start point to the end point of the curve, click to place the center of the arc, and then drag the line handles to adjust the curve.

- **Rectangle, Rounded Rectangle, and Ellipse.** Use Rectangle to draw rectangles and squares with 90-degree corners, Rounded Rectangle to draw rectangles and squares with rounded corners, and Ellipse to draw ellipses and circles.

  To use these tools: Click the Rectangle, Rounded Rectangle, or Ellipse button, and then, in the options box at the bottom of the toolbox, click the fill style you want. Drag at an angle to define the outer edges of the shape. To restrict the shape to a square or circle, hold down the Shift key while dragging.

- **Polygon.** Use this tool to draw a multi-sided shape, such as a triangle or star.

  To use this tool: Click the Polygon button, and then, in the options box at the bottom of the toolbox, click the fill style you want. Drag to draw one side of the shape, click to set each angle, and then double-click to complete the shape. To restrict angles to multiples of 45 degrees, hold down the Shift key while drawing the shape.

Windows Help and Support includes useful information and troubleshooting instructions for Paint. You can access program-specific information from within Paint by clicking Help Topics on the Help menu.

See Also For more information about Windows Help and Support, see "Finding Solutions to Common Problems" in Chapter 15, "Identifying and Solving Problems."

In this exercise, you will use the Paint tools to create and save a simple graphic. There are no practice files for this exercise.

BE SURE TO log on to Windows Vista before beginning this exercise.

1. On the **Start** menu, click **All Programs**, click **Accessories**, and then click **Paint**.

   An untitled Paint window opens.

Current primary and secondary colors   Color palette   Blank canvas

Toolbox   Status bar

Tip The default Paint canvas size is 512 × 384 pixels. If you have worked on a picture with a different size, the new canvas might open at that size.

2. On the **Image** menu, click **Attributes**.

The Attributes dialog box opens.

> **Troubleshooting** Your Units setting might be different than shown here. You can set the default to inches, centimeters, or pixels, depending on your needs.

3. In the **Attributes** dialog box, click **Default**, and then click **OK** to resize the canvas to match the one shown in our graphics.

Rounded
Rectangle

4. In the toolbox, click the **Rounded Rectangle** button.

> **Troubleshooting** If the toolbox is not visible, click Tool Box on the View menu.

The Rounded Rectangle border and fill options appear at the bottom of the toolbox.

The default option, which you will use at this time, is to create an outline with no fill.

5. Point to the upper-left corner of the blank drawing canvas.

The coordinates of the pointer in relation to the upper-left corner of the canvas appear near the center of the status bar. The coordinates are shown in pixels, regardless of the default Units setting.

6. Drag toward the lower-right corner of the canvas to draw a rectangular outline. While still dragging, press and hold the [Shift] key to change the outline to a rounded square.

The starting coordinates of the object you are drawing appear near the center of the status bar. The horizontal and vertical dimensions (in pixels) appear near the right end of the status bar.

Starting coordinates   Dimensions

7. Release the mouse button when the square approximately fills the vertical space of the canvas.

The rounded square will form the outline of a business logo.

Rectangle

8. In the toolbox, click the **Rectangle** button. Then at the bottom of the toolbox, click the option to create a filled rectangle with no outline.

9. In the color palette above the canvas (officially referred to as the *Color Box*), click the blue square (the third square from the right end of the bottom row) to specify this as the fill color.

At the left end of the color palette, the top box changes to the selected primary color. The bottom box indicates your current secondary color. (White is the default.) You change the secondary color by right-clicking a square in the color palette.

> **Tip** How your primary and secondary colors function depends on what tools and options you select. For example, the primary color might be used to fill an object, and the secondary color might be used for an outline.

10. Near the center of the outline, drag to create a filled rectangle.

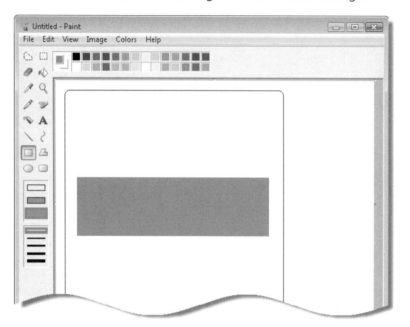

This shape has no outline and is filled with the primary color.

> **Troubleshooting** The objects you draw in Paint cannot be selected and resized as they can in more-sophisticated programs. You can use the Undo command on the Edit menu (or click Ctrl+Z) to remove objects from the drawing canvas or to undo other changes, such as resizing the canvas. You can undo only the last 10 changes.

11. In the color palette, click the red square (the fifth square from the left end of the top row) to set it as the primary color, and right-click the pink square (below the red square) to set it as the secondary color.

Ellipse

12. In the toolbox, click the **Ellipse** button. Then click the option to create a filled outline, and click the thickest line option.

13. Point to the lower-left corner of the filled rectangle. Press and hold the ⟨ Shift ⟩ key, and then drag down and to the right to create a circle. Repeat the process, dragging down and to the left from the lower-right corner of the rectangle, to create two "wheels" of approximately equal size.

The primary color (red) is used for the outline, and the secondary color (pink) is used for the fill.

14. In the toolbox, click the **Rectangle** button, and then click the option to create only an outline. In the color palette, click the gold square (the seventh square from the left end of the top row) to set the primary color. Then drag to draw a vertical rectangle near the upper-right corner of the blue rectangle.

15. In the toolbox, click the **Polygon** button.

Polygon

16. Point to the space at the top of the frame, above the gold rectangle. Then drag down and to the right to begin drawing a line. Press and hold the ⟨ Shift ⟩ key to restrict the line to a 45 degree angle. Without releasing the ⟨ Shift ⟩ key, release the mouse button when the end of the line is just below the top of the gold rectangle.

17. Drag to the left side of the gold rectangle, and release the mouse button.

You will not see the gold line being drawn as you drag, but when you release the mouse button, a horizontal line appears.

18. Release the ⟨Shift⟩ key, point to the beginning point of the shape, and click once to create a triangle.

Fill With Color

19. In the toolbox, click the **Fill With Color** button.

The pointer changes to a paint bucket.

20. With gold still selected as the primary color, click inside the triangle to make it a solid gold color.

Airbrush

21. In the toolbox, click the **Airbrush** button.

The pointer changes to a spray canister.

22. At the bottom of the toolbox, click the large spray pattern option. Then in the color palette, click the light purple square (at the right end of the bottom row).

23. Click several times to the left of the gold arrow to create a smoke trail. Experiment with clicking and dragging for different distances to see the effects you can create.

Text

24. In the toolbox, click the **Text** button, and at the bottom of the toolbox, click the option to insert text with a transparent background. Then in the color palette, click the white square (at the left end of the bottom row) to change the primary color.

25. Drag to draw a rectangular insertion box on top of the blue rectangle.

The floating Fonts toolbar appears. Unlike floating toolbars in other programs, you cannot dock this floating toolbar at the side of the Paint program window. You can, however, move it to any location on the screen.

26. On the **Fonts** toolbar, click the **Font** arrow.

The Font list that appears reflects the fonts installed on your computer.

27. In the **Font** list, click **Comic Sans MS**, and in the **Font Size** list, click **24**.

28. Click in the insertion box to activate the insertion point, and then type Wingtip Toys.

    While the insertion box is active, you can make changes to the box and to its contents.

Bold

29. Press Ctrl+A to select the contents of the insertion box. Then on the **Fonts** toolbar, click the **Bold** button.

30. Point to the top edge of the insertion box, and when the pointer changes to an arrow, drag the box so that the words appear in the approximate center of the blue rectangle. Then click away from the insertion box.

    The Fonts toolbar closes, and your drawing is complete. You now have a simple drawing with which to work through the rest of this chapter.

31. On the **File** menu, click **Save As**.

The Save As dialog box opens. Because you are saving a picture, the default location is your *Pictures* folder.

32. Browse to the *Documents\Microsoft Press\WindowsVistaSBS_Dlx\Graphics* folder. Type WingtipToys in the **File name** box, and then click **Save**.

Paint saves the file as *WingtipToys.jpg*.

 CLOSE the *WingtipToys* file.

Changing the Content, Size, and Orientation of Graphics

You can effect simple changes to any type of graphic file (including photographic images) by using Paint. You can cut, copy, paste, change colors, and so on. You can select an existing shape or text by using the selection rectangle or lasso and then move it, but you can't select and activate a shape or text to edit it. You can delete objects either by selecting and deleting them, by filling the area with the surrounding color, or by doing both.

On a broader scale, you can change many aspects of the dimensions and orientation of a graphic. For example, you can:

● Change the size of the canvas by dragging its move handles or by specifying its exact dimensions in the Attributes dialog box.

● Enlarge or shrink the image horizontally, vertically, or entirely, by a specific percentage.

● Skew the image horizontally or vertically.

● Flip the image horizontally or vertically.

● Rotate the image in 90-degree increments.

See Also For information about changing the file size of a graphic, see "Saving Graphic Files in Different Formats" later in this chapter.

To make it easier to work on small areas of a graphic, you can view your picture at up to 800 percent of its original size. This is useful when you want to work with only a few pixels or need to precisely position an element.

In this exercise, you will open and make changes to an existing graphic. You will experiment with different ways of looking at a picture at different zoom levels, and then you will change the picture's size and orientation.

BE SURE TO start Paint before beginning this exercise.

USE the *ToyTrain* image. This practice file is located in the *Documents\Microsoft Press\ WindowsVistaSBS_Dlx\Graphics* folder.

1. On the **File** menu, click **Open**. In the **Open** dialog box, browse to the *Documents\ Microsoft Press\WindowsVistaSBS_Dlx\Graphics* folder. Click the *ToyTrain* image file, and then click **Open**.

   See Also For information about opening files from Windows Explorer, see "Specifying the Default Program for a Type of File" in Chapter 7, "Working with Programs."

   Paint displays a simple train image. Move handles appear at each side and corner of the canvas.

Move handles

2. Point to the move handle located on the right side of the canvas. When the pointer changes to a double-headed arrow, drag the handle to the right until the canvas is approximately twice as wide as the image.

Select

3. In the toolbox, click the **Select** button. Then at the bottom of the toolbox, click the transparent background option.

— Filled background

— Transparent background

4. Drag to draw a selection box around the image of the train.

When you release the mouse button, resize handles appear at each side and corner of the selection box.

Resize handles

5. Point to any corner resize handle. When the pointer changes to a double-headed arrow, drag toward the center of the image, releasing the mouse button when the image is approximately two-thirds the height of the canvas.

The image becomes proportionally smaller.

> **Troubleshooting** Using the corner resize handle does not restrict the resizing to a proportional change (in other words, you can drag horizontally or vertically as well). When using this method to resize an image, take care to drag inward or outward along an imaginary diagonal line between two corners in order to maintain the original aspect ratio of the image.

6. With the selection box still active, point inside it. When the pointer changes to a four-headed arrow, drag the resized image to the lower-right corner of the canvas.

7. On the **View** menu, point to **Zoom**, point to **Custom**, and then click **200%**. Then enlarge or scroll the program window to display the lower-right corner of the canvas.

> **Tip** The fastest way to change the zoom level is by using the keyboard commands Ctrl+Page Up to zoom out and Ctrl+Page Down to zoom in.

8. With the **Select** tool still active, drag to draw a selection box around only the blue car and red wheels of the train. Press Ctrl+C to copy the selection to the Clipboard, and then press Ctrl+V to paste a copy into the canvas. While the copy is still selected, drag it to the left of the original, aligning the tops of the two blue rectangles.

Fill With Color

9. In the toolbox, click the **Fill With Color** button.

   The pointer changes to a paint bucket.

Pick Color

10. In the toolbox, click the **Pick Color** button.

    The pointer changes to an eyedropper.

11. Point to a blue area of the left train car (the copy you created in step 8), and then click once.

    The fill color is set to the color you clicked, and the pointer reverts to a paint bucket.

    By using this method, you can replicate any existing color.

12. Point to the white square in the left train car, and then click once.

    The white square fills with blue and is no longer visible. In fact, it no longer exists. Only a blue vertical line remains in the train car. At this magnification, it might be difficult to exactly position the paint bucket pointer to fill the dark blue line.

Magnifier

13. In the toolbox, click the **Magnifier** button.

The pointer changes to a magnifying glass in the center of a rectangular magnification area.

14. Point to the dark blue line, and then click once.

The zoom level increases, and the location you clicked moves to the center of the program window.

Zoom slider   Magnifier selection box

15. In the toolbox, click the **Fill With Color** button, and then with the paint can pointer, click the dark blue line once to make it part of the surrounding rectangle.

16. On the **View** menu, point to **Zoom**, point to **Custom**, and then click **200%**. Then enlarge or scroll the program window to display the lower-right corner of the canvas.

> **Tip** To view an entire picture that is larger than your work area, click View Bitmap on the View menu, or press Ctrl+F (for *full screen*). Your picture is displayed in full-screen mode. Any extra space is filled with your Windows desktop background color. To return to Paint, click the primary mouse button.

Eraser/Color
Eraser

17. In the toolbox, click the **Eraser** button. Then at the bottom of the toolbox, click the largest square eraser.

18. Using the eraser, click six times in the left train car to create a row of "windows."

19. On the **View** menu, point to **Zoom**, point to **Custom**, and then click **100%** to view the picture at full size.

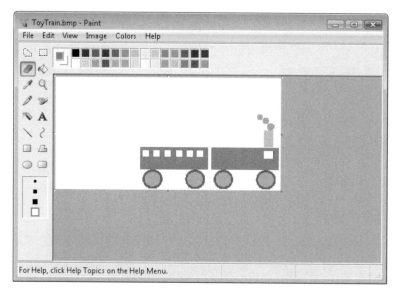

The picture contains a significant amount of white space.

20. In the toolbox, click the **Select** button. Then drag to draw a selection box around the train and its car.

21. On the **Image** menu, click **Flip/Rotate**.

The Flip And Rotate dialog box opens.

22. With **Flip horizontal** selected, click **OK**.

The train turns to point toward the left. If you choose this command without selecting a specific part of the image, the entire canvas flips.

23. With the train still selected, drag it to the upper-left corner of the canvas.

24. Click away from the selection to release it and to activate the resize handles on the canvas. Point to the lower-right handle, and when the pointer changes to a double-headed arrow, drag up until the canvas is approximately the same height as the train. Then drag to the right until the canvas is approximately twice as wide as the existing train.

25. With the **Select** tool active in the toolbox, drag to draw a selection rectangle around the train car (not the train). Press and hold the Ctrl key, and then drag the selection to the right.

A copy of the selected image is created.

26. Without releasing the Ctrl key, drop the copy to the right of the train car. Then drag the selected copy (now the second car) to the right to create a third car.

You now have an entire train.

27. Click away from the selection to release it, and then resize the canvas to fit the train.

28. Save the file in the *Documents\Microsoft Press\WindowsVistaSBS_Dlx\Graphics* folder as ToyTrain2.bmp.

 CLOSE the *ToyTrain2* image.

Using Custom Colors

The standard color palette displayed in Paint includes 28 colors. In the Edit Colors dialog box, you can select from a total of 48 basic colors, or you can create your own by selecting a color; by entering the RGB value (which indicates the amounts of red, green, and blue that are combined to create the color); or by entering the hue, saturation, and luminosity values.

The hue, saturation, and luminosity can best be understood when looking at the Edit Colors dialog box. A color's hue is a horizontal range from red to green to blue to red across the color palette. Its saturation is a vertical range of purity (how much gray it contains). Its luminosity is a range of brightness from pure white to pure black in the slider to the right of the color palette.

Using a Graphic as Your Windows Desktop

Paint provides a way to set a graphic as your Windows Vista desktop background. Open the graphic you want to use for the background in Paint. Then on the File menu, click one of the following options:

- **Set As Background (Tiled)** places multiple copies of the picture in a tile pattern across the entire desktop. The number of copies necessary to fill the desktop will be used; copies that don't fit entirely will be cut off.

- **Set As Background (Centered)** places one copy of the picture in the center of your desktop, on top of your usual desktop background color or picture.

- **Set As Background (Stretched)** places one copy of the picture on your desktop and stretches it to fill the available space. If the picture aspect ratio is different from that of the display, the picture will appear distorted.

To revert to a standard Windows Vista desktop or a simple background color, right-click the desktop, click Personalize, and then click Desktop Background to display your options.

See Also For more information about applying backgrounds to your desktop, see "Changing the Desktop Background" in Chapter 4, "Personalizing Windows Vista."

Saving Graphic Files in Different Formats

There are many different graphic file formats. Some programs save graphics in proprietary formats; others are for general use. Each file format has its own restrictions regarding the colors and compression that it uses, which means that certain file formats support more colors than others, and certain file formats create smaller files than others. The file format that you choose depends on the type of graphic you are saving and what you want to do with it. For example, graphics that will be printed have different requirements than graphics that will be displayed on a computer screen.

With Paint, you can save graphics in several formats, including four types of bitmaps (monochrome, 16-color, 256-color, and 24-bit), GIF, JPEG, PNG, and TIFF. You can also open, view, and print certain icon (.ico) graphics, but you can't save graphics in the icon format from Paint.

In this exercise, you will save a picture in a variety of formats and note the differences in quality and file size.

> **BE SURE TO** open Windows Explorer before beginning this exercise.
>
> **USE** the *TeamPhoto* image. This practice file is located in the *Documents\Microsoft Press\ WindowsVistaSBS_Dlx\Graphics* folder.

1. In **Windows Explorer**, browse to the *Documents\Microsoft Press\WindowsVistaSBS_ Dlx\Graphics* folder.

2. Right-click the *TeamPhoto* file, point to **Open With**, and then click **Paint**.

   Paint displays a photo of America's Finest Publishing Team. The photo is saved as a JPG image.

3. On the **File** menu, click **Save As**.

4. In the **Save as type** list, click **Monochrome Bitmap**.

5. Click in the **File name** box, press Home, type mono_, and then click **Save**.

Paint warns you that saving the picture in this format will cause some loss of color information.

6. In the warning box, click **Yes**.

The picture changes to black and white and is saved with the new name. The color palette also changes to reflect the black-and-white options.

7. On the **File** menu, click **Open**. In the **Open** dialog box, browse to the folder, click the *TeamPhoto* file, and then click **Open**.

The original photo opens.

8. Repeat steps 3 through 7, saving the file as **256 Color Bitmap** and appending 256_ to the beginning of the file name. Then repeat steps 3 through 6, saving the file as **GIF** and typing gif_ at the beginning of the file name.

Close

9. In the upper-right corner of the Paint program window, click the **Close** button to close all the open files and return to the practice files folder.

10. In Windows Explorer, click the **Views** arrow, and then click **Details** to see the size of each of the files you saved.

The file sizes are as follows:

File	Size
TeamPhoto.jpg (original)	139 KB
256_TeamPhoto.bmp	401 KB
gif_TeamPhoto.gif	158 KB
mono_TeamPhoto.bmp	50 KB

 CLOSE Windows Explorer.

Understanding Graphic Formats

The BMP (bitmap) format stores graphics as a series of dots, or pixels. The different types of BMP files reflect the number of bits per pixel needed to store information about the graphic—the greater the number of colors, the greater the number of bits needed.

The GIF (Graphics Interchange Format) format is common for images that appear on Web pages because they can be compressed with no loss of information and groups of them can be animated. GIFs work well for line drawings, pictures with blocks of solid color, and pictures with sharp boundaries between colors. GIFs store, at most, 8 bits per pixel, so they are limited to 256 colors.

The JPEG (Joint Photographic Experts Group) format is a compressed format that works well for complex graphics such as scanned photographs. Some information is lost in the compression process, but often the loss is imperceptible to the human eye. Color JPEG images store 24 bits per pixel, so they are capable of displaying more than 16 million colors. Grayscale JPEG images store 8 bits per pixel.

The PNG (Portable Network Graphic) format has the advantages of the GIF format but can store colors with 8, 24, or 48 bits per pixel and grayscales with 1, 2, 4, 8, or 16 bits per pixel. A PNG file can also specify whether each pixel blends with its background color and can contain color correction information so that images look accurate on a broad range of display devices. The PNG format is also better than GIF for the progressive display of images.

The TIFF (Tag Image File Format) format can store compressed images with a flexible number of bits per pixel. Using tags, one multi-page TIFF file can store several images, along with related information such as type of compression, and orientation.

Printing Graphics

You can print graphics from Paint with the same options that you have when printing from other Windows-based programs. You can set up an image to appear on the printed page at the size and location you want it, and then print to any available local or network printer.

In this exercise, you will prepare a photo for printing from Paint.

> USE the *Red Flower* picture. This practice file is located in the *Documents\Microsoft Press\ WindowsVistaSBS_Dlx\Graphics* folder.
> BE SURE TO install a local or network printer before beginning this exercise.
> OPEN the *Red Flower* picture in Paint.

Maximize

1. If the Paint program window is not already maximized, click the **Maximize** button.

   The entire picture does not fit in the window. This is a good indication that it might not fit onto a piece of paper.

2. On the **File** menu, click **Print Preview**.

   The Print Preview window opens, displaying only one corner of the photo.

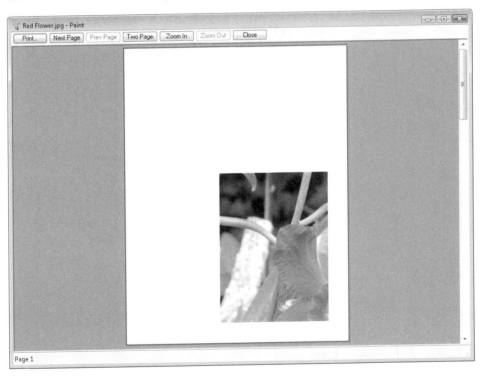

> **Tip** If you know that your picture will fit onto the page the way you want and that your printer settings are already set the way you want them, it is not necessary to preview the picture before printing it. On the File menu, click Print (or press Ctrl+P) to go directly to the Print dialog box.

3. On the toolbar of the **Print Preview** window, click the **Two Page** button.

The Print Preview window now displays two corners of the photo across two pages.

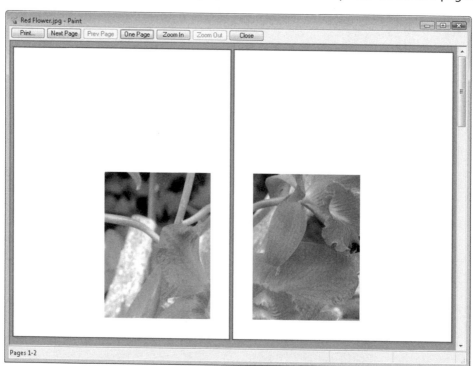

4. On the toolbar, click the **Next Page** button once to display the second and third pages, and again to display the third and fourth pages. Then click the **Close** button.

5. On the **File** menu, click **Page Setup**.

   The Page Setup dialog box opens.

The preview area indicates the way the photo will be printed with the current settings.

6. In the **Scaling** area, click **Fit to**, and then enter 1 in each of the corresponding boxes.

The preview now indicates that the entire picture fits onto one page.

7. In the **Page Setup** dialog box, click **OK**.

8. On the **File** menu, click **Print Preview**.

The Print Preview window now displays the entire picture on one page.

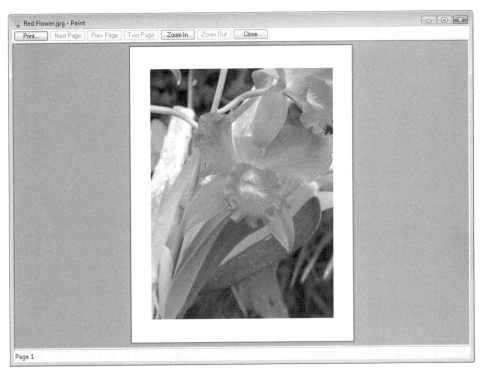

9. On the toolbar of the **Print Preview** window, click the **Print** button.

The standard Windows Print dialog box opens with your installed printers listed in the Select Printer area. A green check mark indicates the default printer.

10. If you want to print to a printer other than the default, click that printer in the **Select Printer** area. Then click **Print**.

Paint prints the picture to the selected printer.

 CLOSE the *Red Flower* file.

Creating Simple Documents

WordPad is a simple word processing program in which you can create formatted documents. It offers a number of options that you can use to embellish your document to best fit your needs.

Windows Help And Support includes useful information and troubleshooting instructions for WordPad. You can access program-specific information from within WordPad by clicking View Help on the Help menu.

See Also For more information about Windows Help And Support, see "Finding Solutions to Common Problems" in Chapter 15, "Identifying and Solving Problems."

In this exercise, you will start WordPad and create a basic document. There are no practice files for this exercise.

BE SURE TO log on to Windows Vista before beginning this exercise.

1. On the **Start** menu, click **All Programs**, click **Accessories**, and then click **WordPad**.
   WordPad starts, displaying a blank document.

   The blinking line in the upper-left corner of the document window indicates the location of the insertion point.

2. Type The Garden Company, and then press ⌈Enter⌋ to move to the next line.

3. Type 1234 Oak Street, and then press ⌈Enter⌋.

4. Type Seattle, WA 10101, and then press ⌈Enter⌋ twice to leave a blank line between the address block you just created and the following text.

5. Type the following paragraph, and then press ⌈Enter⌋ twice:

   The Garden Company offers a variety of classes on plant selection for your geographic area, general and seasonal plant care, and garden-related crafts and activities. This month we are pleased to offer the following classes:

6. Type September 1, press ⌈Tab⌋, type Landscaping with Volcanic Rock, and then press ⌈Enter⌋.

7. Type September 12, press ⌈Tab⌋, type Natural Scandinavian Gardens, and then press ⌈Enter⌋.

8. Type September 20, press ⌈Tab⌋, type Treating Slug and Snail Damage, and then press ⌈Enter⌋ twice.

9. Type Space is limited, so register early! to complete the sample text.

You now have a simple promotional document.

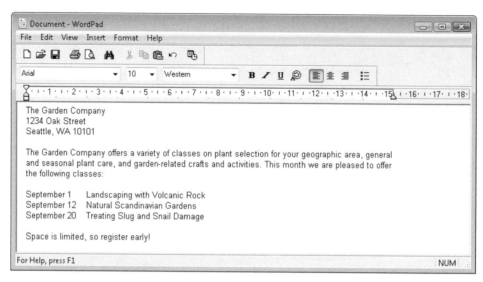

10. On the **File** menu, click **Save As**.

The Save As dialog box opens. Because you are saving a document, the default location is your *Documents* folder.

11. Browse to the *Documents\Microsoft Press\WindowsVistaSBS_Dlx\Graphics* folder.

12. Type **MyDocument1** in the **File name** box, and then click **Save**.

The file is saved as *MyDocument1.rtf*.

CLOSE the WordPad window to exit the program.

Formatting Words and Paragraphs

The way letters, numbers, and characters look on the screen and in print is governed by a number of factors. The basic look is determined by the *font*. You can refine the look by changing the size of the characters and formatting them—for example, by making them bold, italic, or underlined.

The default character formatting used in WordPad documents is 10-point Arial. You cannot change the default font, as you can in Microsoft Office Word, but if you change the font settings at the beginning of the document, later text is inserted in the new font.

The default paragraph formatting used in WordPad documents is for single-spaced, left-aligned paragraphs. You can change the way paragraphs look by changing their alignment and indentation, and by adding bullets.

In this exercise, you will format the characters and paragraphs in an existing document to add structure, emphasis, and clarity.

BE SURE TO start WordPad before beginning this exercise.

USE the *GardenCompany* document. This practice file is located in the *Documents\ Microsoft Press\WindowsVistaSBS_Dlx\Graphics* folder.

Open

1. On the toolbar, click the **Open** button. In the **Open** dialog box, browse to the *Documents\Microsoft Press\WindowsVistaSBS_Dlx\Graphics* folder. Click the *GardenCompany* document, and then click **Open**.

   The document opens in WordPad.

2. On the **Edit** menu, click **Select All** to select the entire text of the open document.

   > **Tip** You can also select all the text in a document by pressing Ctrl+A.

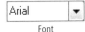

Font

3. On the Format bar, click the **Font** arrow to display the list of available fonts.

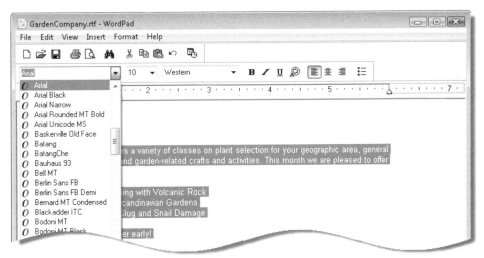

The Font list varies depending on the fonts installed on your computer.

4. In the **Font** list, click **Verdana**.

   The selected text changes from Arial to Verdana.

5. Point to the left end of the first line of text (the company name), and when the pointer changes to a right-pointing arrow, drag to select the first three lines of text (the address block).

Center

6. On the Format bar, click the **Center** button.

The address block moves horizontally to the center of the page.

Color

7. With the address block still selected, click the **Color** button to display the list of available text colors.

Bold

8. In the **Color** list, click **Green**. Then on the Format bar, click the **Bold** button.

The selected text changes to a bold version of the Verdana font. The color change isn't immediately obvious because the text is selected.

9. Press the [Home] key to move the insertion point to the beginning of the address block.

Now you can see that the address block text is green.

10. Triple-click anywhere in the first line to select the paragraph containing the company name.

Font Size

11. On the Format bar, in the **Font Size** list, click **12**.

The company name is now larger than the address.

Italic

12. At the bottom of the document, select the last line of text. Then on the Format bar, click the **Italic** button.

The selected text changes to an italic version of the Verdana font.

Bullets

13. Select the three lines of text listing the upcoming classes. Then on the Format bar, click the **Bullets** button.

The text is formatted as a bulleted list with a hanging indent (which will be obvious later in this chapter). A tab separates the bullet and the date.

14. At the left end of the Ruler, drag the upward-pointing triangle two marks to the left so that the hanging indent is at ¼ inch. (Don't release the mouse button yet.)

> **Troubleshooting** If the Ruler is not visible, click Ruler on the View menu.

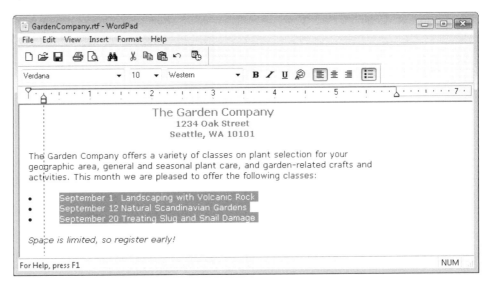

The dotted line indicates the position to which the indent will move.

> **Tip** You can display measurements in WordPad in inches, centimeters, points, or picas. To change the measurement units, click Options on the View menu. In the Options dialog box, click the Options tab, click the units you want to display, and then click OK.

15. Release the mouse button to change the hanging indent from ½ inch to ¼ inch.

Because the class dates and class names are separated by tabs, the space between them increases by ¼ inch.

16. Click away from the bulleted list to release the selection.

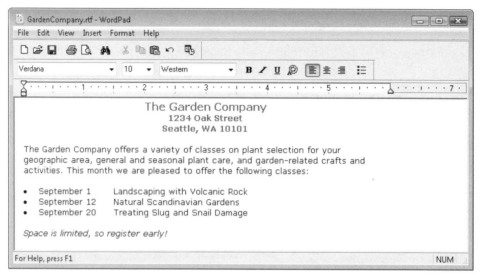

17. Save your document in the *Documents\Microsoft Press\WindowsVistaSBS_Dlx\ Graphics* folder as MyDocument2.

CLOSE the WordPad window to exit the program.

Inserting Text and Graphics

With WordPad, you can import a wide variety of objects into a document, including bitmap-format graphics, text, charts, slides, sound clips, and video clips.

If you are reusing a small part of one document in another document, it makes sense to simply copy and paste text from one to the other. However, if you are reusing an entire document in another document, or if several people are contributing documents to a central project, it is easier and more efficient to import the text from the source document(s) into the host document.

> **Tip** You can insert the current date or time into a document by clicking the Date/Time button on the toolbar and then clicking the date or time format you want.

In this exercise, you will insert text and graphics from external files into an existing document.

> **USE** the *Brochure* and *ClassDesc1* through *ClassDesc3* documents, and the *GCLogo* image. These practice files are located in the *Documents\Microsoft Press\WindowsVistaSBS_Dlx\ Graphics* folder.
>
> **OPEN** the *Brochure* document in WordPad.

1. Click at the end of the first bulleted paragraph, and then press ⏎ Shift + ⏎ Enter to insert a line break.

   The paragraph's hanging indent is now apparent, because the insertion point aligns with the date rather than with the bullet character.

2. On the **Insert** menu, click **Object**.

   The Insert Object dialog box opens, listing a variety of objects you can insert into or link to your document.

> **Tip** The available objects will vary based on the programs installed on your computer.

3. Click **Create from File**.

The Insert Object dialog box changes to enable you to enter or browse to the location of the object you want to insert.

4. Click **Browse**. In the **Browse** dialog box, navigate to the *Documents\Microsoft Press\ WindowsVistaSBS_Dlx\Graphics* folder, click the *ClassDesc1* document, and then click **Open**.

5. In the **Insert Object** dialog box, click **OK** to insert the contents of the *ClassDesc1* document into the *Brochure* document.

A description of the class is inserted into the current document, in a separate frame. The inserted content is editable separately from the host content.

Troubleshooting When you insert content from a source file that does not include a blank paragraph at the end, the character formatting might not appear correctly in the host document.

6. Repeat steps 1 through 5 for the second and third bulleted paragraphs, inserting *ClassDesc2* and *ClassDesc3*, respectively.

7. Double-click the first class description to open it in an editing box.

8. Click to position the insertion point after the word *class*, type a comma, and then click outside the editing box to close it.

The change is reflected in the inserted content.

9. Select the paragraph containing the company name.

10. Repeat steps 2 through 5, this time inserting the *GCLogo* image. Then click a blank area of the document to display the results.

The Garden Company's logo is inserted in place of the selected company name.

11. Save your document in the *Documents\Microsoft Press\WindowsVistaSBS_Dlx\ Graphics* folder as MyDocument3.

 CLOSE the WordPad window to exit the program.

Printing Documents

You can print documents from WordPad with the same options that you have when printing from other Windows-based programs. For example, you can specify which pages to print, how many copies to print, whether to print on both sides of the paper, and whether to print vertically (portrait) or horizontally (landscape) oriented pages.

In this exercise, you will print a document from WordPad.

USE the *FinalBrochure* document. This practice file is located in the *Documents\Microsoft Press\WindowsVistaSBS_Dlx\Graphics* folder.

BE SURE TO install a local or network printer before beginning this exercise.

OPEN the *FinalBrochure* document in WordPad.

1. On the **File** menu, click **Page Setup**.

The Page Setup dialog box opens, displaying the current paper size, orientation, and margins.

2. In the **Page Setup** dialog box, in the **Orientation** area, click **Landscape**. In the **Margins** area, change the **Top** setting to .75. Then click **OK**.

3. On the **File** menu, click **Print Preview**.

The Print Preview window opens, displaying the document as it will look on the printed page. Dotted lines indicate the page margins.

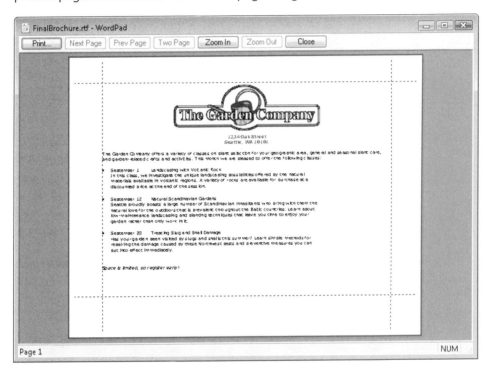

> **Tip** If you know that your document will fit onto the page the way you want and that your printer settings are already set the way you want them, it is not necessary to preview the document before printing it. On the File menu, click Print (or press Ctrl+P) to go directly to the Print dialog box.

With the current settings, this document fits neatly onto one page.

4. On the toolbar of the **Print Preview** window, click the **Print** button.

The standard Windows Print dialog box opens with your installed printers listed in the Select Printer area. A green check mark indicates the default printer.

5. If you want to print the document to a printer other than the default, click that printer in the **Select Printer** area. Then click the **Print** button.

WordPad prints the document to the selected printer.

 CLOSE the WordPad window to exit the program.

Key Points

- The Windows Vista operating system comes with Paint, a program you can use to create and edit graphics, and WordPad, a program you can use to create and format documents.

- Using Paint, you can save graphics in a variety of formats that are ideal for different uses. You can save an edited graphic in its original format or in an alternate format of your choice.

- Documents created in WordPad are not limited to plain text: You can format the font, size, and color of characters; format paragraphs; and insert graphics. You can save WordPad documents as Text or Rich Text Format files.

- When printing graphics from Paint or documents from WordPad, you have the same print options as you do in other Windows-based programs.

Keyboard Shortcuts

Press this	To do this in Paint
Ctrl+C	Copy the selection to the Clipboard.
Ctrl+F	Display a full-screen view of a graphic.
Ctrl+P	Open the Print dialog box.
Ctrl+V	Paste an item from the Clipboard.
Ctrl+Page Down	Zoom in.
Ctrl+Page Up	Zoom out.

Press this	To do this in WordPad
Ctrl+A	Select all text in the active document.
Ctrl+P	Open the Print dialog box.
Ctrl+End	Move to the end of a document.
Ctrl+Home	Move to the beginning of a document.

Chapter at a Glance

View, catalog, and fix pictures, **page 368**

Play music, **page 375**

Burn audio and data discs, **page 385**

12 Working with Digital Media

In this chapter, you will learn to:

- ✔ View, catalog, and fix pictures.
- ✔ Play music.
- ✔ Configure Windows Media Center options.
- ✔ Burn audio and data discs.
- ✔ Share pictures and other digital media files.

These days, most people use their computers for more than simply creating documents, performing calculations, sending messages, and browsing the Internet. You might want to manage, manipulate, and print photographs; download, catalog, and listen to music; watch and create movies; and share digital pictures and media files with colleagues, friends, and family.

Windows Vista comes with built-in tools to help you make the most of your increasingly available digital media options. Whether you're working with media for personal or business purposes, you can use these tools to achieve professional results.

In this chapter, you will view and catalog pictures, play music, burn an audio CD or photo disc, and share pictures with other people on your network.

See Also Do you need only a quick refresher on the topics in this chapter? See the Quick Reference section at the beginning of this book.

Important Before you can use the practice files in this chapter, you need to install them from the book's companion CD to their default location. See "Using the Companion CD" at the beginning of this book for more information.

Viewing, Cataloging, and Fixing Pictures

Windows Vista includes a powerful tool for viewing, cataloging, and editing pictures, called Windows Photo Gallery. Photo Gallery is a substantial upgrade of the Windows Picture And Fax viewer available in Windows XP. In addition to viewing, rotating, saving, and opening image files, you can do the following from the Photo Gallery window, without opening the file:

- Create and manage image collections.
- Delete, rename, or copy a file.
- View and edit file properties, including keywords.
- Adjust photo exposure and color settings.
- Fix red eye effects.
- Precisely crop images to standard or custom proportions.

Photo Gallery is designed for use with digital pictures from cameras and scanners, When opening a file from Photo Gallery you can select the image-editing program you want to use from those installed on your computer. You can print pictures, order prints from a professional printing vendor, send pictures in e-mail, or burn them to a disc—all from the simple Photo Gallery interface. If your computer system supports Windows Movie Maker, which also comes with Windows Vista, you can assemble pictures into a movie and view and catalog videos through Photo Gallery.

> **Tip** To run Movie Maker, your video card must support DirectX 9, and you must have video drivers designed for Windows Vista installed.

Photo Gallery supports the following file formats:

Image formats	**Video formats**
Bitmap (.bmp)	Advanced Systems Format (.asf)
Joint Photographic Experts Group (.jpeg)	Audio Video Interleave (.avi)
JPEG File Interchange Format (.jfif)	Microsoft Digital Video Recordinger-MS (.dvr-ms)
Portable Network Graphics (.png)	Moving Picture Experts Group (.mpeg)
Tagged Image File Format (.tiff)	Microsoft Windows Media Video (.wmv)
Windows Portable Devices (.wpd)	

Troubleshooting Pictures saved in other formats, including the reasonably common Graphics Interchange Format (.gif files), will not display in Photo Gallery even if they are stored in a cataloged folder. To see and work with a .gif file in Photo Gallery, you must first convert it to a supported format.

Double-clicking any file of a type associated with Windows Photo Gallery opens Photo Gallery and displays the file along with information and commands specific to the file.

- The toolbar displays buttons and menus of commands for working with the displayed picture.

- The Info pane displays properties of the selected image; you can add and edit information within the pane. You can hide the Info pane by clicking the X button in its upper-right corner, and redisplay it by clicking the Info button on the toolbar.

- You can use the View controls at the bottom of the Photo Gallery window to move forward or backward in the folder containing the selected file, display a slideshow of the images, reduce or magnify the image view, and rotate or delete selected images.

Toolbar

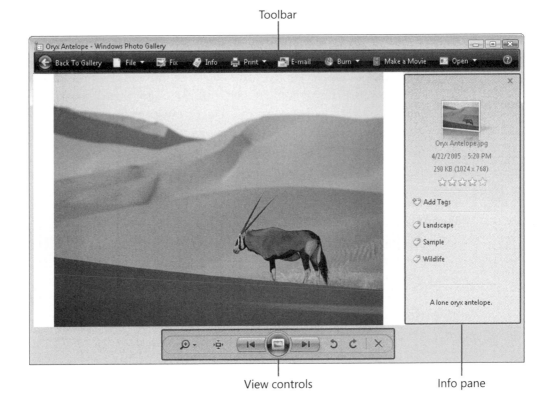

View controls   Info pane

When you click the Add Folder To Gallery or Go To Gallery button while viewing a picture in Photo Gallery, or when you click Windows Photo Gallery in the All Programs list on the Start menu, a Photo Gallery window opens in which you can view and work with all the supported-format pictures in all the folders you have added to the gallery. From this window, you can do the following:

- Select and work with one or more pictures.
- Sort all the pictures that have been added to the gallery, regardless of which folder they are stored in, by keyword (tag), date, or rating.
- View the pictures in a particular folder.

In this exercise, you will display a photo in Photo Gallery and then add the folder in which the photo is stored to the gallery. Then in the Photo Gallery window, you will sort and filter the files in various ways to find the ones you want. You will also add tags and adjust the properties of some photos so that they are easier to find.

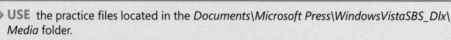

USE the practice files located in the *Documents\Microsoft Press\WindowsVistaSBS_Dlx\ Media* folder.
BE SURE TO log on to Windows Vista before beginning this exercise.

1. On the **Start** menu, click **All Programs**, and then click **Windows Photo Gallery**.

   Windows Photo Gallery start, displaying large thumbnails of the sample pictures and videos that come with Windows Vista. The Filter pane on the left displays a multitude of ways in which you can select pictures to display in the gallery. You can view all pictures and video in all cataloged folders, or only those meeting certain criteria such as the tags assigned, the date taken, or the file location.

View

2. Click the **View** button located to the left of the **Search** box to display a list of options for viewing, grouping, and sorting pictures.

3. On the **View** menu, click **Thumbnails with Text** to see that view, and then click **Tiles**.

4. If the Info pane isn't open, click **Info** on the toolbar.

5. Scroll the content pane to view information about the movies and pictures shown in it.

   For each item, Photo Gallery displays the file name, date and time the movie or picture was taken, file size, length (for movies only), rating (if you've assigned one), and any captions you have assigned to the item.

6. Point to any item that interests you.

   After a moment, Photo Gallery displays a larger thumbnail of the item.

7. In the **Filter** pane, expand the filter categories and experiment with filtering the gallery contents by different criteria. When you finish, click **All Pictures and Videos**.

   Notice that the available filter categories specifically map to the cataloged pictures and videos.

8. On the **File** menu, click **Add Folder to Gallery**.

9. In the **Add Folder to Gallery** dialog box, navigate to the *Documents\Microsoft Press\WindowsVistaSBS_Dlx\Media* folder, and then click **OK**.

   Windows Photo Gallery adds the folder to the gallery and displays a confirmation message. The Filter list changes to include the properties assigned to the items in the folder you added. At the bottom of the Navigation pane, the *Media* folder appears in the list of folders that are part of the gallery, along with your personal *Pictures* and *Videos* folders and the *Public Pictures* and *Public Videos* folders.

10. In the **Add Folder to Gallery** message box, select the **Don't show this message again** check box, and then click **OK**.

11. In the content pane, double-click the *Arizona10* image.

   Windows Photo Gallery displays the picture and its properties.

12. On the toolbar, point to the **File**, **Print**, and **Burn** buttons to see the actions you can take with the displayed picture. Then click **Fix**.

   The Info pane displays actions you can take to change the picture

13. In the **Info** pane, click **Auto Adjust**.

    The colors of the picture change, with the background becoming less blue and the photo elements becoming much more clear.

14. At the bottom of the **Info** pane, click **Undo**, and then click **Redo**, noticing the effect of the automatic adjustment.

15. Experiment with other picture fixes that interest you. When you finish exploring, click **Back To Gallery**.

> **Troubleshooting** If a displayed picture is not yet part of a gallery, the Add Folder To Gallery button appears in place of the Back To Gallery button.

16. At the top of the **Navigation** pane, under **Tags**, click **cactus**.

    The content pane changes to display only pictures from the *Media* folder.

17. With the *Arizona10* image selected, look at the file properties displayed in the **Info** pane.

    The *cactus* tag is one of the four tags associated with this image.

18. In the **Navigation** pane, under **Tags**, click **Flowers**.

    The content pane displays 13 items—12 pictures and a video—which are stored in several folders on your computer.

19. In the **Navigation** pane, under **Tags**, click **Wildlife**.

    The content pane displays four pictures and three videos. The videos are indicated by filmstrip markings on the left and right edges of the opening image of the video.

    Obviously, tagging files with keywords provides a powerful way to locate pictures and videos about a particular subject. But it works best only when you tag all your images.

20. At the bottom of the **Navigation** pane, under **Folders**, click the *Media* folder. Then in the content pane, click the *Frog* image.

The selected image does not have any tags assigned.

21. In the **Info** pane, click **Add Tags**. Then in the box that appears, type wi.

After a short pause, Windows Photo Gallery displays a list of existing tags that begin with these letters.

22. In the list, click **Wildlife**, and press Enter to apply the selected tag to the *Frog* image.

23. In the content pane, click the *Cat* image, hold down the Ctrl key, and then click the *Crow* image.

24. Repeat step 21 to add the **Wildlife** tag to both images at once.

25. In the **Navigation** pane, click the **Wildlife** tag.

The frog, cat, and crow pictures appear among the other Wildlife-tagged pictures.

26. Click the **X** in the upper-right corner of the **Info** pane to close the pane, and then press Ctrl+Home to move to the top of the folder.

Play Slide Show

27. At the center of the **View** controls at the bottom of the window, click the **Play Slide Show** button.

Photo Gallery displays a full-screen slide show of the pictures in the Wildlife category, shown in the order they appear in the content pane.

28. After viewing the slides once through, right-click the displayed image, and then click **Shuffle**.

The slide display changes to a random order.

29. Press the Esc key to end the slide show.

CLOSE Windows Photo Gallery.

Playing Music

Windows Media Player is an easy-to-use program for managing catalogs of music, pictures, and videos, including recorded television programs. You can play or display any of these types of media by simply inserting a CD or DVD into your computer's CD or DVD drive, or by selecting the media you want to play from the Windows Media Player catalog or from a file on your computer. No special instructions are necessary for this simplest use of Windows Media Player. In this topic, we will discuss ways in which you can refine Player performance.

The first time you start Windows Media Player—for example, by inserting an audio CD into your CD drive and clicking Play in the AutoPlay dialog box—you have the option of manually setting up Windows Media Player. You can change the initial settings at any time, so it is simplest to click Express Settings and then click Finish, to get started with the most commonly used settings.

You can display the Player on your computer screen in any of these five modes:

- **Full mode.** The default mode. The CD plays in a window that includes a toolbar with navigation buttons and tabs that provide access to tasks you might want to perform with the media, a video display, a List pane displaying information about the media, and controls for playing the media and changing the window size.

Toolbar

Player controls   List pane

The video pane can display the album cover art or a visualization of the music, or remain blank. To change the display, click the Now Playing arrow, point to Visualizations, and then click the option you want.

● **Compact mode.** Displays only the Player controls. You switch between full mode and compact mode by clicking the Switch Mode button in the lower-right corner of the Windows Media Player.

View Full Screen
Switch Mode

● **Mini Player mode.** Minimizes the Player to the Windows taskbar with access to the Player controls and other information. To display the Mini Player, right-click the Windows taskbar, click Toolbars, and then click Windows Media Player. To switch back to the previous mode, click the Restore button.

Show videos and visualizations

Restore to the previous mode

● **Full-screen mode.** Makes a video or picture fill the entire screen. Moving the mouse displays the Player controls. To switch to full-screen mode, click the View Full Screen button in either full or compact mode. Click the button again to switch back to the previous mode.

● **Skin mode.** Displays a small Player window with full controls. Can be customized with "skins" by means of which the Player takes on the shape and look of radios or other gadgets, mythical creatures, movie characters, or other animated graphic themes.

To switch to skin mode from full mode, right-click a blank area of the tab area or Player controls, point to View, and then click Skin Mode. The Player appears in the current skin in the upper-left corner of the desktop. To change the skin, click Skin Chooser on the View menu, select the skin you want, and then click Apply Skin.

To return to full mode, right-click the skin mode Player, click Switch To Full Mode, and then click the Now Playing tab.

> **Tip** You can download skins from the Web by clicking More Skins in Skin Chooser.

In full mode, the Windows Media Player toolbar includes tabs for the following tasks:

- **Now Playing.** Clicking this button displays a menu from which you can play the current CD, show and hide the List pane, enhance the audio quality, display visual accompaniment to music, and download and install plug-in (helper) programs.

- **Library.** Clicking this button lists the audio files stored on your computer that you have added to the library. They are cataloged by album, artist, and genre. Your *play lists* (compilations of tracks from various CDs and other sources) are also listed. You use commands on the tab's menu to create play lists, view the various types of media stored on your computer, add media files to the library, share media files, and download updated information about your media files from the Internet.

- **Rip.** Clicking this button displays the tracks on the CD currently installed in your CD drive. You can select the tracks you want and rip (copy) them to your computer so that you can play them without the CD being inserted in the drive. Commands on this tab set the format and bit rate of the copy (which affects the size of the file and quality of the sound), and determine whether CDs are automatically ripped and whether the CD is ejected after ripping.

- **Burn.** Clicking this button lists the audio files in the library so that you can select tracks to create a burn list. Commands on the tab enable you to specify whether the disc is ejected after burning and whether the sound should be adjusted so that it is consistent across tracks.

- **Sync.** Clicking this button lists the audio files in the library so that you can select tracks to copy to a portable music device. You can also copy files from the device to your computer. In this way, any changes you make to one are synchronized with the other.

- **Media Guide.** Clicking this button connects you to the Windows Media Web site, which includes links to various entertainment options. It is well worth having a look around this site.

Most of the tabs feature Layout Options and View Options menus at the top of the content window. From these menus, you can change the appearance and organization of the Windows Media Player program window.

> **Tip** You must be in full mode to display the classic menu bar.

In this exercise, you will view the Windows Media Player settings, display the menu bar, and personalize the look and feel of the Player by changing the skin.

> **BE SURE TO** have an active Internet connection before beginning this exercise.

1. On the **Start** menu, click **All Programs**, and then click **Windows Media Player**.

> **Troubleshooting** If this is the first time you have started Windows Media Player, click Finish to accept the default Express Settings installation option.

Windows Media Player starts.

> **Tip** If your computer is part of a private network (such as a home network), Windows Media Player might offer to connect to other computers on your network, for the purpose of finding and sharing music, pictures, and video. You can click the notification to turn on media sharing, or you can turn it on at any time from the Network And Sharing Center.

2. If Windows Media Player starts in compact mode, click the **Switch Mode** button to display the entire interface in full-screen mode.

3. On the toolbar, point to each button in turn. First click the button's arrow to display the list of page options, and then click the button to display the page.

4. Click the **Rip** arrow, and then click **More Options**.

The Options dialog box opens with the Rip Music tab active.

5. Explore the tabs of the **Options** dialog box, noticing how you can customize many different types of Player settings.

6. Make any changes you want, and then click **OK**, or simply click **Cancel** to close the dialog box without making any changes.

7. Click the **Layout Options** button, and then click **Show Classic Menus**.

   The available commands are arranged on the menu bar in five menus: File, View, Play, Tools, and Help.

8. Click the **File** menu, and then point to each menu in turn to see its commands. Then on the **View** menu, click **Skin Chooser**.

   The window changes so that you can choose a skin. The available skins are listed on the left, and a preview of the selected skin appears on the right.

9. Click **More Skins**.

   The Skins For Windows Media Player page opens in your Web browser.

10. Scroll the list of skins, and follow the directions to download a few that you like.

    For the purposes of this exercise, download only skins created by Microsoft. You can come back and explore other skins later.

11. When you finish downloading skins, close your browser window.

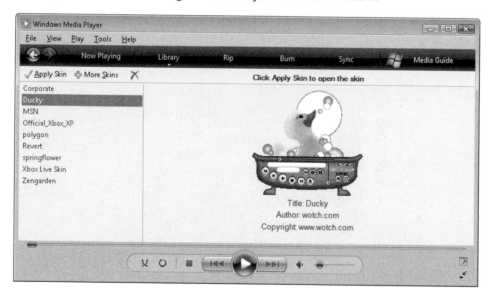

12. In the **Skin Chooser** window, click your favorite skin, and then click **Apply Skin**.

Windows Media Player changes to reflect your selection and switches to skin mode. For example, the *XBox Live* skin looks like a game controller, and displays a cool animation when you open it.

> **Tip** Move the mouse pointer over the buttons on the skin you select to learn what features are available for that skin.

Return to Full
Mode

13. On the skin, click the **Return to Full Mode** button.

> **Troubleshooting** The appearance of the Return To Full Mode button changes to match the skin, but the icon is the same for all skins.

BE SURE TO apply the skin you want to use and, if you want to, repeat step 7 to hide the menu bar before continuing.

CLOSE the Windows Media Player window.

Configuring Windows Media Center Options

You no longer need to purchase a separate edition of the operating system to enable the powerful Windows Media Center functionality on your computer or designated media server—it is built right into Windows Vista. Although it provides capabilities for viewing and cataloging photographs that are superior to those of Windows Photo Gallery and capabilities for collecting and playing music and videos that are superior to those of Windows Media Player, the main appeal of Windows Media Center is its ability to expand your television into a total entertainment center that accesses content on or through your computer. With a built-in or external analog or digital TV tuner, you can use Windows Media Center to pause, rewind, and record television programs (more than one at a time), including high-definition television (HDTV). And you can do it all from across the room with a remote control.

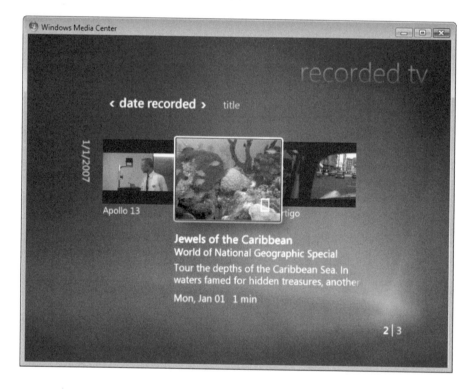

As with Windows Media Player, you can choose an Express or Custom setup the first time you start Windows Media Center. The Express setup takes less than one minute, and you can immediately get started. For example, you can display a dramatic slide show of photos, with Media Center automatically panning, zooming, and transitioning in a highly professional fashion. By default, Windows Media Center scans your *Music*, *Pictures*, and *Videos* folders for media files. You add or remove any folders you like.

At any time after you complete the initial setup process, you can change settings for all of your media-related tasks through the Windows Media Center. To configure the options, open Windows Media Center from the Start menu, go to Tasks, and then click Settings.

General settings include:

- **Startup and Window Behavior.** Automatically start Media Center when you log on and control window and taskbar interactions.

- **Visual and Sound Effects.** Control transitions between screens and images, sounds, color scheme, and the background color displayed behind images or videos.

- **Program Library Options.** Control which of the programs installed on your computer are available from within Media Center and whether those programs can control content and access media information through Media Center.

- **Windows Media Center Setup.** Manually set up the Internet connection, TV signal, speakers, and display used by Media Center.

- **Parental Controls.** Block the display of content you deem inappropriate for your children. You can temporarily unblock content by entering a four-digit access code of your choosing.

- **Automatic Download Options.** Retrieve media display information from the Internet manually or automatically.

- **Optimization.** Schedule regular maintenance of Windows Media Center at a time that is convenient to you.

- **Privacy.** Control the sending of anonymous usage and reliability information from your computer system to Microsoft, and prevent Media Center from keeping track of the shows you view the most.

If your computer system has a built-in or external TV tuner, you can watch and record television programs on your computer. Windows Media Center downloads television program listings from the Internet. TV settings include:

- **Set Up TV Signal.** Configure Media Center as a television receiver.
- **Configure Your TV or Monitor.** Control the way Media Center displays content on your monitor or another display you connect to the computer.
- **TV Audio.** Choose the audio output you want; available options depend on your system.
- **TV Closed Captioning.** When watching television programs through Media Center, you control the display of closed captioning (when available).

When displaying a slide show of images from your *Pictures* folder or another folder you select, you can control the following settings:

- **Show pictures in random order.** Display a slide show of pictures in the order they appear in the folder or in random order.
- **Show pictures in subfolders.** Include or exclude images stored in subfolders of your *Pictures* or other selected folder.
- **Show caption.** If caption information is saved with an image, you can display it as part of a slide show.
- **Show song information during slide show.** If a slide show is accompanied by music, you can display the song title and artist during each song or only at the beginning and end.

When playing music through Windows Media Center, you can display graphic visualizations of the melody, and show the song title, artist, and other available information during the song or at its beginning and end.

DVD settings include:

- **DVD Language.** You can select language preferences for subtitles, audio tracks, and menus. Your preferences will be automatically selected when viewing a DVD with alternative language selections.
- **Closed Captioning.** Control the display of closed captioning when available on a DVD.
- **Remote Control Options.** Program the actions of remote control buttons.

If you are a serious collector of digital photos, music, and movies, or a television aficionado, you will likely find the Windows Media Center experience a delight.

Burning Audio and Data Discs

With CD and DVD burners becoming increasingly standard with new computer systems and increasingly affordable additions to older ones, *burning* audio and data CDs and DVDs is becoming more common as a means of backing up documents, pictures, and music. You don't need to buy a special program to burn your own discs—all the necessary software is part of Windows Vista.

You can create CDs and DVDs in one of two formats:

- **Live File System.** This new disc format is the Windows Vista default format for saving data to a disc. Files are copied, rather than burned, to the disc, without being "staged" in an area of your computer's memory first. You can copy additional files to the disc at a later time and erase files you no longer need from the disc. When you eject the disc from the drive, Windows Vista finalizes the session before opening the drive. Live File System discs are compatible only with Windows XP and later computers.

- **Mastered.** This disc format was the standard when burning discs with Windows XP. A Mastered disc creates a closed session, meaning that no additional data can be added to the disc after you burn it. Files are first gathered into a Temporary Burn Folder and then burned to the disc in one session. After burning the files, the disc is closed and you cannot add or delete data. Mastered discs are compatible with earlier versions of Windows.

To burn a folder of picture files from Windows Explorer:

1. In Windows Explorer, navigate to the folder containing the files you want to burn to CD or DVD. Select either the entire folder or individual files, and then on the toolbar, click **Burn**.

   Windows Vista copies the selected files to a Temporary Burn Folder, opens your disc burner drive, and prompts you to insert a writable disc. If you view the disc burner drive in Windows Explorer, you can see the files that will be burned to the disc.

2. Insert a blank CD or DVD in the drive.

   After scanning the inserted disc, the Burn A Disc dialog box opens.

> **Troubleshooting** If the disc you insert is write-protected due to a previous mastered burn attempt, Windows Vista rejects the disc and asks you to insert another.

3. In the **Burn a Disc** dialog box, enter a name in the **Disc title** box. This is the name that will appear next to the drive letter in Windows Explorer when the disc is in a drive.

4. If you don't intend to burn more data to the disc or want to ensure that the disc is compatible with older operating systems and with CD or DVD players, click the **Show formatting options** button, and in the expanded **Burn a Disc** dialog box, click **Mastered** option.

5. Click **Next**.

   If you are creating a Live File System disc, Windows Vista formats the disc and copies the selected files to it, and then displays the files in Windows Explorer under the heading Files Currently On The Disc. You can leave the disc in the drive and continue to update its contents, or remove the disc from the drive. When you eject the disc from the drive, Windows Vista first prepares the disc by closing the session.

   To copy additional data to a Live File System format disc, insert the disc in the drive, and then either select the files you want to copy in Windows Explorer and click the Burn button, or display the disc contents in Windows Explorer and drag additional files to it.

If you are creating a Mastered disc, Windows Explorer displays the drive, with the selected files listed under the heading Files Ready To Be Written To The Disc, and you then need to click Burn To Disc on the toolbar to initiate the burn.

> **Tip** You can delete files from the Files Ready To Be Written To The Disc list, and add others, before burning the disc.

To burn music tracks to disc from Windows Media Player:

1. In full mode, click the **Burn** tab.

2. Drag the album, play list, or tracks you want to burn into the **Burn List** area of the **List** pane.

3. At the bottom of the **List** pane, click **Start Burn**.

4. When prompted, insert a writable CD or DVD into your computer's disc burner.

   Windows Media Player burns the music files to the disc, and after burning the last track, it finalizes (closes) the disc and then ejects it.

Retrieving Images from a Digital Camera or Scanner

If you have a digital camera or a scanner, you can easily download photographs to a computer that is running Windows Vista. If your camera or scanner is a USB device, Windows Vista recognizes the device and installs the drivers for it the first time you connect it. If your camera or scanner is not a USB device or a Plug And Play device, after connecting the device to your computer, open Control Panel, click Hardware And Sound, and then click Scanners And Cameras to start the Scanner And Camera Installation wizard, which will lead you through the connection process.

Your camera or scanner might come with special software to enable enhanced features. Some manufacturers recommend that you install this software before connecting the device to your computer, so it's a good idea to read the camera or scanner's manual first.

After Windows installs the drivers for your camera, the AutoPlay dialog box guides you through the process of importing or viewing photographs whenever you connect the camera to your computer. If you choose to import the photos, they are copied to your *Pictures* folder or another location you choose. Many digital cameras not only take photos but can also record video clips. You can download these clips in the same way you do photos.

> **Tip** If your digital camera stores images on some kind of removable memory media such as a compact flash card, you can transfer the images to your computer by using an appropriate adapter. Some computers come equipped with built-in card reader drives for this purpose.

After Windows installs the drivers for your scanner, you can use Windows Fax And Scan, a program that comes with Windows Vista, to scan your photographs and store them on your computer.

See Also For information about Windows Fax And Scan, see "Faxing and Scanning Documents" in Chapter 9, "Communicating with Other People."

Sharing Pictures and Other Digital Media Files

If several people work on your computer, you can make your pictures, music, and video files available to them by storing them in your computer's *Public* folders. If your computer is connected to a network, you can share the folders in which you store your media files so that other people on your network can access them.

See Also For information about sharing folders, see "Sharing Drives and Folders" in Chapter 8, "Making Connections."

You can also use Windows Photo Gallery or Windows Media Player to share a collection of media files with other computers running Windows Vista. Usually this type of sharing happens on a home network.

In Windows Photo Gallery, you turn on media sharing by clicking the File button on the toolbar and then clicking Share With Devices. In Windows Media Player, you click the Library arrow and then click Media Sharing. In either case, the Media Sharing dialog box opens. However, in the case of Windows Media Player, you can look for media files that have been shared by other people in addition to sharing your own media files.

In this exercise, you will use Windows Photo Gallery to share your media files with other people on your network.

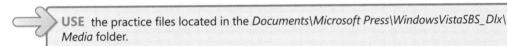

USE the practice files located in the *Documents\Microsoft Press\WindowsVistaSBS_Dlx\ Media* folder.

1. On the **Start** menu, click **All Programs**, and then click **Windows Photo Gallery**.

2. On the toolbar, click the **File** button, and then click **Share With Devices**.

    The Media Sharing dialog box opens.

3. Under **Sharing settings**, select the **Share my media** check box, and click **OK**. Then in the **User Account Control** dialog box, if you're logged on as an administrator, click **Continue**. Otherwise, enter an administrator password, and click **OK**.

The Media Sharing dialog box expands so that you can allow or deny specific users.

4. In the expanded dialog box, click **Settings**.

The Media Sharing - Default Settings dialog box opens.

In the **Share media as** box, you can change the name of the collection of media files you are sharing.

5. Select or clear the check boxes under **Media types**, **Star ratings**, and **Parental ratings** to include only the specific media files you want to share.

6. Click **OK** to close the **Media Sharing – Default Settings** dialog box, and then click **OK** to close the **Media Sharing** dialog box.

   Nothing appears to have happened, but the specified media files are now available to other people on your network.

7. Display **Control Panel**, click **Network and Internet**, and then click **Network and Sharing Center**.

   Under Sharing And Discovery, Media Sharing is now turned on.

 CLOSE the Control Panel and Windows Photo Gallery windows.

Key Points

- With Windows Photo Gallery, you can view, catalog, search, and sort all the pictures stored on your computer.
- With Windows Media Player, you can create play lists of music tracks from various sources and play music in various modes on your computer.
- Windows Vista makes it easy to burn CDs and DVDs without third-party software. You can burn additional files to a disc at a later time.
- You can share digital media that meets specific criteria with other people on your network without having to share drives or folders.

Keyboard Shortcuts

Press this	To do this in Windows Media Player
Ctrl+M	Show or hide the menu bar.
Ctrl+2	Switch to skin mode.
Shift when you insert a CD	Stop a CD from playing automatically.

Press this	To do this in Windows Photo Gallery
Ctrl+F	Open the Fix pane.
Ctrl+P	Print the selected picture.
Enter	View the selected picture at a larger size.
Ctrl+I	Open or close the Details pane.
Ctrl+period (.)	Rotate the picture clockwise.
Ctrl+comma (,)	Rotate the picture counter-clockwise.
F2	Rename the selected item.
Ctrl+E	Search for an item.
Alt+Left Arrow	Go back.
Alt+Right Arrow	Go forward.
Plus sign (+)	Zoom in or resize the picture thumbnail.
Minus sign (-)	Zoom out or resize the picture thumbnail.
Ctrl+B	Best fit.
Left Arrow	Select the previous item.
Down Arrow	Select the next item or row.
Up Arrow	Previous item (Easel) or previous row (Thumbnail).
Page Up	Previous screen.
Page Down	Next screen.
Home	Select the first item.
End	Select the last item.
Delete	Move the selected item to the Recycle Bin.
Shift+Delete	Permanently delete the selected item.
Left Arrow	Collapse node.
Right Arrow	Expand node.
J	Move back one video frame.
K	Pause the video playback.
L	Move forward one video frame.
I	Set the start trim point.
O	Set the end trim point.
M	Split a video clip.
Home	Stop and rewind all the way back to the start trim point.

Alt+Right Arrow	Advance to the next video frame.
Alt+Left Arrow	Go back to the previous video frame.
Ctrl+K	Stop and rewind video playback.
Ctrl+P	Play video from the current location.
Home	Move the start trim point.
End	Move to the end trim point.
Page Up	Seek to nearest split point before the current location.
Page Down	Seek to nearest split point after the current location.

Chapter at a Glance

Administer Windows user accounts, **page 396**

Make changes to Angel's account

Change the account name
Create a password
Change the picture
Set up Parental Controls
Change the account type
Delete the account

Manage another account

Angel
Administrator

Manage your Windows user account, **page 401**

Make changes to your user account

Tasks

Create a password reset disk
Manage your network passwords
Manage your file encryption certificates
Configure advanced user profile properties
Change my environment variables

Create a password for your account
Change your picture
Change your account name
Change your account type

Chris
Administrator

Manage another account
Turn User Account Control on or off

See also

Limit access to the computer, **page 405**

Control when Dana will use the computer

Click and drag the hours you want to block or allow.

☐ Allowed
■ Blocked

13 Managing Computer Security

In this chapter, you will learn to:

- ✔ Administer Windows user accounts.
- ✔ Manage your Windows user account.
- ✔ Limit access to the computer, to programs, and to the Internet.
- ✔ Analyze your computer's security.
- ✔ Configure Internet security zones.

In the old days, computers were isolated from each other, and the only way to transfer information among them was on a floppy disk (now referred to as "sneaker net"). With the advent of networks, information transfer became easier, but so did the possibility that the information stored on a computer would be accessed inappropriately or even illegally from another computer. As networks have grown from small to large, and worldwide access to local area networks has become simple and commonplace, concerns about information security have also increased.

Computer security is a hot topic these days. The proliferation of Internet access and e-mail in homes and workplaces around the world has provided a new (and relatively simple) avenue for malicious intrusion into our lives. It is important to be aware of the possible security vulnerabilities of each computer you work on, whether at home, at school, at work, or in a public place such as an Internet café. It is also important to protect yourself on all these computers through correct network setups, appropriate virus scanning software, and informed computing habits.

In this chapter, you will create user accounts, change user account information, restrict user account access, and manage some of your computer's security settings.

See Also Do you need only a quick refresher on the topics in this chapter? See the Quick Reference section at the beginning of this book.

Important Before you can use the practice files in this chapter, you need to install them from the book's companion CD to their default location. See "Using the Companion CD" at the beginning of this book for more information.

Administering Windows User Accounts

Windows Vista protects the information on your computer through a system of *user accounts* and *passwords*, which at one time were available only for computers that were part of a domain. Windows Vista extends this account and password system to workgroup computers so that more than one person can use the same computer. For example, if you manage your family's financial records on a home computer that is also used by your children to do their homework, you can set up separate accounts for your children so that they can't view confidential information or change your files.

The great thing about user accounts and passwords is that they help keep your information private. You can prevent other users from reading or altering your documents, pictures, music, and other files by storing them in the subfolders automatically set up under your user folder. You can share files by placing them in a *Public* folder or any folder outside of your user folder. (You can also specifically share the subfolders under your user folder, but you don't have to.) With Windows Vista, each user can personalize his or her own working environment and have easy access to frequently used files and applications without worrying about other people making changes to personal settings.

The user account and password system also means that Windows Vista can help you protect your computer from unauthorized changes. Windows Vista supports two levels of computer-specific privileges: Administrator and Standard. The first user account created on your computer is designated as an administrator account. This type of account has higher-level permissions than a standard account, which means that an administrator account owner can perform tasks on your computer that a standard account owner cannot.

Administrator account permissions are necessary to do things such as:

- Create, change, and delete accounts.
- Make system-wide changes.
- Install and remove programs.
- Access all files.

Tasks that require administrator permissions are indicated by a Windows security icon.

Standard account permissions allow a user to do things that affect only his or her own account, including:

- Change or remove the password.
- Change the user account picture.
- Change the theme and desktop settings.
- View files he or she created and files in the *Public* folders.

> **Tip** Windows creates a special account called *Guest*, which is inactive by default and disabled on computers that are part of a domain. You can activate the Guest account to give people limited access to your computer without having to create individual user accounts.

If you have an administrator account, it is a good idea to also create a standard account for your day-to-day computing. Logging on with a standard account will not prevent you from installing software or taking other administrator-level actions, because when Windows Vista requires administrator permissions to complete a task, it displays the User Account Control dialog box, requiring that you enter an administrator password to continue, or if you are logged on as an administrator, confirm that you want to continue the restricted task. (Any administrator can enter his or her password.) After receiving the password, Windows continues with the task.

The advantage of logging on with a standard account is that if malicious software (malware) or spyware sneaks onto your computer or if another person gains access to your computer (either in person or over the Internet) while you are logged on as a standard user, they are blocked from performing administrative tasks because they can't supply the administrator password. If you are logged on as an administrator, you have already supplied the password, leaving you vulnerable to these types of intrusions.

A computer running Windows Vista supports multiple user accounts. Every account has an associated *user account name* and a *user account picture*. Any user can change his or her own account name and picture and can create or change his or her own password; users with administrator permissions can change any user's account name and picture.

> **Important** If your computer is part of a domain, network permissions are administered through your domain account. You might be able to create a new account on your local computer, but you cannot create or modify a domain user account.

In this exercise, you will create a new user account with administrative privileges on your computer, change its privileges, and create a password. You will then delete the account. There are no practice files for this exercise.

BE SURE TO log on to Windows Vista before beginning this exercise.

OPEN Control Panel.

1. In **Control Panel**, under **User Accounts and Family Safety**, click the **Add or remove user accounts** task. Then in the **User Account Control** dialog box, if you're logged on as an administrator, click **Continue**. Otherwise, enter an administrator password, and click **OK**.

> **Troubleshooting** If you are running Windows Vista Business Edition, you have a User Accounts category rather than User Accounts And Family Safety. The steps to complete the tasks in this chapter vary slightly from those given.

The Manage Accounts window opens.

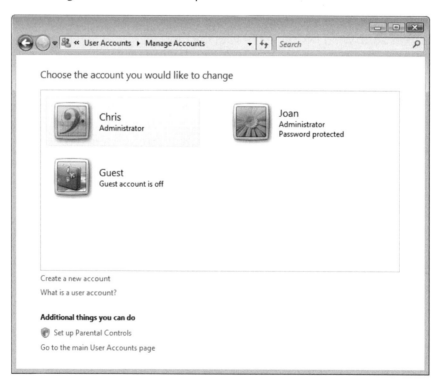

2. Click the **Create a new account** task.

The Create New Account page opens.

3. In the **New account name** box, type Angel. Click **Administrator**, and then click **Create Account**.

Windows Vista creates a new account called *Angel*, and assigns a user account picture to the account, which now appears in the Manage Accounts window.

4. In the **Manage Accounts** window, click **Angel**.

The Make Changes To Angel's Account page displays the options for changing the selected account.

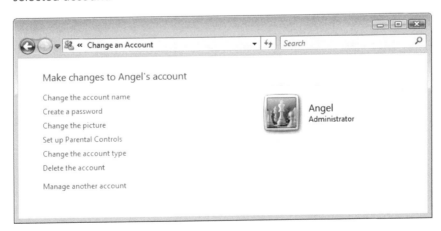

5. Click the **Change the account type** task.

6. On the **Choose a new account type for Angel** page, click **Standard user**, and then click **Change Account Type**.

   On the Make Changes To Angel's Account page, *Standard user* appears under Angel's user account name.

7. Click the **Create a password** task.

   The Create A Password For Angel's Account page opens.

8. In the **New password** box, type Meow! and then press the [Tab] key to move to the next field.

   To ensure the secrecy of the password, the characters are displayed as dots as you type.

9. In the **Confirm new password** box, retype Meow!

10. In the **Type a password hint** box, type What does Angel say?

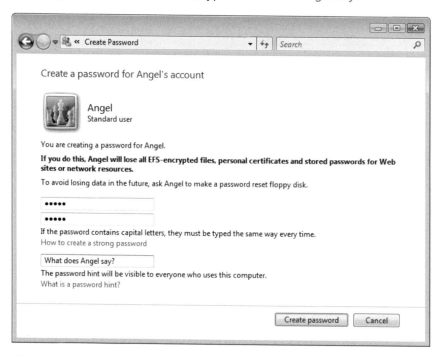

11. Click **Create password** to save the password as part of Angel's user account profile.

    On the Make Changes To Angel's Account page, *Password protected* appears under Angel's user account type.

12. Click the **Delete the account** task.

> **Troubleshooting** You cannot delete a user account while it is logged on to the computer; you must switch to that user account and log it off before you can delete it.

When you delete a user account, you can choose to keep the content of selected personal folders, to ensure that you don't delete files that person might want to keep.

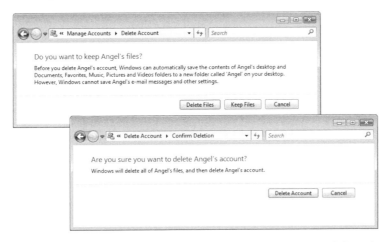

13. Angel has not created any files that you care about, so click **Delete Files**. Then on the **Confirm Deletion** page, click **Delete Account**.

Angel's account no longer appears among the active accounts.

 CLOSE the Manage Accounts window.

Managing Your Windows User Account

On the logon screen, each user account is represented by the user account name and also by a user account picture. Windows Vista comes with 12 user account pictures, representing a variety of animals, sports, and interests. You can select the picture that most closely matches your personality or interests. If none of the default pictures is to your liking, you can use a picture of your own.

You can use *bitmap (BMP)* files, *Graphic Interchange Format (GIF)* files, *Joint Photographic Expert Group (JPEG)* files, or *Portable Network Graphics (PNG)* files as user account pictures. The original graphic can be any size, but the user account picture is always displayed at 48 pixels high by 48 pixels wide. If you select a graphic whose height and width are not the same, the graphic will be stretched or cropped to a square shape when displayed.

In this exercise, you will first change your user account picture to one provided by Windows Vista, and then you will switch to a custom graphic.

USE the *Angelic* image. This practice file is located in the *Documents\Microsoft Press\ WindowsVistaSBS_Dlx\Security* folder.
OPEN Control Panel.

1. In **Control Panel**, click **User Accounts and Family Safety**, and then under **User Accounts**, click the **Change your account picture** task.

The Change Your Picture window displays the built-in user account picture options.

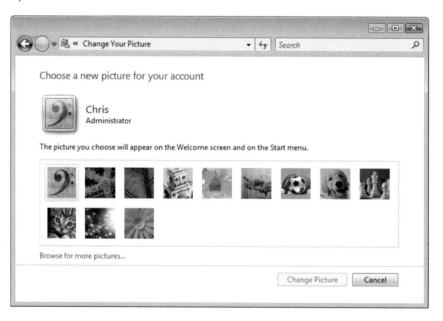

2. Click any picture that you like, and then click **Change Picture**.

   Your new user account picture is shown in the User Accounts window. You can also see it at the top of the Start menu.

3. In the **User Accounts** window, click the **Change your picture** task. Then in the **Change Your Picture** window, click **Browse for more pictures**.

   The Open dialog box displays the contents of your *Pictures* folder.

4. In the **Favorite Links** list, click **Documents**, and then navigate to the *Microsoft Press\WindowsVistaSBS_Dlx\Security* folder.

5. Click the *Angelic* image, and then click **Open**.

   The User Accounts window displays your custom picture.

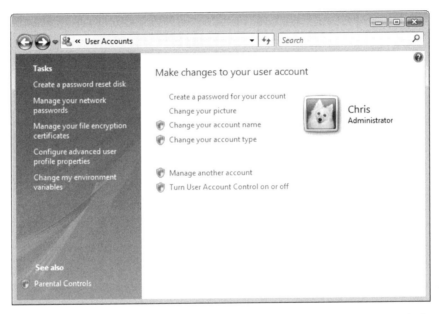

The custom picture is also now available in the Change Your Picture window.

CLOSE the User Accounts window.

Backing Up Your Windows Password

When you protect your Windows Vista user account by assigning a password, you have the option of creating a password hint. Windows Vista displays the password hint if you enter an incorrect password. If you didn't save a password hint, you can reset your password—but in order to do so you must first have created a password reset disk.

> **Tip** You can create a password reset disk only for a local user account, not for a domain user account.

If you password-protect your account, you might want to create a password reset disk in the event that you lose or forget your password. (It might sound unlikely, but it can happen, especially in an environment that requires you to change your password on a regular basis.) You can save the password reset file on either a USB flash drive or a floppy disk (but not on a CD).

To create a password reset disk:

1. Insert a USB flash drive or floppy disk in your computer.
2. In **Control Panel**, click **User Accounts and Family Safety**, and then click **User Accounts**.
3. In the **Tasks** list, click the **Create a password reset disk** task.

   The Forgotten Password wizard starts.
4. On the **Welcome** page, click **Next**.
5. On the **Create a Password Reset Disk** page, select the USB flash drive or floppy disk drive you want to use, and then click **Next**.
6. On the **Current User Account Password** page, enter the password you use to log on to Windows Vista, and then click **Next**.
7. When the **Progress** bar displays *100% complete*, click **Next**. Then click **Finish**.

Be sure to store the password reset disk in a safe place, because anyone can use it to reset your password and gain access to your computer.

Limiting Access to the Computer, to Programs, and to the Internet

If you want to allow or encourage your children to use the computer but are concerned about the amount of time or the hours of the day they might spend "surfing" the Web or playing games, you can set time limits on their computer use and restrict access to games, to specific programs, and to Web sites displaying objectionable content. After setting up parental controls, you can generate activity reports to follow up on actual computer usage. And although this level of policing might not be necessary, perhaps just knowing that you can do it will provide some reassurance to you or reinforcement for your children.

> **Tip** Windows Vista parental controls are available only on computers that are part of a workgroup, not on computers that are part of a domain. Domain computers are administered centrally.

Windows Vista recognizes game ratings such as those assigned by the Entertainment Software Rating Board (ESRB), which indicate the minimum age recommendation for the game. Content ratings include those listed in the following table.

Rating symbol	Recommended for	Description
EC (Early Childhood)	Ages 3 and older	Contains no material that parents would find inappropriate.
E (Everyone)	Ages 6 and older	May contain minimal cartoon, fantasy, or mild violence; and/or infrequent use of mild language.
E10+ (Everyone 10+)	Ages 10 and older	May contain more cartoon, fantasy, or mild violence; mild language; and/or minimal suggestive themes.
T (Teen)	Ages 13 and older	May contain violence, suggestive themes, crude humor, minimal blood, simulated gambling, and/or infrequent use of strong language.
M (Mature)	Ages 17 and older	May contain intense violence, blood and gore, sexual content, and/or strong language.
AO (Adults Only)	Ages 18 and older	May include prolonged scenes of intense violence and/or graphic sexual content and nudity.

See Also For more information about software and game ratings, visit *www.esrb.org*.

Additional content descriptors may indicate the specific reason or reasons for the rating. The ESRB employs 30 descriptors, including Alcohol Reference, Blood and Gore, Cartoon Violence, Crude Humor, Nudity, Real Gambling, Sexual Violence, and Strong Language. These descriptors can help you to determine whether a specific game is suitable.

You can set parental controls to allow all games considered by a game rating board to be appropriate for a child of a specific age, or you can specifically allow or restrict games with specific types of content.

> **Important** Anyone with an administrator account on your computer can set up, alter, or remove parental controls. For the controls to be fully effective, protect each administrator account with a password and disable the Guest account if it is not password-protected.

In this exercise, you will limit the amount of time that another person is allowed to use your computer. There are no practice files for this exercise.

BE SURE TO set up a standard user account on your computer, and log on as an administrator, before beginning this exercise.

1. Display **Control Panel**, and under **User Accounts and Family Safety**, click **Set up parental controls for any user**. Then in the **User Account Control** dialog box, if you're logged on as an administrator, click **Continue**. Otherwise, enter an administrator password, and click **OK**.

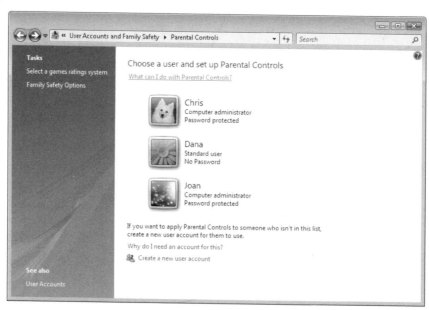

2. In the Parental Controls window that opens, click the user you want to set a time limit for.

The User Controls window opens.

3. Under **Parental Controls**, click **On, enforce current settings**, and then in the **Windows Settings** area, click **Time limits**.

The Time Restrictions window opens.

4. Click each hour in the grid that you want to block.

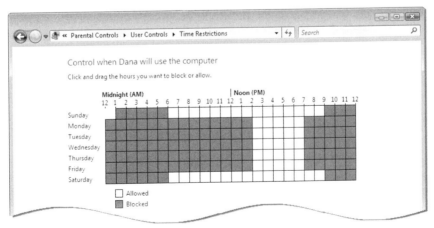

During the blocked time periods, if the selected user tries to log on to his or her account, Windows Vista denies access to the account and displays a message that the user account is blocked at that time.

5. In the **Time Restrictions** window, click **OK**.

6. In the **User Controls** window, with **On, collect information about computer usage** selected under **Activity Reporting**, click **View activity reports**.

The Activity Viewer displays the current (blank) report.

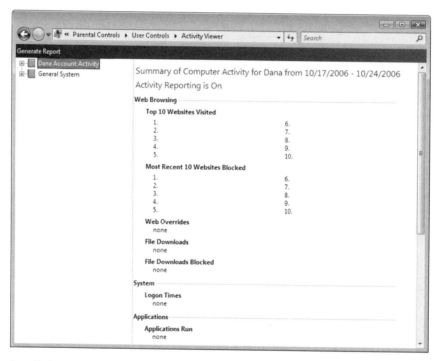

7. Scroll the report to see the kinds of activities it tracks. Then in the upper-left corner of the **Activity Viewer** window, click the **Back** button.

Back

8. Under **Windows Settings**, investigate the **Windows Vista Web Filter**, **Games**, and **Allow and block specific programs** controls. Adjust the parental controls as you want, and then click **OK**.

 BE SURE TO turn off the parental controls if you don't want to use them.

CLOSE the Parental Controls window.

See Also For information about limiting access to objectionable Internet content on a broader scale, see "Restricting Objectionable Content" in Chapter 6, "Safely and Efficiently Accessing the Internet."

Analyzing Your Computer's Security

Most people think of security in terms of protecting a computer and the information stored on it against attacks by malicious programs such as *viruses* and malicious people known as *hackers*. Windows Vista is the most secure Microsoft operating system to date. It helps you protect your computer from these and other external threats with a number of built-in security features, including:

- *Windows Firewall*, which helps you prevent unauthorized transmissions to and from your computer.
- *Windows Defender*, which helps you detect software that might pose a potential threat to your privacy or your computer.
- *Windows Security Center*, which monitors the types of protection on your system.
- *User Account Control*, which requires specific acknowledgment and an administrator password when accessing settings that could disrupt your computer or affect its users.
- *Windows Update*, which makes it easy for you to ensure that your computer has the latest security tools.

> **Important** Windows Vista does not include a virus scanning program, so you will need to purchase and install one yourself. Many commercial software packages that detect and treat computer viruses are available.

Any computer that is connected to the Internet, whether full-time or intermittently, is exposed to the risk of attack. This risk should always be taken seriously. You can protect your system in the following ways:

- **Work behind a firewall.** If you have a direct Internet connection, the firewall that is built into Windows Vista forms a secure bridge between the external Internet and your computer. If you are working on a home network, your firewall might be installed on the computer that controls communications between your home network and the Internet. If you're working on a domain, the firewall is a secure bridge between the Internet and your organization's intranet, to which your computer is connected. In all cases, the firewall protects your computer from intrusion.

   Windows Vista includes Windows Firewall, a program that protects your computer from initiating or receiving unauthorized external connections, such as those attempted by certain kinds of computer viruses. With Windows Firewall, the only connections that can be made to your computer are those either initiated or approved by you. Windows Firewall is turned on by default for all users and all connections to your computer, including local area network (LAN), Virtual Private Network (VPN), and dial-up connections. Windows Firewall settings are controlled from the Windows Security Center.

- **Protect your computer with Windows Defender.** While you are connected to the Internet, malicious software (malware) and spyware might try to install themselves on your computer. They can also be attached to CDs and DVDs. Once installed, they can harm your computer or steal information, either immediately or at a future time. Windows Defender, which comes with Windows Vista, helps you protect your computer by alerting you when an installation program starts, or when a program tries to run itself or change your settings.

  As with a virus-protection program, you can use Windows Defender to scan your computer for suspicious software, either manually or on a regular schedule. It can quarantine or remove any malware or spyware it finds. It is important to keep the Windows Defender database of the software you don't want on your computer up to date, because Windows Defender uses this database (which consists of files called *definitions*) to identify the software. Fortunately, you can rely on Windows Update to automatically update the Windows Defender definitions.

- **Install all available security upgrades.** Use Windows Update to automatically keep your Windows Vista computer up to date with official Microsoft-issued product updates and Windows Defender definitions.

  See Also For more information about Windows Update, see "Updating Windows System Files" in Chapter 1, "Getting Started with Windows Vista."

- **Use third-party antivirus software.** Select a program that monitors your hard disk drive and external drives, as well as all incoming and outgoing files.

- **Never open unidentified e-mail attachments.** In particular, don't open any files that have an .exe extension.

  See Also For more information about e-mail security, refer to *Microsoft Office Outlook 2007 Step by Step* by Joan Preppernau and Joyce Cox (Microsoft Press, 2007).

- **Regularly check Windows Security Center.** You can make sure all your computer systems are set for optimal protection in this one handy location.

In this exercise, you will examine your Windows Firewall setting options. Then you will explore and modify the Windows Defender options. Finally, you will view the status of your computer's protection against unauthorized external connections, viruses, spyware, and other threats. There are no practice files for this exercise.

> **OPEN** Control Panel.

1. In **Control Panel**, click **Security**, and then click **Security Center**.

   Windows Security Center opens.

2. In the left pane of the **Windows Security Center** window, click **Windows Firewall**.

   Windows Firewall opens.

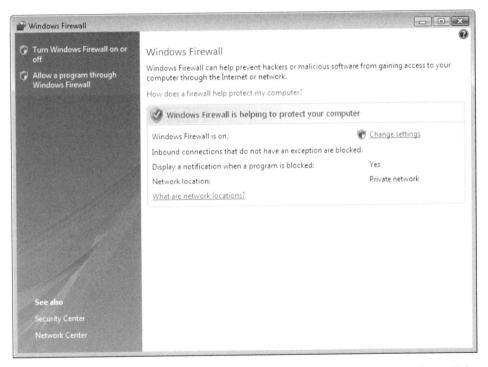

3. Read the information about your current Windows Firewall status, and then click **Change settings**. In the **User Account Control** dialog box, if you're logged on as an administrator, click **Continue**. Otherwise, enter an administrator password, and click **OK**.

The Windows Firewall Settings dialog box opens, displaying the General tab. If your computer is connected to a domain, the settings might be unavailable (gray), indicating that firewall policies are controlled by the domain administrator.

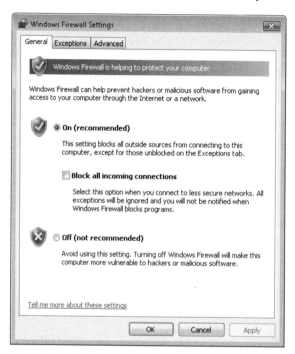

4. Read the descriptions of the three basic options: **On (recommended)**, **Block all incoming connections**, and **Off (not recommended)**.

   Unless you have another firewall protecting your computer, the On option should always be selected. Before you use an unsecured or otherwise risky connection (such as a free Internet connection in a public location), return to this dialog box and select the Block All Incoming Connections check box.

   > **Tip** Clicking the Tell Me More About These Settings link at the bottom of the tab displays the Understanding Windows Firewall Settings topic in Windows Help And Support. You can find further information about Windows Firewall here.

5. In the **Windows Firewall Settings** dialog box, click the **Exceptions** tab. Then scroll the **Program or port** list to see the basic exception types, noting which items are selected.

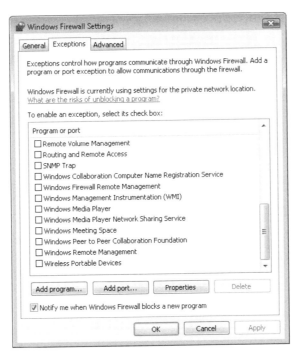

You can specifically allow external communications by certain types of programs by selecting the corresponding check boxes on this tab. When Windows Firewall prompts you to allow or deny a connection from a program you are using, connections that you allow are selected here. (And you can reverse your selection from here.) You can add a specific program or the port it uses to the list, and you can specify whether the program or port is unblocked for external communications with any computer, only the computers on your network, or only specific computers. (If you play interactive Internet games, you might find it necessary to unblock a specific port.)

6. Click the **Advanced** tab to display a list of the network connections currently protected by Windows Firewall.

   You can select each individual network connection to be protected by Windows Firewall. If you are concerned that your firewall protection might be compromised by settings you've changed, you can restore the default Windows Firewall settings at any time.

7. In the **Windows Firewall Settings** dialog box, click **Cancel**. Then close the **Windows Firewall** window.

8. On the **Start** menu, point to **All Programs**, and then click **Windows Defender**.

   Windows Defender starts.

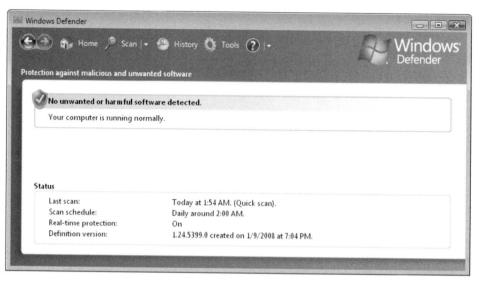

9. On the toolbar at the top of the window, click **Tools**.

The Tools And Settings page opens.

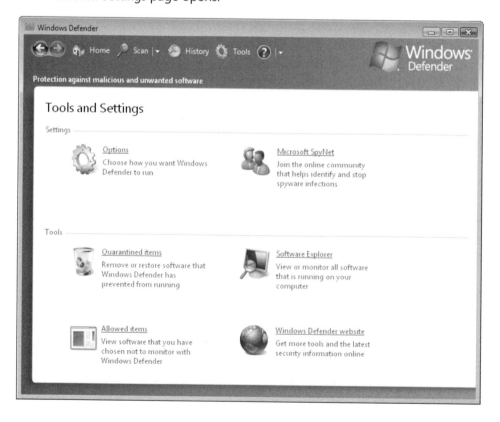

From this page, you can control the way Windows Defender works and monitor the software running on your computer.

10. In the **Settings** area, click **Options**.

The Options page opens.

From this page, you can control the frequency and type of automatic scanning, the actions taken by Windows Defender when encountering a suspicious item, the real-time protection in effect, and other options.

11. Scroll the page and notice the available options. Then in the **Automatic scanning** area, set the frequency and time for automatic scans to occur, select whether to perform a quick scan or full-system scan at that time, and click **Save**. In the **User Account Control** dialog box, if you're logged on as an administrator, click **Continue**. Otherwise, enter an administrator password, and click **OK**.

It is a good idea to keep the default setting to automatically scan your computer, but you can change the frequency and approximate time when you want the scans to take place to match a time your computer will be available.

12. In the **Security** window, click the **Check this computer's security status** task.

Windows Security Center opens, displaying the status of the four security essentials.

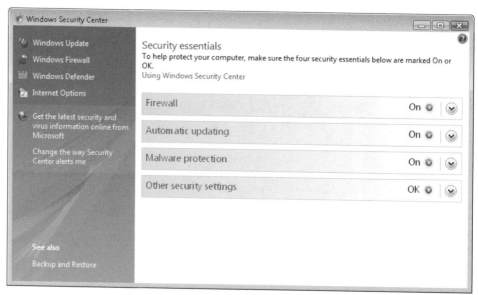

13. Make sure that all four settings are set to **On**. If any are not, click the corresponding **Find a program** button to locate and install the missing security application.

CLOSE the Windows Security Center, Windows Defender, and the Security window.

Configuring Internet Security Zones

With Windows Internet Explorer, you can set different levels of security for different types of Web sites. For example, you might feel perfectly comfortable running programs that originate from your organization's intranet site or from specific Web sites that you trust (such as your own), but not want to allow certain types of programs to run on your computer from the Internet.

Internet Explorer divides the types of Web sites you visit into these four security zones:

- **Internet.** All external Web sites that are not in the trusted or restricted site lists.
- **Local intranet.** All Web sites that are part of your organization's local network.
- **Trusted.** Specific Web sites that you have designated as trustworthy; you believe that content from these sites will not damage your computer or data.
- **Restricted.** Specific Web sites that you have designated as untrustworthy; you believe that content from these sites might damage your computer or data.

You must specifically designate Web sites as part of the Trusted Sites and Restricted Sites zones; otherwise these zones are empty.

You can set the security level for each zone at one of five predefined levels, or you can customize the security level for your own or your organization's needs. The predefined security levels are:

- **High.** This level is appropriate for any Web sites you don't trust, or if you want to have full control over the content that is downloaded to and run on your computer. This is the default security level for the Restricted Sites zone. Internet Explorer prevents potentially harmful content from running on your computer, which might mean that the functionality or display of some Web sites is impaired.
- **Medium-high.** This level is appropriate for most Internet sites, and it is the default security level for the Internet zone. Internet Explorer prompts you before downloading any potentially unsafe content, and it does not download unsigned *ActiveX controls*.
- **Medium.** This is the default security level for the Trusted Sites zone. Internet Explorer does not download unsigned ActiveX controls, and prompts you for permission before downloading potentially unsafe content. Specific settings vary from the Medium-high security level.
- **Medium-low.** This is the default security level for the Local Intranet zone. Internet Explorer does not download unsigned ActiveX controls, but most other content runs without prompts.
- **Low.** This level is appropriate only for sites that you absolutely trust. Internet Explorer provides only minimal safeguards and warnings, and it downloads and runs most content without prompting you for permission.

Most people will find that the default settings are adequate for their needs, but from time to time you might want or need to customize a setting. Even if you never do, it's good to know what your options are so that you are confident that your Web browsing is done in a secure and sensible manner.

In this exercise, you will examine your current Internet Explorer security zone settings, experiment with changing your security options, and add and remove a Web site from the restricted sites list. There are no practice files for this exercise.

> **Important** If you have personalized your Internet security settings for a specific purpose and do not want them to be reset to the default settings, do not complete this exercise.

BE SURE TO display Control Panel before beginning this exercise.

1. In **Control Panel**, click **Security**, and then under **Internet Options**, click the **Change security settings** task.

   The Internet Properties dialog box opens, displaying the Security tab.

> **Tip** You can also display this tab by starting Internet Explorer and then double-clicking the zone name on the status bar.

Depending on your current security settings, the Security level for this zone area displays either a slide control like the one shown here or a custom setting.

2. If your screen shows a custom setting, click **Default level** to return the Internet zone to the default Medium-high security level.

Next you'll try customizing the security options.

3. Click **Custom level** to display the **Security Settings** dialog box for the currently selected Internet zone.

The default security level is shown in the Reset Custom Settings area.

4. Scroll through the options and change a few to see how changing security levels works. (Don't worry; you can undo the changes.) When you're finished making changes, click **OK**.

5. In the **Warning** message box prompting you to confirm your changes, click **Yes**.

In the Internet Options dialog box, the security level for the Internet zone is now set to Custom.

6. In the **Select a zone** area, click **Restricted sites**.

The security level for the Restricted Sites zone is set to High, and cannot be changed.

7. Click **Sites**.

The Restricted Sites dialog box opens.

Depending on your previous Internet Explorer use, the Websites list might already contain one or more site addresses.

8. In the **Add this website to the zone** box, type www.microsoft.com, and then click **Add**.

> **Important** If you do not want to temporarily implement any changes to your Internet zone security settings, skip to step 12.

9. In the **Restricted Sites** dialog box, click **Close**. Then in the **Internet Properties** dialog box, click **OK**.

Start

10. Click the **Start** button, and with the insertion point in the **Start Search** box, type http://www.microsoft.com. Then press Enter .

Internet Explorer starts, and displays the Microsoft Corporation Web site.

The status bar at the bottom of the Internet Explorer window indicates that this is a restricted site.

Site security status

Any scripts (small programs) or active content on this site will not run on your computer.

11. In the **Recent Tasks** list at the bottom of the left pane of the **Security** window, click **Change security settings**. In the **Internet Properties** dialog box, click **Restricted sites**, and then click **Sites**.

12. In the **Websites** list, click **www.microsoft.com**. Click **Remove**, and then click **Close**.

13. In the **Select a zone** area, click **Internet**, and then click **Default level** to return the Internet zone to the default security settings.

14. To implement this security level, click **OK**; otherwise, click **Cancel** to close the **Internet Properties** dialog box without implementing any of the changes.

CLOSE the Security window.

Protecting Yourself from Phishing Sites

Some Web sites are set up to collect information about users who visit them and use that data for fraudulent purposes. These "phishing sites" (so named because they "fish" for information) aren't Web sites that you would visit on purpose; links to them are distributed in e-mail messages, usually purporting to be from a bank or other financial institution. The phishing site link in the message is usually disguised as a valid link, but has code behind it that sends you to a site that is not the one you think you are visiting.

CHASE ♦

Dear customer of JPChase Bank,

Technical services of the JPchase Bank are carrying out a planned software upgrade. We earnestly ask you to visit the following link to start the procedure of confirmation on customers data.

To get started, please click the link below:

https://chaseonline.chase.com/confirm.php?account42649 .

This instruction has been sent to all bank customers and is obligatory to fallow.

Thank you,
Customers Support Service.

Many phishing messages are immediately obvious due to the poor spelling and grammar they contain. Others claim to come from companies you don't actually have a financial relationship with. Even if you do business with the company, don't click the link! Instead, call the company to verify the validity of the request. Most reputable companies would never communicate with you about your personal or financial information in this way.

Internet Explorer 7 comes with a Phishing Filter that helps protect you by blocking known phishing sites. The filter is updated several times per hour using the latest security information from Microsoft and several industry partners. You can also use the filter to report suspicious sites or scams.

In addition to turning off automatic checking of visited sites against the list of known phishing sites, you can disable the Phishing Filter entirely. We would advise you to do this only if you feel confident that you will not be fooled by any phishing messages you receive.

Key Points

- User accounts can have associated passwords to protect the privacy of each person's data. You can back up your password information so that you can reset your password if you forget it.

- If you are concerned about how other people might use your computer, you can set limits on when it can be used, for how long it can be used, and what it can be used to do.

- You can easily analyze and optimize your computer's security settings.

- Internet Explorer has settings specifically designed to help you browse the Web without inadvertently exposing your computer and its information to risk of damage or theft.

Keyboard Shortcuts

Press this	To do this
Ctrl+Esc	Open the Start menu.
Ctrl+Tab	Move through dialog box tabs.
Ctrl+Shift+Tab	Move backwards through dialog box tabs.
F1	Display Help.
Windows logo key	Open or close the Start menu.

Chapter at a Glance

Improve your computer's performance, **page 437**

Turn Windows features on and off, **page 444**

Remove unnecessary files, **page 447**

14 Optimizing Your Computer System

In this chapter, you will learn to:

✔ Locate system information.

✔ Monitor and improve your computer's performance.

✔ Turn Windows features on and off.

✔ Manage cached files.

✔ Remove unnecessary files.

You don't have to be a power user to be concerned about your computer's performance. Whether you use your computer for work, for gaming, or for occasionally browsing the Internet and sending e-mail messages to friends, you might find that your computer isn't as fast as you would like it to be. You can improve the performance of your computer and make the most of its resources in several ways. Some of them, such as increasing your computer's RAM, involve hardware. But you might get appreciable increases in speed and reliability just by giving your computer a system tune-up.

In this chapter, you will locate various types of information about your computer system, learn about your computer's Windows Experience Index, fine-tune some performance settings, turn off Windows features you never use, remove obsolete files, and rearrange files on your hard drive so that they can be accessed faster.

See Also Do you need only a quick refresher on the topics in this chapter? See the Quick Reference section at the beginning of this book.

> **Important** No practice files are required to complete the exercises in this chapter. For more information about practice files, see "Using the Companion CD" at the beginning of this book.

Locating System Information

From time to time, you will want or need to locate information about the components that make up your computer system. Very basic information about your computer is shown in the Welcome Center that appears each time you start your computer (until you turn off this feature). The System window displays additional information about your computer hardware and operating system, including the following:

- Operating system edition, version, and type (32-bit or 64-bit)
- *Windows Experience Index* base score
- Processor speed
- Installed memory (RAM)
- Computer name
- Domain and workgroup identification
- Windows activation status, product ID, and validation

The Windows Experience Index base score shown in the System window is not a cumulative rating; it is the lowest of five individual ratings scored by your system components. An individual subscore is awarded for each of the following components:

- Processor speed
- Installed RAM
- General desktop graphics
- 3-D gaming graphics
- Primary hard disk data transfer rate

The highest score currently available is 5.9; higher scores will be introduced as necessary to keep up with hardware advances.

See Also   For more information about the Windows Experience Index, see "Improving Your Computer's Performance" later in this chapter.

You can view information about hardware devices installed on your computer from Device Manager. You can view and set properties for each device and locate devices and device drivers that are not functioning properly.

In this exercise, you will locate information about your computer's internal and external devices. There are no practice files for this exercise.

BE SURE TO log on to Windows Vista before beginning this exercise.

OPEN Control Panel.

1. In **Control Panel**, under **System and Maintenance**, click **Get Started with Windows**.

   The Welcome Center opens. In the top panel, the Welcome Center displays information about the operating system edition, processor speed, memory, and video card, as well as the computer name.

2. In the upper-right corner, click **Show more details**.

The System window opens. This window displays more specific information about the components mentioned in the Welcome Center, the Windows Experience Index base score, information about the domain or workgroup to which your computer is connected, and the Windows activation status.

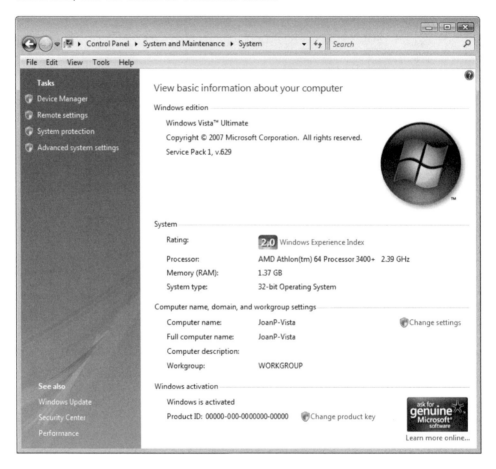

3. In the **System** area, click **Windows Experience Index**.

The Performance Information And Tools window opens, displaying your computer's Windows Experience Index.

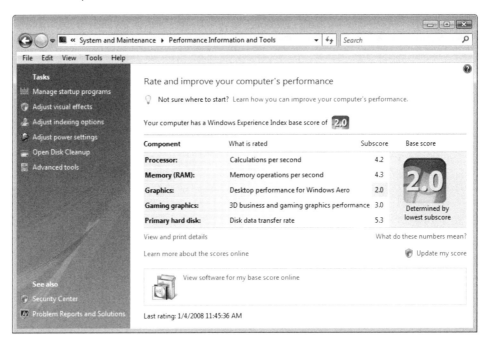

On this page, you can view the individual subscores for each of the five components that affect how well your computer runs, and whether it can implement Windows Aero features. The lowest subscore, which is also your base score, is emphasized.

See Also For information about evaluating and improving your Windows Experience Index scores, see "Improving Your Computer's Performance" later in this chapter.

4. In the **Tasks** list, click **Advanced Tools**.

The Advanced Tools window opens. Specific recommendations for improving your system performance may be shown at the top of the window.

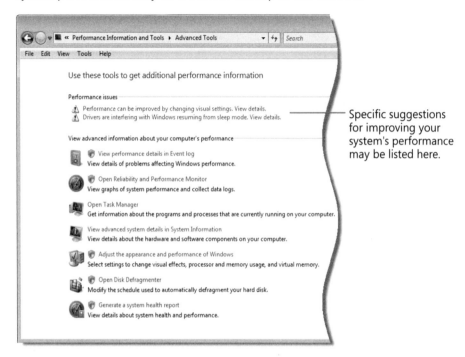

Specific suggestions for improving your system's performance may be listed here.

From this window, you can access many types of information about your computer and your computer's performance.

5. Experiment with the tools available from this window, if you want to. When you finish, return to Control Panel. (Return to Control Panel from this window by clicking the left-facing chevrons in the address bar and then in the list clicking **Control Panel.**)

6. In **Control Panel**, click **Hardware and Sound**, scroll the window if necessary, and then click **Device Manager**. In the **User Account Control** dialog box that appears, if you're logged on as an administrator, click **Continue**. Otherwise, enter an administrator password, and then click **OK**.

Device Manager starts. Information about the internal and external devices installed on your computer is available from this window.

7. Click the plus sign to the left of **Display adapters** to expand the category.

The graphics card on which your Windows Experience Index Graphics subscore is based is shown here. If your computer has multiple graphics cards (for example, to support a multi-display system), they will all be shown here.

8. Right-click the display adapter.

A context menu presenting basic options appears.

From this menu, you can update the device driver, disable or uninstall the device, or view and modify additional properties. A similar menu of options is available in Device Manager for each installed device.

9. Expand various categories to view the devices installed on your machine, and the properties of the devices.

 CLOSE the Device Manager and Control Panel windows when you finish.

Monitoring Your Computer's Performance

If it interests you, you can easily monitor many aspects of your computer's performance. Through Software Explorer (a feature of Windows Defender), you can view information about programs and processes that start automatically when you log on to Windows, programs currently running on your computer, and programs that are accessing the network. From Software Explorer, you can prevent programs from starting automatically, exit programs and end processes, and block incoming network connections.

From Windows Task Manager, you can view and control the programs, processes, and services running on your computer. You will be familiar with the programs, but you might be surprised by the number of processes and services that run in the background without your awareness or involvement. When you experience a problem with an application, Task Manager is a good place to start looking for solutions. For example, if an application stops responding, you can force it to shut down from Task Manager. If a conflict arises due to multiple instances of a program running, you can stop the associated process from Task Manager. You can also identify and control who is logged on to the computer.

You can gain a more in-depth view of the resources the computer is using from the Resource Monitor window. From this window, you can closely monitor CPU usage, disk activity, network utilization, and memory usage.

In this exercise, you will examine the programs and processes running on your computer and your resource utilization. There are no practice files for this exercise.

 OPEN Control Panel.

1. In **Control Panel**, under **Programs**, click **Change startup programs**.

Software Explorer starts, and displays only those programs that automatically start each time you log on to your computer. The programs in this list are specific to your user account and are grouped by publisher.

Details for the program selected in the left pane are shown in the right pane. If you can remove or disable a program, those buttons become active below the right pane when you select the program.

> **Tip** You can start Software Explorer at any time by clicking Windows Defender on the All Programs menu, clicking Tools, and then clicking Software Explorer.

2. Scroll the list to view the startup programs. Click the name of any program to see its details.

3. If you want to prevent a program that is on the list from starting automatically in the future, click the program name, and then click the **Remove** button.

4. In the lower-left corner of the Windows Defender window, click **Show for all users**. In the **User Account Control** dialog box that appears, if you're logged on as an

administrator, click **Continue**. Otherwise, enter an administrator password, and then click **OK**.

Software Explorer displays the programs that start when any user logs on to the computer. (When you install a program, you can choose to make it available only for you, or for anyone who logs on.)

5. In the **Category** list, click **Currently Running Programs**, and scroll the list that appears. Click any program that interests you to view information about it in the right pane.

Software Explorer displays a list of running programs and processes, grouped by publisher. You might be surprised at the number of programs and processes running on your computer. Some programs require many supporting processes that run silently in the background and utilize resources without you being aware of them.

6. In the lower-right corner of the Windows Defender window, click the **Task Manager** button.

Windows Task Manager starts.

> **Tip** You can start Windows Task Manager at any time by pressing Ctrl+Alt+Delete and then clicking Task Manager on the Windows Vista screen that appears.

7. Click the **Applications** tab, if it is not already active.

This tab displays the programs currently running on your computer. You can switch to or exit a program by clicking it in the list and then clicking the appropriate button in the lower-right corner of the window.

> **Tip** You can start a program and run it as an administrator by clicking the New Task button, entering or browsing to the program, and then clicking OK.

8. Click the **Processes** tab.

This tab displays information about the processes currently running in your Windows Vista session, including the file name and process name or description, who started the process, and the amount of CPU and memory the process is using. You can display all the processes running on the computer by selecting the Show Processes From All Users check box. You can stop a process by clicking the process and then clicking the End Process button.

The Services tab displays similar information for the services running on the computer. Clicking the Services button on this tab starts the Microsoft Management Console and displays the Services snap-in, from which you can manage the automatic and manual services that run on the computer.

9. Click the **Performance** tab.

This tab displays a constantly updating overview of the resources your computer is using.

10. On the **Performance** tab, click the **Resource Monitor** button. In the **User Account Control** dialog box that appears, if you're logged on as an administrator, click **Continue**. Otherwise, enter an administrator password, and then click **OK**.

The Resource Monitor opens, displaying the Resource Overview section.

Notice that Task Manager remains open on top of the Resource Monitor window.

11. Close **Windows Task Manager** so that it doesn't block your view of the Resource Monitor window.

> **Tip** Windows Task Manager includes two additional tabs: Networking and Users.
>
> The Networking tab displays a visual representation of network utilization, but the information available from the Resource Monitor is far more useful.
>
> The Users tab shows the status of all local and remote users logged on to the computer. From this tab, you can disconnect or log off any user, or send a message to the user. (The message appears on the user's screen in an information window.)

The Resource Overview section at the top of the Resource Monitor window displays continuously updating charts tracking CPU usage, disk activity, network utilization, and memory usage. Each of the corresponding section headers (the vertical bars) displays green and blue indicators of the activity in that area.

12. Click the **Resource Overview** heading to hide the charts, and then click each of the resource area headings to view current and historical usage data for that area.

> **Tip** Additional resources are available from the Learn More section at the bottom of the Resource Monitor window.

 CLOSE the Resource Monitor, Windows Defender, and Control Panel windows when you finish.

Improving Your Computer's Performance

If your productivity isn't what you think it should be and you suspect your computer is part of the problem, Windows Vista can give you information about your computer's performance and ways in which you might be able to improve it through the Windows Experience Index base score. The higher the base score, the better your computer's overall performance.

See Also For information about the Windows Experience Index, see "Locating System Information" earlier in this chapter.

The base score you need depends a lot on what you intend to do with the computer. For example, you might receive a base score of 1 because you don't have a high-powered graphics card, even though you receive subscores of 3 or 4 in the processor, memory, and hard disk categories. Your computer would be more than adequate to run office applications such as word processing and spreadsheet programs; it just wouldn't be powerful enough to adequately display Windows Aero or sophisticated games. To optimize your computer for those purposes, you would need to upgrade your graphics card.

> **Tip** You can use the base score as an indicator of programs that will run well on your computer. Avoiding programs that require a higher base score than your computer's Windows Experience Index will help you avoid disappointing performance. In conjunction with the rating program, Windows Vista provides a link to software that will perform well on your computer.

If the Windows Experience Index memory subscore indicates that you would do well to upgrade your computer's memory, you don't necessarily have to crack open your computer's case to install new sticks of RAM or pay someone to do it for you. With a Windows Vista feature called *Windows ReadyBoost*, some types of *USB flash drives* can double as memory-expansion devices. If you insert a flash drive in a USB port, the AutoPlay dialog box that appears includes a Speed Up My System option. Clicking this option displays the ReadyBoost tab of the Properties dialog box for your flash drive, which tells you whether your flash drive has the type of "fast" flash memory that can be used for this purpose. If it does, you can select how much of your flash drive's capacity you want to use as auxiliary memory.

> **Tip** When considering your desktop computer's performance, don't forget the most basic principle: keep it clean. The fans that keep your computer from overheating pull in air from outside the computer. With that air comes dust, dirt, pet hair, and other bits and pieces. This sediment clogs the fans and settles on the internal components, contributing to increased heat and decreased performance. Every three months or so, open the computer case. (Most cases now have a slide-off panel on the side, but if it's not obvious, consult the computer's manual.) With a vacuum hose or crevice tool, carefully vacuum the inside and outside of the case. Pay particular attention to both sides of the fan or fans. If you have had your computer for more than six months and haven't yet done this, you might be quite surprised at what you find inside!

Short of upgrading your computer system's hardware, some of the things you can do to improve performance are:

● Minimize the number of programs and services that start automatically when you log on to the computer.

● Speed up screen refresh rates by simplifying the visual effects Windows Vista has to create.

● Adjust your computer's power settings—for example, so that it wakes from a powered-down or sleeping state more readily.

> **Tip** If you use a mobile computer such as a laptop or Tablet PC, you can adjust the battery usage to prolong the period of time you can go without recharging.

● Streamline the indexing of files to focus on the ones you are most likely to want to find.

See Also For information about searching for files, see "Finding Specific Information" in Chapter 3, "Working with Folders and Files."

● Increase file access speed by consolidating files (defragmenting the hard disk) and removing files you don't need.

See Also For information about removing files you don't need, see "Removing Unnecessary Files" later in this chapter.

There can be times when there is nothing specifically wrong with your computer, but it is not operating at its peak efficiency. You might think that your computer is simply not as fast as it used to be, and although perceived speed can be a function of your own level of patience, it might be true that your system has slowed down since it was new. Unlike a sewing machine or a blender, a slow computer probably isn't due to the parts getting old and worn out; it might simply be that your hard disk has become cluttered and its contents *fragmented*.

Each time you save information to your hard disk, Windows Vista writes the information to the currently available space on the disk. When you delete information, the space that information used to occupy becomes free, and more information can take its place. When a file that you save to your hard disk doesn't entirely fit in one empty space, it is divided into "fragments" across multiple spaces. Accessing fragmented information takes more time than accessing the same information when it is stored contiguously.

You can use *Disk Defragmenter* to analyze all the data stored on your hard disk and then consolidate fragmented files into contiguous chunks. The benefits are faster file access and larger areas of available space in which to store new files. Each drive on your computer can be *defragmented* separately. By default, Windows Vista runs Disk Defragmenter every week. You can change this schedule, or you can run the program manually at any time.

> **Tip** Depending on the size of your hard disk, Disk Defragmenter can take up to an hour to run.

In this exercise, you will examine the way Windows handles visual effects, and your computer's power settings. Then you will defragment your hard drive. There are no practice files for this exercise.

OPEN Control Panel.

1. In **Control Panel**, click **System and Maintenance**, and then click **Performance Information and Tools**.

   The Performance Information And Tools window opens.

2. In the **Tasks** list in the left pane, click the **Adjust visual effects** task. In the **User Account Control** dialog box, if you're logged on as an administrator, click **Continue**. Otherwise, enter an administrator password, and then click **OK**.

   The Performance Options dialog box opens, displaying the Visual Effects tab. You can allow Windows Vista to select the optimum settings for your computer, or you can control the settings yourself. You can choose standard packages of settings configured to produce the best visual appearance (at the expense of speed) or the best performance (at the expense of looks). Or you can set each performance option individually.

3. If you want to adjust the settings to improve your computer's performance, on the **Visual Effects** tab, click **Adjust for best performance**, and then click **Apply**.

4. In the **Performance Options** dialog box, click the **Advanced** tab.

From this tab, you can change the allocation of processor resources and the size of the paging file. You can manually set the paging file size for each drive, or have Windows Vista handle this for you.

5. In the **Performance Options** dialog box, click **Cancel**. Then in the **Tasks** list in the left pane of the **Performance and Information Tools** window, click the **Adjust power settings** task.

The Power Options window opens, displaying three default power plans offering energy savings, performance, or a balance between the two.

> **Tip** The available power options may vary based on your computer.

6. Click **High Performance**, and then under that option, click **Change plan settings**.

   In the Edit Plan Settings window, you can adjust the period of time you want Windows Vista to wait while the computer is idle before turning off the display and before putting the computer into Sleep mode, as well as the display brightness.

7. Click **Change advanced power settings**.

   The Power Options dialog box opens, with the High Performance options listed. You can change any option to suit the way you work.

> **Troubleshooting** Don't be concerned if your list of options is different from the one shown. Windows Vista identifies the power settings that you can adjust for your computer and lists only those options.

Back

8. Click **Cancel** to close the **Power Options** dialog box. Then click the **Back** button in the upper-left corner of the **Edit Plan Settings** window to return to the Power Options window.

9. If you want to change the power plan settings for your computer, select the option that represents the closest fit, and then to fine-tune the settings, click **Change plan settings**. When you finish making changes, click **Control Panel** in the Address Bar.

10. In **Control Panel**, click **System and Maintenance**. Scroll the **System and Maintenance** window if necessary, and then under **Administrative Tools**, click **Defragment your hard drive**. In the **User Account Control** dialog box, if you're logged on as an administrator, click **Continue**. Otherwise, enter an administrator password, and then click **OK**.

   The Disk Defragmenter window opens. By default, Windows Vista runs Disk Defragmenter once each week.

> **Tip** If your computer has more than one hard disk drive, each will be listed in the Disk Defragmenter window with its own schedule.

11. Click **Modify schedule** to display the current schedule. Make any changes that you want to, and then click **OK**.

   The Disk Defragmenter window shows the updated details of the scheduled defragmentation.

12. In the **Disk Defragmenter** window, click **Defragment now**. If your computer has multiple storage disk drives, select the check boxes for the disks you want to defragment in the dialog box that appears, and then click **OK**.

   Disk Defragmenter begins the defragmentation process.

13. When the defragmentation process is complete, click **OK** to close the **Disk Defragmenter** window.

 CLOSE the System And Maintenance window.

Turning Windows Features On and Off

Some of the features that come with Windows Vista are installed on your computer but are not immediately available for use because they are not turned on by default. Some features are turned on only in specific editions of Windows Vista, and some features aren't turned on in any edition. You can turn on a missing feature, such as Removable Storage Management, at any time. Or if your computer's performance seems unsatisfactory, you can try turning off Windows features you don't use to conserve system resources. You can always turn them back on if you find you need them.

In this exercise, you will explore the Windows Features dialog box so that you know how to turn Windows features on and off. There are no practice files for this exercise.

> **OPEN** Control Panel.

1. In **Control Panel**, click **Programs**, and then under **Programs and Features**, click the **Turn Windows features on or off** task. Then in the **User Account Control** dialog box, if you're logged on as an administrator, click **Continue**. Otherwise, enter an administrator password, and click **OK**.

   The Windows Features dialog box opens, and after a few seconds, a list of all the features appears. If all components of a feature are installed, its check box is selected. If some components of a multi-component feature are installed, its check box is shaded.

2. Scroll the features list, noticing which ones are installed and which aren't.

3. If you are not using an installed feature that you know it is safe to remove (such as Games), clear its check box, and then click **OK**.

A message box tells you that configuring the change might take several minutes. When the process is complete, the message box and the Windows Features dialog box close.

 CLOSE the Programs window.

Managing Cached Files

When you visit a Web page, the page and its graphics are stored, or *cached*, in the *Temporary Internet Files* folder on your hard disk. The folder size is limited by default to 50 MB; you can increase (up to 1 GB) or decrease (down to 8 MB) the folder size to control how often the folder is purged. If you do a lot of Web surfing, particularly of graphic-intensive sites, the folder can fill up relatively quickly; after it is full, older files are deleted when newer files are cached.

> **Tip** If you would prefer that Internet Explorer not cache any temporary files, select the Empty Temporary Internet Files Folder When Browser Is Closed check box on the Advanced tab of the Internet Properties dialog box.

In this exercise, you will view your temporary Internet files and associated settings. There are no practice files for this exercise.

 OPEN Control Panel.

1. In **Control Panel**, click **Security**, and then under **Internet Options**, click **Delete browsing history and cookies**.

The Internet Properties dialog box opens, displaying the General tab.

2. In the **Browsing history** area, click **Settings**.

The Temporary Internet Files And History Settings dialog box opens.

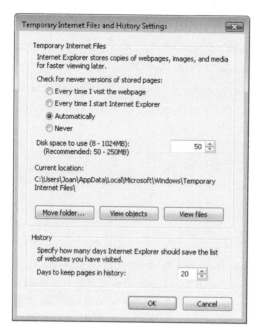

In this dialog box, you can specify how often Internet Explorer looks for updated versions of cached pages, and how much storage space is available for your temporary Internet files.

3. Click **View files**.

Your *Temporary Internet Files* folder opens, probably displaying a wide variety of cached files.

4. Close the **Temporary Internet Files** window, and then click **View objects**.

Your *Downloaded Program Files* folder opens. This folder might contain very few (or no) files, depending on your Internet browsing habits.

5. Close the **Downloaded Program Files** window, and then click **Cancel** in the **Temporary Internet Files and History Settings** dialog box.

 CLOSE the Internet Properties dialog box and the Security window.

> **Tip** You can clear the file cache by clicking Delete in the Browsing History area. Internet Explorer will recache any previously visited pages and cookies the next time you visit those sites. To delete only selected items—for example, to delete temporary files but retain cookies—display the *Temporary Internet Files* folder, select the desired files, and then press Delete. You can sort files by file type to quickly locate specific groups of files.

Removing Unnecessary Files

Every time you open a file, access a Web page, install a program, or download a file, Windows Vista creates a temporary file on your computer. In the case of program files such as documents, the temporary files contain autorecover information. Most of these temporary files are deleted automatically when they are no longer needed. However, poorly behaved programs sometimes don't clean up after themselves, resulting in megabytes of unnecessary files on your hard disk.

Other types of unused files can also clutter up your hard disk. A common culprit is the Recycle Bin—by default, deleted files are stored in the Recycle Bin until you empty it.

> **Tip** To delete a file without temporarily storing it in the Recycle Bin, press Shift+Delete instead of Delete. To always bypass the Recycle Bin, right-click the Recycle Bin, click Properties, select the Do Not Move Files To The Recycle Bin check box, and then click OK.

See Also For more information about the Recycle Bin, see "Rearranging and Deleting Items on the Desktop" in Chapter 2, "Working Efficiently in Windows Vista."

You can use *Disk Cleanup* to free up space on your hard disk by removing downloaded program files, temporary files, and offline files; compressing old files; and emptying the Recycle Bin. It is a good idea to use the *Task Scheduler* to schedule Disk Cleanup to run regularly. Then you don't have to remember the last time you ran it or when it's time to run it again.

> **Tip** To start Task Scheduler, open the System And Maintenance window, and then under Administrative Tools, click Schedule Tasks.

In this exercise, you will run the Disk Cleanup utility on your computer. There are no practice files for this exercise.

 OPEN Control Panel.

1. In **Control Panel**, click **System and Maintenance**, scroll the window if necessary, and then under **Administrative Tools**, click **Free up disk space**.

   The Disk Cleanup Options dialog box opens, prompting you to choose whether you want to clean up only your files or the files used by all users of your computer.

2. Click **My files only**. If your computer has multiple storage disk drives, click the drive you want to clean up in the dialog box that appears, and then click **OK**.

   After calculating the amount of disk space you can recover, the Disk Cleanup dialog box opens.

3. Scroll the **Files to delete** list. Click the name of each category of files in turn (not the category check box) to display its description.

   These descriptions will help you identify the categories that you can safely tell Disk Cleanup to delete. If a list of the files to be deleted is available, a View Files button is also displayed.

4. Click **Recycle Bin**, and then click **View Files**.

   The Recycle Bin window opens, giving you the opportunity to restore files before Disk Cleanup deletes them.

5. Close the **Recycle Bin** window.

6. Select the check boxes of all the categories of files you want to delete.

   The total amount of disk space you will gain is recalculated to reflect your selections.

7. Click **OK**. Then click **Delete Files** to confirm that you want to delete the selected categories of files.

> **Tip** Depending on the number of files to be compressed and deleted, Disk Cleanup can take from one to ten minutes to run.

As Disk Cleanup completes the selected operations, a progress bar indicates how the cleanup is proceeding. You can cancel the cleanup at any point during the operation. The Disk Cleanup dialog box closes when the operation is complete.

 CLOSE Control Panel.

Key Points

- Windows Vista makes it easy to locate information about the internal and external devices installed on your computer.

- You can monitor resource usage on an ongoing basis, and adjust the way Windows Vista works to achieve the best possible performance from your computer.

- You can decrease the time it takes your computer to start up by removing any unnecessary programs and services from the startup process.

- Turning off some visual effects and optimizing your power settings are two other ways to increase performance.

- You might be able to improve the performance of your computer system by turning off Windows features that you do not use.

- Deleting unnecessary files and defragmenting your hard disk are easy ways to increase hard disk access speeds.

- Keeping your computer physically clean inside and out is another way to ensure that it operates at peak efficiency.

Keyboard Shortcuts

Press this	To do this
Delete	Delete the selected item and move it to the Recycle Bin.
Shift+Delete	Delete the selected item without moving it to the Recycle Bin first.
Ctrl+Esc	Open the Start menu.
Windows logo key	Open or close the Start menu.

Chapter at a Glance

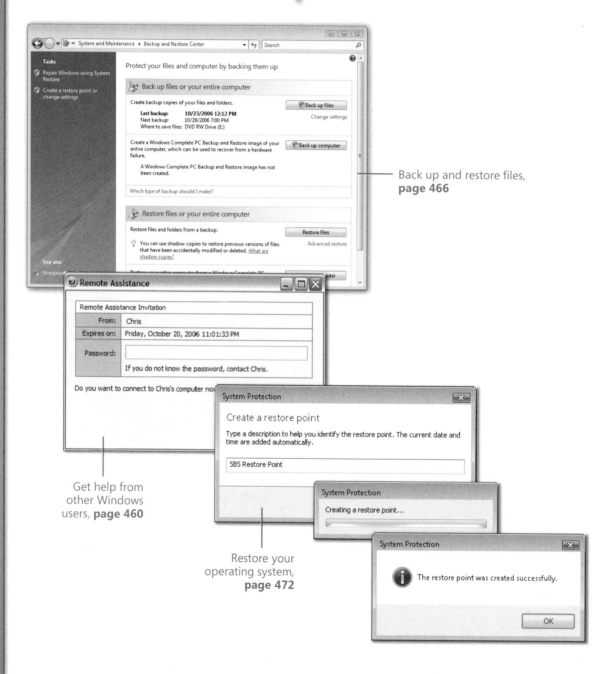

Back up and restore files, **page 466**

Get help from other Windows users, **page 460**

Restore your operating system, **page 472**

15 Identifying and Solving Problems

In this chapter, you will learn to:

- ✔ Find solutions to common problems.
- ✔ Find information through a newsgroup.
- ✔ Get help from other Windows users.
- ✔ Back up and restore files.
- ✔ Restore your operating system.
- ✔ Transfer software, settings, and files to another computer.

It's easier than ever to find and use the Windows Vista tools and features that can help you maintain your computer. However, the fact that maintenance is easy doesn't mean that you won't ever experience a problem while using your computer. One of the first things you learn about skiing is how to recover safely and gracefully from a fall; this is also a good thing to learn in computing. Knowing where to look for solutions to problems is the key to safe recovery. It is also wise to take a few precautions to help you avoid problems as much as you can.

If you do run into technical difficulty with your Windows Vista computer, your first recourse is to look in Windows Help And Support for information. For more complex problems, you might need to seek help from other computer users. And if your system has become really unstable, you might need to restore it to a point in the past where it worked reliably.

Computer problems are frustrating, but most stop short of being disasters unless they involve loss of data. Windows Vista goes to great lengths to make it easy for you to regularly back up and restore your valuable files. It also makes it easy to transfer your system setup, programs, and files to a new computer so that you can be up and running in the least possible time.

In this chapter, you will learn how to use the available free support options. For those times when nothing seems to solve an operating system problem, you will learn how to roll your system back to its state before the problem occurred. Then you will learn how to back up files stored on your computer, and how to transfer programs, settings, and files from one computer running Windows Vista to another.

See Also Do you need only a quick refresher on the topics in this chapter? See the Quick Reference section at the beginning of this book.

> **Important** Before you can use the practice files in this chapter, you need to install them from the book's companion CD to their default location. See "Using the Companion CD" at the beginning of this book for more information.

Finding Solutions to Common Problems

It is fairly common for people to purchase furniture, toys, bikes, or other things that require assembly, and then neglect to read the instruction manual until they actually have a problem. Along the same lines, many people never consult a program's Help file, because they don't realize how much good information can be found there.

Windows Help And Support is the place to go when you're having trouble. This is more than just a common Help file. It includes general and task-oriented articles cross-referenced to related articles and resources, a comprehensive glossary, tutorials and demonstrations, and links to most of the tools that you need to keep your computer running smoothly. You can choose from a list of common topics on its main page, search by keyword or phrase, or look up specific topics in the table of contents. If the information you need isn't in Windows Help And Support, you can at least find pointers to other resources.

Windows Help And Support displays static content that is stored on your computer, and dynamic content that it accesses over the Internet. By including online content resources in your searches, you can be confident that you are getting current information.

If your question is of a more technical nature, you can follow a link from Windows Help And Support to the Microsoft Help And Support site, which hosts an in-depth library of Knowledge Base articles written in response to customer inquiries.

You open Windows Help And Support by clicking the Help And Support link on the Start menu. Many Windows Vista windows and dialog boxes contain links to context-sensitive Help files that provide information about the currently displayed feature or program, and assist you in deciding which options you should choose.

> **Tip** Pressing the F1 key opens Windows Help And Support to a related topic, or opens the Help file for the currently active Microsoft program. Pressing the F1 key from within a Microsoft Office Word file opens the Word Help file, pressing the F1 key from within a Microsoft Office Excel file opens the Excel Help file, and so on. Many software manufacturers have made their context-sensitive help available through the F1 key, which is why context-sensitive help is often referred to as F1 Help.

In this exercise, you will open Windows Help And Support and search for useful information. There are no practice files for this exercise.

> **BE SURE TO** log on to Windows Vista before beginning this exercise.

1. On the **Start** menu, click **Help and Support**.

   The Windows Help And Support window opens. You can display categories of information by clicking the icons in the Find An Answer area and explore support options by clicking the links in the Ask Someone area. To locate topics containing a specific word or phrase, enter the word or phrase in the Search Help box, and then click the Search Help button or press Enter.

2. At the right end of the toolbar at the top of the window, click **Options**, and then in the list, click **Settings**.

3. In the **Help Settings** dialog box, ensure that the **Include Windows Online Help and Support** check box is selected. Then click **OK**.

Browse Help

4. On the toolbar, click the **Browse Help** button.

If you don't know precisely what information you are looking for, you can locate information by general topic from this page.

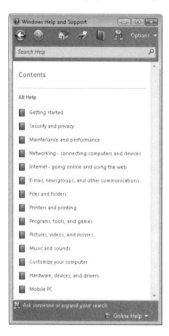

5. Click **Getting started**, click **If you are new to Windows–the basics**, and then click **Help and support**.

Notice that the path you followed to get to this page is displayed above the topic list. You can click any link in the path to return to that page.

Maximize

6. On the **Help and support** page, click **Getting help (overview)**. In the **Windows Help and Support** window, click the **Maximize** button if necessary.

The displayed topic contains in-depth information about ways of getting help with Windows Vista.

> **Tip** At the bottom of most Help topics, you have the opportunity to provide feedback about the usefulness of the information provided in the topic. Click the appropriate button, provide any additional information requested, and then click Finish to send your comments to the Microsoft support team, who continually refine the Help topics based on this feedback.

Search box

Search Help

7. Scan the topic. When you finish, type getting help in the **Search Help** box, and then click the **Search Help** button.

> **Tip** Search terms are not case-sensitive; typing *Getting Help* produces the same results.

A list of the first 30 topics that fit your search term appears. At the bottom of the list is a link to the next 30 topics.

Back

8. Click any topic link that interests you. Then in the upper-left corner of the **Windows Help and Support** window, click the **Back** button.

You can move back and forth between visited topics in the same way that you do in Windows Explorer and Windows Internet Explorer.

Home

9. On the toolbar, click the **Home** button to return to the starting page. Then explore on your own.

CLOSE Windows Help And Support when you finish browsing the Help file.

Reporting Problems

When your computer experiences a hardware or software problem, Windows Vista creates a problem report containing information such as when the problem occurred and what software program or hardware device was involved, and sends the report to Microsoft. If you prefer, you can have the tool ask you before sending the problem reports. In some cases, the problem-reporting tool might request permission to send additional information that will help to identify the problem and develop a solution. You are always given the opportunity to view the additional information before you give permission to send it, and you can deny permission. Personal information from your computer is not transmitted, unless it is contained in a document you specifically authorize the tool to send.

If the Microsoft support database contains a solution to or other information about your reported problem, the problem-reporting tool returns with the information. You can choose whether to implement any reported solutions.

You can view transmitted and unsent problem reports and collected solutions in the Problem Reports And Solutions window. You can send the collected reports manually at any time.

To display the Problem Reports And Solutions window:

→ In **Control Panel**, click **System and Maintenance**, and then click **Problem Reports and Solutions**.

To turn off automatic reporting:

1. In the **Problem Reports and Solutions** window, click **Change settings**.
2. On the **Choose how to check for solutions to computer problems** page, click **Ask me to check if a problem occurs**, and then click **OK**.

To manually submit problem reports:

→ In the **Problem Reports and Solutions** window, click the **Check for new solutions** task.

   Windows Vista sends reports about the currently logged issues to Microsoft, and reports any solutions that it finds.

You can implement any of the reported solutions; Windows Vista does not implement them for you.

Finding Information Through a Newsgroup

Windows Vista newsgroups are online forums where Windows Vista users and experts from around the world interact to discuss their experiences with the operating system and all manners of problems and solutions. These newsgroups are not officially monitored by Microsoft, and Microsoft is not responsible for any of the information available there. You can find discussion threads about many common and uncommon problems. You might find an answer to a question or an interesting discussion that you want to keep up with or join.

Newsgroups are free of charge, and you can join or quit them at any time. You can follow a link to the newsgroups through Windows Mail or through a Web-based newsgroup reader. After joining the newsgroup, you can interact with a newsgroup in several different ways:

- You can visit a newsgroup to read messages.
- You can post a new message and wait for a response.
- You can post a reply to a message to the newsgroup; your message then becomes part of the discussion thread and is available to anyone who visits the newsgroup.
- You can send an e-mail message to the person who posted a specific message, or forward the message to someone else through e-mail.
- You can subscribe to a newsgroup and have all its messages sent to you via e-mail.
- You can subscribe to a specific discussion thread, in which case you will receive an e-mail message notifying you when a new message has been posted to the thread.

A word of warning about newsgroups: Some people see them as a forum for blowing off steam without actually communicating information that is useful or interesting to anyone else. You might find that it takes quite a while to wade through all the available messages before you find information that is pertinent to your situation. On the bright side, although Microsoft does not officially monitor the newsgroups, there do appear to be a fair number of "experts" who post useful information or respond to valid queries.

To locate Windows Vista newsgroups:

1. On the **Start** menu, click **Help and Support**.

   The Windows Help And Support window opens.

2. Under **Ask someone**, click **Windows communities**.

   The Windows Vista Newsgroups page opens in your default Web browser.

You can search for a newsgroup by topic, or click Getting Started With The Web-Based Newsreader for more information about using the newsgroup interface.

> **Getting Help from Microsoft Product Support**
>
> If you can't solve a problem by searching the Windows Help And Support topics, you can click the Microsoft Customer Support link under Ask Someone in the Windows Help And Support window to log specific problems with the Microsoft support staff, who then reply to your problem online. This method of handling product support is very efficient, both for you and for Microsoft.
>
> Along with a description of your problem, you will be asked to send information about your computer that the product support technician might need to diagnose the problem and offer a useful solution. You can either allow your system information to be collected automatically by tools that come with Windows Vista, or you can stipulate which information can be sent to Microsoft. You are not required to send anything other than your product key, but because known issues often affect only certain computer models, sound cards, graphics cards, and so on, information about your computer can be useful.
>
> Your problem report is assigned a tracking number so that you can follow up on your request for help. You can return to the Online Assisted Support site at any time to view the status of your support request, or you can ask to be notified by e-mail when an answer has been posted.

Getting Help from Other Windows Users

If you've tried to solve a problem on your own and have not been successful, you can turn to a friend or co-worker for help. Simple problems can frequently be diagnosed in a phone, e-mail, or instant messaging (IM) conversation; others are difficult for other people to identify or fix when they are not working on the affected computer. If it isn't convenient for someone to physically work with your computer to troubleshoot the problem, you can allow him or her to take control of your computer from another Windows computer by using the Windows Remote Assistance feature. By the same means, you can offer assistance to other Windows Vista users. (If you ask for assistance from Microsoft product support staff, a product support technician might also use Remote Assistance to troubleshoot technical problems with your computer.)

You initiate a *remote assistance* session by sending an invitation. To protect your computer from unauthorized access, the invitation is valid for a specific length of time—from 1 minute to 99 days—and can require a password, which you would send separately. You can send a remote assistance invitation through e-mail or IM to anyone with a computer running Windows Vista or Windows XP.

> **Tip** If you are running Windows Live Messenger, you can request remote assistance directly through the instant messaging program.

In this exercise, you will request remote assistance. There are no practice files for this exercise.

BE SURE TO enlist the help of a friend or co-worker running Windows Vista or Windows XP.

1. On the **Start** menu, point to **All Programs**, click **Maintenance**, and then click **Windows Remote Assistance**.

   Windows Remote Assistance starts.

2. Click **Invite someone you trust to help you**.

3. If you have configured Windows Mail, Microsoft Office Outlook, or another e-mail program on your Windows Vista computer, click **Use e-mail to send an invitation**, enter and confirm the password you want your remote assistant to use, and click **Next**; then skip to step 6. Otherwise, click **Save this invitation as a file**.

Windows Remote Assistance creates an invitation file containing the information another computer needs to begin a remote assistance session.

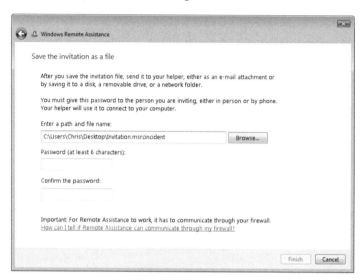

By default, the invitation file is saved to your desktop, but you can save it to another location if you prefer.

4. In the **Password** box, type a string of six or more characters you want your remote assistant to enter in order to gain access to your computer. Then click **Finish**.

The Windows Remote Assistance dashboard opens, and the remote assistance invitation file is created and saved to your desktop.

5. Start or switch to your e-mail program, and send the remote assistance invitation file to the person you want to assist you. Then contact him or her separately with the remote assistance password.

When your remote assistant receives the invitation, she or he accepts the invitation by entering the password, and then clicking Yes.

6. After the invitation is accepted, click **Yes** to allow your remote assistant to view your screen and chat with you.

The Windows Remote Assistance window opens on your computer.

A window also opens on the remote assistant's computer. At this point, the two of you can chat by typing messages, or if you both have microphones and speakers, by talking. You can also send files. Your remote assistant can see everything you do on your computer, so you can open files or demonstrate the steps that lead up to a problem and then ask for advice.

7. On the toolbar, click the **Chat** button, and in the box at the bottom of the window, tell your remote assistant to take control of your computer.

He or she will need to click the Request Control button on the Remote Assistance toolbar. You will then receive a message asking if you would like to share control of your computer.

8. Click **Yes**.

You both now have control of the mouse on your computer. However, you should not both try to move it at the same time.

9. When you decide that you no longer want to share control of your computer, on the toolbar, click the **Stop sharing** button.

You now have exclusive control of your mouse.

10. When you finish the Remote Assistance session, click the **Disconnect** button.

CLOSE the Windows Remote Assistance window.

Starting Your Computer in Safe Mode

If your computer experiences a serious problem, you might need to start Windows Vista in safe mode in order to troubleshoot it. In safe mode, Windows Vista operates with a minimum level of functionality, running only the devices and drivers necessary for you to use internal and external drives and your display, keyboard, and mouse.

If the problem is due to the installation of a program, after starting in safe mode, you can run System Restore and roll back to the restore point created before the installation. If the problem is due to a device or device driver, you can identify problems, update drivers, and configure devices from Device Manager. If the problem is due to a program running on your computer, starting in safe mode is a good way to identify the cause of the problem, because programs that are set up to start automatically when you log on do not start automatically in safe mode. You can start each program individually to identify which is the likely culprit.

If you have a problem with a device driver and need to install a new one, you can start Windows Vista in safe mode with networking. In this mode, you can make network and Internet connections so that you can download and install updated drivers.

To start Windows in safe mode:

1. Remove any media from the drives, and then restart the computer.

2. After the computer restarts, but before the Windows logo appears, press `F8`.

3. On the **Advanced Boot Options** screen, use the arrow keys to highlight the safe mode option you want, and then press `Enter` to continue the startup operation.

While the computer is operating in safe mode, the words *Safe Mode* appear in the corners of the display.

Enabling and Disabling Remote Assistance

The Remote Assistance option is turned on by default. If you are uncomfortable with the idea that other people might be able to access your computer over the Internet, you can block Remote Assistance connections to your Windows Vista computer.

If you want, you can stipulate the number of minutes, hours, or days a remote assistance invitation that you send to another Windows user is valid, and you can limit remote assistance to only computers running Windows Vista.

To display the Remote Assistance settings:

→ In **Control Panel**, click **System and Maintenance**. Then under **System**, click the **Allow remote access** task. In the **User Account Control** dialog box, if you're logged on as an administrator, click **Continue**. Otherwise, enter an administrator password, and click **OK**.

The System Properties dialog box opens, displaying the Remote tab.

To completely disable Remote Assistance:

→ In the **Remote Assistance** area, clear the **Allow Remote Assistance connections to this computer** check box, and then click **OK**.

To limit Remote Assistance access:

1. In the **Remote Assistance** area, click **Advanced**.

2. In the **Remote Assistance Settings** dialog box, set the access level, invitation duration, and access type as you want, and then click **OK**.

Backing Up and Restoring Files

When *file* and *folder* were terms used to describe things made of paper, it was possible for your important documents to be permanently destroyed by fire, water, coffee, toddlers, accidental shredding, or a variety of other natural and unnatural disasters. With the advent of electronic files and folders, it is still possible for the files containing your information to be destroyed, but if you have recently backed up the information, you can recover from the loss with relatively little trouble.

Backing up is the process of creating a copy of your files somewhere other than on your computer so that you can restore them if an event such as a virus attack, hard disk failure, theft, fire, or other loss should occur. Most people aren't convinced of the necessity of backing up the various types of information they create and work with until they suffer a disaster—and then they become evangelists. Your organization should have an automated system in place to regularly back up all the information stored on servers, but might or might not back up information stored on each and every individual computer—and few people have a system set up at home to protect family records, correspondence, digital photographs, and other personal information.

One key factor in useful data backups is frequency—information that has not been backed up is not protected. For continuous data protection, you can rely on an online data backup service such as Datacastle (*www.datacastlecorp.com*), which securely backs up incremental changes from your computer over the Internet at regular intervals. Implementing this type of solution ensures that you never lose more than a few minutes' work, and addresses another key factor in useful data backups—the storage location. Backing up your information to a CD, DVD, tape, or removable hard drive protects you from data loss only if the backup is also protected. For example, if you store your backup in your laptop bag and your laptop bag is stolen, you are not protected. Similarly, storing your backup in a location where it might be damaged or destroyed by environmental factors does not provide adequate protection.

If you prefer to back up information to physical media such as CDs or DVDs, or to another computer on your network, you can do so by using Windows Backup. You can back up information manually, or have Windows Vista do it automatically according to a schedule you establish.

> **Tip** Automatic backups are not available with Windows Vista Home Basic Edition.

The backup schedule you choose should reflect the rate at which you create and change files. If you work on your computer only on weekends, a daily backup will probably not be necessary. On the other hand, if you work from your home office, store all your work on your computer, and could lose significant time or income if your computer crashes, a daily backup is a good idea. You can schedule automatic backups on a regular basis, and supplement them with manual backups when important. Keep in mind that your computer must be turned on at the scheduled time for Windows to be able to complete the backup.

You should routinely back up only the files you create, not program files or system files. Program files do not change very often and can usually be reinstalled from the original installation CDs. You can make a backup of your system files, but this is usually necessary only in rare circumstances.

If your computer is connected to other computers over a network or if you have more than one hard drive, you can choose one of those locations for the backup. If your computer is not connected to other computers and has only one hard drive, the computer must have a CD or DVD burner to create a backup. You cannot back up to a flash drive, to the disk containing the files you are backing up, or to the disk that Windows is installed on. If you are backing up to a CD or DVD, you must be present to insert a new disk at the scheduled time. If you are not, Windows will put the backup on hold and will prompt you to insert the CD or DVD to continue the process.

> **Tip** Even if you have more than one internal hard drive, you might want to back up to a location away from your computer in case of disaster.

When you back up your files, Windows creates a folder in the designated backup location called *Backup Set [date] [time]*. The first time you create a backup, Windows performs a full backup of all files of the designated type. Thereafter, it updates the backup set with the files that you have created or changed since the last backup. You might want to create a new full backup periodically to start afresh.

If you need to restore a file from a backup set, you display the Backup And Restore Center, indicate the required files or folders and the restoration location, and Windows does the rest.

> **Tip** If you have made changes to a file and need to revert to a previous version, you might not need to restore it from a backup. If you have used System Protection to create a restore point, Windows automatically saves "shadow" copies of your files as part of the restore point. These copies are listed on the Previous Versions tab of each file's Properties dialog box. You can right-click the file and then click Restore Previous Version to display this tab of the dialog box, where you can select the version you want. The previous version then overwrites the current version.

In this exercise, you will back up a document to a removable storage device. You will also set a schedule for future backups. Then you will delete a file and restore it from the backup.

> **Troubleshooting** You must be logged in as an administrator to back up or restore files.

USE the *BookBeat* document. This practice file is located in the *Documents\Microsoft Press\WindowsVistaSBS_Dlx\Solutions* folder.

BE SURE TO log on to Windows Vista as an administrator and have a blank writable CD or DVD or the location of a network computer available before beginning this exercise.

OPEN Control Panel.

1. In **Control Panel**, under **System and Maintenance**, click **Back up your computer**.

   The Backup And Restore Center opens.

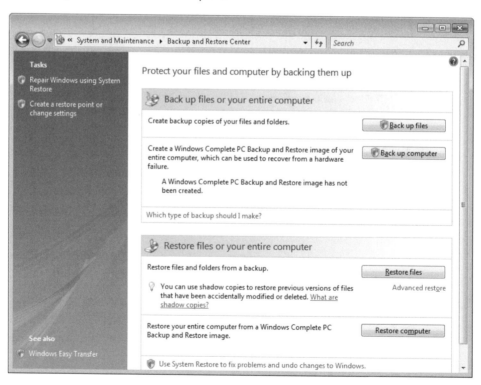

> **Troubleshooting** If automatic backup is already set up on your computer, your Backup And Restore Center will look different. To the right of Create Backup Copies Of Your Files And Folders, click Back Up Files, and when the process is complete, click OK. Then skip to step 9.

2. Under **Back up files or your entire computer**, click **Back up files**. Then in the **User Account Control** dialog box, click **Continue**.

The Back Up Files wizard searches your system for an appropriate backup device—either an alternative hard disk drive, a CD writer, or a DVD writer.

3. Select the hard disk or other drive where you want to save the backup, and then click **Next**.

The Back Up Files wizard indicates the types of files you might want to back up. Pointing to a category displays a description in the Category Details box.

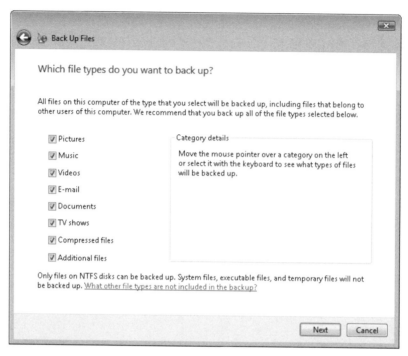

4. For this exercise, clear all the check boxes except **Documents**, and then click **Next**.

You are prompted to establish a schedule for backing up the selected types of files.

5. Adjust the **How often**, **What day**, and **What time** settings to the way you want them by clicking each one in turn and selecting from the list.

6. If you are backing up to a CD or DVD, insert a blank disk into your CD or DVD drive; otherwise skip this step.

7. Click **Save settings and start backup**.

   The backup starts, and a progress box displays the status of the backup process.

   > **Troubleshooting** If you are asked to insert a blank disk or to format the disk, click OK.

8. When the process is complete, close the **Backup Status and Configuration** dialog box.

   The Backup And Restore Center provides information about the most recent backup and the next scheduled backup.

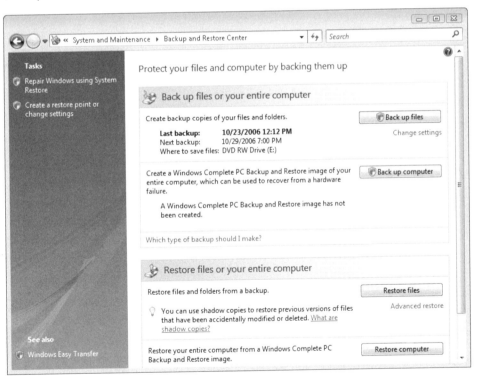

9. Open your *Documents* folder in Windows Explorer, navigate to the *Microsoft Press\ WindowsVistaSBS_Dlx\Solutions* folder, and then delete the *BookBeat* document. Leave the window open.

Now you will restore the file from your backup.

10. On the Windows taskbar, click the **Backup and Restore Center** taskbar button.

11. Under **Restore files or your entire computer**, click **Restore files**.

The Restore Files wizard asks what you want to restore.

12. With **Files from the latest backup** selected, click **Next**.

13. On the wizard's next page, click **Add files**. Then with the contents of your *Documents* folder displayed in the **Add files to restore** dialog box, navigate to the *Microsoft Press\WindowsVistaSBS_Dlx\Solutions* folder, double-click the *BookBeat* document, and then click **Next**.

14. On the next page, leave **In the original location** selected, and then click **Start restore**.

15. When Windows reports that the file has been successfully restored, click **Finish**.

16. Close the **Backup and Restore Center**.

In the Windows Explorer window, you can see that the file has been restored from the backup.

 CLOSE the Windows Explorer window.

Restoring Your Operating System

In the beginning, you start with a clean computer with a brand new operating system. As time goes by, you install new programs, delete programs, change your system settings, and upgrade to new versions of programs. Gradually, things change, and sometimes things fail, and you might find yourself wishing you could go back to the way things were. Now you can! You can use System Restore to roll back your system to the condition it was in at a prior point in time. You can roll back to any of these types of checkpoints and restoration points:

- Windows Vista creates an install restore point each time you install a program or device driver, and each time Windows Update installs an update.
- Windows Vista creates a system checkpoint when you back up or restore your computer.
- You can create a manual restore point at any time.

You can turn System Restore on or off for each hard disk in your computer, as long as the disk is at least 1 GB. (System Restore will not run on smaller disks.) Each hard disk must have 15 percent of its total space free for its restore points, which are saved on the individual disks. When the allocated restore point storage space is full, older restore points are deleted.

Restoring your computer restores Windows Vista and the programs that are installed on your computer to the state they were in at the time of the selected restore point. Your personal files (including your saved documents, e-mail messages, address book, Windows Internet Explorer Favorites, and History list) are not affected. All the changes made by System Restore are completely reversible, so if you don't like the results, you can restore the previous settings and try again.

System Restore also creates shadow copies of files and folders that have been changed since the previous restore point. If you make a change to a file or folder that you wish you hadn't, you can open the shadow copy and save it as a new file. Similarly, you can open versions of files that have been saved during a backup. To view available shadow copies and backup versions, right-click the file or folder, click Properties, and then in the Properties dialog box, click the Previous Versions tab.

> **Tip** Each of the System Restore checkpoints and restoration points is the equivalent of a large-scale file backup. If a virus-infected file is stored as part of a restoration point, it could inadvertently be restored along with the rest of your system settings if you choose to restore your system to that particular restoration point.
>
> While the System Restore feature is enabled, the backup files are protected from detection or cure by virus scanning programs. Prior to running a system-wide virus checker, disable the System Restore feature to ensure that all files are checked and cured or deleted as appropriate.

In this exercise, you will create a manual restore point and see how to restore your computer to a previous state. There are no practice files for this exercise.

BE SURE TO display Control Panel before beginning this exercise.

1. In **Control Panel**, click **System and Maintenance**, and then click **System**.

2. In the **Tasks** list on the left side of the **System** window, click **System protection**. In the **User Account Control** dialog box, if you're logged on as an administrator, click **Continue**. Otherwise, enter an administrator password, and click **OK**.

> **Tip** You can also access System Restore by clicking Undo Changes To Your Computer With System Restore in Windows Help And Support, or by clicking System Restore in the See Also area of the Performance And Maintenance window.

The System Properties dialog box opens, displaying the System Protection tab.

3. Click **Create**, and then in the **System Protection** box, type SBS Restore Point to identify the purpose of the restore point.

4. In the **System Protection** box, click **Create**.

5. After Windows Vista creates the restore point, click **OK** in the **System Protection** box.

6. In the **System Properties** dialog box, click **System Restore**.

The System Restore wizard starts.

The restore point of the most recent software or driver installation is selected as the recommended restore point.

7. Click **Choose a different restore point**, and then click **Next**.

The System Restore wizard displays the available restore points and checkpoints.

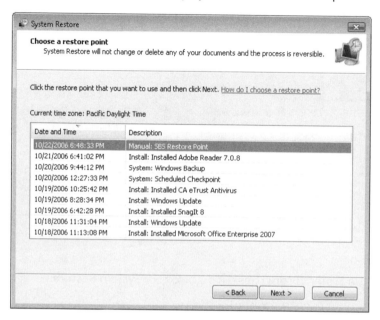

You can restore your computer to any of these points.

8. On the **Choose a restore point** page, click **Cancel** to exit the wizard without restoring your computer to a previous point.

 CLOSE the System Properties dialog box and the System window.

Transferring Software, Settings, and Files to Another Computer

Have you put off purchasing a new computer or switching to a different one because you dread the task of installing all the programs you use, customizing all your settings, and moving all your data files? You might not even be sure exactly what you should transfer in order to have everything you need. *Windows Easy Transfer* helps you choose what to transfer and leads you step by step through the process. It does not delete information from the old computer, so you don't need to worry that accidentally transferring the wrong file means it is lost forever.

You can transfer the following types of files and settings from a computer running Windows XP or Windows Vista to a computer running Windows Vista:

- Folders and files
- E-mail settings, contacts, and messages
- Program settings
- User accounts and settings
- Internet settings and favorites

You can transfer files, but not settings, from a computer running Windows 2000 to a computer running Windows Vista.

You can use several methods to get the information from one computer to the other, including over a network; via DVD, CD, or USB flash drive; or by using an *Easy Transfer Cable* (a USB cable that connects two computers together).

> **Troubleshooting** While the transfer is taking place, you will not be able to use either computer. Because the transfer can take several hours, you cannot start the process from a mobile computer that is running on battery power; you must first plug it in.

To begin the transfer process:

1. Log on to your computer as an administrator.

2. On the **Start** menu, point to **All Programs**, click **Accessories**, click **System Tools**, and then click **Windows Easy Transfer**. Then in the **User Account Control** dialog box, click **Continue**.

3. Follow the instructions in the **Windows Easy Transfer** wizard to specify the transfer media or method, the information you want to transfer, and the password for recovering that information.

4. If you are transferring files and settings via removable media, start **Windows Easy Transfer** on the second computer, and click **Continue transfer in progress**.

5. Provide the information requested by the wizard. When prompted to do so, insert the transfer disk into the second computer, select the destination drive, enter the password, and then click **Next**.

   The files transfer to the new computer.

Key Points

- If you need help with Windows Vista, you can find locally stored and online information through Windows Help And Support.

- You can get help from other people through a newsgroup, from an online product support provider, or by inviting a person to provide Remote Assistance.

- It is a good idea to periodically back up your important files. If you have a serious computer problem, you can restore files or even your entire operating system to an earlier state.

- Setting up a new computer is no longer a daunting task with Windows Easy Transfer, which helps you transfer all your programs, settings, and files from a computer running Windows XP or Windows Vista to another computer running Windows Vista.

Keyboard Shortcuts

In Windows Help And Support, press this	To do this
Alt+C	Display the Table of Contents.
Alt+N	Display the Connection Settings menu.
F10	Display the Options menu.
Alt+Left Arrow	Move back to the previously viewed topic.
Alt+Right Arrow	Move forward to the next (previously viewed) topic.
Alt+A	Display the customer support page.
Alt+Home	Display the Windows Help And Support home page.
Home	Move to the beginning of a topic.
End	Move to the end of a topic.
Ctrl+F	Search the current topic.
Ctrl+P	Print the current topic.
F3	Move to the Search box.

Glossary

activating A security measure that requires you to validate your copy of Windows Vista online or by telephone within 30 days of first use.

ActiveX control A set of technologies that enables software components to interact with one another in a networked environment, regardless of the language in which the components were created.

Address bar In Windows Explorer, a text box containing the navigation path to the current folder, beginning with the Windows symbol representing the overall Windows storage structure. The arrow after each folder name links to a list of its subfolders. In Windows Internet Explorer, a text box containing the Web address of the currently displayed Web page.

administrative privileges The highest level of permissions that can be granted to a user account. A computer administrator can perform tasks affecting the computer and all the user accounts on it. Administrative privileges are required to perform any tasks relating to or affecting computer security.

alias A unique name used to identify a user on a domain. In an e-mail address, the alias is the portion of the address that appears before the at sign (@).

aspect ratio In computer displays and graphics, the ratio of the width of an image or image area to its height.

attachment A file, picture, digital signature, or other external data sent in conjunction with an e-mail message.

Audio Description A Windows Vista accessibility program that narrates videos as they play, if this feature is available within the video file.

autorun file A file that automatically starts an installation program when you insert the installation disc or browse to the folder containing it.

background tabs In Internet Explorer tabbed browsing, a page tab that opens in the background, so that the tab you are currently working with stays in the foreground.

backing up The process of creating a copy of your files somewhere other than on your computer so that you can restore them if an event such as a virus attack, hard disk failure, theft of a laptop, fire, or other loss should occur.

bitmap (BMP) A data structure in memory that represents information in the form of a collection of individual bits. A bitmap image represents images as dots, or pixels, on the screen and is saved in the bitmap (.bmp) format.

blog Short for *Weblog*. A personal Web site created for the purpose of sharing information and opinions with other Internet users. Blogs range from personal diaries and ways for communities to keep in touch to sources of information on a specific topic.

BMP See *bitmap (BMP)*.

browser See *Web browser*.

browsing Navigating through a folder hierarchy, for example in a dialog box or in Windows Explorer, to select a folder or file.

burning Copying a file, such as an image or audio file, to a CD or DVD.

byte A unit of information that is the equivalent of one character.

cable A type of broadband Internet connection that uses cable television lines.

caching The process of storing information in a computer's memory, or storing a Web page on a computer's hard disk, for rapid retrieval at a later time.

CD key A unique combination of letters and numbers that identifies a product license.

clicking The action of pressing and releasing the primary mouse button.

command An instruction to the computer's operating system.

compressing To reduce the size of a set of data, such as a file or a communications message, so that it can be stored in less space or transmitted with less bandwidth.

computer system A complete, working computer, including the hardware, the operating system, and any other software or peripheral devices that are necessary to make the computer function.

contact group A contact record that combines individual contacts into a single group. In Windows Contacts, contact groups are stored as .group files in each user's personal *Contacts* folder.

contact record A collection of information about a person, usually accessible from an e-mail program. Windows Contacts stores contact records as .contact files in each user's personal *Contacts* folder.

content pane Displays files and folders stored in the currently selected folder or storage device.

context menu A context-sensitive menu of commands that appears when you right-click an item.

credentials The user name and password you use to connect to a domain, Web site, folder, or other secure location.

defragmentation The process of consolidating data stored on a hard disk drive into contiguous chunks, for the purpose of increasing file access speed.

desktop An on-screen work area that uses icons and menus to simulate the top of a desk.

desktop shortcut See *shortcut*.

device driver A software component that permits a computer system to communicate with a device.

DHCP server A computer running the Microsoft DHCP service, which allows IP addresses to change as needed.

dialog box A window that contains buttons and various kinds of options through which the user can carry out a particular command or task.

dial-up connection A connection from your computer to another computer using two modems and an ordinary telephone line. The remote computer usually belongs to the Internet service provider (ISP) with whom you have set up your user account.

Digital Subscriber Line (DSL) A type of high-speed Internet connection using standard telephone wires; also referred to as a *broadband connection*.

Disk Cleanup A program that frees up space on your hard disk by removing downloaded program files, temporary files, and offline files; compressing old files; and emptying the Recycle Bin.

Disk Defragmenter A program that analyzes all the data stored on your hard disk and then consolidates fragmented files into contiguous chunks. The benefits are faster file access and larger areas of available space in which to store new files.

DLL See *dynamic-link library (DLL)*.

DNS See *domain name system (DNS)*.

docking To move a toolbar to the edge of an application window so that it attaches to and becomes a part of the application window.

domain A logical (rather than physical) group of resources—computers, servers, and other hardware devices—on a network, that are centrally administered through Microsoft Windows Server. Also, the domain name used as the base of Web site addresses and e-mail addresses.

domain name system (DNS) The hierarchical system by which hosts on the Internet have both domain name addresses and IP addresses. The domain name address is used by human users and is automatically translated into the numerical IP address, which is used by the packet-routing software.

double-clicking Pressing and releasing the primary mouse button twice in quick succession.

dragging The process of moving an item to another place on the screen by selecting the item and then pressing and holding down the mouse button while moving the mouse.

driver See *device driver.*

DSL See *Digital Subscriber Line (DSL).*

dynamic-link library (DLL) An operating system feature that allows executable routines to be stored separately as files with .dll extensions and to be loaded only when needed by a program.

Easy Transfer Cable A USB cable that connects two computers together.

e-mail address A series of characters, consisting of an alias and a domain name, that identifies an e-mail account.

e-mail alias See *alias.*

e-mail server See *mail server.*

e-mail signature A block of text, usually providing your contact information, that you manually or automatically append to the end of an e-mail message.

executable file A program file that can be run. Files that have .exe extensions are executable.

expansion slot A socket in a computer, designed to hold expansion boards and connect them to the system bus (data pathway) as a means of adding or enhancing the computer's features and capabilities.

external peripherals Devices installed by connecting them to ports without having to open up your computer. Examples are your computer's monitor, keyboard, mouse, and speakers.

Filter Keys A keyboard feature that causes Windows to ignore brief or repeated keystrokes, or slows the repeat rate.

font A set of characters. Traditionally the term *font* referred to a specific size and style within a font family, such as 10-point italic Verdana. Now the term commonly refers to the entire family.

fragmentation The scattering of parts of the same file over different areas of the disk. Fragmentation occurs as files on a disk are deleted and new files are added. It slows disk access and degrades the overall performance of disk operations, although usually not severely.

gadget A device displayed in Windows Sidebar that provides constantly updated information, such as the time.

GB See *gigabyte (GB).*

GIF See *Graphics Interchange Format (GIF).*

gigabyte (GB) 1,024 megabytes, though often interpreted as approximately one billion bytes.

Graphics Interchange Format (GIF) A graphics file format developed by CompuServe and used for transmitting raster images on the Internet. An image in this format may contain up to 256 colors, including a transparent color. The size of the file depends on the number of colors actually used.

graphical user interface (GUI) User interface incorporating visual elements such as a desktop, icons, and menus.

group An account that contains other accounts, called *members*. Permissions and rights granted to a group are also granted to its members.

hacker A person who attempts to gain access to computers or software programs through illegal means, often with the malicious intent of damaging computer data through the introduction of a virus.

hardware The physical components of a computer system, including any peripheral equipment such as printers, modems, and mouse devices.

High Contrast A program that changes the display of your screen from the usual muted Windows colors to a starker color scheme to make individual items on the screen stand out more from others.

home page In Internet Explorer, the page or pages that open automatically when you start your browser. For Web sites, the first page displayed when you connect to a site.

HTML See *Hypertext Markup Language (HTML)*.

HTTP See *Hypertext Transfer Protocol (HTTP)*.

hub In a network, a device joining communication lines at a central location, providing a common connection to all devices on the network.

hyperlink A link from a text or graphic element to another location in the document, to another document, or to a Web page.

Hypertext Markup Language (HTML) An e-mail message format that supports paragraph styles, character styles, and backgrounds. Most e-mail programs support the HTML format.

Hypertext Transfer Protocol (HTTP) A protocol used to access information from the Internet.

icon A small image displayed on the screen to represent an object that can be manipulated by the user. Icons serve as visual mnemonics and are used to control certain computer actions without the user having to remember commands or enter them through the keyboard.

IEEE 1394 A port used for the high-speed transfer of audio and video data.

IMAP See *Internet Message Access Protocol (IMAP)*.

Information Bar A bar that appears at the top of the Internet Explorer content pane, notifying you when potentially risky actions, such as downloading an ActiveX control, require your permission to continue.

input language A Regional And Language Options setting that specifies the combination of the language being entered and the keyboard layout, IME, speech-to-text converter, or other device being used to enter it.

Internet Message Access Protocol (IMAP) An e-mail–handling protocol that organizes messages on the server, and you choose messages to download by viewing their headers.

instant messaging (IM) A real-time electronic communication system that allows you to "chat" with contacts by typing in a window on your computer screen.

internal peripherals Devices that have to be installed inside your computer. The internal component might be in the form of a card that provides a new connection at the back of the computer, or it might be a new hard disk drive, DVD drive, or tape backup drive that is accessed from the front of the computer.

Internet protocol address See *IP address*.

Internet service provider (ISP) A business that supplies Internet connectivity services to individuals, businesses, and other organizations.

IP address A 32-bit address used to identify a node on an IP network. Each node on the IP network must be assigned a unique IP address, which is made up of the network ID and a unique host ID. This address is typically represented with the decimal value of each 8 bits separated by a period (for example, 192.168.7.27).

ISDN A digital phone line used to provide a high-bandwidth Internet connection. An ISDN line must be installed by the telephone company at both the calling site and the called site.

ISP See *Internet service provider (ISP)*.

Joint Photographic Expert Group (JPEG) An image compression mechanism designed for compressing either full-color or grayscale still images. It works well on photographs, naturalistic artwork, and similar material. Images saved in this format have .jpg or .jpeg file extensions.

JPEG See *Joint Photographic Expert Group (JPEG)*.

KB See *kilobyte (KB)*.

keyboard shortcut A combination of keys that when pressed together implement a command in Windows or in a program.

kilobyte (KB) 1,024 bytes of data storage; in reference to data transfer rates, 1,000 bytes.

LAN See *local area network (LAN)*.

license terms The terms defining the legal relationship between you and the manufacturer of a software program, the terms under which you may use the software, and the extent of the manufacturer's liability, that you must agree to before installing or running a software program.

local area network (LAN) The process of connecting to a computer on your network that has been set up to provide Internet access; connections to upstream providers are handled for you by that computer.

local printer A printer that is connected directly to your computer.

local/locally A term referring to the computer you are currently using.

locking Making your Windows desktop inaccessible to other people; most effective when your user account is protected by a password.

logging off The process of disconnecting a computer from a network domain without affecting other users' sessions.

logging on The process of starting a computer session.

Magnifier See *Microsoft Magnifier*.

mail server A network-accessible computer running Microsoft Exchange Server or another mail server program, responsible for the management of the e-mail system as well as the routing and storage of e-mail messages and other information.

mapping a drive The process of assigning a drive letter to a specific computer or shared folder on your network. This is commonly done to create a constant connection to a network share but can also be used to maintain a connection to an Internet location.

MB See *megabyte (MB)*.

megabyte (MB) 1,024 kilobytes of data storage; in reference to data transfer rates, 1,000 kilobytes.

menu bar The toolbar from which users can access the menus of commands.

Microsoft Magnifier A Windows Vista accessibility program that opens a magnification panel in which the screen under the mouse pointer is displayed, magnified up to nine times. You can adjust the size and location of the magnification panel.

Microsoft Narrator A Windows Vista accessibility tool that converts on-screen text to spoken audio in order to read menu commands, dialog box options, and other screen features out loud. It also reads keystrokes as they're typed and identifies the location as you move around.

Microsoft Paint A drawing program with which users can create simple or elaborate drawings. These drawings can be either black and white or color, and can be saved as bitmap files. It can also be used to work with *.jpg* and *.gif* files. Paint pictures can be pasted into another document, or used as a desktop background.

middleware A type of software that connects two or more otherwise separate applications, which could be software programs or system applications.

modem A device that allows computer information to be transmitted and received over a telephone line. The transmitting modem translates digital computer data into analog signals that can be carried over a phone line. The receiving modem translates the analog signals back to digital form.

Mouse Keys A Windows Vista accessibility tool that allows you to move the cursor around the screen by pressing the Arrow keys on the numeric keypad.

Narrator See *Microsoft Narrator.*

Navigation pane Displays your personal folders and when you expand the Folders list, displays a hierarchical view of the entire storage structure of your computer.

network A group of computers that communicate with each other through a wired or wireless connection.

network printer A printer that is not connected directly to your computer. Instead, you access the printer through a network or workgroup as a free-standing networked printer, through someone else's computer, through a print server, or through a printer hub.

network share A folder on a different computer on your network.

newsgroup A collection of messages posted by individuals to a news server (a computer that can host thousands of newsgroups).

Notepad A basic text editor used to create simple documents or Web pages.

notification area The area on the taskbar to the right of the taskbar buttons that displays information about the status of programs, including those running in the background (programs you don't need to interact with), as well as links to certain system commands.

OEM See *original equipment manufacturer (OEM).*

offline Not connected to a network or to the Internet. Also used to describe time that you will be away from your computer.

online Connected to the Internet.

On-Screen Keyboard A Windows Vista tool that displays a visual representation of a keyboard from which you can select individual keys by using your mouse, pen, or other device.

operating system The underlying program that tells your computer what to do and how to do it. The operating system coordinates interactions among the computer system components, acts as the interface between you and your computer, enables your computer to communicate with other computers and peripheral devices, and interacts with programs installed on your computer.

original equipment manufacturer (OEM) The maker of a piece of equipment.

Paint See *Microsoft Paint.*

parallel port An input/output connector that sends and receives data eight bits at a time, in parallel, between a computer and a peripheral device.

password A security measure used to restrict access to user accounts, computer systems, and resources. A password is a unique string of characters that must be provided before access is authorized.

password reset disk A disk (or other piece of removable media, such as a USB flash drive) created by the user from within Windows. If a password is forgotten or lost, the disk allows the user to create a new password.

path The route followed by the operating system through the directories in finding, sorting, and retrieving files on a disk.

peripheral device A device, such as a disk drive, printer, modem, or joystick, that is connected to a computer and is controlled by the computer's microprocessor.

personal folder A folder that you open by clicking your user name at the top of the Start menu. You can save documents, spreadsheets, graphics, and other files in your personal folder. As you work on your computer and personalize Windows, it saves information and settings specific to your individual user profile in this folder.

pinned programs area A special area at the top of the left side of the Start menu to which users can drag program icons and shortcuts.

pixel The individual dots that make up the picture displayed on your computer. Each pixel displays one color. See also *screen resolution*.

play list A compilation of tracks from various CDs and other sources.

Plug and Play A phrase meaning that the operating system can locate any necessary drivers itself.

PNG See *Portable Network Graphics (PNG)*.

pointing Moving the mouse pointer over an object.

POP3 See *Post Office Protocol 3 (POP3)*.

pop-up The small Web browser window that opens on top of (or sometimes below) the Web browser window when you display a Web site or click an advertising link.

port An interface through which data is transferred between a computer and other devices, a network, or a direct connection to another computer.

Portable Network Graphics (PNG) A file format for bitmapped graphic images, designed to be a replacement for the GIF format without the legal restrictions associated with GIF.

Post Office Protocol 3 (POP3) A popular protocol used for receiving e-mail messages. This protocol is often used by ISPs. In contrast to IMAP servers, which provide access to multiple server-side folders, POP3 servers allow access to a single Inbox.

primary display In a multi-monitor setup, the monitor that includes the Windows logon screen and the taskbar.

printer driver A software program designed to enable other programs to work with a particular printer without concerning themselves with the specifics of the printer's hardware and internal language.

product key A unique combination of letters and numbers that identifies a program's product license.

program icon See *icon*.

program shortcut See *shortcut*.

Quick Launch toolbar A customizable toolbar optionally displayed on the Windows taskbar, from which users can or start programs or utilities with a single click.

read receipt An electronic receipt delivered to a message sender when the recipient has displayed the message. This is useful when sending time-critical information, or any time you need confirmation that a message has been received.

recently opened programs list A list on the Start menu of the last several programs started by the user.

Recycle Bin The place where Windows temporarily stores files you delete. When the Recycle Bin is empty, the icon depicts an empty trash can; when you delete items (but don't empty the Recycle Bin), the icon depicts pieces of paper in the trash can.

remote access server A host on a LAN that is equipped with modems so that users can connect to the network over telephone lines.

remote assistance A convenient way for a friend or trusted person to connect to a local computer from a remote computer and help troubleshoot a problem. To protect your computer from unauthorized access, the invitation is valid for a specific length of time—from 1 minute to 99 days—and can require a password, which is sent separately.

Remote Desktop A means of accessing a Windows session that is running on one computer from another computer.

restore point A snapshot of your computer system settings taken by Windows Vista at regular intervals as well as prior to any major change such as installing a program or updating system files. If you experience problems with your system, you can restore it to any saved restore point without undoing changes to your personal files.

right-clicking The action of pressing and releasing the secondary mouse button.

root The highest or uppermost level in a hierarchically organized set of information. The root is the point from which subsets branch in a logical sequence that moves from a broad or general focus to narrower perspectives.

root directory The place where folders and files are stored directly on a drive. The root directory often contains system files that should not be modified or moved in any way.

router A device connecting computers on a network or connecting multiple networks, that receives data and forwards it.

screen resolution The fineness of detail attained by a monitor in producing an image, measured in pixels, expressed as the number of pixels wide by the number of pixels high. See also *pixels*.

screen saver Static or moving images that are displayed on your computer after some period of inactivity.

ScreenTip The small text box that appears when pointing to an icon (positioning the mouse pointer over it), and contains identifying information.

scroll bar A vertical or horizontal bar that users move to change the position of content within a window.

secondary display In a multi-monitor setup, the monitor on to which you can expand programs so that you can expand your work area.

shared drive A drive that has been made available for other people on a network to access.

shared folder A folder that has been made available for other people on a network to access.

shortcut An icon on the desktop that a user can double-click to immediately access a program, a text or data file, or a Web page.

shortcut menu See *context menu*.

shutting down A process that closes all your open applications and files, ends your computing session, closes network connections, stops system processes, stops the hard disk, and turns off the computer.

signature See *e-mail signature*.

Simple Mail Transfer Protocol (SMTP) A member of a suite of protocols that governs the exchange of electronic mail between message transfer agents.

Sleep mode A Windows Vista feature that saves any open files and the state of any running programs to memory and to your hard disk, and then puts your computer into a power-saving state.

SMTP See *Simple Mail Transfer Protocol (SMTP)*.

software Programs with which users perform tasks (such as creating documents or playing games) on a computer.

software piracy The illegal reproduction and distribution of software applications.

sound card A type of expansion board on PC-compatible computers that allows the playback and recording of sound.

Sound Sentry A Windows Vista feature that flashes the screen element you specify (your choices are the active caption bar, active window, or desktop) every time the system's built-in speaker plays a sound.

Speech Recognition Allows you to control Windows, control open programs, and dictate text by speaking into a microphone.

Start menu A list of options that is your central link to all the programs installed on your computer, as well as to all the tasks you can carry out with Windows Vista.

stationery An electronic message template that can include a background, fonts, font colors, and custom margins.

Sticky Keys A Windows Vista accessibility feature that makes it easier to use the keyboard with one hand by causing the Ctrl, Shift, and Alt keys to "stick" down until you press the next key.

surfing the Web To browse information on the Internet.

switch box An enclosure that contains a selector switch. It looks similar to a hub but allows only one active connection at a time.

synchronizing Copying changed items between a mailbox or address book on a server and its corresponding offline folder so that both are up to date.

system cache An area in computer memory where Windows Vista stores information it might need to access quickly.

system date The current date according to the operating system.

system folders The folders created when Windows Vista was installed. The folders are Program Files, Users, and Windows. See the index to locate specific information about each of these folders.

system time The current time according to the operating system. The system time controls a number of behind-the-scenes settings and is also used by Windows and by programs to maintain an accurate record of events.

tabbed browsing A feature in Internet Explorer with which you can browse different Web sites on different tabs, easily and quickly switching between them.

tabs Multiple windows located within the Internet Explorer program window that can each display a different Web site.

task pane A fixed pane that appears on one side of a program window, containing options related to the completion of a specific task.

Task Scheduler Program with which you can schedule regular hard disk maintenance tasks.

taskbar Displays buttons you can click to run programs, utilities, and commands, as well as buttons representing the windows of open programs and files.

taskbar buttons Buttons on the taskbar representing each open window, file, or program.

theme A set of visual elements that applies a unified look for the computer desktop. Each theme can include a desktop background color or picture; a color scheme that affects title bars and labels; specific fonts used on title bars, labels, and buttons; sounds associated with specific actions; and other elements.

tilt-wheel mouse A mouse that incorporates a wheel that scrolls not only vertically, but also horizontally.

time server A computer that periodically synchronizes the time on all computers within a network. This ensures that the time used by network services and local functions remains accurate.

title bar The horizontal bar at the top of a window that displays the window name. It may also display the program icon, the Maximize, Minimize, and Close buttons, and the optional question mark button for context-sensitive Help. To display a menu with commands such as Restore and Move, right-click the title bar.

Toggle Keys A Windows Vista accessibility feature that sounds an audio signal when you press the Caps Lock, Num Lock, or Scroll Lock key. A high-pitched sound plays when the keys are activated, and a low-pitched sound plays when the keys are deactivated.

toolbar Presents menus and buttons specific to the content of the current window. When more buttons are available than can be shown, a chevron (>>) appears at the right end of the toolbar; clicking the chevron displays a list of other commands.

turning off The process of shutting down Windows so users can safely turn off the computer power. Many computers turn the power off automatically.

UI See *user interface (UI)*.

UNC See *Universal Naming Convention (UNC)*.

Uniform Resource Locator (URL) An address for a resource on the Internet. URLs are used by Web browsers to locate Internet resources.

Universal Naming Convention (UNC) The system of naming files among computers on a network so that a file on a given computer will have the same path when accessed from any of the other computers on the network.

Universal Serial Bus (USB) A connection that provides both data transfer capabilities and power to a peripheral device.

upgrading The process of updating your computer's operating system files to a newer version, without disturbing information that is stored on your computer, such as documents, spreadsheets, and data files.

URL See *Uniform Resource Locator (URL)*.

USB See *Universal Serial Bus (USB)*.

USB flash drive A portable flash memory card that plugs into a computer's USB port and stores up to 2 GB of data.

user account On a secure or multi-user computer system, an established means for an individual to gain access to the system and its resources.

User Account Control A Windows Vista security feature that requires specific acknowledgment and an administrator password when accessing settings that could disrupt your computer or affect its users.

user account name See *user name*.

user account picture An individual graphic representing a specific computer user account. User account pictures are available only on computers that are members of a workgroup or are stand-alone, and are not available on computers that are members of a network domain.

user interface (UI) The portion of a software program with which a user interacts.

user name A unique name identifying a user's account to Windows. An account's user name must be unique among the other group names and user names within its own domain or workgroup.

user profile A computer-based record maintained about an authorized user of a multi-user computer system. It describes the way the computer environment looks and operates for that particular user.

users A collective term used to refer to people who use computers.

utility A small program that provides additional features to the computer user; for example, the Magnifier utility that enlarges a portion of the screen in a separate window.

vCard A friendly term for a .vcf file; an electronic business card format for contact information. The vCard format is compatible with a variety of e-mail messaging systems.

virtual private network (VPN) The extension of a private network. VPN connections provide remote access and routed connections to private networks over the Internet.

virus A program that infects computer files or other programs by inserting copies of itself into the files, and might execute some harmful or inconvenient action. A program that inserts itself into an e-mail program and sends copies of itself to everyone in the address book is an example of a virus.

VPN See *virtual private network (VPN)*.

Web An abbreviated term for *World Wide Web*; a worldwide network consisting of millions of smaller networks that send and receive data among each other.

Web browser Software that lets a user view HTML documents.

Welcome screen The screen that appears when you start your computer, containing links to each of the active user accounts.

wildcard character A keyboard character that can be used to represent one or many characters when conducting a query. The question mark (?) represents a single character, and the asterisk (*) represents any number of characters.

window A portion of the screen where programs and processes can be run. Users can open several windows at the same time. Windows can be closed, resized, moved, minimized to a button on the taskbar, or maximized to take up the whole screen.

Windows Classic The menu style found in Windows 2000 and earlier. If you are unable to adjust to the changed look of the Windows Vista menu, you have the option of changing back to the Classic version.

Windows Defender A Windows Vista security feature that helps you detect software that might pose a potential threat to your privacy or your computer.

Windows Easy Transfer A program that leads you step by step through the process of transferring files to a new computer.

Windows Experience Index Measures hardware and assigns a base score that reflects the lowest of a set of subscores for your processor, memory, graphics card, and hard disk.

Windows Firewall A built-in Windows security feature that helps to prevent unauthorized transmissions to and from your computer.

Windows ReadyBoost A Windows Vista feature that makes it possible to increase the available system memory by using USB flash drives as memory-expansion devices.

Windows Security Center A Windows Vista security feature that monitors the types of protection on your system.

Windows Sidebar A desktop pane that keeps useful tools and current information readily accessible.

Windows Update A utility that scans your computer, confers with the Microsoft Update online database, and recommends or installs any updates that are available for your operating system, your software programs, or your hardware.

wizard A program that walks you through the steps necessary to accomplish a particular task.

workgroup A logical group of computers that is not centrally administered but communicates through a network.

Index

Symbols

.wcinv files, 289
3-D view of open windows, 53

A

Access to files and folders, limiting, 94
Accessibility dialog box, 200
accessibility features, 22. *See also* Ease Of Access
    center
    recommendations on, 25
accounts. *See* user accounts
activating Windows, 7, 10
    checking status of, 9
    defined, 479
    grace period for, 7
activation status, identifying, 426
ActiveX controls, 479
activity reports, viewing, lxxvi
ad hoc wireless networks, 250
    disconnecting from, lxi, 250
    distance limitation, 250
    setting up, lx, 250
    temporary nature of, 250
ad windows, blocking. *See* Internet Explorer
    Pop-up Blocker
Add A Favorite dialog box, 203
Add Folder To Gallery button, 373
Add Input Language dialog box, 156
Add Or Change Home Page dialog box, 198
Add To Favorites button, 203
Address Bar, 42
    defined, 479
    displaying, 56
address book. *See* Windows Contacts
addresses, Web site. *See* URLs
administrative privileges
    defined, 479
    software installation and, 224
administrator account, 3, 396
administrator tasks, 396
Advanced Sharing dialog box, lxii, 262

advanced startup options, 464
Advanced Tools window, 430
Aero. *See* Windows Aero
Airbrush button (Paint), 334
alias, 479
Animations, turning off, 22
antivirus programs, 410
AOL e-mail accounts, connecting Windows Mail
    to, 267
Appearance And Personalization window, 114
Appearance Settings dialog box, 122
applications. *See* software
appointments, 314
    creating, 319
approved sites in Content Advisor, 215
arranging windows, 50
aspect ratio
    defined, 479
    for viewing movies on screen, 144
assistance, remote. *See* remote assistance
attachments, 479
Audio Description, 22, 479
audio devices. *See also* speakers
    syncing Windows Media Player with, 377
audio files, sharing, 389
audio input jack, 180
    identifying, 181
audio notes, 304
audio output jack, 176
authentication on e-mail servers, 271
auto arranging shortcuts and icons, 71
AutoComplete for Tablet PCs, turning
    on/off, 164
automatically starting software, 229
AutoPlay dialog box, 375, 388
autorun files, 223. *See also* software installation,
    defined, 479

B

Back button, 101, 103, 193
    Windows Explorer, 77, 83, 87
    Windows Help And Support, lxxx, 457
Back Up Files wizard, 469

background, desktop
changing, xlvii–xlix, 126
default, 6
graphics as, 345
picture as, 128
reverting to original, 345
solid color as, 129
background images, turning off, 22
background tabs, 193. *See also* tabbed browsing
defined, 479
background, Web page, 200
backgrounds, graphic, transparent, 339
backing up, 466
before upgrading to Windows Vista, xviii
changed files only, 467
defined, 479
frequency of, 466
system files, 467
Backup And Restore Center, xv, 468
backup sets, restoring files from, lxxxii, 472
backups
locations for, 467
scheduling, lxxxii, 466, 471
balloons. *See* ScreenTips
BE SURE TO paragraphs, xxx
BitLocker Drive Encryption, xvi
bitmap (BMP) files
creating, 100
defined, 348, 479
editing, 100
file format, 345
saving, 347
as user account pictures, 402
blank page, setting as home page, 199
blocking Internet content. *See* parental controls
blogs, 186
defined, 479
updates, viewing. *See* RSS feeds
BMP files
creating, 100
defined, 348, 479
editing, 100
file format, 345
saving, 347
as user account pictures, 402
bolding text, 356
in graphics, 336
boom microphones. *See* microphones
broadband connections, 187
Browse For Files Or Folders dialog box, 68
Browse For Folder dialog box, 132

Browse Help button, lxxx, 456
browsers. *See* Internet Explorer; Internet Explorer 7; Web browsers
browsing, 43
defined, 479
folders, 43
browsing history, deleting, 445
browsing the Internet, 185
bulleted lists, creating, 357
Burn A Disc dialog box, 385
Burn button, 385
burning CDs, 377, 385
defined, 479
of media files, lxxiv
of pictures, lxxiv
business cards, electronic, 305
buttons
margin icons for, xxx
taskbar. *See* taskbar buttons
bytes, 97
defined, 479

C

cable Internet connections
connecting with, 187
defined, 479
caching, 445. *See also* Temporary Internet Files folder
defined, 480
turning off, 445
Calculator, 38
Calendar. *See* Windows Calendar
calendar terminology, 314
cameras. *See* digital cameras
Caps Lock key, audio signal when pressed, 23
cascading windows, 50
casual copying, 7
CD, companion to book. *See* companion CD
CD keys, 223, 480
CDs
burning, 377, 385
playing. *See* Windows Media Player
ripping music from, 377
centering
background pictures, 128
text, 356
Certificate of Authenticity sticker, 11
Change Your Picture window, 402
chapter thumb tabs, how to use, xxix

characters
  international, 154
  non-standard. *See* symbols
Chat button (Remote Assistance), lxxxi, 463
chatting during remote assistance, lxxxi, 463
chatting (IM), 284, 482
check boxes, xxvi
  selecting items with, 127
checkpoints. *See* System Restore
Choose Details dialog box, 89
Classic version
  defined, 489
  of Start menu, 33, 36
cleaning computer interior, 438
cleaning up hard disk. *See* Disk Cleanup
clearing
  Internet Explorer history, 205
  system cache, 21
clicking, xxiv
  defined, 480
  speech recognition command for, 62, 63
clock. *See* system time
Clock gadget, 296
Close button, 48, 99, 195, 205
Close button (Windows Explorer), 84
CLOSE paragraphs, xxx
Close Tab button, 195
closing
  Favorites Center, 205
  Internet Explorer 7, 195
  lists, without making selection, 83
  Sidebar, 301
  speech recognition command for, 67
  tabs, in Internet Explorer 7, 195
  windows, xliii, 48, 84
  windows, all in group, 50
  Windows Explorer, 84
color depth, 122
color schemes. *See also* themes; Windows
    Aero
  changing, xlviii, 119
  high-contrast, 22
color, text, 356
Colors dialog box, 200
colors
  custom, 344
  primary and secondary in Paint, 332
  on Web pages, changing, 200
column charts. *See also* charts
combo boxes, xxvii
command buttons, xxvi

commands
  defined, xxvi, 480
  displaying on Windows folder toolbars, 307
compact mode (Windows Media Player), 376
companion CD
  practice files on, xxxi
  resources available on, xxxiii
compressed folders, 97
  creating, 101
compressing files, xlvi, 97, 101
compression, 480
computer, controlling by voice commands, 57
Computer folder, renaming, xlix, 138
Computer Management console, 227
computer name
  changing, xlix, 137
  identifying, 426
  viewing, xlix, 137
computer system
  defined, 480
  improving performance, 430
Computer window, opening, 44
conferences online. *See* Windows Meeting
    Space
configuring
  Content Advisor, lviii
  Windows Media Center, 383
Connect To A Network wizard, 188, 246
connecting
  devices. *See* devices
  to domains, 251. *See also* domains
  to network connections, 189
  to network resources, 82
  to the Internet, 186, 189
  to workgroups, lx
contact group, 480
contact program. *See* Windows Contacts
contact records, 304, 480
Contacts folder toolbar, 307
contacts, Windows. *See* Windows Contacts
Content Advisor, 212
  approved or denied sites, adding, 215
  blocked content, viewing, lviii
  categories, setting restriction levels for, 215
  configuring, lviii, 214
  supervisor password, creating, 216
  turning off, lviii, 218
Content Advisor dialog box, 215
content descriptors, 405
Content pane, 42, 480
content ratings, 405

content, restricting, 212
context-sensitive help, 455
Control Panel, 48
controlling access to files and folders, 94
Cookies, deleting, 445
copying
    files, xlvii
    files, for backup. *See* backing up
    folders and files, 102
    software. *See* software piracy
    speech recognition command for, 67
CPU usage, monitoring, 234, 435
Create Shortcut wizard, 68, 70
Create Supervisor Password dialog box, 216
Credentials, 480. *See also* network passwords;
        passwords; user names
critical updates, 13
cursor, moving with keyboard, 23
custom colors, 344
Customize Start Menu dialog box, 36
customizing
    notification area, 55
    Start menu, 34
    user interface, 120, 126
    Windows Aero, 122
    Windows Explorer, 84
    Windows Media Player, 379
customizing Windows Vista for ease of
        use, 22
custom security zones, 419. *See also* Internet
        security zones
cutting
    files, 104
    speech recognition command for, 67

D

daisy-chaining devices, 143
Datacastle data backup service, 466
date. *See* date and time; system date
date and time. *See also* system date; system
        time
    changing, xlix
    defined, 487
    display of, turning off, 55
Date And Time dialog box, 134
deactivating. *See* turning off
default folder view, setting, 91
default printer
    changing, 171
    setting, 170

default programs. *See* middleware
Default Programs window, 235
default Windows programs, changing, 235
Defender. *See* Windows Defender
defragmenting hard disk. *See* Disk
        Defragmenter
Delete Home Page dialog box, 199
Deleted Items folder (Windows Mail), 267
deleting
    browsing history and cookies, 445
    bypassing Recycle Bin when, 447
    columns, from views, 90
    e-mail messages, 283
    files, xlvi, 97, 102
    folders, 102
    home page, 199
    Internet Explorer history, 205
    programs, 225
    shortcuts, xliv, 68, 72
    software, 225
    speech recognition command for, 67
    unused files, 447
    user accounts, lxxv, 401
denied sites in Content Advisor, adding, 215
desktop, 29, 30
    appearance of, 4
    background, default, 6
    defined, 480
    displaying, 53
    high-contrast color scheme, 22
    icons. *See* icons
    shortcuts on, arranging, 71
    showing, 32
desktop background
    changing, xlvii, xlviii, xlix, 126
    graphics as, 345
    picture as, centering, 128
    pictures as, 128
    reverting to original, 345
    setting, lxxii
    solid color as, 129
    videos on, 7
Desktop Background page, 126
desktop shortcuts. *See* shortcuts
Details pane
    displaying/hiding, 84, 86
    opening, 93
Details view, 85
    displaying, 88
    filtering files in, 88
    sorting columns in, xlvi
    sorting files in, 88

device drivers, 142, 175
  defined, 480
  installing, in safe mode, 464
  updating, lxxix
Device Manager, 430
devices, 141
  connecting sequentially, 143
  connecting to ports, 143
  connecting, when insufficient number of
    ports, 143
  connecting, with hubs or switch boxes, 143
  daisy-chaining, 143
  defined, 484
  external, 141
  internal, 142
  internal, installing, 142
  managing, lxxix
  mobile PCs and, 150
  Plug and Play, 141
  software for, 142
DHCP servers, 480
dial-up connections
  connecting with, 187
  defined, 480
dialog boxes, xxvi, 30
  Accessibility, 200
  Add A Favorite, 203
  Add Input Language, 156
  Add Or Change Home Page, 198
  Advanced Sharing, lxii, 262
  Appearance Settings, 122
  AutoPlay, 375, 388
  Browse For Files Or Folders, 68
  Browse For Folder, 132
  Burn A Disc, 385
  Choose Details, 89
  Colors, 200
  Content Advisor, 215
  Create Supervisor Password, 216
  Customize Start Menu, 36
  Date And Time, 134
  defined, 480
  Delete Home Page, 199
  Disk Cleanup, 448
  Disk Cleanup Options, 448
  Display Settings, 145
  Feed Settings, 211
  Folder Options, 85, 90
  Help Settings, lxxx, 455
  Internet Options, 194, 214, 218
  Internet Properties, 418
  Internet Time Settings, 136
  Media Sharing, 389
  Mouse Properties, 151
  Open With, 233
  Options, 164, 379
  Pen And Input Devices, 162
  Performance Options, 440
  Photo Screen Saver Settings, 132
  Pop-up Blocker Settings, 197
  Power Options, 442
  Press And Hold settings, 162
  Print, 207
  Properties, 93, 94
  Regional And Language Options, 155
  Remote Assistance Settings, lxxxii, 465
  Remove Properties, 96
  Restricted Sites, 420
  Screen Saver Settings, 131
  Security Settings, 419
  Select Users Or Groups, lxii, 262
  Set Program Access And Computer
    Defaults, 235
  Sound, 178
  Stored Credential Properties, 259
  System Properties, xlix, lxxxiii, 138, 243,
    256, 475
  Tabbed Browsing Settings, 195
  Tablet PC Settings, 160
  Taskbar And Start Menu Properties, 35, 54, 56
  Temporary Internet Files And History
    Settings, 445
  Text Services And Input Languages, 156
  Theme Settings, 115
  User Account Control, 10, 15, 137
  Windows Features, 444
  Windows Firewall Settings, 412
dictating text, 23
digital cameras, 388
Digital Subscriber Line (DSL), 480
  Internet connections, 187
disabling. See turning off
Disconnect button, lxxxi
disconnecting
  from ad hoc wireless networks, lxi, 250
  from mapped drives, xlv
  from Remote Desktop session, 255
  remote assistance, lxxxi, 464
  users, 437
Disk Cleanup
  defined, 480
  deleting files with, 449
  running, lxxviii
  scheduling, 447

Disk Cleanup dialog box, 448
Disk Cleanup Options dialog box, 448
disk configuration, 227
Disk Defragmenter, 439
    default schedule of, 439
    defined, 480
    opening, 443
    scheduling, lxxix, 443
disk drives, 42-43
Disk Management
    Help file, 229
    information, lix
    snap-in, 227
disk volumes, 228
display devices. *See* monitors
display resolution. *See* screen resolution
Display Settings dialog box, 145
DLLs. *See* dynamic link libraries (DLLs)
DNS. *See* domain name system (DNS)
docking
    defined, 480
    Input Panel, on Tablet PCs, 165
    taskbar, 51
document libraries, 260
documents
    date and time, inserting, 358
    line breaks, inserting, 359
    opening, in WordPad, 355
    page setup, 362
    printing, 362
    saving, in WordPad, 354
    scanning, 285
    sharing. *See* shared drives; shared folders
    text, 98
Documents folder, 2, 103
    opening, xlv, 76, 80
domain, identifying, 426
domain name system (DNS), 481
domains, 3
    connecting to, lxi, 251
    defined, 481
    logging on to, 1, 3
    logging on with, 3
    machine accounts, 251
    parental controls and, 405
    remote passwords for. *See* network passwords
    user accounts, 251
    vs. workgroups, 241
    working remotely, 241. *See also* virtual
        private network (VPN) connections

double-clicking, xxiv
    defined, 481
    speech recognition command for, 62–63
double-click speed, changing, 152
Downloaded Program Files folder, opening, 446
downloading
    device drivers, 175
    screen savers, 131
    Windows Media Player skins, 377, 380
Drafts folder (Windows Mail), 267
dragging, xxiv
    defined, 481
    files, 104
    with secondary mouse button, 231
drivers. *See* device drivers
    printer. *See* printer drivers
drives, 42–43
    mapping. *See* mapping drives
    shared. *See* shared folders
    viewing. *See* Windows Explorer
drop-down list boxes, xxvii
drop shadow. *See* shadow effect
DSL. *See* Digital Subscriber Line
dual monitors. *See* monitors, multiple
dynamic link libraries (DLLs), 75, 481

E

e-mail
    accounts, 269, 271
    addresses, 268, 481
    attachments, 479
    alias, 479
    programs. *See* Windows Mail
    protocols, 268
    servers, 268, 271, 483
    signature, 481
e-mail messages. *See also* Windows Mail
    creating, 280
    deleting, 283
    formatting, 278
    icons for, 51, 279
    opening, 276, 279, 281
    responding to, 279, 282
    selecting multiple, 283
    sending, 281
    sending, in Windows Mail, 278
e-mailing Web pages, lvii, 208-209
Ease of Access Center, xv, 23

Ease Of Access icon, 23
ease of use recommendations, 25
Easy Transfer Cable, 477, 481
Edit Plan Settings window, 442
editing graphics, 100
editing text, speech recognition commands
    for, 64
efficiency. *See* performance
electronic business cards. *See* Windows
    Contacts
electronic notes. *See* Sticky Notes
Ellipse button (Paint), 333
emptying Recycle Bin, 32
end-user license agreements (EULAs), 224. *See*
    also software installation
entering passwords, 5
Entertainment Software Rating Board, 405
environment. *See* user interface
Eraser button (Paint), 342
EULAs. *See* end-user license agreements
    (EULAs)
events, 314, 319
executable files, 75, 222, 481
Expand button, 157
expansion slots, 143, 481. *See also* ports
exporting Sticky Notes, 302
extended display for multiple monitors, 148
extensions. *See* file, name extensions
external display for multiple monitors, 148
external peripherals, 141, 481. *See also* devices

F

F1 help, 455. *See also* Windows Help And
    Support
Fast User Switching, xli, 17
Favorite Links list, 79
Favorites Center, 202
    adding pages to, 203
    closing, 205
    History page, displaying, 204
    opening, 204
    opening permanently, 205
    pinning to window, lvii
Favorites Center button, 204
Favorites, Internet Explorer, 192
Favorites list
    adding sites to, lvii
    searching, lv, 192
fax program. *See* Windows Fax And Scan

faxes, 284-85
Feed Headlines gadget, 297
Feed Settings dialog box, 211
file associations. *See* software associations
file cache, 447. *See also* caching
file compression. *See* compressing files
file formats for graphics, 345, 348
file location
    default for saving new files, 97
    for program files, 75
file name extensions, 232. *See also* file types
    displaying, 92
    displaying by default, 85
    programs associated with. *See* software
        associations
file properties
    displaying, 88
    removing, 96
    viewing, 93–94
File Sharing wizard, 261
file types, 97. *See also* file name extensions
    conflicts with, 232
files
    backing up. *See* backing up
    compressing, xlvi
    copying, xlvii, 102
    creating, 97
    cutting, 104
    deleting, xlvi, 75, 97, 102
    dragging, 104
    executable. *See* executable files
    limiting access, 94
    moving, 102
    names, changing, 98
    navigating to, 76
    opening, 99
    organizing, 97
    pasting, 103
    properties, removing, xlvi
    renaming, 97
    restoring, from backup sets, lxxxii, 472
    restoring, previous versions, 467
    restoring, from Recycle Bin, 102
    saving, 99
    ScreenTips, viewing, 93
    sharing, 396
    size of, 99
    size, viewing, 347
    sorting, 103
    tags, adding, 95
    temporary, 97

files (continued)
titles, adding, xlvi, 93
types of, 75
viewing. *See* Windows Explorer
viewing properties, 93
views, changing, xlvi
views of, 84. *See also* Windows Explorer
working with, 75
fill colors in Paint, 331, 334
Fill With Color button (Paint), 340
filtering
folder contents, 88
search results, 107
Filter Keys, 23, 481
Fire Wire ports, 143
firewall programs, 409. *See also* Windows
Firewall
flash drives
as memory-expansion devices, 438
defined, 488
flashing screen when sounds played, 22
flicks, configuring for Tablet PCs, 163
flipping graphics, 342
Folder Options dialog box, 85, 90
folder properties
displaying, 88
viewing, 93
folder templates, applying, 307
folders
browsing, 43
compressed, 97
compressed, opening, 101
copying, 102
creating, 96–98
deleting, 97, 102
limiting access, 94
moving, 102
navigating, xlv, 81
navigating to, 76
opening, xlv
personal. *See* user profile folders
Program Files. *See* Program Files folder
renaming, 97
setting folder types, 307
as templates, 96
viewing. *See* Windows Explorer
views, 84. *See also* Windows Explorer
views, changing, xlvi
views, setting default, 91
working with, 75

Folders list
contents, 79
displaying, 45, 78
expanding folders in, 42
navigating in, 81
fonts, 354
changing, 355
defined, 481
selecting, for graphic text, 336
size, changing, 356
in title bars and menus, changing, 22
Fonts toolbar, 335
Forgotten Password wizard, 404
formatting
e-mail messages, 278
text, in graphics, 336
Forward button (Windows Explorer), 77, 83
fragmentation, 439, 481. *See also* Disk
Defragmenter
frames, xxv
fraudulent sites. *See* phishing sites
full-screen mode for
graphics, 342
Windows Media Player, 375–376

G

gadgets, 29, 221, 295. *See also* Sidebar
adding to Sidebar, 298
defined, 481
detaching from Sidebar, 300
game ratings, 405
games, 236
accessing, 39
installing, 236
linking on Start menu, lix, 236
playing, 237
Games link, adding to Start menu, 39
GB (gigabyte), 97, 481
genuine Windows validation, 426
GIF (Graphic Interchange Format) files
defined, 348, 481
saving, 347
as user account pictures, 402
Windows Photo Gallery and, 369
gigabytes (GB), 97, 481
glossary terms, formatting of, xxx
gmail e-mail accounts, connecting Windows
Mail to, 267

Go button, 5, 191
Google Reader, RSS feeds on, 212
Graphic Interchange Format (GIF) files.
    See GIF (Graphic Interchange Format)
    files
graphical user interface (GUI), 30, 481
graphics
    airbrush effect, 334
    attributes, viewing, 330
    backgrounds, transparent, 339
    bitmap. *See* bitmap (BMP) files
    canvas size, changing, 337
    copying, 343
    creating, 100, 326
    editing, 100
    file formats, 345, 348
    fill colors, 331, 340
    flipping, 342
    full-screen mode, 342
    GIF format. *See* GIF (Graphic Interchange
        Format) files
    JPEG format, 348
    move handles, 338
    opening, 338, 347
    PNG format, 348
    printing, 348
    printing setup, changing, 350
    printing on single page, 351
    properties, viewing, 347
    resizing, 337, 339
    rotating, 342
    saving, 337
    selecting, in Paint, 339
    as slide shows, displaying, 104
    text, adding, 335
    TIFF format, 348
    as Windows desktop, 345
    zooming in on, 340, 341
graphics adapter, 120
graphics card, and screen resolution, 144
graphics files, default software association, 232
grouped windows, 50
grouping
    of taskbar buttons, 49
    turning off, 55
groups, 482
Guest account, 397
GUI (graphical user interface), 30

H

hackers, 409, 482
handwriting recognition, 23.
    See also Tablet PCs
hanging indents, 357
hard disk
    cleaning up. *See* Disk Cleanup
    configuration of, 227
    contents, viewing, 79
    defined, 42
    fragmentation, 439. *See also* Disk
        Defragmenter
    managing, 227
    size of, typical, 97
hardware, 141
    cleaning, 438
    defined, 482
Hardware And Sound window, 177
hardware devices, viewing properties, 427
hardware performance. *See* performance
hardware specifications, checking, 119
headlines, displaying, 297
headphone jack, 176
headset microphones. *See* microphones
Help. *See* Microsoft Help and Support site;
        Windows Help And Support
help with book/companion CD, xxxix
Help Settings dialog box, lxxx, 455
hidden files, 75
hiding
    clock, 55
    Details pane, 86
    Navigation pane, 86
    Quick Launch toolbar, 55
    system time, 133
hierarchical storage structure, 42
High Contrast, 22, 482
hints for passwords, 400, 404
history, Internet, 445
History list, 192
    changing, lv
    clearing, 204, 205
    searching, 192
    viewing, 204
Home arrow, 198
Home button (Windows Help And
        Support), 457

home page, 198
blank page as, lvi, 199
changing, lvi, 198
defined, 482
deleting, 199
displaying, lvi
multiple, setting up, lvi, 199
setting current page as, 198
horizontal scrolling with mouse wheel,
configuring, 153
Hotmail and Windows Mail, 266
HTML (Hypertext Markup Language), 482
HTTP (Hypertext Transfer Protocol), 482
hubs
connecting devices with, 143
defined, 482
hue, 344
hyperlinks, 190, 193, 482
Hypertext Markup Language (HTML), 482
Hypertext Transfer Protocol (HTTP), 482

I

Icon views, 85
icons, 30, 31
auto arranging, 71
defined, 482
ellipsis (...) in name of, 32
resizing, 69
Speech Recognition, 61
Identify Monitors button, 145
IE. *See* Internet Explorer 7
IEEE 1394, 143, 482
images. *See* graphics
IMAP (Internet Message Access Protocol),
268, 482
Important paragraphs, xxx
importing text into WordPad, 358
improving system performance, 430
Inbox (Windows Mail), 266
indenting text, 357
index of book, how to use, xxix
index of data files, 105
individualized settings. *See* user profiles
Information Bar, 197, 482
information storage, 42
input languages. *See* keyboard input
languages
insertion point width, changing, 22
installed memory, identifying amount, 426

installing
digital camera drivers, 388
games, 236
internal devices, 142
keyboard input languages, 156
local printers, lii, 166
ports, 143
practice files, xxxvi
printers, 169
printer drivers, 170
scanner drivers, 388
software. *See* software installation
instant messaging (IM), 284, 482
interface elements in exercises, formatting
of, xxx
internal peripherals, 142. *See also* devices
defined, 482
installing, 142
international settings for keyboard.
See keyboard input language
Internet
blocking content. *See* parental controls
connecting to, 186, 188-89
history of, 185
temporary files, viewing, lxxviii
Internet Content Rating Association (ICRA),
212, 213
Internet Explorer
advanced options, 218
browsing history, 445
cached files. *See* caching; Temporary Internet
Files folder
favorites, 192
History list, 192
history, viewing, lvii
home page, changing, lvi
new window, opening, 193
searching Favorites and History lists, 192
security settings, lxxvii
security zones. *See* Internet security zones
starting, lv, 52
Internet Explorer 7
background color, changing default, 200
closing, 195
default page. *See* home page
Favorites Center. *See* Favorites Center
font size, changing default, 200
History list, clearing, 204–205
home page. *See* home page
HTML editing program, default, 190
links in. *See* hyperlinks

Live Search, 202-203
multiple Web sites, viewing in tabs.
    See tabbed browsing
navigating forward and back in, 193
objectionable content, restricting, 212
program settings, default, 190
recently visited pages, viewing list of, 194
RSS feeds, 210
sessions, multiple, 190
starting, 191, 199
tabs in. *See* tabbed browsing
text color, changing default, 200
updating, 196
Web sites, opening in new tabs, 191
Internet Explorer Pop-up Blocker, 196
    allowing pop-ups from certain sites, 197
    audio alert, turning off, 197
    configuring, 197
    turning off, 197
Internet Message Access Protocol (IMAP),
    268, 482
Internet Options dialog box, 194, 214, 218
Internet Properties dialog box, 418
Internet protocol (IP) address, 482
Internet security zones, 416
    custom, setting, 419
    default level, setting, 419
    displaying, 418
    security levels for, 417
Internet service providers (ISPs), 187
    defined, 482
    setting up connection, 187
Internet time, 136
Internet Time Settings dialog box, 136
intranet firewall programs, 409
inviting attendees to meetings
    Windows Calendar, 320
    Windows Meeting Space, 290
IP addresses, 482
ISDN Internet connections, 187, 483
ISPs. *See* Internet service providers (ISPs)
italicizing text, 356

J

Japanese keyboard, 154. *See also* keyboard
    input languages
JPEG. *See* Joint Photographic Expert Group
    (JPEG) files
Join A Domain Or Workgroup wizard, 243, 251

joining a meeting, 289
joining newsgroups, 459. *See also* newsgroups
Joint Photographic Expert Group (JPEG)
    files, 348
    defined, 483
    as user account pictures, 402
junk e-mail, filtering, 273

K

KB. *See* kilobyte (KB)
kernel memory usage, monitoring, 435
keyboard input languages
    defined, 482
    installing, li, 156
    removing, lii
    screen abbreviations for, 158
    switching, 155
    viewing available, 157
keyboard shortcuts
    defined, 483
    speech recognition commands for, 63
    underlining in command names, 23
keyboards
    alternatives to, 23
    full-size, connecting to mobile PCs, 150
    moving cursor with, 23
    On-Screen, 23
kilobytes (KB), 97
    defined, 483

L

Landscape button, 206
landscape orientation, printing Web pages
    in, 206
Language bar, 159
Languages, for keyboard input. *See* keyboard
    input languages
LANs. *See* local area networks (LANs)
laptop computers. *See* mobile PCs
Launch Internet Explorer Browser button, 19,
    52, 199
left mouse button. *See* primary mouse
    button; secondary mouse button
library (Windows Media Player), display-
    ing, 377
license terms, defined, 483
limiting access to files and folders, 94

line breaks, inserting, 359
lines, drawing. *See* graphics
links to programs. *See* shortcuts
List view, 85
lists, closing, without making selection, 83
Live File System format, 385
Live Search, 202–203
    search providers, finding additional, 203
local area networks (LANs), 187
    connecting with, 187
    defined, 483
local, defined, 483
local drive letters, 82
Local Intranet zone, 417. *See also* Internet
        security zones
local printers, 166
    defined, 483
    installing, lii, 166
    sharing, 166. *See also* network printers
locally, defined, 483
Lock button, 19
locking
    defined, 483
    taskbar, xliii
    computer, xli, 18–19
logging off, xlii, 1, 18, 231
    defined, 483
    other users, 437
    from Remote Desktop, 255
logging on, 1–3
    defined, 483
    to domains, 1, 3
    with domains, 3
login names. *See* user account names
look and feel. *See* user interface
luminosity, 344

M

machine accounts, 3, 251
Magnifier, 22
    defined, 483
Magnifier button (Paint), 341
magnifying screen, 22
mail servers
    addresses, 267
    defined, 483
mailboxes, 268
malware, protecting against. *See* Windows
        Defender

Manage Accounts window, 398
mapping drives, xlv, 43, 82
    defined, 483
margins, adjusting when printing, 206
mass e-mails. *See* e-mail messages
Mastered file format, 385
Maximize button, xxv, 47, 456
maximized windows, moving between dual
        monitors, 148
maximizing
    speech recognition command for, 67
    windows, xxv, 47, 349
MB. *See* megabytes (MB)
Media Center. *See* Windows Media Center
media files, sharing, 389
Media Sharing dialog box, 389
Medium Icons view, 87
meeting requests, 322
Meeting Space. *See* Windows Meeting Space
meetings
    inviting attendees, 320
    removing attendees, 321
    meetings, online, 287. *See also* Windows
        Meeting Space
megabytes (MB), 97
    defined, 483
memory, upgrading, 438
Menu bar, displaying/hiding, 84
menu bars, xxv
    defined, 483
menus, 30
    font, changing, 22
    right-pointing arrows next to items, 34
message boxes, xxviii
messages, e-mail. *See* e-mail messages
mice, 151
    buttons, configuring, 151
    buttons, switching primary and secondary, 151
    configuring, 153
    double-click speed, changing, 152
    Web pages, navigating with, 153
microphones, 180
    adjusting, 58
    connecting, liv
    jacks, identifying, 181
    setting up, 58, 181
    troubleshooting, 182
    types of, 180
    USB, installing, 180
    volume, adjusting, 181

Microphone Setup wizard, 181
Microsoft Help And Support site, 454. *See also* Windows Help And Support
Microsoft Magnifier. *See* Magnifier
Microsoft Narrator. *See* Narrator
Microsoft Notepad, 99
Microsoft Office Outlook. *See* Outlook
Microsoft Outlook Express. *See* Windows Mail
Microsoft Paint. *See* Paint
Microsoft Press Knowledge Base, xxxix
Microsoft Product Support, 460
Microsoft Product Support Services, xxxix
Microsoft Windows Firewall. *See* Windows Firewall
Microsoft Windows Update, 13. *See also* updating Windows
Microsoft Windows Vista. *See* Windows Vista
Microsoft Windows XP. *See* Windows XP
Microsoft WordPad. *See* WordPad
middleware, 235
    defined, 483
    included with Windows Vista, 235
    settings, changing, lix, 235
Minimize button, xxv, 48, 116
minimizing
    Remote Desktop window, 255
    speech recognition command for, 67
    windows, xliii
    windows, all, xliii, 32, 54
minimizing windows, 48
    all, 53
    in group, all, 50
Mini Player (Windows Media Player), 376
mirrored display for multiple monitors, 148
mobile PCs. *See also* Tablet PCs
    batteries, conserving when using multiple monitors, 148
    devices, adding to, 150
    full-size devices, connecting to, 150
    widescreen display on, 144
modems, defined, 484
monitors, 144
    color depth, setting, 122
    display area, 144
    full-size, connecting to mobile PCs, 150. *See also* monitors, multiple
    maximum number you can attach, 147
    multiple, display options for, 148
    multiple, identifying which is which, 145
    multiple, moving displays of, 149
    multiple, moving maximized windows between, 148

multiple, primary and secondary display, 148
multiple, requirements for, 148
multiple, setting up, 147
primary, changing, l
screen refresh rate, 121
screen refresh rate, changing, 121
screen savers. *See* screen savers
monitors, multiple, on mobile PCs, 150
mouse actions, xxiv
mouse, connecting to mobile PCs, 150
mouse grid, speech recognition command for displaying, 63
Mouse Keys, 23
    defined, 484
mouse pointer
    configuring, l, 152
    default, restoring, 152
Mouse Properties dialog box, 151
mouse wheel
    configuring, li, 153
    horizontal scrolling with, configuring, 153
    vertical scrolling with, configuring, 153
move handles on graphics, 338
Movie Maker. *See* Windows Movie Maker
moving
    files to new computer, 476
    folders and files, 102
music
    playing. *See* Windows Media Player
    sharing, 389
Music Details folder, 103
Music folder, opening, 76
Music Icons folder, 103
My Documents folder. *See* Documents folder
My MSN, RSS feeds and, 212
My Yahoo!, RSS feeds on, 212

N

naming printers, 166
narrating videos, 22
Narrator, 22
    defined, 483
navigating. *See* browsing
    folders, xlv, 81
    to folders and files, 76
    in Folders list, 81
    Web pages, lv
    windows, xxv
    Windows Help And Support, lxxx, 457
    wizards, 169

Navigation pane, 42
  defined, 484
  displaying/hiding, 84
  Folders list, displaying in, 78
  hiding, 86
Network And Internet window, 245
network connections
  connecting to, 189
  displaying, 188
network drives, mapping. *See* mapping drives
Network File And Sharing Center, defined, xv
network passwords, 259
  storing, lxii, 259
network printers, 173
  connecting to, 173
  connecting to, by entering name directly, 174
  defined, 484
  drivers, installing, 174
  naming, 166
network shares, 43
  defined, 484
network software installation, 223
network utilization, monitoring, 437
networks, 3
  connecting to, 82
  defined, 484
new computer, transferring files to, 476
news headlines, displaying, 297
newsgroups, 283. *See also* Windows Mail
  defined, 484
  interacting with, 459
  joining, 459
  locating, lxxxi, 459
  subscribing to, 459
  on Windows Vista topics, 459
newsreaders. *See* RSS feeds
non-standard characters. *See* symbols
notebook computers. *See* mobile PCs
notebooks, OneNote, 205
Notepad, 99
  defined, 484
notes. *See* Sticky Notes
notification area, 50
  customizing, 55
  defined, 484
  hidden icons in, 50
  message icon, 51
  printer icon, 51
  Speech Recognition icon, 61
  Windows Security icon, 51

notifications, length of, specifying, 22
numbered steps, formatting conventions
    used in, xxx
Num Lock key, audio signal when pressed, 23

O

objectionable content, restricting, 212
objects, inserting in WordPad, 359. *See*
    also drawing objects
OEM. *See* original equipment manufacturer
Offline, defined, 484
offline work in Windows Mail, 266
On-Screen Keyboard, 23
  defined, 484
on-screen meetings, 287
OneNote, Web pages, sending to notebook,
    205
online, defined, 484
online meetings, 287. *See* Windows Meeting
    Space
On The CD icon, xxx
opening
  compressed folders, 101
  Computer window, 44
  Control Panel, 48
  Disk Defragmenter, 443
  Document folder, 76
  documents, in WordPad, 355
  Documents folder, 80
  Downloaded Program Files folder, 446
  e-mail messages, 276, 279, 281
  Favorites Center, 204
  files, 99
  folders, xlv
  graphics, 338, 347
  Music folder, 76
  Paint, 329
  personal folders, 76
  Pictures folder, 76
  Print Preview, 349
  Sidebar, 296
  speech recognition command for, 67
  Start menu, 32, 35
  Sticky Notes, 302
  Temporary Internet Files folder, 446
  Windows Contacts, 306
  Windows Defender, 413
  Windows Explorer, 77
  Windows Firewall, 411

Windows Help And Support, 454–455
Windows Mail, 269
Windows Security Center, 411, 416
WordPad, 353
OPEN paragraphs, xxx
Open With dialog box, 233
operating system
    defined, xxiii, 484
    identifying edition, version, and type, 426
option buttons, xxvi
optional updates, 13
Options dialog box, 164, 379
Organize menu, 86, 93, 98, 103
organizing files, 97
orientation. *See* screen orientation
original equipment manufacturer (OEM), 31
    defined, 484
Outbox (Windows Mail), 266
Outlook, 266
Outlook Express. *See* Windows Mail
overriding Web page text and background
    appearance, 200

P

Page button, 208
page orientation, 363
page setup, 362
paging file size, setting, 441
Paint, 100
    airbrushing in, 334
    canvas, resizing, 337, 343
    canvas size, default, 329
    changing image dimensions, lxix
    changing image orientation, lxix, lxxi
    Color Box, 331
    colors, copying, 340
    colors, custom, 344
    colors, picking, 340
    displaying the toolbox, lxix
    duplicating images, lxxi
    Ellipse button, 333
    erasing in, 342
    fill colors, 331, 334
    fitting an image to a page, lxxii
    moving images, lxxi
    opening, 329
    opening images, lxix
    outlines, creating, 331
    pointer coordinates, 330
    Polygon button, 333

    primary and secondary colors, 332
    printing graphics from, 348
    Rectangle button, 331
    resizing canvas, lxix
    resizing graphics in, 332
    resizing images, lxxi
    Rounded Rectangle button, 330
    saving images, lxix
    selecting custom color, 327
    selecting graphics in, 339
    setting primary color, lxix
    setting secondary color, lxix
    setting zoom level, 327
    text, adding, 335
    viewing images full-screen, lxx
Paint toolbox, 326
    displaying, 330
Paint tools
    Airbrush, 328
    Brush, 327
    Ellipse, 328
    Eraser, 327
    Fill With Color, 327
    Free-Form Select, 326
    Line, 328
    Magnifier, 327
    Pencil, 327
    Pick Color, 327
    Polygon, 328
    Rectangle, 328
    Rounded Rectangle, 328
    Select, 327
    Text, 328
paragraph formatting in WordPad, 355
parallel ports, 143
    defined, 484
parental controls, 405
    configuring, lxxvi
    domain computers and, 405
    information collection, 408
    setting up, 406
    time limits, 405, 407
Parental Controls
    defined, xv
    window, 407
password protecting
    Content Advisor, 216
    session, 18, 19
password reset disk, 4
    creating, 404
    defined, 484

Password Reset wizard, 4
passwords, 396
  assigning, lxxv, 400
  defined, 484
  entering, 5
  on exiting screen saver, requiring, 133
  hints, creating, 400, 404
  network. *See* network passwords
  for Remote Desktop, storing, lxii, 258
  resetting, lxxvi, 4, 404
pasting
  files, 103
  speech recognition command for, 67
paths, 42
  defined, 484
  displaying, 81
Pen And Input Devices dialog box, 162
pen, configuring for Tablet PCs.
    See Tablet PCs
People Near Me, 287
  opening, lxiv
performance
  evaluating. *See* Windows Experience Index
  improving, 438
  monitoring, 435
Performance Information And Tools
    window, 429
Performance Options dialog box, 440
peripheral devices. *See* devices
permissions, for shared folders,
    restricting, 262
personal folders, 8, 43. *See also* user profile
    folders
  defined, 485
  displaying, 42, 79
  opening, 76
personal information, protecting, 196
Personalization window, 120, 145
personalized settings. *See* user profiles
phishing e-mails, filtering, 273
Phishing Filter, 422
phishing sites, 422
Photo Gallery. *See* Windows Photo Gallery
Photo Screen Saver Settings dialog box, 132
photographs. *See* pictures
physical memory, monitoring usage, 234, 435
Pick Color button (Paint), 340
Picture And Video folder, 104
pictures. *See also* drawing objects; graphics
  burning to CD, lxxiv
  as desktop background, 128
  opening in Windows Photo Gallery, 370

  as screen savers, xlviii, 132
  for user accounts. *See* user account pictures
Pictures And Videos folder, 103
Pictures folder, opening, 76
Pin The Favorites Center button, 205
pinned programs area on Start menu, 33, 40
  adding links to XE, xlii
  defined, 485
  unpinning links from, 41
pinning Favorites Center, to window, 205
pirated software
  avoiding, 11
  probability of viruses with, 12
pixels, 100, 144, 402
  defined, 485
  size of, related to screen resolution, 144
play lists (Windows Media Player)
  defined, 485
  displaying, 377
Play Slide Show button, 374
playing games. *See* games
playing music. *See* Windows Media Player
Plug and Play
  defined, 485
  devices, 141
PNG files, 348
  defined, 485
  as user account pictures, 402
pointing, defined, 485
pointing devices, 30. *See also* mouse
  alternative, xxiv
Polygon button (Paint), 333
Pop-up Blocker, settings, changing, lv. *See
    also* Internet Explorer Pop-up Blocker
Pop-up Blocker Settings dialog box, 197
pop-up windows
  blocking. *See* Internet Explorer Pop-up
    Blocker
  defined, 485
POP3. *See* Post Office Protocol 3
Portable Network Graphics (PNG) files.
    See PNG files
portrait orientation, 206
ports, 141, 143, 413
  defined, 485
  Fire Wire, 143
  installing, 143
  insufficient number of, 143
  parallel, 143
  for printers, selecting, 168
  USB, 143

Post Office Protocol 3 (POP3), 268, 485
Post-It notes. *See* Sticky Notes
posts, blog. *See* blogs
power conservation, 18
Power Options dialog box, 442
Power Options window, 441
power settings, optimizing, lxxviii, 439, 441–442
practice files on companion CD, xxxi
 installing, xxxvi
presentations, multiple monitors for. *See* monitors, multiple
Press And Hold Settings dialog box, 162
Preview pane, displaying, 85, 308
previewing
 screen savers, 133
 Web pages, lvii
 Web pages, in full screen mode, 206
primary and secondary colors in Paint, 332
primary display
 defined, 485
 in dual monitor setup, 148–149
primary hard drive, 42
primary mouse button, switching with secondary, 151
Print arrow, 206
Print dialog box, 207
Print Document button, 207
Print Preview
 full screen mode, 206
 opening, 349
 viewing options, changing, 349
 Web pages, viewing in, 206
printer drivers, 166
 defined, 485
 installing, 170
 for network printers, installing, 174
printer icon, 51
printers. *See also* local printers; network printers
 adding, 168
 default, changing, liii, 171
 default, setting as, 170
 installing, 169
 naming, 166
 port, selecting, 168
 sharing, liii, 171. *See also* network printers
printing
 documents, 362
 graphics, 348
 margins, adjusting, 206

to non-default printers, 352
 page orientation settings and, 363
 Web pages, 205
 Web pages, orientation, 206
privileges, administrative. *See* administrative privileges
problem reports, 458
 sending manually, lxxxi, 458
 turning off, lxxxi, 458
 viewing, 458
Problem Reports And Solutions window, displaying, lxxxi, 458
processes
 currently running, 435
 ending, 435
 identifying those currently running, lxxx
 monitoring, 234
processor resources, allocating, 441
processor speed, identifying, 426
product ID, identifying, 426
product keys, 223
 defined, 485
product support. *See* Microsoft Product Support
profiles. *See* user profiles
Program Files folder, 43, 75
program icons, 49
program interface elements in exercises, formatting of, xxx
program shortcut. *See* shortcuts
programs. *See* software
properties, adding, lxxiii
Properties dialog box, 93, 94
protecting personal information, 196
protocols, e-mail, 268
Public folder, 44, 47, 260
Punctuation, speech recognition commands for, 65

Q

Quick Launch toolbar, 49
 chevron on, 49
 defined, 485
 displaying, 49
 hiding, 55
 program links, adding, 49
Quick Reference, how to use, xxix
Quick Tabs, 202

R

random access memory (RAM)
    identifying amount, 426
    upgrading, 142, 438
rating systems for objectionable content, 213
RAW files, Windows Photo Gallery and, 369
read receipt, defined, 485
reading text out loud. *See* text-to-speech
    tools
ReadyBoost, 438
Really Simple Syndication (RSS) feeds.
    See RSS feeds
Recent Pages button, 77, 194
Recent Pages button (Windows Explorer), 84
Recent Pages list, 84
recently opened programs list, 34
    customizing, xlii
    defined, 485
    removing, 36–37
recently visited sites. *See* History list
recording audio Sticky Notes, 304
Rectangle button (Paint), 331
recurring appointments, 314
Recycle Bin, 32, 97
    bypassing, 447
    defined, 485
    displaying, 102
    emptying, 32
    restoring items from, 102
    turning off, 97
Regional And Language Options dialog
    box, 155
regional settings for keyboards. *See* keyboard
    input languages
registering a product, 7
reminders, 314
remote access servers (RAS)
    defined, 485
    virtual private network (VPN) connections
        and, 245. *See also* virtual private network
        (VPN) connections
remote assistance
    chatting during, lxxxi, 463
    defined, 485
    disabling, 465
    disconnecting, lxxxi, 464
    discontinuing, lxxxi, 464
    initiating, 460
    limiting access to, lxxxii, 465
    requesting control, 463

settings, displaying, lxxxii, 465
    setting up, lxxxi, 462
    starting, lxxxi, 461
    Windows Live Messenger and, 461
Remote Assistance dashboard, 462
Remote Assistance Settings dialog box,
    lxxxii, 465
Remote Assistance window, 463
Remote Desktop, 254
    connections, restricting, lxi
    defined, 486
    disconnecting from, 255
    domain computers, connecting to, 258
    hiding controls, 255
    minimizing window, 255
    password, storing, lxii, 258
    previous versions of Windows and, 254
    remote computer, browsing for name of, 257
    sleep mode and, 256
    users, adding, 256
Remote Desktop Connection window, 257
remote printers. *See* network printers
Remove Properties dialog box, 96
removing software. *See* software removal
renaming
    Computer folder, xlix, 138
    files, 98
    shortcuts, 69
repeated keystrokes, ignoring, 23
reporting on problems. *See* problem reports
Request Control button, 463
resetting passwords, lxxvi, 4, 404
resizing
    canvas, in Paint, 337, 343
    graphics, 337, 339
    icons, 69
    Paint canvases, 329
    taskbar, xliv, 54
    windows, xliii, 47
resolution, screen. *See* screen resolution
Resource Monitor, starting, 435
responding to e-mail messages, 279, 282
restarting
    computer, 21
    software installation and, 225
Restore Down button, xxv, 47
Restore Files wizard, 472
restore points, 15, 467–473. *See also* System
    Restore
    creating, lxxxiii, 474
    defined, 486
    rolling back to, lxxxiii, 476

restoring
   from backup sets, lxxxii, 467, 472
   from backup sets, previous versions, 467
   files, from Recycle Bin, 102
   speech recognition command for, 67
   system, with System Restore. See System
      Restore
   windows, to previous size, 47
Restricted Sites dialog box, 420
Restricted Sites zone, 417. See also Internet
      security zones
   adding sites to, 420
   removing sites from, 421
restricting content, 212
restricting Internet access. See parental
      controls
Return To Full Mode button (Windows Media
      Player), 381
right-clicking, xxiv
   defined, 486
   speech recognition command for, 63
right mouse button. See primary mouse
      button; secondary mouse button
ripping music from CDs, 377
rolling back to previous point. See System
      Restore
root, defined, 486
root directory, 46
   defined, 486
rotating graphics, 342
Rounded Rectangle button (Paint), 330
router, defined, 486
RSS feeds, 210
   adding, 210
   audio alert when Internet Explorer finds, 210
   available, displaying, 210
   directories of, 210
   Google Reader and, 212
   My MSN and, 212
   My Yahoo! and, 212
   subscribing to, 211
   update frequency, specifying, 211
   Web-based readers for, 212
running heads, how to use, xxix

S

safe mode, 464
   with networking, 464
SafeSurf, 213
saturation, 344

saving
   bitmaps, 347
   documents, in WordPad, 354
   files, 99
   GIF files, 347
   graphics, 337
scam Web sites. See phishing sites
Scanner And Camera Installation wizard, 388
scanners, 388
   installing drivers, 388
scanning documents, 285
scanning program. See Windows Fax And Scan
scanning for spyware. See Windows Defender
scheduling backups, lxxxii, 466, 471
screen orientation, changing, lii
screen refresh rate, 121
screen resolution, 144
   changing, 145
   defined, 486
   graphics card and, 144
   maximum, 144
   most popular, 144
   pixel size and, 144
   for widescreen display, 144
screen savers, 130
   default, 131
   defined, 486
   display speed, adjusting, 133
   downloading, 131
   password, requiring on returning from, 133
   pictures as, xlviii, 132
   previewing, 133
Screen Saver Settings dialog box, 131
ScreenTips, 32
   defined, 486
   viewing, 93
scroll bar, defined, 486
scroll box, xxv
Scroll Lock key, 23
scrolling
   speech recognition command for, 62, 67
   with mouse wheel, configuring, 153
Search button, 203
search index, 105
Search Options button, 203
Search pane, 85
search providers, adding to Live Search, 203
searching, xlvii. See also tags
   Control Panel, 48
   Favorites list, 192
   History list, 192
   the Internet, 107. See Windows Live Search

searching (continued)
the Web, 203
Windows Help And Support, 455, 457
Windows Mail, 274
searching your computer, 105, 106
advanced options, 108
filtering results of, 107
with wildcard characters, 108
secondary display
defined, 486
in dual monitor setup, 148–149
secondary mouse button
dragging with, 231
switching with primary, 151
security, 409. See also firewall programs;
passwords; user accounts; virus scanning
programs; Windows Defender; Windows
Security Center
Security Center. See Windows Security Center
security levels, 417
Security Settings dialog box, 419
security status, checking, lxxvii
security upgrades, 410
security zones. See Internet security zones
See Also paragraphs, xxx
Select Users Or Groups dialog box, lxii, 262
selecting
graphics, in Paint, 339
multiple items, 100
speech recognition command for, 62
text, all, 355
sending messages to other users, 437
Sent Items folder (Windows folder), 267
servers, remote access, defined, 485
services
currently running, 435
monitoring, 234
Services snap-in, 435
Set Program Access And Computer Defaults
dialog box, 235
Settings, Control Panel, searching for, 48
Setup.exe file, 222. See also software
installation
Set Up Speech Recognition wizard, 58
shadow copies, viewing, 473. See also System
Restore
shapes, drawing
circles, 328
ellipses, 328
lines, 327–328
polygons, 328

rectangles, 328
squares, 328
triangles, 328
shared drives, 260
defined, 486
shared folders, 260
creating, lxii, 261
defined, 486
permissions, restricting, 262
sharing
drives, limiting access when, 260
files, 396
folders, limiting access when, 260
media files, 389
pictures, from Windows Photo Gallery, lxxiv
printers, liii, 166, 171. See also network
printers
Web pages. See e-mailing Web pages
shortcuts, 31, 68
arranging on desktop, 71
auto arranging, 71
creating, xliv, 68, 70
defined, 486
deleting, xliv, 68, 72
ellipsis (...) in name of, 32
on Quick Launch toolbar, adding, 49
pinning to Start menu, 33, 40
rearranging, xliv
renaming, 69
in Startup folder, adding, 231
unpinning from Start menu, 41
Show Desktop button, 32, 53
Show Hidden Icons button, 51
Shut Down button, 21
Shut Down Options button, 17, 20, 231
shutting down, xlii, 1, 19, 21
defined, 486
side by side windows, 50
Sidebar. See Windows Sidebar
signature. See e-mail signature
Simple Mail Transfer Protocol (SMTP),
268, 486
skin mode (Windows Media Player), 376
skins (Windows Media Player)
changing, 380
downloading, 377, 380
Sleep button, 19
Sleep mode, xiv, xlii, 18
activating, 19
defined, 486
troubleshooting, 18

sliders, xxvii
Slide Show button, 104
slide shows
  as screen saver, 132
  graphics, displaying as, 104
slide shows (Windows Photo Gallery), 374
slow computer, restarting to fix, 21
SMTP. *See* Simple Mail Transfer Protocol
softlifting, 7
software, 141
  copying. *See* software piracy
  currently running, lxxx, 435
  default in Windows, changing, 235
  defined, 486
  displaying installed, 37
  file name extensions. *See* file name extensions
  genuine, identifying, 11
  license infringement, 7
  license terms, 7
  links to. *See* shortcuts
  pirated, avoiding, 11
  pirated, probability of viruses with, 12
  quitting, 234, 435
  recently opened, list of, 34
  recently opened, removing list of from Start
    menu, 36, 37
  shortcuts to. *See* shortcuts
  starting, 221
  starting, on computer startup, lix, 229
  switching to, 435
  unlicensed, ineligibility for support and
    updates, 12
software associations, 232
  changing, 233
  files without, opening, 232
  for graphics files, 232
  multiple, for single file type, 232
software errors, 234
software installation, 222
  administrative privileges and, 224
  for already-installed software, 226
  with CD or DVD, 223
  on first use, 224
  location of files for, 224
  options for, 224
  over Internet, 223
  over network, 223
  product keys and, 223
  restarting computer during and after, 225
  with CD or DVD, 223

software manufacturers, mailing lists,
  removing from, 224
software piracy, 12
  defined, 486
  license infringement as, 7
  protection from, built into Windows Vista, 12
software ratings, 405
software removal, 225
sorting files, 103
sound cards, 176, 486
Sound dialog box, 178
Sound Sentry, 22, 486
sounds, flashing screen when played, 22
spam, filtering, 273
speaker jack, 176
Speaker Setup wizard, 179
speakers, 176
  connecting, liv, 176
  standard setup for, 176
  testing, 179
special characters. *See also* symbols
  inserting in documents, 154
  speech recognition commands for, 65
special needs, features for. *See* accessibility
  features; ease of use
speech commands
  for clicking the screen, 63
  frequently used commands, 62
  for keyboard keys, 63
  for punctuation marks and special
    characters, 65
  for using common controls, 63
  for working with text, 64
  for working with windows and programs, 67
speech profiles, creating specific, 57
Speech Recognition, xv, 23
  configuring, xliv
  defined, 486
  using, xlv
speech recognition
  command reference, 62
  disabling automatic startup, 59
  increasing accuracy, 57
  status, 61
  stopping, 61
  tutorial, 57, 60
Speech Recognition command bar, 61
speech recognition software, 57
spin boxes, xxvii
spyware, protecting against. *See* Windows
  Defender

stacking windows, xliii, 50, 53
standard account, 3
standard user account, 397
Start button, 8, 14, 35, 44, 77, 86, 106,
    159, 188
Start menu, 32
    Accessories folder, 38
    All Programs link, 34
    Classic version, 33
    Classic version, switching to, 36
    customizing, 34
    defined, 487
    games link, adding, lix, 39, 236
    layout of, 34
    opening, 32, 35
    pinned programs area, 33, 40
    pinned programs area, unpinning links
        from, 41
    recently opened programs list, 34
    recently opened programs list, removing,
        36, 37
    starting programs from, xlii
starting
    Calculator, 38
    Internet Explorer, lv, 52
    Internet Explorer 7, 191, 199
    programs, on computer startup, lix
    programs, from Start menu, xlii
    remote assistance, lxxxi, 461
    in safe mode, 464
    software, 221
    software, on computer startup, 229
    Web browser, default, 191
    Windows Media Player, 378
Startup folder, 229
    adding programs to, lix, 231
    for all users, displaying, 230
    personal, displaying, 230
stationery, defined, 487
Step by Step series, conventions used in, xxix
Sticky Keys, 23
    defined, 487
Sticky Notes, 301
    audio, 304
    customizing, 302
    exporting, 302
    forcing window to stay on top, 302
    keeping on top, lxvi
    opening, 302
    pasting into other programs, 302

recording notes, lxvi
    sharing notes, lxvi
    starting, lxvi
    turning on and off, 303
Stop sharing button, lxxxi, 464
storage of information, 42
Stored Credential Properties dialog box, 259
Storing network passwords, 259
subscribing
    to newsgroups, 283. See also newsgroups;
        Windows Mail
    to RSS feeds. See RSS feeds
Subsystem for Unix-based Applications
    (SUA), xvii
surfing the Web, 185. See also World
    Wide Web
    defined, 487
Swedish keyboard, switching to, 155. See
    also keyboard input languages
Switch Between Windows button, 53
switch boxes
    connecting devices with, 143
    defined, 487
switching between user accounts. See Fast
    User Switching
switching windows, 53
symbols, inserting in documents, 154
Sync Center, defined, xv
synchronizing
    defined, 487
    system time over network, 133, 136
    Windows Mail folders, 267
system cache, 21
    defined, 487
system date, 51, 133
    changing, 135
    displaying, 134
    inserting into documents, 358
system files, backing up, 467
system folders, 43
    defined, 487
System, improving performance, 430
system performance, monitoring, 435
System Properties dialog box, xlix, lxxxiii, 138,
    243, 256, 475
System Protection, 467
system resources, viewing utilization, lxxx
System Restore, 472
    accessing, lxxxiii, 474
    checkpoints created by, 473
    hardware requirements, 473

restore points created by, 473
restore points, creating, lxxxiii, 474
restoring from, lxxxiii, 476
shadow copies, viewing, 473
System Restore wizard, 475
system time, 51, 133
changing, 135
for different time zones, adding, 135
hiding, 55, 133
synchronizing over network, 133, 136
System window, 137, 243, 428

T

Tab List, 202
tabbed browsing, 190–191, 193
background tabs, 193
closing Internet Explorer when in use, 195
defined, 487
multiple home pages with, 199
navigating pages, 190
recently viewed pages, viewing for tab, 194
settings, 195
settings, changing, lv
Tab List, 202
tabs, bringing to front, 193
tabs, closing, 195
Tabbed Browsing Settings dialog box, 195
table of contents, how to use, xxix
tables, captions, creating table of. See tables
    of figures
Tablet PCs. See also mobile PCs
AutoComplete, turning on/off, 164
battery usage, optimizing, 439
flicks, configuring, 163
handwriting recognition, training, 161
Input Panel, 160
Input Panel, configuring, 161, 164
Input Panel, docking, 165
Input Panel, opening, 165
Insert button, configuring, 164
optional components, 303
pen, configuring, 161
pen equivalents of mouse actions, setting, lii
pen equivalents of mouse settings,
    configuring, 161
press and hold settings, configuring, 162
screen orientation, configuring, 161
Tablet PC Settings dialog box, 160

tabs
defined, 487
dialog boxes, xxvi
in Internet Explorer 7. See tabbed browsing
tagging photos in Windows Photo Gallery, 373
tags. See also searching
adding, lxxiii
on files, adding, 95
task panes, xxvi
defined, 487
Task Scheduler, 447
defined, 487
tasks, adding to, lxxix
taskbar, 29, 49
customizing, xliii
defined, 487
docked, 51
grouping, turning off, 55
locking, xliii
resizing, xliv, 54
unlocking, xliii, 51, 54
Taskbar And Start Menu Properties dialog
    box, 35, 54, 56
taskbar buttons, 49
clicking, 50
defined, 487
grouping of, 49
maximum number of, 50
tasks
administrator, 396
tracking, 315
teleconferences, 287
teleconferencing. See Windows Meeting Space
television programs, watching on computer.
    See Windows Media Center
templates, folders as, 96
temporary files, 447
Temporary Internet Files And History Settings
    dialog box, 445
Temporary Internet Files folder, 445
deleting contents of, 445
deleting items from, 447
opening, 446
temporary Internet files, viewing, lxxviii
testing speakers, 179
text
bolding, 356
centering, 356
coloring, 356
importing into WordPad, 358

text (continued)
  indenting, 357
  in graphics, adding, 335
  in graphics, formatting, 336
  in graphics, selecting fonts for, 336
  italicizing, 356
  selecting all, 355
text boxes, xxvii
  creating, 328
Text button (Paint), 335
text documents, creating, 98
text editing, speech recognition commands
  for, 64
text editor. *See* Notepad
text on Web pages, 200
Text Services And Input Languages dialog
  box, 156
text-to-speech tools, 22. *See also* Narrator
Theme Settings dialog box, 115
themes, 114. *See also* color schemes
  defined, 487
  Windows Classic, applying, xlvii, 115
  Windows Vista, applying, 116
thumb tabs in book, how to use, xxix
TIFF files, 348
Tiles view, 85, 90
tilt-wheel mice, defined, 487
time. *See also* date and time; system time
  inserting into documents, 358
time limits on Internet usage. *See* parental
  controls
time servers, 133, 137
  defined, 487
time zones, displaying on multiple clocks, 135
Tip paragraphs, xxx
title bars, xxv
  defined, 487
  font, changing, 22
titles, file, adding, 93
Toggle Keys, 23
  defined, 487
toolbars, xxv, 42
  defined, 488
  Quick Launch. *See* Quick Launch toolbar
  Sidebar. *See* Sidebar
Tools, Control Panel, searching for, 48
tracking schedule. *See* Windows Calendar
transferring files to new computer, 476
transparent backgrounds in graphics, 339
transparent windows, enabling, xlviii, 125. *See*
  also color schemes

trash can. *See* Recycle Bin
tray. *See* notification area
tree view, 79
troubleshooting
  microphones, 182
  Sleep mode, 18
troubleshooting reports. *See* problem reports
TRUSTe Privacy Program, 196
Trusted Sites zone, 417. *See also* Internet
  security zones
turning off
  caching, 445
  Content Advisor, lviii, 218
  defined, 488
  Internet Explorer Pop-up Blocker, 197
  problem reports, lxxxi, 458
  Recycle Bin, 97
  remote assistance, 465
  Windows Firewall, 412
turning on
  media sharing, 389
  Windows Firewall, 412
tutorials, speech recognition, 60

U

UI. *See* user interface
Ultimate Extras, 7
UNC. *See* Universal Naming Convention
  (UNC)
Uniform Resource Locator (URL), 56
  defined, 488
  entering directly, 191
Uninstall button, 226
uninstalling
  software. *See* software removal
  Windows features, 445
Universal Naming Convention (UNC)
  address, 3
  defined, 488
Universal Serial Bus (USB)
  defined, 488
  ports. *See* USB ports
unlicensed software. *See also* software piracy
  ineligibility for support and updates, 12
unlocking
  computer, xli
  taskbar, xliii, 51, 54
unused files, deleting, 447

updating
   device drivers, 175
   Internet Explorer 7, 196
   search index, 105
updating Windows, 12–13
   automatically, 13
   automatically downloading updates but
      manually installing, 17
   critical updates, 13
   optional updates, 13
   time setting for installation, changing, 16
updating to Windows Vista. *See* upgrading
   Windows Vista
upgrading
   defined, 488
   RAM, 142
upgrading memory, 438
upgrading Windows Vista, xviii, 12
   backing up files before, xviii
   checking possible issues with, xviii
URGE Web site, 377
URL. *See* Uniform Resource Locator
USB. *See* Universal Serial Bus
USB flash drives
   as memory-expansion devices, 438
   defined, 488
USB ports, 143
   microphones, installing to, 180
USE paragraphs, xxx
User Account Control, 409
   defined, xv, 488
User Account Control dialog box, 10, 15, 137
user account pictures, 8, 397, 401
   changing, lxxv, 402
   default, 401
   defined, 488
   formats acceptable for, 402
   size of, 402
user accounts, 2, 3, 251, 396
   administrator. *See* administrator account
   creating, lxxv, 399
   defined, 488
   deleting, lxxv, 401
   displaying, 46
   Guest. *See* Guest account
   logging in multiple simultaneously. *See* Fast
      User Switching
   names. *See* user names
   parental controls, enabling, 407. *See*
      also parental controls

password-protecting, 400
   standard. *See* standard account
   types, changing, lxxv, 400
User Accounts window, 403
user input in exercises, formatting of, xxx
user interface, 1, 29. *See also* color schemes;
      Sidebar; themes
   customizing, 119–120, 126
   visual effects. *See* visual effects
user interface (UI), defined, 488
user names, 397, 401
   defined, 488
user passwords. *See* passwords
user profile folders
   accessing, 46
   displaying, 79
user profiles, 2, 43, 46
   accessing, 46
   defined, 488
users, 2
   defined, 488
   disconnecting, 437
   logging off, 437
   monitoring, 234, 437
   sending messages to, 437
Users folder, 43
Usenet. *See* newsgroups
Utlilities, defined, 488

V

vacuuming computer, 438
vCard, defined, 488
version control, 260. *See also* document
      libraries
vertical scrolling, with mouse wheel,
      configuring, 153
video cards, multiple monitors and, 148
video files, sharing, 389
videos, narrating, 22
View Full Width button, 206
views, 85
   changing, xlvi
   columns in, adding/deleting, 88
   columns in, deleting, 90
   for folders, setting default, 91
   switching, 87
   tree, 79
Views button, 87

Virtual PC Express, xvii
virtual private network (VPN), defined, 488
virtual private network (VPN) connections,
    241, 245
  creating, lx
  passwords, displaying during setup, 248
  public or private, specifying, 249
  speed of, 245
viruses, 409
  defined, 488
  protecting against, 409
virus scanning programs, 410
Vista. *See* Windows Vista
visual effects
  optimizing performance, lxxviii, 440
  settings, 440
voice commands, 57
volume of microphone, adjusting, 181
VPN. *See* virtual private network (VPN)
    connections; virtual private network

W

waking computer from Sleep mode, 18
Web. *See* World Wide Web
Web browsers, 186. *See also* Internet Explorer
  default, starting, 191
  defined, 489
  tabs in. *See* tabbed browsing
Web conferences, 287
Web conferencing. *See* Windows
    Meeting Space
Web links
  context menu for, 193
  defined, 482
  following, 193
  opening in new tab, 193
  opening in new window, 193
Web logs. *See* blogs
Web pages
  background color, changing, 200
  colors, changing, lvi
  default displayed in Internet Explorer 7.
    See home page
  e-mailing, lvii, 208
  e-mailing, URL only, 209
  Favorites Center, adding to, 203
  links on. *See* hyperlinks
  navigating, lv
  navigating forward and back, 193

  navigating, with mouse, 153
  OneNote notebook, sending to, 205
  previewing, lvii
  previewing in full screen mode, 206
  printing, 205
  printing, adjusting margins when, 206
  printing, in landscape orientation, 206
  printing, in portrait orientation, 206
  Print Preview, viewing in, 206
  recently visited, viewing list of, 194
  RSS feeds for. *See* RSS feeds
  screenshots of all currently open, 202
  setting as home page, 198
  switching quickly between. *See* tabbed
    browsing
  text color, changing, 200
  text size, changing, lvi, 200
Web sites
  in Content Advisor, adding to approved or
    denied sites, 215
  default options, overriding, lvi
  opening, lv
  opening in new tabs, 191
  phishing, 422
  pop-up windows, allowing from, 197
  recently visited. *See* History list
  scam. *See* phishing sites
  URLs, entering directly, 191
Welcome Center, 7, 427
Welcome screen, 3, 5
  defined, 489
wildcard characters
  defined, 489
  in searches, 108
Window Color And Appearance page,
    122, 124
window transparency, enabling, xlviii, 125.
    See also color schemes
windows
  activating, from taskbar buttons, 50
  Advanced Tools, 430
  arranging, 50
  cascading, 50
  closing, xliii, 48, 84
  color and appearance, setting, 124
  defined, xxv, 489
  grouped, closing all, 50
  grouped, minimizing all, 50
  grouping, turning off, 55
  maximized, moving between dual
    monitors, 148

maximizing, xxv, 47, 349
minimizing, 48
minimizing all, xliii, 32, 53–54
navigating, xxv
resizing, xliii, 47
restoring to previous size, 47
side by side, 50
stacking, xliii, 50, 53
switching between, xliii, 53
System, 428
Windows Aero, xiii, xvi, 118
  customizing, 122
  display, 47
  hardware requirements, checking, 119
  hardware requirements for, 118
Windows BitLocker Drive Encryption, xvi
Windows Calendar, xv, 314
  appointments, 314
  changing calendar color, 317
  changing defaults, 316
  creating appointments, lxviii, 319
  creating events, lxviii, 319
  creating meetings, lxviii
  events, 314
  groups, 318
  importing calendars, 317
  inviting meeting attendees, 320
  locating Internet calendars, lxviii
  meeting requests, 322
  multiple calendars, 316
  publishing calendars, 316
  reminders, 314
  sharing calendars, 316
  starting, lxviii
  subscribing to calendars, 317
  terminology, 314
  tracking tasks, 315
Windows Classic theme. *See also* themes
  applying, xlvii, 115
  defined, 489
  of Start menu, 33, 36
Windows Contacts, 278, 304
  adding members to a contact group, lxviii
  contact groups, 304, 306
  contact records, 304
  creating contact groups, lxvii
  creating contact records, lxvii
  creating contacts, 309
  creating groups, 311
  displaying commands, 307

displaying Contacts folder commands, lxvi
electronic business cards and, 305
exporting contacts, lxvii, 305
importing contacts, lxvii, 305
opening, lxvi, 306
ScreenTips in, 311
sending messages, lxviii
setting folder type, lxvi
viewing, 277
Windows Mail and, 266
Windows Defender, 409, 410
  automatic scanning, setting options for, 415
  configuring, lxxvii
  defined, 489
  opening, 413
  options, setting, 415
Windows desktop, reverting to original, 345
Windows DreamScenes, 7
Windows Easy Transfer wizard, lxxxiii,
    476–477
  defined, 489
Windows Experience Index
  base score, 426
  defined, 489
  displaying, 427, 440
  evaluating, 437
  subscore, 426
Windows Explorer
  closing, 84
  customizing, 84
  defined, xiv
  elements of, 77
  opening, 77
Windows Fax and Scan, 284
  scanning printed documents, lxiv
  sending and saving scanned documents, lxiv
  sending faxes, lxiv
Windows features, 444. *See also* specific
    features
  turning on/off, lxxviii, 444
  uninstalling, 445
Windows Features dialog box, 444
Windows Firewall, 409
  blocking all incoming connections, 412
  configuring, lxxvi
  defined, 489
  exceptions, setting, 412
  opening, 411
  ports, unblocking, 413
  turning on/off, 412

Windows Firewall Settings dialog box, 412
Windows folder, 44
Windows Help And Support, 454. *See also* Microsoft Product Support
  browsing, 456
  context-sensitive topics, 455
  F1 key and, 455
  feedback, sending, 456
  navigating in, lxxx, 457
  newsgroups, 459. *See also* newsgroups
  online help, enabling, lxxx, 455
  opening, 454–455
  related topics, opening to, 455
  searching, 455, 457
  starting page, jumping to, 457
Windows Internet Explorer 7. *See* Internet Explorer 7
Windows Live Mail, 266
Windows Live Messenger, 284
  remote assistance and, 461
Windows Live Search, xlvii, lvii
  search providers, adding, lvii
Windows logo key, 58
Windows Mail, 266. *See also* newsgroups
  accessing newsgroups, lxiv
  adding a message sender to Windows Contacts, lxiii
  changing e-mail account configuration, lxiii
  changing the program window layout, lxiii
  connecting to e-mail accounts, lxiii
  connecting to outside e-mail accounts, 267
  defined, xiv
  displaying message contents, lxiii
  filtering messages, lxiii
  folders, creating, 267
  folders in, 266
  Hotmail, unavailability of, 266
  icons in, 279
  junk mail filter, 273
  layout, changing, 274
  newsgroups, connecting to, 283
  opening, 269
  opening e-mail messages in, 276
  options, 267, 278
  searching, 274
  sending e-mail messages in, 281
  sending messages in, 278
  setting up, 266, 270
  sorting messages, lxiii
  starting, lxiii

  synchronizing folders in, 267
  user interface, 271
  welcome message, 275
  Windows Contacts and, 266
  working offline, 266
Windows Media Center, xvi, 382
  configuring, 383
  DVD settings, 384
  slide show settings, 384
  TV settings, 384
Windows Media Player
  appearance, changing, lxxiv
  burning CDs from, lxxiv, 377, 387
  classic menu bar, displaying, 380
  compact mode, 376
  customizing, 379
  full mode, 375
  full-screen mode, 376
  library, displaying, 377
  Mini Player, 376
  play lists, displaying, 377
  playing music with, 375
  ripping CDs, 377
  setting up on first run, 375
  skin mode, 376
  skins, changing, 380
  skins, downloading, 377, 380
  starting, 378
  syncing with portable device, 377
Windows Meeting Space, xvii, 287
  distributing files, lxv
  editing handouts, lxv
  initiating meetings, lxv
  invitation files, 289
  joining meetings, lxiv, 289
  sharing files, lxv
  starting, lxiv
Windows Mobility Center, xvii
Windows Movie Maker, xvi
  hardware requirements, 368
Windows Photo Gallery, 368
  adding folders, lxxiii
  adding tags, lxxiii
  defined, xv
  displaying, 372
  file formats supported by, 368
  filtering, 370
  fixing pictures, lxxiii
  GIF and RAW formats in, 369
  grouping, 370

sharing media files with, 389
sharing pictures from, lxxiv
slide shows, displaying, 374
sorting, 370
starting, lxxiii
tags, adding to photos, 373
tags, filtering photos by, 373
toolbar, 372
viewing, 370
Windows ReadyBoost, 438
  defined, 489
Windows Remote Assistance. *See* remote
  assistance
Windows Security Center, 409
  checking, 410
  defined, 489
  opening, 411, 416
Windows Security icon, 51
Windows Sidebar, 29, 295. *See also* gadgets
  adding gadgets to, lxv, 298
  changing gadget options, lxv
  changing properties, lxvi
  closing, 301
  defined, 489
  detaching gadgets from, 300
  displaying, lxv
  displaying gadgets on the desktop, lxv
  forcing to stay on top, 301
  hiding, lxv
  keeping on top, lxvi
  moving gadgets, lxvi
  opening, 296
  properties, changing, 300
  reattaching gadgets, lxv
Windows SideShow, xvi
Windows Tablet And Touch Technology, xvi
Windows Task Manager, lxxx, 234
  Applications tab, 435
  Networking tab, 437
  Performance tab, 435
  Processes tab, 435
  Services tab, 435
  starting, lix
  Users tab, 437
Windows Update, 409
  defined, 489
  installing available updates from, 14
Windows Vista
  activating. *See* activating Windows
  Aero. *See* Windows Aero
  Business edition, xvii

CD, appearance of authentic, 11
defined, xxiii
edition, checking, 118
Enterprise edition, xvii
Home Basic edition, xiv
Home Premium edition, xvi
new features, xiii
newsgroups for, 459
piracy protection system, 12
Service Pack 1, 6
Speech Recognition, 57
themes, applying, 116. *See also* themes
Ultimate Edition, 7
updating. *See* updating Windows
upgrading to. *See* upgrading to Windows
  Vista
wizards, 68
  Back Up Files, 469
  Connect To A Network, 246
  Create Shortcut, 70
  defined, 489
  File Sharing, 261
  Forgotten Password, 404
  Join A Domain Or Workgroup, 243, 251
  Microphone Setup, 181
  navigating in, 169, 189
  Restore Files, 472
  Scanner And Camera Installation, 388
  Set Up Speech Recognition, 58
  Speaker Setup, 179
  System Restore, 475
  Windows Easy Transfer, lxxxiii, 477
WordPad
  bolding text in, 356
  bulleted lists in, 357
  centering text in, 356
  changing default units of measurement,
    lxxii
  coloring text in, 356
  creating bulleted lists, lxxii
  date and time, inserting, 358
  defined, 352
  displaying the Ruler, lxxiii
  font, changing, 355
  font, changing size, 356
  font, default, 354
  formatting fonts and paragraphs, lxxii
  help, accessing, 352
  importing text into, 358
  indenting text in, 357
  inserting images from files, lxxiii

WordPad (continued)
  italicizing text in, 356
  navigating in, 356
  objects, inserting, 359
  opening, 353
  opening documents in, 355
  paragraph formatting, default, 355
  printing documents from, lxxiii, 362
  saving documents in, 354
  selecting document contents, lxxii
  selecting one paragraph, lxxii
  starting, lxxii
workgroups, 3
  connecting to, lx
  creating, lx, 243
  defined, 489
  vs. domains, 241
  identifying, 426
  network resource management in, 242
  setting up, 242
working remotely. See Remote Desktop; virtual
    private network (VPN) connections
World Wide Web. See also surfing the Web
  defined, 489
  history of, 185
  searching, 203
writing CDs. See burning CDs
WWW. See World Wide Web

Y

Yahoo! e-mail accounts, connecting Windows
    Mail to, 267

Z

zones, Internet. See Internet security zones
zooming, graphics, 340–341

What do you think of this book?

We want to hear from you!

Do you have a few minutes to participate in a brief online survey?

Microsoft is interested in hearing your feedback so we can continually improve our books and learning resources for you.

To participate in our survey, please visit:

www.microsoft.com/learning/booksurvey/

...and enter this book's ISBN-10 or ISBN-13 number (located above barcode on back cover*). As a thank-you to survey participants in the United States and Canada, each month we'll randomly select five respondents to win one of five $100 gift certificates from a leading online merchant. At the conclusion of the survey, you can enter the drawing by providing your e-mail address, which will be used for prize notification only.

Thanks in advance for your input. Your opinion counts!

* Where to find the ISBN on back cover

ISBN-13: 000-0-0000-0000-0
ISBN-10: 0-0000-0000-0

Example only. Each book has unique ISBN.

Microsoft®
Press